THE
SELF AND
MEMORY

STUDIES IN
SELF AND IDENTITY
SERIES

THE
SELF AND
MEMORY

EDITED BY

DENISE R. BEIKE
JAMES M. LAMPINEN
DOUGLAS A. BEHREND

PSYCHOLOGY PRESS
NEW YORK • HOVE

Published in 2004 by
Psychology Press
27 Church Road
Hove, East Sussex
BN3 2FA, UK
www.psypress.com

Published in the USA and Great Britain by
Psychology Press
711 Third Avenue
New York
NY 10017
www.psypress.co.uk

First issued in paperback 2014

Routledge is an imprint of the Tylor and Francis Group, an informa company

Copyright © 2004 by Taylor & Francis Books, Inc.

Psychology Press is an imprint of the Taylor & Francis Group.

10 9 8 7 6 5 4 3 2 1

Library of Congress Cataloging-in-Publication Data

The self and memory / edited by Denise R. Beike,
James M. Lampinen, Douglas A. Behrend.
        p. cm. -- (Studies in self and identity)
    Includes bibliographical references and index.

    ISBN 13: 978-1-84169-078-0 (hbk)
    ISBN 13: 978-1-138-00602-7 (pbk)
    1. Autobiographical memory--Congresses. I. Beike, Denise R. II.
Lampinen, James M. III. Behrend, Douglas A. IV. Series.

BF378.A87S45 2004
153.1'3--dc22   2004009846

Acknowledgments

This volume resulted from a Marie Wilson Howells symposium entitled "Memory and the Self," held in November of 2000 in Fayetteville, Arkansas. The Marie Wilson Howells Endowment to the Department of Psychology funded the symposium. The faculty and graduate students in the Department of Psychology at the University of Arkansas all worked to make the symposium a success. Special thanks go to Dave Schroeder and Eric Knowles, who were involved from the beginning in planning and hosting the symposium. Their advice and support were invaluable to the project.

Contributor List

Jochen Barth
Universiteit Maastricht
The Netherlands

Douglas A. Behrend
University of Arkansas

Denise R. Beike
University of Arkansas

Andrew L. Betz
Progressive Insurance

Pavel Blagov
Emory University

Jessica J. Cameron
University of Manitoba
Canada

John G. H. Cant
University of Puerto Rico Medical
    School

Robyn Fivush
Emory University

Jeffrey D. Green
Soka University

Mark L. Howe
Lakehead University
Canada

Erica Kleinknecht
Pacific University

James M. Lampinen
University of Arkansas

Juliana K. Leding
University of Arkansas

Dan P. McAdams
Northwestern University

Timothy N. Odegard
University of Arkansas

Brad Pinter
University of Washington

Daniel J. Povinelli
University of Louisiana at Lafayette

Michael Ross
University of Waterloo
Canada

Constantine Sedikides
University of Southampton
UK

Jefferson A. Singer
Connecticut College

John J. Skowronski
Northern Illinois University

W. Richard Walker
Winston-Salem State University

Anne E. Wilson
Wilfrid Laurier University
Canada

Erin T. Wirth-Beaumont
University of Arkansas

Contents

1

THE EMERGENCE OF THE SELF AND MEMORY

1

Evolving Conceptions of the Self and Memory

DENISE R. BEIKE
JAMES M. LAMPINEN
DOUGLAS A. BEHREND
University of Arkansas

*T*he present volume was inspired by the three coeditors' independent explorations of the expanding literature on autobiographical memory. One of us is trained as a social psychologist with expertise in the self-concept, another as a cognitive psychologist with expertise in the phenomenology of false memories, and another as a developmental psychologist with expertise in language and cognition. Despite our different backgrounds, the critical role of the self in autobiographical memory became apparent to each of us, as it has to other autobiographical memory researchers. Indeed, serious study of the interrelation of the self and memory is currently at its apex. A breakthrough occurred in 2000 with the publication of Conway and Pleydell-Pearce's article on the self-memory system in *Psychological Review*. This truly seminal article brought together research from clinical, cognitive, developmental, personality, and social psychology, as well as neuroscience. Virtually every psychologist can find research from his or her subfield cited in this article, brought together cogently with research from other subfields into a broad theory of personal memory and the self. Suddenly, a common language was available for researchers from disparate areas to communicate and compare findings. To celebrate and to encourage the exploration of the self and memory, we hosted a symposium at the University of Arkansas in November 2000, inviting the major theorists who are working at the juncture of these two once-separate areas of endeavor. The quest to discover how the self and memory influence one another can be an exercise in trying to pin down elusive concepts, as an analysis of the history of the self and personal memory in psychology attests.

THE SELF

Philosophers and psychologists have long debated the nature of the self, and its relation to memory. Descartes famously postulated, "I think, therefore I am." We might modify this to read, "I remember, therefore I am." Along these lines, Berkeley (1734/1979) posited an entity that "exercises divers [sic] operations, as willing, imagining, remembering. . . . This perceiving, acting being is what I call *mind, spirit, soul, myself* [italics in original]" (p. 43). Hume (1739/1979), however, thought that the idea of a self that unified perceptions and memories was a mere illusion: "We feign the continued existence of the perceptions of our senses, to remove the interruption [i.e., the break from one perception to the next]; and run into the notion of a soul, and self, and substance, to disguise the variation" (p. 61). By the time of James, however, the notion of a self, however fanciful or imagined it might be, had taken hold in the new science of psychology. James claimed that there could be no science of psychology that ignored the self; indeed, "the personal self rather than the thought might be treated as the immediate datum in psychology" (1890/1981, pp. 220–221), because thoughts and perceptions and feelings are perceived as *belonging* to the self. Except for a lengthy reprieve in America during the dominance of behaviorism, a psychology of the self has flourished ever since. The main players in the game of self have been social and personality psychologists, with cognitive psychologists and neuroscientists as very recent entrants.

James is generally credited not only with defining the new science of psychology around the self, but also with introducing an important distinction among senses of the self. He proposed the self as "I" versus the self as "me," the knower versus the object to be known. This distinction continues to be made today (e.g., Brown, 1998; Pinker, 1997). Cognitive scientist Steven Pinker (1997) calls these aspects *sentience* and *self-knowledge*, respectively. Pinker agrees with James that sentience rather than self-knowledge presents the more interesting and mysterious problem. Contributors to the present volume demonstrate, however, the complexity and mystery of both aspects of the self. Some contributors, such as Sedikides, Green, and Pinter, or Cameron, Wilson, and Ross are interested in self-description and self-evaluation, the clear earmarks of the "me" self, or self-knowledge. Others, such as McAdams, Fivush, or Lampinen, Odegard, and Leding are interested in identity and the sense of continuity of the self. These are aspects of the "I" self, or sentience. Many of the contributors to this volume address aspects of both.

How the self should be defined is an ongoing debate in psychology and other social sciences. Current theories emphasize the social and interpersonal nature of the self (e.g., Brewer & Gardner, 1996); its fluidity (e.g., Gergen, 1982); its temporal aspects (Halberstadt, Niedenthal, & Setterlund, 1996; Ross & Wilson, 2002; Ryff, 1991); and its relation to both momentary and enduring goals (e.g., Conway & Pleydell-Pearce, 2000; Emmons & Kaiser, 1996; Singer & Salovey, 1993). Contributors to the present volume reflect this diversity of definitions of the self as well. As a consequence, there is no single definition of the self that can easily be laid out to cover all the senses of the self that are relevant for this volume. It remains for future research to determine which sense of self is most critical for personal memory, or whether all senses are relevant.

PERSONAL MEMORY

Despite the absence of a single agreed-upon definition of the self, research on the self and memory has been underway for decades. Our focus in this volume is on the relationship of the self to a particular subtype of memory, variously called autobiographical, personal, or sometimes episodic memory. As distinguished from memory for facts, personal memory is memory for the events that happen to oneself. As has been noted by numerous scholars of autobiographical memory, memory research progressed mainly through laboratory study of words, pictures, and lists until Neisser (1982) and Tulving (1983) opened the door and challenged the field to take on the neglected but arguably more important topic of personal memories.

A flurry of research followed, resulting in hundreds of journal articles and dozens of volumes on the topic. A 1986 volume on autobiographical memory begins with the following statement clearly linking personal memory and the self: "Autobiographical memory is about the self. . . . Autobiographical memory is the source of information about our own lives, from which we are likely to make judgments about our own personalities and predictions of our own and, to some extent, others' behavior. Autobiographical memory, however, also provides a sense of identity and continuity. . ." (Rubin, 1986, p. 7). Conway (1990) distinguished autobiographical memories from other types of memories by virtue of their high self-reference, the subjective experience of remembering, and the presence of personal interpretation. He further explained the role of the self in personal memory this way: "Remembering . . . events is heavily dependent upon reconstruction and beliefs, theories about the mind, and the self, all of which . . . lead to 'memories' which are consistent with the current state of the cognitive system at the expense of accurately representing the past" (p. 104).

By 1996, Rubin felt the literature justified the claim that autobiographical memory was composed of these components: verbal narrative, imagery, and emotion. The self was not mentioned, nor was it mentioned in the introduction to a 1998 volume on the topic (Thompson, Herrmann, Bruce, Read, Payne, & Toglia, 1998). Perhaps the presence of the self was seen as so self-evident that it was no longer necessary to mention it. Contrary to the unstated role of the self, the introductory chapter in each volume explicitly mentions the narrative nature of autobiographical memory or its study. Some theorists see the narrative quality of personal memory as axiomatic (e.g., Fivush, 1991; McAdams, 1997; Nelson, 1993; Pillemer, 1998), whereas others see it as one of several possible ways that personal memories may be studied (Robinson & Taylor, 1998). Contributors to the present volume take different stances on this issue, with some strongly advocating a narrative approach (Fivush, McAdams) and others taking what might be called a featural or episodic approach (Beike, Kleinknecht, & Wirth-Beaumont; Lampinen et al.; Sedikides et al.). Contributors also differ on how they see features and narratives as being causally related: Do features or episodes exist or are they reconstructed? And are narratives the true representation, or an epiphenomenon of reporting? Aside from the issue of narratives versus episodes, there is the issue of the level of generality of personal memories. Several contributors acknowledge that personal memories exist on multiple levels of a hierarchy (e.g., Singer &

Blagov), reflecting Conway and Pleydell-Pearce's (2000) notion of a three-tiered structure. Still other contributors investigate remembered selves as well as remembered events (e.g., Cameron et al., Skowronski). Past or remembered selves are important cognitive and emotional constructs, and play a vital role in the self-memory system, but have no clear place in a three-tiered system composed of lifetime periods, general events, and specific events. As was the case for the self, it is impossible to construct a definition of personal memory that is sufficiently broad to encompass the contributions to this volume and yet sufficiently narrow to distinguish it from other types of memory.

MAJOR THEMES

Four major themes weave throughout the volume, differentially emphasized by each contributor. These themes became apparent to us as we perused the chapters, so we used them as the organizing framework for this volume. One theme is the *emergence* of autobiographical memory. Barth, Povinelli, and Cant compare the personal memory abilities of nonhuman primates with those of human children and suggest an evolutionary framework for differences in these abilities. Howe discusses his theory that personal memories depend upon the presence of a cognitive self. A second theme is the *narrative* nature of personal memory. Fivush discusses what can be gleaned from the narrative form of the memories of sexual abuse survivors. McAdams reviews his life story model of personal identity, and discusses research on two different types of life stories that might be told, the contamination sequence and the redemption sequence. Singer and Blagov discuss how the stories encapsulated in self-defining memories reveal the nature of the self and its current goals. A third theme is *emotion*. Beike and colleagues discuss the different roles that emotional and nonemotional (what they call open and closed) memories play in the momentary construction of the self. Sedikides and colleagues consider how the need for positive evaluation of the self influences memory for personal events.

A fourth theme is *time*. Skowronski reviews research on how time is represented in autobiographical memory and how memory for time undergirds our concept of our lives and ourselves. Cameron and colleagues present their theory of temporal selves, in which memory for past selves is dependent upon current goals and the desire for a positive self-view. Lampinen and colleagues analyze the basis for a sense of continuity of the self over time, in particular people who describe themselves as no longer being the same self. They refer to the first state of affairs as diachronic disunity and explore its consequences for the representation of personal memories and for adjustment.

COMPARISON TO ISSUES THAT ONCE PREDOMINATED

The present volume, as a time capsule of the state of research and theory on autobiographical memory, reflects the changing focus of the field. Although the primary focus of each chapter varies, common assumptions pervading all of the chapters represent a break with past research and theory. Most notably, two issues that were once of central concern in research on personal memory have faded. One such issue that dominated earlier research was a concern with the *accuracy* of personal memories. Indeed one of the best-known volumes of the early 1990s was titled *Affect and Accuracy in Recall* (Winograd & Neisser, 1992). Although it is often necessary to use errors and distortions as a dependent measure, inaccuracies per se are less integral to theories today than they were in the 1980s and 1990s. A second issue that once dominated was that of *imagery* in personal memory. The presence of sensory images is currently viewed as merely one of many subjective properties of personal memory that may be investigated.

In the new millennium, researchers of the self and personal memory concern themselves with issues of greater breadth than accuracy or imagery. One such issue is the *form* of personal memory representation. Some theorists see it as hierarchical (Conway & Pleydell-Pearce, 2000; McAdams, this volume; Singer & Blagov, this volume), others as narrative (Fivush, this volume; King, 2002), and still others as featural or configural. Relatedly, the *processes* by which personal memories and the self come to bear upon one another are of much greater interest now than they were ten or twenty years ago. Conway and Pleydell-Pearce (2000) are quite specific about this process, as are Cameron and colleagues, Sedikides and colleagues, and Skowronski (all found in this volume).

Another newly emerging theme is that of *subjective experience*. What do personal memories feel like? How do they make the rememberer feel? What are their subjective properties rather than their objective accuracy? Beike and colleages, Lampinen and colleagues, and Singer and Blagov all discuss subjective qualities of personal memories. In addition, a concern with *adjustment* pervades much current research and theory. Given the central role that personal memories play in everyday life, they are now being given a central role in adjustment and mental health. The positive, self-protective skew of the self-memory system is addressed by many of the contributors to this volume (e.g., Cameron et al., Sedikides et al.), and the distinction between healthy and less healthy ways of integrating the self and memory is made by others (e.g., Beike et al., Fivush, Lampinen et al., McAdams, Singer & Blagov).

Finally, the *cross-talk* among theorists in historically separate subfields of psychology (e.g., developmental and social) is finally taking place. We believe the present volume presents a compelling picture of an area of research that is the product of a diverse yet loosely affiliated group of scientists. Self and personal memory is a topic at the full flowering of its development, with theories that address the specifics of process and representation as well as the implications for health and happiness. Klein (2001) noted, "Within academic psychology . . . self and memory historically have been approached as separate areas of inquiry, with one domain largely ignoring the other. Fortunately, this situation has begun to change and research investigating self and memory, though still in its infancy, has produced a general outline of the relation" (p. 26). That general outline may be gleaned from the pages that follow. There are many points of agreement, and many areas that have yet to be decided. These are not merely the finer points; in many cases they are major points, reflecting that there is much work yet to be done. Still, the contents of this volume provide overwhelming support for James's contention that the self is the basic currency of psychology, and for Rubin's claim that personal memory is "not only a record, but a resource" (1986, p. 23) for insight into the self. The inescapable conclusion is that the self and personal memory intertwine to form the core of the human experience.

REFERENCES

Berkeley, G. (1734/1979). A treatise concerning the principles of human knowledge. In R. I. Watson (Ed.), *Basic writings in the history of psychology*. New York: Oxford University Press.

Brewer, M. B., & Gardner, W. (1996). Who is this "We"? Levels of collective identity and self representations. *Journal of Personality and Social Psychology, 71*, 83–93.

Brown, J. D. (1998). *The self*. Boston, MA: McGraw-Hill.

Conway, M. A. (1990). *Autobiographical memory: An introduction*. Milton Keynes: Open University Press.

Conway, M. A., & Pleydell-Pearce, C. W. (2000). The construction of autobiographical memories in the self memory system. *Psychological Review, 107*, 261–288.

Descartes, R. (1637/1978). Discourse on the method of rightly conducting the reason, translated by E. S. Haldane & G. R. T. Ross. In R. I. Watson (Ed.), *Basic writings in the history of psychology* (pp. 12–20). New York: Oxford University Press.

Emmons, R. A., & Kaiser, H. A. (1996). Goal orientation and emotional well-being: Linking goals and affect through the self. In L. L. Martin & A. Tesser (Eds.), *Striving and feeling: Interactions among goals, affect, and self-regulation* (pp. 79–98). Hillsdale, NJ: Lawrence Erlbaum Associates.

Fivush, R. (1991). The social construction of personal narratives. *Merrill-Palmer Quarterly, 37*, 59–82.

Gergen, K. J. (1982). From self to science: What is there to know? In J. Suls (Ed.), *Psychological perspectives on the self*, Vol. 1 (pp. 129–149). Hillsdale, NJ: Lawrence Erlbaum Associates.

Halberstadt, J. B., Niedenthal, P. M., & Setterlund, M. B. (1996). Cognitive organization of different tenses of the self mediates affect and decision making. In L. L. Martin & A. Tesser (Eds.), *Striving and feeling: Interactions among goals, affect, and self-regulation* (pp. 123–150). Hillsdale, NJ: Lawrence Erlbaum Associates.

Hume, D. (1739/1979). A treatise of human nature: Volume 1. In R. I. Watson (Ed.), *Basic writings in the history of psychology*. New York: Oxford University Press.

James, W. (1890/1981). Principles of psychology (2 vols.). In F. Burkhardt (Ed.), *The works of William James*. Cambridge, MA: Harvard University Press.

King, L. A. (2002). Gain without pain? Expressive writing and self-regulation. In S. J. Lepore & J. M. Smyth (Eds.), *The writing cure: How expressive writing promotes health and well-being*. Washington, D.C.: American Psychological Association.

Klein, S. B. (2001). A self to remember: A cognitive neuropsychological perspective on how self creates memory and memory creates self. In C. Sedikides & M. B. Brewer (Eds.). *Individual self, relational self, collective self* (pp. 25–46). Philadelphia, PA: Psychology Press.

McAdams, D. (1997). *The stories we live by: Personal myths and the making of the self.* New York: Guilford Press.

Neisser, U. (1982). Memory: What are the important questions? In U. Neisser (Ed.), *Memory observed* (pp. 3–20). San Francisco, CA: Freeman Press.

Nelson, K. (1993). The psychological and social origins of autobiographical memory. *Psychological Science 4,* 7–14.

Pillemer, D. B. (1998). *Momentous events, vivid memories.* Cambridge, MA: Harvard University Press.

Pinker, S. (1997). *How the mind works.* New York: Norton.

Robinson, J. A., & Taylor, L. R. (1998). Autobiographical memory and self-narratives: A tale of two stories. In C.P. Thompson, D. J. Herrmann, D. Bruce, J. D. Read, D. G. Payne, & M. P. Toglia (Eds.), *Autobiographical memory: Theoretical and applied perspectives* (pp. 125–143). Mahwah, NJ: Lawrence Erlbaum Associates.

Ross, M., & Wilson, A. E. (2002). It feels like yesterday: Self-esteem, valence of personal past experiences, and judgments of subjective distance. *Journal of Personality and Social Psychology, 82,* 792–803.

Rubin, D. C. (Ed.). (1986). *Autobiographical memory.* Cambridge, MA: Cambridge University Press.

Rubin, D. C. (Ed.). (1996). *Remembering our past: Studies in autobiographical memory.* New York: Cambridge University Press.

Ryff, C. D. (1991). Possible selves in adulthood and old age: A tale of shifting horizons. *Psychology and Aging, 6,* 286–295.

Singer, J. A., & Salovey, P. (1993). *The remembered self: Emotion and memory in personality.* New York: The Free Press.

Thompson, C. P., Herrmann, D. J., Bruce, D., Read, J. D., Payne, D. G., & Toglia, M. P. (Eds.). (1998). *Autobiographical memory: Theoretical and applied perspectives.* Mahwah, NJ: Lawrence Erlbaum Associates.

Tulving, E. (1983). *Elements of episodic memory.* New York: Oxford University Press.

Winograd, E., & Neisser, U. (Eds.). (1992). *Affect and accuracy in recall: Studies of "flashbulb memories."* New York: Cambridge University Press.

2

Bodily Origins of SELF

JOCHEN BARTH
Universiteit Maastricht

DANIEL J. POVINELLI
University of Louisiana at Lafayette

JOHN G. H. CANT
University of Puerto Rico Medical School

*T*hirty-five years ago, Gallup (1970) reported the existence of a surprising phylogenetic difference in the capacity of organisms to recognize themselves in mirrors: the ability appeared to be present in chimpanzees, but not in several species of monkeys that he tested. After being exposed to mirrors, he observed chimpanzees apparently using their reflected images to explore parts of themselves that they had never had the opportunity to see before (their eyes, teeth, nose, and ano-genital area, for example). Figure 2.1 provides some examples of these behaviors captured in our own laboratory. To confirm the interpretation of these spontaneous reactions, the chimpanzees were anesthetized and surreptitiously marked with a red dye on the upper portion of their eyebrow ridges and ears (locations that were only visible with the aid of a mirror). Upon recovery, the chimpanzees made no attempt to touch these areas until they were again allowed to observe themselves in a mirror, at which point they immediately began touching the marked regions of their faces (see also Povinelli et al., 1997). Gallup concluded that the chimpanzees had learned to recognize themselves in mirrors. Gallup (1970) also tested several species of Old World monkeys using the same procedures. Surprisingly, the monkeys, although initially interested in the mirror, neither exhibited the self-exploratory behavior, nor touched the red spots on their faces during the mark test.

Reports from a number of laboratories replicated Gallup's (1970) findings with chimpanzees, and continued to fail to find evidence for mirror self-recognition in

11

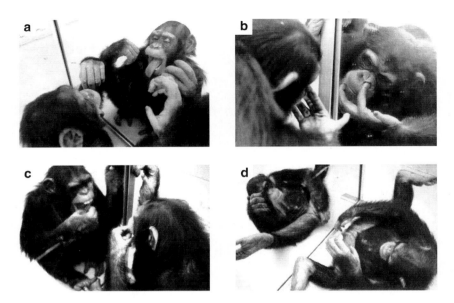

FIGURE 2.1. A 5-year-old chimpanzee (a) exhibiting exaggerated facial expressions and (b–d) otherwise invisible parts of her body while observing herself in a mirror.

lesser apes and a wide array of other nonhuman primates (review by Anderson & Gallup, 1999). Other research extended the presence of the capacity for mirror self-recognition to another great ape species, orangutans, but somewhat surprisingly, not gorillas (e.g., Suarez & Gallup, 1981). More recently, the final species of great ape, bonobos (*Pan paniscus*) has been tested and reported to exhibit evidence for mirror self-recognition, as well (although these latter tests have lacked important controls; Hyatt & Hopkins, 1994; Walraven, Elsacker, & Verheyen, 1995).

THE BODY IN THE MIRROR

As time passed and evidence continued to suggest a robust difference in the capacity for self-recognition in mirrors between chimpanzees, orangutans, and humans on the one hand and other primates on the other, Gallup (e.g., 1977) increasingly favored the provocative conclusion that differences in the capacity of organisms to recognize themselves in mirrors might reflect differences in the presence of self-awareness, what he defined as the ability to become the object of one's own attention. His common-sense interpretation of the results was that it was impossible to know who it was you were seeing in a mirror unless you first had a concept of self. Later Gallup (1982) further speculated that if chimpanzees and orangutans were self-aware in this sense, they might also have the capacity to reflect upon their own experiences and, by inference, the experiences of others as well.

Gallup's empirical findings concerning the phylogenetic distribution of the phenomenon of mirror self-recognition have withstood the test of time (see below, and recent review by Anderson & Gallup, 1999). However, until recently, the accounts of why these kinds of reactions to seeing the self in a mirror were restricted to chimpanzees, orangutans, and humans were sparse (and troubling) — as were detailed theories of the cognitive mechanisms supporting the ability. On the face of it, the fact that this ability was limited to the great apes and humans seemed odd, especially given the difficulty in imagining an ecological context in which evolution would have favored the ability to recognize oneself in a mirror. Rather, self-recognition in mirrors was seen as a by-product of selection for some other, unspecified abilities (e.g., Humphrey, 1976). Reasoning in this manner, some scholars attempted to link the phenomenon with a higher degree of social intelligence, but this account left unexplained why the ability was not found in the dozens of other highly social primates, but was present in highly solitary orangutans.

The first integrated evolutionary account of why the capacity for self-recognition in mirrors was restricted to the great apes and humans was provided a decade ago by Povinelli and Cant (1995). Their explanation took a surprising turn, essentially amounting to an account (contra ideas by Gallup, 1982) of how the great apes evolved a more explicit representation of their *bodies*, not their minds. Povinelli and Cant argued that the unique aspects of the self-concept that evolved in the ancestor of the great apes and humans (aspects that are reflected in the mirror test), were largely *kinesthetic* ones (see Gallup, 1970). They speculated that an explicit representation of some aspect of the kinesthetic component of the self evolved as a result of a peculiar convergence of organismal and ecological factors faced by the common ancestor of the great apes and humans. In particular, they hypothesized that the fourfold difference in the body mass of the great apes (chimpanzees, bonobos, orangutans, and gorillas) as compared to other highly arboreal (tree-dwelling) primates, generated substantial challenges for these animals as they evolved their larger body masses. Povinelli and Cant proposed that this evolutionary increase in body mass rendered the habitat increasingly difficult to traverse, primarily because of the severe deformation of supports (tree limbs) caused by this body mass. Using aspects of the morphology and behavior of modern orangutans as a rough model of the common ancestor, they highlighted how the orangutan's extreme body mass forces it to spend a nontrivial amount of time engaged in locomotor activities that appear to require a great deal of flexibility and planning in the translocation of the body through the arboreal habitat in which it travels. Finally, they speculated that this process of locomotion required the coevolution of a more elaborated representation of the body and its actions to assist in planning and deploying the orangutans' movements. For purposes of clarity, we shall hereafter refer to this particular body image[1] and its attendant systems in large-bodied arboreal primates in highly compliant environments as Self Evolved for Locomotor Flexibility (SELF). Povinelli and Cant further speculated that this self-representational system might have established a quite explicit self concept, one which allows for the behaviors characteristic of mirror self-recognition, and one which may have served as the point of departure for the more elaborate, psychological aspects of the self-concept so characteristic of humans. In this chapter we revisit this model, and clarify and refine certain of its features. We also describe several new predictions that can be derived from the model, along with some preliminary investigations we have conducted to test them.

We begin by reviewing the current evidence concerning species differences in mirror self-recognition. We then provide a brief account of a class of causal models of the phenomenon, and show why self-recognition in mirrors may depend, fundamentally, upon an explicit, kinesthetic representation of the self (SELF) that initially evolved to subserve behavioral solutions to the problems created by the large body mass that evolved in the ancestor of the great apes and humans. Next, we explore the distribution of other abilities in chimpanzees and the great apes which may also either depend upon or be greatly facilitated by the SELF system purported to be uniquely present in these species. In doing so, we describe a preliminary attempt to test the generality of one component of the model by testing whether the SELF system of chimpanzees (and presumably orangutans, as well) expresses itself in situations other than mirror self-recognition (in this case, a tool-using situation).

A SHORT COURSE ON MIRROR SELF-RECOGNITION IN PRIMATES AND OTHER ANIMALS

Three challenges have been raised in response to Gallup's claim that mirror self-recognition is restricted to the great apes and humans: (1) chimpanzees do not really display the behaviors Gallup reported, (2) chimpanzees do exhibit these behaviors, but so do other nonhuman primate species (including gorillas and certain species of monkeys), and (3) regardless of whether other primates do or do not exhibit self-recognition, certain nonprimate taxa (such as dolphins) can do so. We briefly examine each of these claims in turn.

Do Chimpanzees "Recognize" Themselves in Mirrors? — Yes

Gallup's (1970) interpretation of the spontaneous self-exploratory behaviors exhibited by chimpanzees (in conjunction with the subjects' responses to the marks tests) was that chimpanzees were capable of using mirrors to explore parts of their bodies that were not previously visible to them. In a widely circulated series of reports, Heyes (1994, 1995, 1998) challenged this (and other aspects) of Gallup's (1970) interpretation. She hypothesized that the spontaneous self-exploratory behaviors reported by Gallup and others were inherently ambiguous, and that the increase of mark-directed touches from the control to the test period could be explained in other ways. In particular, she argued that chimpanzees normally engage in a significant level of ambient face-touching behavior (e.g. scratching and self-grooming), and therefore speculated that a likely effect of the anesthesia used in the marking procedure would be to depress these baseline levels of face-touching behaviors. She thus argued that the elevation in touches to the marked regions during the test period that Gallup (1970) and others reported may have been due to a decline in the effects of the anaesthetic agent across the control and test period. This amounted to a claim that the entire phenomenon of self-recognition in chimpanzees was a methodological artifact.

Povinelli and colleagues (1997) tested several competing predictions that can be derived from Heyes's model versus the self-recognition model, and in each case found clear and unambiguous support for the predictions of the self-recognition model. Indeed, the results were incompatible with every empirical prediction that can be derived from Heyes's model. First, during the mark tests, the chimpanzees selectively touched the marked areas of the face, as compared to the contralateral, unmarked areas (see Figure 2.2). Second, unlike the pattern predicted by a gradual recovery from anesthesia (a gradual increase in touches to the marked areas of the face), there was a clear temporal spike in the chimpanzees' touches to the marked regions *coincident with the uncovering of the mirror* (see Figure 2.2). Finally, after spiking, the number of touches to the marks *declined* across the test (as opposed to increasing and stabilizing at some ambient level, as predicted by Heyes), presumably because the animals discovered their inconsequential nature (see Figure 2.2).

Although the predictions of Heyes's proposal have been empirically falsified, it should be noted that investigations with larger numbers of chimpanzees of different ages have suggested that certain qualifications of Gallup's (1970) original conclusions are nonetheless warranted. First, there is a much more rapid onset of self-recognition in mirror-naive animals than reported by Gallup (Povinelli et al., 1993). Second, there are developmental dissociations among some types of mirror-mediated, self-directed behaviors and others (Povinelli et al., 1993; Eddy, Gallup, & Povinelli, 1996). Third, only certain types of mirror-mediated behaviors (e.g., self-exploratory behaviors) are associated with passing the mark test (Povinelli, Rulf, Landau, & Bierschwale, 1993; Eddy, Gallup, & Povinelli, 1996). And finally, not all chimpanzees exhibit behaviors diagnostic of self-recognition (Swartz & Evans, 1991; Povinelli et al., 1993; de Veer, van der Bos, Theall, Gallup, & Povinelli, 2002). None of these facts, however, suggests that the general phenomenon as reported by Gallup (1970) is unreliable. Indeed, test–retest measures have suggested stability of this trait in many individual animals for up to 8 years (de Veer et al., 2002).

Is Self-Recognition Absent in Lesser Apes and Monkeys? — Apparently So

Literally hundreds of monkeys, representing a wide array of species, have been tested in the 35 years since Gallup's (1970) original report (see Anderson & Gallup, 1999). Furthermore, the range of techniques that have been employed to try to "pry" this capacity out of monkeys is impressive (see Anderson & Gallup, 1999), if for no other reason than that these attempts stand as a constant reminder that

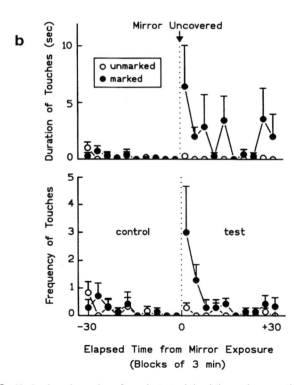

FIGURE 2.2. Method and results of mark test: (a) while under anesthesia, regions of the subject's face are targeted to be marked with a red dye (shaded areas) and contralateral facial regions (unshaded areas) are targeted as control areas, and upon full recovery (b) subject is exposed to a covered mirror for 30 minutes, followed immediately by 30 minutes of exposure to a mirror. Note that in (b) touches to the facial regions are selective to the marked areas, coincident with the uncovering of the mirror, and decline after the subject discovers that the marks are inconsequential.

the phylogenetic difference in the capacity does not appear to be a trivial one. This is not to say that no one has claimed to have found the capacity in species of nonhuman primates outside the great ape/human group. Perhaps the most celebrated of these was a report by Hauser and colleagues (1995) that reported to have demonstrated self-recognition in virtually every cotton-top tamarin tested. However, after the original videotapes of this study were made available, and the methodology and interpretation of this study were criticized (e.g., Anderson & Gallup, 1997), the authors later reported a series of failures to replicate their results (Hauser, Miller, Liu, & Gupta, 2001).

Naturally, there are two ways of interpreting the inability to detect the capacity for self-recognition in primates outside the great ape/human group. One approach is to try to understand what this difference might mean about the self-representational systems of species (or individual organisms) that do and do not exhibit evidence of self-recognition in mirrors. The other approach is to assume that the differences that have been observed to date do not reflect significant, underlying cognitive differences among species, but instead are superficial artifacts of minor attentional, motivational, and/or perceptual differences. With respect to the latter strategy, numerous methodological explanations have been offered as possible reasons why monkeys do not display mirror-mediated self-exploratory behaviors or pass the mark test. In our estimation, however, none of these possibilities has survived empirical scrutiny (see Anderson & Gallup, 1999).

Let us briefly examine just two of the most frequently raised methodological concerns surrounding the empirical findings with monkeys. First, it has been widely suggested that because direct eye contact is typically a threatening signal in monkeys, they avoid closely inspecting their mirror images, and hence fail to learn as much about their mirror-image as do chimpanzees and orangutans (see, e.g., Gallup, Wallnau, & Suarez, 1980). A study by Anderson and Roeder (1989) examined this idea by confronting capuchin monkeys with two mirrors placed at a 60 degree angle to each other, thus allowing them to look at themselves without having to make direct eye contact. Despite extended exposure, the capuchins showed no evidence for mirror self-recognition (see also Anderson & Gallup, 1999, for other attempts to test this hypothesis).

Second, many skeptics have suggested that perhaps monkeys, lesser apes, and even gorillas, are simply not as interested in their bodies as are chimpanzees and orangutans. Thus, perhaps they do not pass the mark test simply because they do not care about the appearance of these marks. Gallup, Wallnau, and Suarez (1980) tested this hypothesis by marking monkeys on their abdomens, as well as on their ears and foreheads. Upon recovery from anesthesia, the monkeys exhibited an intense interest in touching and inspecting the marks on their abdomens (the ones they could directly see), but not the ones they could only observe through the mirror (the ones on their faces), thus ruling out the idea that they were simply uninterested in such marks. A similar study by Suarez and Gallup (1981) inv four gorillas exposed these animals to mirrors for a total of 80 hours. Desp extended interaction with mirrors, these gorillas did not attempt to to experimentally applied marks on their faces during the mark test, ever they exhibited considerable interest in marks that were placed on their wrists (see also Shillito, Gallup, & Beck, 1999). This procedure has since emerged as an important motivational control for the mark test in species (or individuals) that do not exhibit evidence of self-recognition (e.g., Povinelli et al., 1993).

Are Gorillas a Puzzling Case? — Yes and No

Gallup's (1970) initial assumption was that the ability for self-recognition might be restricted to the great apes and humans. Extensive testing of gorillas, however, has revealed that these great apes typically do not exhibit the kinds of spontaneous self-exploratory behaviors in front of mirrors displayed by chimpanzees and orangutans, nor have they exhibited evidence of passing properly controlled[2] mark tests (see Suarez & Gallup, 1981; Ledbetter & Basen, 1982; Shillito, Gallup, & Beck, 1999). On the face of it, this should be puzzling, given the phylogenetic relationships of the great apes and humans (Figure 2.3). The orangutan lineage diverged earliest from the last common ancestor of this group, whereas chimpanzees, gorillas, and humans are more closely related. Given the presence of the ability in most species of great apes, but its absence in all other primate species tested thus far (see Figure 2.3), the most parsimonious analysis suggests that the capacity evolved in the last common ancestor of the great ape/human group, and that this capacity was subsequently lost in the gorilla lineage (see Povinelli, 1994). Although the loss of this ability in gorillas may at first seem odd, as we discuss below, this fact turns out to be consistent with the evolutionary model offered by Povinelli and Cant (1995). In other words, the absence of self-recognition in mirrors in gorillas may be understandable in the context of the clambering hypothesis.

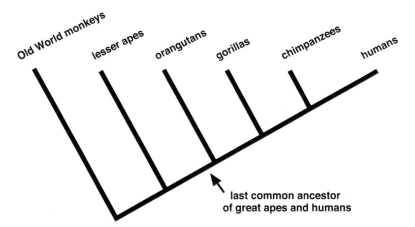

FIGURE 2.3. Phylogeny of the great apes and humans showing lesser apes (gibbons and siamangs) and Old World monkeys as outgroups. The split between the orangutans and the African apes and humans occurred approximately 15–20 million years ago.

Can Dolphins Recognize Themselves in Mirrors? — Maybe, Maybe Not

Numerous species outside the primate order have been assessed for their reactions to their mirror images (see Gallup, 1968, for a review), but only a handful of them have actually been tested using Gallup's (1970) procedure. Furthermore, until recently, none had been reported to exhibit patterns of behavior suggestive of self-recognition (e.g., elephants: Povinelli, 1989). An exception may be dolphins. Reiss and Marino (2001) reported positive evidence of "self-directed" mirror-mediated behavior in two bottle-nosed dolphins, where self-directed referred to elevations in the amount of time dolphins spent looking at themselves in mirrors, and the adoption of certain postures while marked. It is important to note, however, that the evidence for self-recognition in dolphins derives from measurements that are not strictly comparable to those used with primates. Two dolphins were repeatedly either marked or sham-marked (i.e., the experimenters merely pretended to mark them) while fully conscious. Dolphins were then reported to swim to a preexisting mirror faster[3] when they were marked (or sham-marked) and were reported to spend more time in front of a mirror when marked than when not marked. However, the fact that an organism may increase the amount of time spent looking in a mirror after having been marked does not necessarily indicate self-recognition. For example, over 20 years ago Gallup and his colleagues showed that rhesus monkeys will exhibit elevated levels of looking at a mirror after having been marked without exhibiting spontaneous self-exploratory behavior or attempting to touch the marks on their faces (e.g., Gallup, Wallnau, & Suarez, 1980). It is as if the monkey in the mirror has become interesting again because of the novelty of its marked face! Nonetheless, despite the reservations we have expressed here, if the findings of Reiss and Marino (2001) are replicated with a design that surmounts the interpretative problems we have expressed, the capacity for self-recognition in dolphins would constitute a remarkable case of convergent evolution, and could point to an alternative evolutionary route for evolving a SELF system.

BODY MASS, HABITAT DEFORMATION, AND THE EVOLUTION OF SELF

With respect to the phylogenetic distribution of the capacity for self-recognition in mirrors, the evidence just reviewed continues to point in the direction suggested by Gallup over three decades ago: spontaneous, mirror-mediated, self-exploratory patterns of behavior, and positive results using the mark test, appear to be limited to the great apes and humans (with the caveats concerning gorillas and dolphins described above). This means that 15–20 million years ago, some ability evolved in the common ancestor of the great apes and humans that now manifests itself as the capacity for self-recognition in mirrors. But what exactly was this ability, and what was the evolutionary context that produced it? Any attempt to answer this question must begin by providing a clearer specification of what the task is measuring in the first place.

Theory of the Mirror Self-Recognition Task

As his thinking about the task developed, Gallup (e.g., 1977) increasingly assumed that the patterns of behavior exhibited by chimpanzees in front of mirrors are generated by an inference of the sort, "That's me!" But what dimensions of "me" must necessarily be represented in order to respond to mirrors in this way? Gallup (1982, 1985, 1998) has emphasized the role of reflecting on one's own mental states. Further, he and others have suggested that the capacity for self-recognition in mirrors in both human infants and chimpanzees may be connected with the emergence of an objective perspective on the self's past and future, by attempting to link the onset of self-recognition in human toddlers (occurring at around 18–24 months of age) with the emergence of autobiographical memory (see Brooks-Gunn & Lewis, 1984; Gallup, 1982, 1998; Howe & Courage, 1993, 1997; Howe, this volume).

But do the behaviors exhibited by chimpanzees and young children in front of mirrors really depend upon representing these psychological and temporal dimensions of the self? Both Mitchell (1993) and Povinelli (1995) have offered alternatives to these views, and have provided detailed analyses of the mirror task which both suggest that mirror-mediated self-exploratory behavior (including passing the mark test) may most directly depend on an explicit representation of one's kinesthetic states — one's body image. Indeed, this general idea seems consistent with Gallup's (1970) original view of the task: ". . . self-directed and mark-directed behaviors would seem to require the ability to project, as it were, proprioceptive information and kinesthetic feedback onto the reflected visual image so as to coordinate the appropriate visually guided movements via the mirror" (p. 87). However, the exact mechanisms by which infants (and chimpanzees) come to understand the explicit connection between their body and their mirror image has been a matter of some debate, with several theories currently under consideration. In order to gain some insight into the nature of the self-representation that may have evolved in the last common ancestor of the great apes and humans, it is necessary to briefly explore causal theories of the phenomenon of mirror self-recognition in humans.

Mitchell (1993) argued that the young child (or chimpanzee, for that matter) must first learn that mirrors contingently reflect objects in front of them before they can apply this idea to the case of their own body, and offered two theories about how this might be accomplished. The existing data would seem to suggest that this premise is incorrect; it is not necessary to understand how mirrors work in order to pass the mark test (discussion by Povinelli, 1995). Research with human infants, for example, has consistently shown that there is no correlation between whether infants pass the mark test and whether they can solve a simple task of turning around to look at a toy that is presented in a mirror (Loveland, 1986; Robinson, Connell, McKenzie, & Day, 1990). Thus, passing the mark test would not seem to depend upon understanding the pragmatics of mirror use. Further, human infants raised in cultures without mirrors pass the mark test at the same age as infants raised in cultures with mirrors, after only a brief (5-minute) pretest exposure to their mirror images (Priel & de Schonen, 1986).

Povinelli's (1995) theory of self-recognition in human infants also emphasizes the role of the kinesthetic dimension of the self, but, unlike Mitchell's theory, specifies that understanding the pragmatics of how mirrors work is not necessary to exhibit patterns of self-exploratory behavior, or to pass a mark test. Instead, his theory pinpoints the existence of an explicit representation of the integrated body image as the critical factor. Once an organism can hold in mind a representation of the current state of its body, it is in the position to begin to form explicit relations among objects of perception (e.g., the image in a mirror) and the body image. One such relation that seems critical to exhibit the patterns of behavior that are taken to be criterial for self-recognition in mirrors, is an equivalence relation: *that thing (image in the mirror)* is equivalent to *my body*.[4] In analyzing the mirror task, Gallup (1970), Mitchell (1993), and others have emphasized the role of a system that matches (commonly codes) kinesthetic and visual information. While not denying the role that such common coding must play in the self-recognition task, Povinelli has noted that various forms of imitation are present well before 18 months, some even at birth (see Meltzoff & Moore, 1999, for a review). Therefore, such systems are not likely to be the limiting factor for the self-recognition task.

The above considerations can be interpreted to suggest that a crucial advance in the development in self-representation in human infants occurs when the kinesthetic aspect of the body is raised to a level of explicitness that it can be held in mind as an object of attention in its own right (Povinelli, 1995). This kind of "on-line" representation of the self's bodily actions can be contrasted with an even more advanced understanding of the self as a thing that has repeated instantiations across time — a continuous history.

The Present Self, Extended in Time

Since the early 1990s, Povinelli and colleagues have been attempting to better understand the kind of on-line, kinesthetic self-representation supporting mirror self-recognition in human infants, by contrasting it with a more temporally extended self-representation that emerges later in development (see Povinelli, 2001, for a review of this research). In one extended series of studies, they explored the role that temporal contingency plays in supporting mirror self-recognition in young children. For example, when the images observed by the young child were not live (as they are in a mirror) but slightly delayed, this strongly affected the children's ability to exhibit evidence of recognizing themselves. In one series of studies, Povinelli, Landau, and Perilloux (1996) exposed 2-, 3-, and 4-year-old children to both live and briefly delayed visual images of themselves. In one experiment, each child was videotaped as he or she played a distinctive and novel game with an experimenter. During the game, the experimenter praised the child, and used this as the opportunity to secretly place a large, brightly-colored sticker on top of the child's head. Three minutes later, the children were either shown the video recording of the events that had just happened including a clear depiction of the experimenter placing the sticker on their head. The results were striking. None of the 2-year-olds, and only 25% of the 3-year-olds reached up to search for the sticker. Although it might be tempting to think that the children simply did not notice the sticker in the delayed video, this was not the case. Many of them spontaneously commented or laughed when the video depicted the sticker being placed on their head. Furthermore, after the video playback was over, we drew their attention to the sticker on their image in the video, and asked them, "What is that?" The majority of the children responded, "It's a sticker," or something comparable. But significantly, this did not lead them to reach up to their own head to search for it. Even when we asked them if they could get it, they typically looked at the image, shrugged their shoulders and replied, "I can't." In another experiment, the same basic procedures were used to directly compare how 2- to 3-year-old children would react to seeing themselves in the standard delayed image, versus a live image. Most of the children in the live condition reached up to remove the sticker, whereas very few children in the delayed condition did so.

We must be careful here. In one sense, 2- to 3-year-old children can recognize themselves in delayed video or photographs. For example, when asked "Who is that?" even the youngest of preschoolers we tested replied, "me!" or stated their proper names (see Povinelli et al., 1996, Exp. 2; Povinelli & Simon, 1998; Povinelli et al., 1999, Exp. 1). However, this recognition seems to occur at the level of their physical features (perhaps most strongly their facial features). For example, when asked, "Where is that sticker?" they frequently made reference to the "other" child: "It's on *her* [or *his*] head." It was as if the children were attempting to say that, "Yes, that *looks* like me, but it's not *me* — she's not doing what I'm doing." One 3-year-old girl summarized this psychological conflict quite succinctly: "It's Jennifer," she stated — but then hurriedly added, "Why is she wearing my shirt?" Coupled with the results of the mark test, our conclusion from these data are that at any given moment, there are multiple dimensions of the self that might or might not be explicitly represented or recognized, and it should not be surprising that at various points in development not all of these aspects of the self may be available to the child.

So when does the child develop a more autobiographical or historical stance toward the self? Our tests reveal that by about 4 years of age a significant majority of children begin to pass our tests of delayed self-recognition, implying that they understand the historical-causal linkage between past and present versions of themselves. Unlike their younger counterparts, 4- to 5-year-olds typically reach up to remove the sticker when they observe the delayed images of themselves. Also, no longer do they refer to "him" or "her" when talking about the images, nor do they state their proper names. The transition in performance on our test at 4 years of age is generally consistent with the suggestions by Nelson (1992), Fivush (2001), Welch-Ross (1999), and others, that autobiographical memory may not

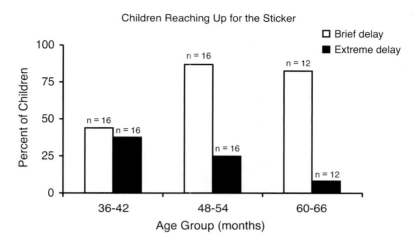

FIGURE 2.4. Results of a test to determine if 3-, 4-, and 5-year-olds can distinguish between the relevance of videotape showing a sticker having been placed on their heads 7 days earlier (extreme delay) versus 3 minutes earlier (brief delay). As shown here, 4- and 5-year-olds appreciate that only the briefly delayed images are causally relevant to their current appearance. See text for details.

emerge until 3.5 to 4.5 years of age — considerably later than the 18- to 24-month mark others have suggested based in large part on the age at which children begin to recognize themselves in mirrors (e.g., Brooks-Gunn & Lewis, 1984; Howe & Courage, 1993, 1997; Gallup, 1998).

Perhaps the most dramatic confirmation of our interpretation of the delayed self-recognition tests came from a study in which we invited 3-, 4-, and 5-year-old children to visit our center twice, with each visit separated by a week (see Povinelli & Simon, 1998). During the first visit, each child played a novel, distinctive game in a playroom with two experimenters. As in our previous studies, we secretly placed a sticker on each of their heads. However, at the end of the game, rather than letting them watch the video, we surreptitiously removed the sticker and the child went home. On the second visit, the child played a different game in a different room, during which we once again placed a sticker on his or her head. At this point, the critical manipulation of the study occurred: half of the children in each age group were shown the video recording of what had just happened, whereas the other half were shown the video from one week earlier. The 4- and 5-year-old children understood the difference. In these age groups, the children who saw the briefly delayed video reached up to their heads to search for the sticker, whereas the ones who viewed the week-old tape did not (see Figure 2.4). In direct contrast, not only did the 3-year-olds reach up less than half of the time, they did so with equal frequency whether they had been shown the 3-minute-old video or the week-old one (see Figure 2.4). Apparently, not only did the younger children generally not appreciate that the delayed images could be relevant to their current appearance, even the ones who did reach up to their heads did not take into account the critical variable: when the events had occurred in causal relation to the present moment.

Summary of the Self-System that Underwrites the Mirror Task

To recap, our theory of the mirror task is that the behaviors that are taken as evidence of self-recognition in chimpanzees and very young children are supported by an explicit mental representation of the actions of their bodies (possibly their agency) — not their mental states. We have argued that the mirror-mediated behaviors exhibited by chimpanzees and orangutans on the one hand, and young children, on the other, are, at their foundation, derived from an ability to form an explicit equivalence relation between what they see in the mirror and what they directly experience in their own behavior. Every time they act, the mirror (or live video) acts with them. An organism possessing an explicit representation (a concept, as it were) of this kinesthetic experience, ought to be able to conclude that "Everything that's true of this (my body) is also true of that (the mirror image) — and vice versa." Thus, unlike other species, chimpanzees and orangutans may possess an explicit or integrated enough representation of their bodies to have a concept (my body) onto which they can map what they see occurring in a mirror. Note that this is not meant to imply that for 18- to 24-month-old human children the *only* aspect of the self explicitly represented is the body; rather, it is simply meant to suggest that regardless of whether other aspects of the self (say, the mental aspects) are represented or not, these other representations would not appear to play a pivotal role in eliciting behaviors diagnostic of passing the mirror test. From this perspective, the fact that in human infants the capacity for self-recognition in mirrors is correlated with certain kinds of knowledge of the psychological linkages between self and others, such as those underpinning the self-conscious emotions, synchronic imitation, and empathy (Asendorpf & Baudonniere, 1993; Bischof-Köhler, 1988; Johnson, 1982; Lewis, Sullivan, Stanger, & Weiss, 1989) is all the more intriguing, because it suggests that in human development, at least, this level of explicitness of the self's physical aspect is linked in important ways to other kinds of equivalencies between self and other. Whether these equivalences are present in the same fashion in other species that exhibit evidence of self-recognition in mirrors, such as chimpanzees, remains unclear.

Evolutionary Origins of SELF: A Body Too Heavy for the Trees?

But then why do humans, chimpanzees, and orangutans possess this integrated and explicit bodily self-concept in the first place, while other animals — such as monkeys — do not? This question amounts to asking what evolutionary forces sculpted this bodily representation in the last common ancestor of the great ape/human group.

Clearly, any viable theory of the evolution of the kind of body image that we are talking about must begin with the recognition that all organisms with a reasonably developed nervous system must possess dedicated systems for monitoring the effects of external stimuli on the body. In the case of organisms with complex central nervous systems, quite elaborated mechanisms for proprioceptive and kinesthetic feedback are present (see Berlucchi & Aglioti, 1997). This includes, of course, human infants (for discussions of the "ecological" self of human infants, see Butterworth, 1992, 1995). Furthermore, it stands to reason that specific proprioceptive and kinesthetic systems are differentially elaborated in different lineages. However, there would seem to be no a priori reason why these aspects of the self would necessarily need to be represented as objects of knowledge in the central cognitive system in order to function effectively. (Indeed, for what it is worth, such systems are typically taxonomized under the construct of the body schema, and therefore placed outside the purview of the system of intentional action; see Gallagher, 1986.)

Thus, to make progress, we must be prepared to accept a distinction between systems that *embody* proprioceptive and kinesthetic information — that is, systems that are self-specifying for bodily senses — versus systems that represent the body as an object in its own right (akin to the distinction between self-perception and self-conception; see Butterworth, 1992). With this distinction in mind, we need to ask, What factors could have led to the selection for a more robust and integrated representation of the body? or, Why would the ancestors of the great ape/human group, in particular, have needed to evolve a greater capacity to reason about the ongoing effects of the body on the environment during locomotion? As noted earlier, Povinelli and Cant (1995) proposed that this system — what we have for purposes of convenience and clarity labeled the SELF system — evolved to cope with a specific set of organismic and ecological factors that converged in the ancestors of the great apes and humans.

One clue as to why such an explicit representation of the body might have evolved when it did lies in the large difference in body mass between the great apes and other primates. Consider orangutans, whose body mass and arboreal lifestyle may represent the closest living approximation to the condition of the last common ancestor of the great apes and humans. Povinelli and Cant (1995) noted that these 40 kg (female) to 80 kg (male) animals face specific problems in moving from one location to another that are not faced to an appreciable degree by other arboreal primates with smaller body masses. For example, as orangutans attempt to cross from one tree to the next, they not only encounter natural gaps in the canopy, but, due to their extreme body mass acting to deform the limbs of trees, they create gaps, as well. Of course, as any arboreal animal moves outward from the center of a tree, its body mass can, depending on the morphology of the branches, deform the habitat around it, opening gaps between adjacent habitat structures. However, the deformation caused by the very large body mass of orangutans (especially adults) as they attempt to move from one resource patch to the next, creates unusually severe problems because, unlike smaller-bodied arboreal primates, the gaps they create are likely to be larger, and they cannot simply leap across such gaps (in fact, orangutans do not leap at all). Thus, what might be a more or less continuous path for a primate of smaller body mass (punctuated by gaps that they can leap across) will be experienced as a discontinuous path for the orangutan. We also suggest that the combination of the greater deformation caused by greater body mass with variable spatial arrangements of branches and lianas (themselves varying in compliance) creates greater diversity of gap-crossing challenges for very large animals. Finally, because the relative strength of the habitat is reduced as body mass increases, and each support is less stable as it deforms downward, orangutans must be more selective about the structures they utilize. In summary, we propose that the different nature of discontinuity in the canopy for an arboreal mammal of very large mass, coupled with a general reduction in relative habitat strength and stability, combine to create unique challenges to effective locomotion. Thus an evolutionary increase in one dimension of the animal's body — its mass — has had cascading effects on its locomotion-related activities (see Figure 2.5).

Reflecting on the interacting factors just discussed, Povinelli and Cant (1995) hypothesized that the dramatic increase in body mass that occurred during the evolution of the ancestor of the modern great apes and humans, resulted in selection for what we are calling the SELF system, a system that enhances locomotor capacities. The potentially great selective importance of these capacities is apparent from Cant's (1992a) observation that the basic components of reproductive success, such as finding food and mates and avoiding predators, depend directly on the effectiveness with which an animal negotiates its habitat. Thus, one may reason that as body mass evolved in the great ape/human lineage past some deformation-related limit, and degree of arboreality remained constant, selection would have favored those individuals that could deploy effective new solutions to these problems. The SELF system as we envision it integrates explicit representation of the body, with systems for planning and executing locomotor actions in a highly deformable habitat in which supports used by the animal change their locations not only relative to the animal as it moves, which is true for all moving animals, but in relation to each other due to the loads imposed by the animal itself.

Povinelli and Cant (1995) proposed that one of the principal solutions to the problems described above was the increasing dependence upon a particular mode of locomotion called "orthograde clambering." However, it now seems clear that emphasizing a particular *mode* of locomotion may have diverted attention from the key distinction (admittedly, more difficult to quantify) in the arboreal locomotion of orangutans — a distinction involving a unique *process* of locomotion through highly compliant habitat structures — and caused us to focus on a behavior (clambering) that is too broadly defined to be useful in this context. Povinelli and Cant proposed that this organismal–ecological interface entailed the coevolution of a more integrated, explicit representation of the body, along with attendant systems for planning and executing these actions in an arboreal environment: what we have now labeled the SELF system.

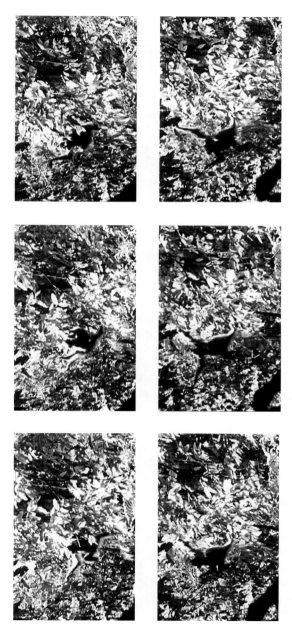

FIGURE 2.5. An adult female orangutan crossing a gap between two trees by clambering.

It is crucial to note our belief that the problems solved by the SELF system are rarely, if ever, encountered by certain smaller-bodied arboreal primates who live in the same habitat as Sumatran orangutans. Consider long-tailed macaques. Their body mass (3.5–5.5 kg) is generally too small to generate difficult gaps, and thus for them the canopy functions as a more or less continuous substrate. In those cases where natural gaps are encountered, these smaller-bodied primates can simply leap across them — for scaling reasons, an option not available to 40–80 kg orangutans! Thus, for long-tailed macaques, over 90% of their daily locomotion can be described by highly stereotyped modes of locomotion (walking, running, leaping, etc.; see Cant, 1988). An intermediate, and therefore interesting case, is the siamang, which may weigh as much as 11 kg. Even this body mass would appear to be large enough to make travel along the top of branches less stable as the siamang's primary mode of locomotion, brachiation, is suspension below branches. However, siamang body mass is apparently not so large as to require the unique process of locomotion practiced by orangutans as they travel through a network of arboreal structures that severely deform under the loads created by their body mass. Siamangs typically cross large gaps in the travel path by leaping on a downward trajectory or dropping (Fleagle, 1976). Furthermore, like long-tailed macaques and other primates, a high proportion of siamang loco-motion can be described by stereotyped modes of locomotion. Thus, in contrast to orangutans, other arboreal primates inhabiting the same habitat have apparently not crossed a body mass threshold (the value of which is presently unknown) where deformation of habitat structure becomes so severe that a more explicit body image becomes necessary to keep track of the body's moment-to-moment effect on the surrounding environment.

Although such problem-solving activities of orangutans during locomotion have been qualitatively described elsewhere (Cant, 1992b; Chevalier-Skolnikoff, Galdikas, & Skolnikoff, 1982; Povinelli & Cant, 1995), what is needed now is the development of methods that can produce *quantifiable* estimates of the difference in the complexity of habitat deformation and the orangutan's response to it during bouts of locomotion through highly compliant portions of the arboreal habitat, on the one hand, and locomotion in other contexts where habitat deformation is mild to nonexistent (e.g., locomotion along large, horizontal tree limbs), on the other. A critical component of such research efforts will be the development of reliable methods for describing, and then comparing, the maximum complexity of habitat deformation created by the very large bodied orangutans, to that created by the considerably smaller-bodied arboreal lesser apes and New World monkeys (such as spider monkeys and woolly monkeys) whose body mass (although four times smaller than female orangutans) is still considerable enough to create a nontrivial degree of habitat deformation. Inter-specific comparisons of this kind should allow us to identify the unique "signatures" of habitat deformation generated by very large-bodied apes, as well as their behavioral response to such deformation, with the ultimate aim of more clearly specifying the unique challenges faced by these animals.

TABLE 2.1. Mirror Self-Recognition Status, Body Mass, and Complexity of Arboreal Locomotion in the Extant Great Apes

Species	Mirror Self-Recognition Status	Body Mass Rank[a] (kg, male/female)	Complexity of Arboreal Travel[b]
Orangutan	+	2 (78/35)	1
Bonobo	+	4 (45/33)	2
Chimpanzee	+	3 (50/41)	3
Gorilla	−	1 (169/80)	4 (terrestrial)

[a] Body mass in kg from Fleagle (1999, Table 7.2, body mass among subspecies was averaged). [b]Species ranks for arboreal travel are derived from estimates of time spent in complex positional behavior while crossing from one tree to the next.

Arboreal Gap-Crossing and Life History Parameters in Comparative Perspective

Focusing just on the four species of extant great apes (chimpanzees, bonobos, orangutans, and gorillas), our model posits a relationship between arboreality, body mass, and body image. (Humans, of course, are a special case that we shall examine in a moment.) Table 2.1 organizes what is currently known about degree of arboreality, body mass, and mirror self-recognition in the extant great apes. Using the last common ancestor of the great ape/human group as a reference, orangutans appear to have become quite specialized in their behavioral responses to the deformation caused by their body mass while moving through the canopy, gorillas have moved in the opposite direction, essentially becoming reterrestrialized, with chimpanzees and bonobos somewhere intermediate of these two extremes.

The most intriguing aspect of the data summarized in Table 2.1 concerns gorillas. Although there are individual differences in mirror self-recognition among chimpanzees and orangutans[5] (see e.g. Povinelli et al., 1993), at least three well-controlled studies with lowland gorillas have failed to produce even a single animal that has exhibited compelling evidence of self-recognition (see earlier discussion). Not surprisingly, the gorilla's readaptation to a terrestrial way of life appears to have had consequences for certain aspects of their life history. Compared to orangutans, gorillas exhibit an accelerated pattern of development in virtually all areas: they locomote independently at a younger age, they are weaned sooner, and exhibit earlier menarche and age at first birth. Although the data are not excellent, chimpanzees and bonobos again appear to be somewhat intermediate (see Povinelli & Cant, 1995). Finally, and perhaps more importantly, gorillas appear to develop certain aspects of physical maturity not just absolutely faster, but also when compared to certain aspects of intellectual development (e.g., Antinucci, 1990; Chevalier-Skolnikoff, 1983; Parker, 1999; Redshaw, 1978; Spinozzi & Natale, 1989).

One possible conclusion from these data is that as the gorilla lineage was evolving towards a more terrestrial way of life, they no longer needed the SELF system (which evolved to sub-serve a behavioral solution to the habitat deformation occurring during arboreal locomotion), and hence were free to trade off this system in favor of more rapid physical maturation. Indeed, data which suggest that gorillas exhibit accelerated physical maturation relative to intellectual development (see above), provide some circumstantial evidence in support of this view (see discussion by Povinelli, 1994). If these data are corroborated, substantial weight would be added to the hypothesis that the basic genetic instructions for those systems are still present in modern gorillas, but are turned off due to shifts in the rate and timing of development (for empirical details which support this possibility, see Povinelli, 1994). However, we should quickly add that it remains unclear what aspects of the SELF system, precisely, might have been traded off during the evolution of gorilla development. It is possible that gorillas possess a body image[6] indistinguishable from primates outside the great ape/human group. However, it is also possible that they retain a more integrated body image than other primates, but one that differs in substantial enough ways from the ancestral SELF system to preclude the establishment of an equivalence relation between their body and a contingent mirror image of themselves (see above). In other words, only certain developmental pathways relevant to the SELF system may have been turned off during the course of the evolution of the gorilla lineage, and thus these animals may still retain a considerably more developed body image than other primates.

Some researchers have pointed out that the fact that humans are even more readapted to a terrestrial way of life than are gorillas could represent a stumbling block for the clambering theory (e.g., Gallup, 1998). As explained above, however, terrestriality is relevant only insofar as it is a marker of selection for more rapid physical maturation relative to intellectual development – that is, to the extent that it suggests that certain later-emerging systems may have been turned off due to changes in the rate and timing of development of other systems. Clearly, this is not true in the human case. In fact, it seems obvious that selective forces that operated during human evolution pushed our species in the opposite direction, developmentally speaking, from gorillas. Rather than accelerating physical development, humans evolved an extended period of physical immaturity *and* pushed aspects of general intellectual development considerably later, with all key life history parameters delayed relative to the great apes. To provide a concrete example, humans exhibit independent locomotion at a much later stage of cognitive development than do any of the great apes (e.g., Antinucci, 1990). Indeed, if anything, the overall pattern of development in humans suggests an extended period for the elaboration of the self-concept (along many dimensions), not a truncation of this period.

Other "Fingerprints" of SELF

Although the nature of the SELF system is at present only weakly specified, several key aspects of Povinelli and Cant's (1995) theory can now be highlighted.

First, the hypothesis posits that the great apes and humans possess a body image that is, in some contexts, available as a concept, or object of knowledge in its own right. Whereas many species have proprioceptive and kinesthetic systems that have evolved to regulate complex patterns of movement through space, it may be the case that only the great apes and humans have elevated knowledge of the body as an object of knowledge in itself.

Second, it may be that the SELF is the fundamental platform of the more elaborated dimensions of the self which exist in humans — dimensions that may or may not exist in great apes, and other species. If so, even now it may still be the body, not the mind, which is first and foremost available to the developing human infant, and thus this dimension of the self may retain a kind of phenomenological primacy as other, psychological aspects of the self begin to emerge (see Povinelli, 2001).

Third, if the SELF evolved as an adaptation for coping with the problem that increasing body mass generated for arboreal locomotion in the last common ancestor of the great apes and humans, then its detection millions of years later by Gallup (1970) and his mirror test was curiously serendipitous. After all, if our model has merit, then in attempting to discover whether chimpanzees might be able to recognize themselves in mirrors, Gallup would have inadvertently uncovered a system honed by natural selection millions of years earlier for a completely unrelated function; it just so happened that some of the properties of mirrors happen to engage the SELF system! On this view, we should expect that other abilities may be dramatically facilitated by, or in some cases, even allowed for, by the SELF system. Many authors, for example have discussed the connection between the representation of one's body and imitation (Meltzoff, 1990; Merleau-Ponty, 1962; Mitchell, 1993). Although many acts of imitation may be possible without the presence of the kind of body image we are describing, it seems increasingly clear that reproduction of another's actions (broadly construed) can be achieved through multiple routes. Thus, it is possible that the emergence of the SELF system, by adding a level of explicitness to the self, incidentally augmented the tendencies for orangutans and chimpanzees to reproduce the actions of others. Another example may be the case of tool-use. Although many species use, and even fashion tools, in certain species, the presence of the SELF system may facilitate the discovery and deployment of tools as objects separate and explicitly distinct from the thing that deploys them (for example, "my hand") (see Povinelli, 2000, pp. 328–337). In short, the SELF system, which initially evolved as an adaptation to subserve effective locomotion in primates with very large body masses, may express itself (imperfectly) in many contexts, only one of which is mirror self-recognition.

Importantly, the flip side of this coin may be true as well. It may be that the surprising within-species individual differences in mirror self-recognition among chimpanzees and orangutans (see above) are both real and a reflection of the fact that the fundamental cognitive system that supports mirror self-recognition, evolved for other purposes, and therefore only imperfectly map on to the mirror test (or any other test not specifically related to the evolutionary context in which it evolved). In short, individual differences in the robustness of the SELF system that have little or no consequence on the ability to negotiate through highly compliant arboreal habitat may have large differences on tests of mirror self-recognition. This fact may also help explain the previously puzzling findings of declines in mirror self-recognition in adulthood in chimpanzees (see de Veer et al., 2002; Povinelli et al., 1993). After all, what is declining might either be the robustness of the system (not typically used in captivity) or incidental factors which allow for self-recognition, but are not essential to the kinesthetic self needed for effective arboreal locomotion. In addition, this helps to flesh out our earlier explanation of why the absence of behavioral patterns indicative of self-recognition in gorillas may not be so surprising.

It should be emphasized that at present our model is merely a framework pointing to a particular ecological problem (travel through extremely compliant, arboreal habitats by very large-bodied apes) that may have driven a more explicit representation of the body and a suite of motor planning systems designed to subserve effective locomotion. It does not specify (a) the scope of this SELF system, or (b) the extent of the evolutionary "redescription" (Karmiloff-Smith, 1992) that the proprioceptive, kinesthetic, or both systems have undergone. Furthermore, it does not specifically indicate which motor planning systems were most affected, elaborated, or both by the evolution of the SELF system. In short, at present, the hypothesis fails to specify a causal account of what specific cognitive systems are necessary to support the process of locomotion we have identified as crucial to our model. Because of this present level of ambiguity in the theory, and the theoretical difficulties in reducing that ambiguity, for the time being we advocate a broad-based approach to understanding how the evolutionary forces that sculpted the unique process of arboreal locomotion exhibited by modern orangutans might have affected the representation and use of the body image, broadly construed.

NOVEL TESTS OF THE SELF HYPOTHESIS

If, as we have been speculating, the mirror test is just one (albeit straightforward) way of tapping into the SELF system, then a particularly profitable method of testing the clambering hypothesis might be to determine if the great apes differ in as-of-yet undefined ways from other primates in areas related to the use and/or reasoning about the body image. In what follows, we focus on one approach along these lines that we have pursued. First, we describe how the SELF system may have endowed organisms with a tool-using tendency that, until now, has not been widely recognized. Second, we describe a simple experiment that we conducted to determine if chimpanzees, at least, possess this ability.

Tool-Use, Tool-Discovery, and the SELF

Previously, we had speculated that if chimpanzees and orangutans possess a SELF system, this could explain why they are such expert tool-users: they may possess a more explicit representation of their bodies and their actions, and hence they may more clearly consider self-object relations (see Povinelli, 2000, pp. 228–337). Tool-use exists in a wide range of animal species (see Beck, 1980, for a broad overview), and we are certainly not suggesting that a SELF system is required to produce such behaviors. Rather, the hypothesis is simply that the more explicitly the distinction between self and object can be represented, the more rapidly tool-use will emerge. The sheer diversity of the tool-kits of chimpanzees in the wild, and the remarkable tool-using and tool-making capacities of chimpanzees and orangutans in captivity suggest that a more explicit representation of the self's body and actions may dramatically speed up the discovery and use of tools.[7]

The prototypical case of tool-use involves the animals using a tool as an extension of the hand in order to rake an out-of-reach object close enough that it can be grasped with the hand. For the purposes of the present research, however, we were interested in the opposite case: where an object of interest is within reach, but the animal does not wish to directly touch it because it is alarming in some way. Would the chimpanzees spontaneously appreciate that a tool could be used to move the alarming object out of the way, or to gather information about it, so that they did not have to touch it directly? It occurred to us that if chimpanzees and orangutans really do possess a more explicit representation of their bodies (by virtue of their possession of the SELF system), then they might exhibit such behavior spontaneously (see Povinelli, 2000, p. 335). After all, if these species really do represent their bodies more explicitly, then as they act upon an object with a tool, they may have at their disposal separately accessible representations of (a) their hand acting on the tool, and (b) the tool acting on the object.[8]

AN EXPERIMENTAL TEST

To explore this idea, we tested seven captive adult chimpanzees (Barth & Povinelli, 2004), all of whom have had an exceptional amount of experience with using tools in a wide variety of tasks (see Povinelli, 2000, for details on their rearing and testing history). The subjects were tested behind a Plexiglas® partition that contained three openings through which the subjects could freely respond (a procedure with which they were intimately familiar). When the chimpanzees entered, they always found three sticks on the floor of the test unit, always in the same position. Most of the trials were *standard tool-using trials*, where a piece of food was sitting on the other side of the partition, out of the chimpanzees' immediate reach. On these trials, the chimpanzees easily demonstrated an understanding that they could use one of the sticks to rake in the reward (a hardly surprising feat, given their previous experience; see Povinelli, 2000).

The key findings, however, came from the *test trials* that were administered at certain intervals between the standard tool-using trials. On these trials, a large box with the open side facing the subject was present on the floor directly in front of the Plexiglas partition, and was always positioned the same distance from the subject. A highly desirable food reward (either an apple or a banana), an alarming object, or both were then positioned just inside the box so that they were clearly visible to the chimpanzee and easily within his or her reach. The alarming objects included furry toy animals, rubber snakes, and spiders (the alarming potential of the objects was tested informally on a different group of chimpanzees prior to the beginning of the experiment).

A total of six different kinds of test trials were used (with each animal receiving four trials of each kind). Four of these six conditions consisted of the trials just described: (1) food-only, (2) alarming-object-only, (3) food-beside-alarming-object, and (4) food-behind-alarming-object. Two other conditions were also used that were identical to the food-only and alarming-object-only conditions except that the entire box was covered by a cloth so that the subject did not know what was inside unless he or she removed the cloth: (5) covered/food-only and (6) covered/alarming-object-only. As before, the sticks were present, available to the subjects if they chose to use them. Thus, the chimpanzees were free to make contact with the food, the object, or both either by using their hands, using one of the tools as a mediator, or to ignore the situation altogether. The significant aspect of this design was that on all test trials, the food and the alarming objects were always the same distance from, and easily within reach of, the individual chimpanzees.

We reasoned that in the food-beside-alarming-object and food-behind-alarming-object conditions, an organism with a SELF system would be highly likely to make the inference that it could use the tool to push the alarming object out of the way and thus avoid having to make direct bodily contact with the object as it reached for the food. Similar logic applied to the two conditions in which the box was covered, and the chimpanzees were therefore ignorant of what was inside: they ought to use the tool to remove the cloth before reaching with their hands. Finally, on the alarming-object-only trials we reasoned that in the absence of food, the subjects would be interested in exploring the alarming object, but that they ought to use the tool, not their hands, to do so. All of these conditions could be contrasted with the food-only condition, in which we expected that the subjects would simply reach directly with their hands to take the food. On the other hand, if the subjects simply conceived the tool as an extension of their arms, they would be expected to be quite hesitant to contact the alarming object, even with the tool. Our primary measure was the number of bouts that the subjects used their hands versus the tools across the six conditions.

The two conditions in which the contents of the box were covered turned out to be the most pivotal. Three of our seven apes consistently used one of the provided tools to uncover the concealed box before they reached with their hands in these two conditions (see Figure 2.6). The remaining four apes either removed the cloth by hand or did not respond at all. The behavior on these covered conditions predicted their behavior on the other conditions. The chimpanzees that uncovered the box by using a tool also used the tool consistently on the conditions in which an alarming object was present, but not on the food-only trials. They used the tool to move the object away from the food (or the food away from the object) and they used the tool to explore the object. They only rarely made contact

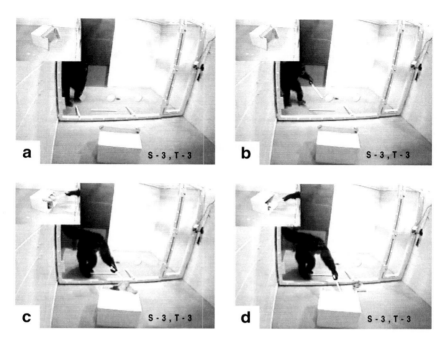

FIGURE 2.6. Covered box condition: A chimpanzee subject (a) encounters a covered box and (b–d) spontaneously uses a provided stick to uncover it in order to explore its contents.

with the object by using their hands, and if they did, only *after* they first explored it with the tool. Likewise, they only rarely retrieved the food directly without first increasing the distance between food and object by using the tool. In contrast, the four apes that reached to unveil the box with their hands in the covered conditions, also only used the tool randomly with respect to the other conditions, if they used it at all.

Importantly, all of the apes directly retrieved the food from the box by using their hands in the food-only condition. This demonstrates that the three apes who used the tool only when the alarming object was present, and when they did not know what was in the box, clearly distinguished between the conditions and did not simply use the tool for idiosyncratic reasons, such as overestimating the distance between themselves and the box. Rather, they used the tool only on those trials during which their hands would have to touch, or come too close to touching, an alarming object.

Although the results are preliminary, they suggest that at least three of our chimpanzees provided reliable evidence of utilizing an explicit representation of their hands when they used the tool as a mediator between their hand and the object. Not all of our apes did so, however. Indeed, our apes could be classified into two groups, those that did use the tool as a mediator and those that did not.

This difference cannot be explained by individual differences in tool-using exper-tise, as all of the apes were proficient tool-users with an exceptional amount of practice and experience on a wide variety of tasks (see Povinelli, 2000). More directly, in the present study, all of the subjects used the tools to retrieve the food reward easily on the standard tool-using trials (see above). So, why did only about half of them use the tool as a mediator? As noted above, perhaps it is because the SELF system we are probing evolved in a different context, one that only imper-fectly maps itself into the present test situation.

Although we have not yet conducted our test with other species — in partic-ular, those that do not exhibit evidence of self-recognition — comparative tests of this sort (especially a direct comparison between great apes and several species of old and new world monkeys) would be of great interest. At present, we offer these data as a possible illustration of how the SELF system we hypothesize to exist in the great apes and humans — a system that has heretofore been explored only through the mirror test — may express itself in other contexts as well.

CONCLUDING REFLECTIONS ON SELF

In this essay, we have elaborated upon a hypothesis first put forward by Povinelli and Cant (1995) that the evolutionary origins of the self-concept may be found in a unique set of ecological circumstances faced by the ancestors of the great apes and humans — a set of factors that selected for the development of an explicit representation of their bodies and an understanding of their bodies' ongoing effects on the environment. In doing so, we have not sought to downplay the importance of the myriad, implicit kinesthetic and proprioceptive systems that allow organisms to function in the environments they inhabit. Indeed, a wealth of research in devel-opmental psychology, cognitive neuroscience, and motor planning has explored the nature of the body image/schema, elucidating the mechanisms that allow organisms ranging from human infants to bats to fishes to elephants to integrate somatosensory and visual information, and distinguish self from environment.

Nonetheless, it seems likely that a fundamentally new representation of the self — what we have labeled the SELF system — evolved for roughly the reasons outlined almost a decade ago by Povinelli and Cant. But this new, integrated representation of the body may have done more than endow those organisms to exhibit the rather remarkable ability for self-recognition in mirrors. It may have pre-adapted these species for more elaborated forms of tool-use, new ways of relating to the bodily acts of others, and more flexible use of manual-based signals, just to name a few. And, if we are right, this may just be the tip of the iceberg; it may be that when it comes to cascading effects of the evolution of the SELF, there may exist numerous (and as-of-yet unexplored) species differences between the great apes and humans on the one hand, and most other forms of life on the other. A subtle, but distinct thread may thus run through the actions of humans and the other great apes, a kinematic signature of a SELF we share due to our common ancestry.

ENDNOTES

1. We use the term *body image* in connection with the conceptual system that evolved in response to selection for a more explicit, conceptual representation of the body and its movements (i.e., the SELF system) that evolved in the ancestor of the great apes and humans. In subsuming the SELF system under the umbrella of the concept of the body image, we attempt to follow the standard convention in distinguishing between the concepts of body image and body schema (see, for example, Gallagher, 1986). Although we are not fully comfortable with that distinction as applied here, if one of the central distinctions between body image and body schema is that the former is a conceptual structure whereas the latter is not, then the SELF system, as we envision it, would fall under the rubric of body image. One of the only other axes of contrast between body image and body schema in the human literature is the conscious versus subconscious distinction — a dichotomy of little practical use in dealing with nonhuman primates. A more interesting point of theoretical difficulty is that body schema is typically used when referring to unconscious systems that play a dynamic role in monitoring and governing posture and movement (e.g., Head, 1920).

2. Three properly controlled tests have not elicited any evidence of self-recognition in gorillas (Ledbetter & Basen, 1982; Shillito, Gallup, & Beck, 1999; Suarez & Gallup, 1981), despite some rather extreme efforts to rule out methodological artifacts (see especially the report by Shillito et al., 1999). Despite this, there have been numerous claims for self-recognition in gorillas (see review by Swartz, Sarauw, & Evans, 1999). However, data supporting the existence of mirror self-recognition in gorillas are derived from tests that have not implemented key control procedures that are necessary in order to draw strong conclusions as to the presence or absence of the capacity (see Gallup, 1994, for a detailed discussion of the logic of various procedures). This is not to rule out the possibility that gorillas, under certain abnormal circumstances could exhibit evidence of self-recognition (see Povinelli, 1994), but thus far the best evidence suggests that normally reared, socially housed gorillas do not.

3. One dolphin was also reported to expose the part of its body that had been marked as the first behavior when it reached the mirror, but this was only true in 6/8 cases, with 2 cases excluded because they were ambiguous. If the 2 ambiguous cases are included as negative instances, this would constitute only 6/10 cases. Because no data concerning how unmarked dolphins typically present their bodies to a mirror were provided, it is not clear how to compare these data to a baseline performance. The authors also stress the fact that the same dolphin exhibited no social behavior to the mirrors. However, as the authors themselves note, the subjects were thoroughly habituated to the mirrored surfaces in their tanks. Finally, the authors also report that no social behavior was observed when mirrors were reintroduced. Unfortunately, no systematic data appear to have been collected to support this point. In any event, although it has been speculated that the presence or absence of social behavior to mirrors is related to self-exploratory behaviors (e.g., Suarez & Gallup, 1986), empirical data suggest that this measure does not predict whether chimpanzees exhibit evidence of self-recognition (see Povinelli, Rulf, Landau, & Bierschwale, 1993).

4. We concede that the presence of the notion of the possession of the body (implied here by the phrase "my body," as opposed to "this body"), raises difficult philosophical

problems which we do not pretend to have solved (see, for example, Martin, 1995). With respect to the mirror task, Davis (1989) has provided a detailed analysis of the minimal kind of self-concept that needs to be ascribed to the organism that passes it. He concludes that the test at least demonstrates the existence of a concept of "my body" that includes material properties (color, shape, contour, texture, location, movement, etc.).

5. Although there would appear to be reliable individual differences in the capacity for mirror self-recognition among chimpanzees (see deVeer et al., 2002; Povinelli et al., 1993; Swartz & Evans, 1991), several researchers have construed the existing data in a highly questionable manner. For example, at least three separate reviews of the self-recognition literature have cited the most definitive population-level study to date, Povinelli et al. (1993), as having produced evidence that only 30/92 (33%) of chimpanzees exhibited behavioral evidence of self-recognition (SR+), and/or only 13/42 (31%) passed the mark test (see Heyes, 1994; Swartz et al., 1999; Westergaard & Hopkins, 1994). These numbers were obtained by collapsing across all age groups that Povinelli et al. tested: a grossly flawed procedure given the strong ontogenetic trends that were reported, and highlighted, by the original authors. For example, most of the chimpanzees tested by Povinelli et al. were under 5 years of age, and the data set clearly reveals that the onset of the capacity peaks at around 8–16 years of age (at which 70–80% of all animals, based on stringent behavioral criteria, exhibited the capacity). Furthermore, the mark tests *specifically targeted* an equal sample size of subjects who were classified as SR+ or SR–: they were not selected at random as implied by the reviews cited above. To be clear, the analytical technique used by these reviews is analogous to combining data from a large number of 10-month-old human infants with data from a handful of 5-year-old children and adults, in order to obtain an estimate for the percentage of humans that are capable of recognizing themselves in mirrors.

6. Given that it is not clear what aspects of the SELF system have been modified, it is unclear whether the term *body image* or *body schema* is most appropriate here. See endnote 1.

7. A contrast between orangutans and gorillas is of interest here. Orangutans do exhibit tool-making and tool-use in the wild (e.g., van Schaik, Fox, & Sitompul, 1996), but they are certainly not as extensive as chimpanzee tool-making and tool-use. If the definition of tool is expanded to include the remarkable use the deformation of smaller tree trunks to assist in the translocation of their bodies through space (tree-swaying), then the amount of orangutan tool-using behavior might easily exceed that of chimpanzees. Indeed, in captivity, orangutans seem to be remarkably preadapted to tool-making and tool-use (e.g., Lethmate, 1982). In contrast, gorillas almost never use tools in the wild (even under the broadest definitions available), and although they certainly can and do learn to use tools in captivity, the extent of such behavior does not appear to be as elaborated as in orangutans and chimpanzees (see Boysen et al., 1999; Fontaine, Moisson, & Wickings, 1995). This later claim, however, is largely based on subjective impressions, rather than quantitative data obtained from extensive surveys of zoological collections.

8. The use of such explicit representations could be contrasted with, for example, studies with monkeys that have shown that when a monkey uses a tool to retrieve distant objects the neuronal schema that codes for the hand extends to include the space around the distant object (Iriki, Tanaka, & Iwamura, 1996). Across trials,

objects that were represented as being in the extrapersonal space, become coded as near objects, if a physical extension of the body (a tool) is used. Although this coding of far objects as near objects in bimodal neurons during tool-use has also been found in humans (Berti & Frassinetti, 2000; Farne & Ladavas, 2000), we posit an additional representation in humans and the great apes that allows for the representation of "my hand" to mediate these lower-level representations.

REFERENCES

Anderson, J. R., & Gallup, G. G., Jr. (1997). Self-recognition in Saguinus? A critical essay. *Animal Behaviour, 54,* 1563–1567.

Anderson, J. R., & Gallup, G. G., Jr. (1999). Self-recognition in nonhuman primates: Past and future challenges. In M. Haug & R. E. Whalen (Eds.), *Animal models of human emotion and cognition* (pp. 175–194). Washington, D.C.: American Psychological Association.

Anderson, J. R., & Roeder, J.-J. (1989). Responses of capuchin monkeys (*Cebus apella*) to different conditions of mirror-image stimulation. *Primates, 30,* 581–587.

Antinucci, F. (1990). The comparative study of cognitive ontogeny in four primate species. In S. T. Parker & K. R. Gibson (Eds.), *"Language" and intelligence in monkeys and apes: Comparative developmental perspectives*. New York: Cambridge University Press.

Asendorpf, J. B., & Baudonniere, P. -M. (1993). Self-awareness and other-awareness: Mirror self-recognition and synchronic imitation among unfamiliar peers. *Developmental Psychology, 29,* 88–95.

Barth, J., & Povinelli, D. J. (2004). Explicit body representation and tool-use in chimpanzees. Manuscript submitted for publication.

Beck, B. B. (1980). *Animal tool behavior.* New York: Garland.

Berlucchi, G., & Aglioti, S. (1997). The body in the brain: neural bases of corporeal awareness. *Trends in Neurosciences, 20,* 560–564.

Berti, A., & Frassinetti, F. (2000). When far becomes near: Remapping of space by tool use. *Journal of Cognitive Neuroscience, 12,* 415–420.

Bischof-Köhler, D. (1988). On the connection between empathy and the ability to recognize oneself in the mirror. [German]. *Schweizerische Zeitschrift für Psychologie, 47,* 147–159.

Boysen, S. T., Kuhlmeier, V. A., Halliday, P., & Halliday, Y. M. (1999). Tool use in captive gorillas. In S. T. Parker & R. W. Mitchell (Eds.), *The mentalities of gorillas and orangutans: Comparative perspectives* (pp. 179–187). New York: Cambridge University Press.

Brooks-Gunn, J., & Lewis, M. (1984). The development of early visual self-recognition. *Developmental Review, 4,* 215–239.

Butterworth, G. (1992). Origins of self-perception in infancy. *Psychological Inquiry, 3,* 103–111.

Butterworth, G. (1995). An ecological perspective on the origins of self. In J. L. Bermudez & A. J. Marcel (Eds.), *The body and the self* (pp. 87–105). Cambridge, MA: MIT Press.

Cant, J. G. (1987). Positional behavior of female Bornean orangutans (*Pongo pygmaeus*). *American Journal of Primatology, 12,* 71–90.

Cant, J. G. H. (1988). Positional behavior of long-tailed macaques in northern Sumatra. *American Journal of Physical Anthropology, 76,* 29–37.

Cant, J. G. H. (1992a). Positional behavior and body size of arboreal primates: A theoretical framework for field studies and an illustration of its application. *American Journal of Physical Anthropology, 88*, 273–283.

Cant, J. G. H. (1992b). Positional behavior of arboreal primates and habitat compliance. In B. Thierry, J. R. Anderson, J. J. Roeder & N. Herrenschmidt (Eds.), *Current primatology. Vol. 1. Ecology and evolution* (pp. 187–193). Strasbourg: Université Louis Pasteur.

Cartmill, M. (1974). Rethinking primate origins. *Science, 184*, 436–443.

Chevalier-Skolnikoff, S. (1983). Sensorimotor development in orang-utans and other primates. *Journal of Human Evolution, 12*, 545–561.

Chevalier-Skolnikoff, S., Galdikas, B. M. F., & Skolnikoff, A. (1982). The adaptive significance of higher intelligence in wild orang-utans: A preliminary report. *Journal of Human Evolution, 11*, 639–652.

Davis, L. H. (1989). Self-consciousness in chimps and pigeons. *Philosophical Psychology, 2*, 249–259.

de Veer, M. W., Gallup, G. G., Jr., Theall, L. A., van der Bos, R., & Povinelli, D. J. (2002). An eight-year longitudinal study of self-recognition in chimpanzees (*Pan troglodytes*). *Neuropsychologia, 41*, 229–234.

Eddy, T. J., Gallup, G. G., Jr., & Povinelli, D. J. (1996). Age differences in the ability of chimpanzees to distinguish mirror-images of self from video images of others. *Journal of Comparative Psychology, 110*, 38–44.

Farne, A., & Ladavas, E. (2000). Dynamic size-change of hand peripersonal space following tool use. *NeuroReport, 11*, 1645–1649.

Fivush, R. (2001). Owning experience: Developing subjective perspective in autobiographical narratives. In C. Moore & K. Lemmon (Eds.), *The self in time: Developmental perspectives* (pp. 35–52). Mahwah, NJ: Lawrence Erlbaum.

Fleagle, J. (1976). Locomotion and posture of the Malayan siamang and implications for hominoid evolution. *Folia Primatologica, 26(4)*, 245–269.

Fleagle, J. (1999). *Primate adaptation and evolution.* San Diego: Academic Press.

Fontaine, B., Moisson, P. Y., & Wickings, E. J. (1995). Observations of spontaneous tool making and tool use in a captive group of western lowland gorillas (*Gorilla gorilla gorilla*). *Folia Primatologica, 65*, 219–223.

Gallagher, S. (1986). Body image and body schema: A conceptual clarification. *Journal of Mind & Behavior, 7*, 541–554.

Gallup, G. G., Jr. (1968). Mirror-image stimulation. *Psychological Bulletin, 70*, 782–793.

Gallup, G. G., Jr. (1970). Chimpanzees: Self-recognition. *Science, 167*, 86–87.

Gallup, G. G., Jr. (1977). Self recognition in primates: A comparative approach to the bidirectional properties of consciousness. *American Psychologist, 32*, 329–338.

Gallup, G. G., Jr. (1982). Self-awareness and the emergence of mind in primates. *American Journal of Primatology, 2*, 237–248.

Gallup, G. G., Jr. (1985). Do minds exist in species other than our own? *Neuroscience and Biobehavioral Reviews, 9*, 631–641.

Gallup, G. G., Jr. (1994). Self-recognition: Research strategies and experimental design. In S. T. Parker & R. W. Mitchell (Eds.), *Self awareness in animals and humans: Developmental perspectives* (pp. 35–50). New York: Cambridge University Press.

Gallup, G. G., Jr. (1998). Self-awareness and the evolution of social intelligence. *Behavioural Processes, 42*, 239–247.

Gallup, G. G., Jr., Wallnau, L. B., & Suarez, S. D. (1980). Failure to find self-recognition in mother-infant and infant-infant rhesus monkey pairs. *Folia Primatologica, 33,* 210–219.

Hauser, M. D., Kralik, J., Botto-Mahan, C., Garrett, M., & Oser, M. (1995). Self-recognition in primates: Phylogeny and the salience of species-typical features. *Proceedings of the National Academy of Science, 92,* 10811–10814.

Hauser, M. D., Miller, C. T., Liu, K., & Gupta, R. (2001). Cotton-top tamarins (*Saguinus oedipus*) fail to show mirror-guided self-exploration. *American Journal of Primatology, 53,* 131–137.

Head, H. (1920). *Studies in neurology* (Vol. 2). London: Oxford University Press.

Heyes, C. M. (1994). Reflections on self-recognition in primates. *Animal Behaviour, 47,* 909–919.

Heyes, C. M. (1995). Self-recognition in primates: Further reflections create a hall of mirrors. *Animal Behaviour, 50,* 1533–1542.

Heyes, C. M. (1998). Theory of mind in nonhuman primates. *Behavioral & Brain Sciences, 21,* 101–134.

Howe, M. L., & Courage, M. L. (1993). On resolving the enigma of infantile amnesia. *Psychological Bulletin, 113,* 305–326.

Howe, M. L., & Courage, M. L. (1997). The emergence and early development of autobiographical memory. *Psychological Review, 104,* 499–523.

Humphrey, N. K. (1976). The social function of intellect. In P. P. G. Bateson & R. A. Hinde (Eds.), *Growing points in ethology* (pp. 303–317). Cambridge, England: Cambridge University Press.

Hyatt, C. W., & Hopkins, W. D. (1994). Self-awareness in bonobos and chimpanzees: A comparative perspective. In S. T. Parker & R. W. Mitchell (Ed.), *Self-awareness in animals and humans: Developmental perspectives.* New York: Cambridge University Press.

Iriki, A., Tanaka, M., & Iwamura, Y. (1996). Coding of modified body schema during tool use by macaque postcentral neurons. *NeuroReport, 7,* 2325–2330.

Johnson, D. B. (1982). Altruistic behavior and the development of the self in infants. *Merrill-Palmer Quarterly, 28,* 379–388.

Karmiloff-Smith, A. (1992). *Beyond modularity: A developmental perspective on cognitive science.* Cambridge, MA: MIT Press.

Larson, S. K. (1988). *Individual differences in physiology, behavior, and temperament over the first 15 months of life.* Urbana-Champaign: University of Illinois Press.

Ledbetter, D. H., & Basen, J. A. (1982). Failure to demonstrate self-recognition in gorillas. *American Journal of Primatology, 2,* 307–310.

Lethmate, J. (1982). Tool-using skills of orang-utans. *Journal of Human Evolution, 11,* 49–64.

Lewis, M., Sullivan, M. W., Stanger, C., & Weiss, M. (1989). Self development and self-conscious emotions. *Child Development, 60,* 146–156.

Loveland, K. A. (1986). Discovering the affordances of a reflecting surface. *Developmental Review, 6,* 1–24.

Martin, M. G. F. (1995). Bodily awareness: A sense of ownership. In J. L. Bermudez, A. J. Marcel & E. Naomi (Eds.), *The Body and the self.* Cambridge, MA: The MIT Press.

Meltzoff, A. N. (1990). Foundations for developing a concept of self: The role of imitation in relating self to other and the value of social mirroring, social modeling, and self practice in infancy. In D. Cicchetti & M. Beeghly (Eds.), *The self in transition: Infancy to childhood.* (pp. 139–164). Chicago: University of Chicago Press.

Meltzoff, A. N., & Moore, M. K. (1999). Persons and representation: Why infant imitation is important for theories of human development. In J. Nadel & G. Butterworth (Eds.), *Imitation in infancy: Cambridge studies in cognitive perceptual development* (pp. 9–35). New York: Cambridge University Press.

Merleau-Ponty, M. (1962). *Phenomenology of perception*. London: Routledge and Kegan Paul.

Mitchell, R. W. (1993). Mental models of mirror-self-recognition: Two theories. *New Ideas in Psychology, 11,* 295–325.

Nelson, K. (1992). Emergence of autobiographical memory at age 4. *Human Development, 35,* 172–177.

Parker, S. T. (1999). The life history and development of great apes in a comparative perspective. In S. T. Parker & R. W. Mitchell (Eds.), *The mentalities of gorillas and orangutans: Comparative perspectives* (pp. 43–69). New York: Cambridge University Press.

Povinelli, D. J. (1989). Failure to find self-recognition in Asian elephants (*Elephas maximus*) in contrast to their use of mirror cues to discover hidden food. *Journal of Comparative Psychology, 103,* 122–131.

Povinelli, D. J. (1994). How to create self-recognizing gorillas (but don't try it on macaques). In S. T. Parker & R. W. Mitchell (Eds.), *Self awareness in animals and humans: Developmental perspectives* (pp. 291–300). New York: Cambridge University Press.

Povinelli, D. J. (1995). The unduplicated self. In P. Rochat (Ed.), *The self in infancy: Theory and research. Advances in psychology, 112* (pp. 161–192). Amsterdam, the Netherlands: North-Holland/Elsevier Science Publishers.

Povinelli, D. J. (2000). *Folk physics for apes*. New York: Oxford University Press.

Povinelli, D. J. (2001). The self: Elevated in consciousness and extended in time. In C. Moore & K. Lemmon (Eds.), *The self in time: Developmental perspectives* (pp. 75–95). Mahwah, NJ: Lawrence Erlbaum.

Povinelli, D. J., & Cant, J.G.H. (1995). Arboreal clambering and the evolution of self-conception. *The Quarterly Review of Biology, 70,* 393–421.

Povinelli, D. J., Landau, K. R., & Perilloux, H. K. (1996). Self-recognition in young children using delayed versus live feedback: Evidence of a developmental asynchrony. *Child Development, 67,* 1540–1554.

Povinelli, D. J., Landry, A. M., Theall, L. A., Clark, B. R., & Castille, C. M. (1999). Development of young children's understanding that the recent past is causally bound to the present. *Developmental Psychology, 35,* 1426–1439.

Povinelli, D. J., Gallup, G. G., Jr., Eddy, T. J., & Bierschwale, D. T. (1997). Chimpanzees recognize themselves in mirrors. *Animal Behaviour, 53,* 1083–1088.

Povinelli, D. J., Rulf, A. B., Landau, K. R., & Bierschwale, D. T. (1993). Self-recognition in chimpanzees (*Pan troglodytes*): Distribution, ontogeny, and patterns of emergence. *Journal of Comparative Psychology, 107,* 347–372.

Povinelli, D. J., & Simon, B. B. (1998). Young children's understanding of briefly versus extremely delayed images of the self: Emergence of the autobiographical stance. *Developmental Psychology, 34,* 188–194.

Priel, B., & de Schonen, S. (1986). Self-recognition: A study of a population without mirrors. *Journal of Experimental Child Psychology, 41,* 237–250.

Redshaw, M. (1978). Cognitive development in human and gorilla infants. *Journal of Human Evolution, 7,* 133–141.

Reiss, D., & Marino, L. (2001). Mirror self-recognition in the bottlenose dolphin: A case of cognitive convergence. *Proceedings of the National Academy of Science, 98,* 5937–5942.

Robinson, J. A., Connell, S., McKenzie, B. E., & Day, R. H. (1990). Do infants use their own images to locate objects reflected in a mirror? *Child Development, 61,* 1558–1568.

Shillito, D. J., Gallup, G. G., Jr., & Beck, B. B. (1999). Factors affecting mirror behaviour in western lowland gorillas, *Gorilla gorilla. Animal Behaviour, 57,* 999–1004.

Spinozzi, G., & Natale, F. (1989). Early sensorimotor development in gorilla. In F. Antinucci (Ed.), *Cognitive structure and development in nonhuman primates.* Hillsdale, NJ: Lawrence Erlbaum.

Suarez, S. D., & Gallup, G. G., Jr. (1981). Self-recognition in chimpanzees and orangutans, but not gorillas. *Journal of Human Evolution, 10,* 175–188.

Suarez, S. D., & Gallup, G. G., Jr. (1986). Social responding to mirrors in rhesus macaques (*Macaca mulatta*): Effects of changing mirror location. *American Journal of Primatology, 11,* 239–244.

Sugardjito, J., & Van Hooff, J. A. (1986). Age-sex class differences in the positional behaviour of the Sumatran orang-utan (*Pongo pygmaeus abelii*) in the Gunung Leuser National Park, Indonesia. *Folia Primatologica, 47,* 14–25.

Swartz, K. B., & Evans, S. (1991). Not all chimpanzees (*Pan troglodytes*) show self-recognition. *Primates, 32,* 483–496.

Swartz, K. B., Sarauw, D., & Evans, S. (1999). Comparative aspects of mirror self-recognition in great apes. In S. T. Parker & R. W. Mitchell (Eds.), *The mentalities of gorillas and orangutans: Comparative perspectives* (pp. 283–411). New York: Cambridge University Press.

van Schaik, C. P., Fox, E. A., & Sitompul, A. F. (1996). Manufacture and use of tools in wild orangutans. *Naturwissenschaften, 83,* 186–188.

Walraven, V., Elsacker, L., & Verheyen, R. (1995). Reactions of a group of pygmy chimpanzees (*Pan paniscus*) to their mirror-images: Evidence of self-recognition. *Primates, 36,* 145–150.

Welch-Ross, M. K. (1999). Preschoolers' understanding of mind: Implications for suggestibility. *Cognitive Development, 14,* 101–131.

Westergaard, G. C., & Hopkins, W. D. (1994). Theories of mind and self-recognition. *American Psychologist, 49,* 761.

3

Early Memory, Early Self, and the Emergence of Autobiographical Memory

MARK L. HOWE
Lakehead University

*I*t is well accepted that our self-concept plays a critical role in autobiographical memory (e.g., Conway & Pleydell-Pearce, 2000; Habermas & Bluck, 2000; Howe, 2000, 2003). Indeed, who we are influences what we attend to, encode, and store about our everyday experiences. As well, who we are influences what we retrieve at the time of remembering these autobiographical events. Our current needs, wishes, aspirations, and intents often control what is reported to others about our life experiences, if not the actual memories themselves that are being retrieved.

Our self-concept is also contingent on memory (see also Ross & Wilson, 2000). That is, recollections of ourselves in the context of a past play a critical role in our understanding and conceptualization of who we are today. Unfortunately, memory may not be a particularly dependable base upon which to build our self-concepts. Indeed, it is now well-known that memory does not behave as if it were a passive video recorder. Rather, its content is influenced by our self-conceptualization at the time the event occurred, changes to our self-concept over time, as well as our self-concept at the time we are remembering our past selves. Moreover, because both memory and self are dynamical systems, neither remain static during the interval between event encoding and autobiographical recall. In fact, both the content of memory and the elements that constitute the self are thought to change as a function of new experiences, knowledge, and reorganization of what already exists. Interestingly, such changes can include the creation of false memories about past events, false memories that tend to be constrained by our self-concept. In particular, false memories about our past are more easily thought to be authentic if they are consistent with our current view of ourselves (e.g., Mazzoni, Loftus, & Kirsch, 2001).

45

Clearly, then, memory and the self exist in a symbiotic relationship. Because this relationship is critical to both the existence of the self and to memory for experiences in our past, the question arises as to whether this self and its attendant autobiographical memory repository exist at birth (or even before) or whether it emerges sometime after birth. Of course, much of the debate concerning the early existence of the self and autobiographical memory depends on how we define *self* and whether we can measure autobiographical memory prior to the onset of productive language. The focus of this chapter will be on these and related issues that concern the convergence of the development of the self and memory, developments that culminate in the emergence of autobiographical memory. I will begin by outlining what is known about the nature of self from birth to two years. Following this, I will provide a brief synopsis of developments in memory that occur simultaneously very early in life. Finally, I will show how changes in the self are linked to the onset of autobiographical memory and show that autobiographical memories do exist prior to the time they can be articulated using language. Findings from a variety of studies will be used throughout to help illustrate the points made about the nature of the early self and its pivotal role in the establishment of autobiographical memory.

PREAMBLE

Prior to turning to these more detailed sections, I provide a conspectus of the general arguments that will be the basis of this chapter. As I have contended previously (e.g., Howe, 2000; Howe & Courage, 1997), it is the emergence of the cognitive self in the second year of life that is the key event that launches autobiographical memory. Further, although considerable development occurs in language (both receptive and productive) during this same period of time, I will argue that these achievements do not directly affect the *onset* of autobiographical memory. Rather, they come to provide an expressive outlet for those recollections as autobiographical memory continues to evolve and mature into the childhood years. In that capacity, language serves to preserve (e.g., through rehearsal, reinstatement) or potentially alter (e.g., through reconstruction) memory records of personally experienced events, but is not a prerequisite to their foundation. Indeed, as the infant memory literature I will review indicates, early memories are not necessarily represented linguistically at all. For older children and adults, memory representations can be instantiated symbolically in a number of ways at input and at output (e.g., verbal, imaginal), though these formats should not be confused with how this information is *represented* in memory. One implication of this observation (i.e., that the manner in which information is output is not necessarily isomorphic with how it is represented in storage) is that the strong correlation between improvements in autobiographical recall and children's linguistic and narrative skills is likely an artifact of the verbal tools we use to measure autobiographical memory. Finally, it is reasonably well accepted that children must already have concepts of objects and events, as well as relational notions about them, in order for language about these objects, events, and relations to be acquired (see Mandler, 1992; Slobin, 1985). As the literature on infant categorization demonstrates clearly, concepts are often formed in memory well before the child becomes a language user (e.g., see Mandler & McDonough, 1993). Even after the onset of language children have been found to use gestures before words to indicate certain new conceptual understandings in the domain of problem-solving. Such discrepancies between gesture and word may provide "windows on the mind" of a child in a transitional state of knowledge acquisition in which new knowledge that can be expressed in the gestural mode is still unavailable for expression in the verbal mode (e.g., see Goldin-Meadow, Alibali, & Church, 1993).

Similar arguments can be made about the emergence of the self and language about the self. For example, Bates (1990) noted that the acquisition of any natural language requires a preexisting theory of the self. In a similar vein, Damasio (1999) pointed out that "language — that is, words and sentences — is a translation of something else, a conversion from nonlinguistic images which stand for entities, events, relationships, and inferences. If language operates for the self and for consciousness in the same way it operates for everything else, that is, by symbol-izing in words and sentences what exists first in nonverbal form, then there must be a nonverbal self and a nonverbal knowing for which the words 'I' and 'me' or the phrase 'I know' are the appropriate translations in any language" (p. 108). He goes on to say that "the idea that the self and consciousness would emerge *after* language, and would be a direct construction of language, is not likely to be correct . . . if self and consciousness were born de novo from language, they would constitute the sole instance of words without an underlying concept" (p. 108).

In light of these theoretical views, it is probably more than coincidental that infants first reveal their awareness of the cognitive sense of self nonverbally. At about 18 months, they use the gestural mode (i.e., mark-directed behavior to their mirror image, self-referent pointing) to communicate an early awareness of the self that is the cornerstone of autobiographical memory. During this time infants begin to understand self-referent pronouns that only later can be expressed in productive language about the self. It is my contention that only following the emergence of the cognitive self as expressed through gestures will infants be able to consolidate their knowledge about the self and to move on to a new level of competence which will enable them to use self language and narrative skills to report autobiographical memories in speech. Finally, although the onset of the cognitive self defines the lower boundary for the personalization of event memory, it does not guarantee that these memories will be encrypted as autobiographical. However, if we accept the argument that the self emerges prior to language about the self and is influential in the creation of autobiographical memory, and if we accept this distinction between symbols and the memorial representations they stand for, then several important questions arise. What is the nature of this early self and when does it emerge? Is there any empirical evidence that the emergence of autobiographical memory is linked to the timing and nature of this early self? What is the role of language in autobiographical memory *after* its genesis in the preverbal child?

EARLY SELF

Conjecture about the nature and function of the self has a long tradition (e.g., Bowlby, 1969; Darwin, 1877; Freud, 1959; James, 1890/1961; Mead, 1934; Piaget, 1954) that is rife with controversy concerning appropriate ways to measure this elusive concept. Despite this controversy, the developmental course of the self is still the focus of intense research activity (e.g., Cicchetti & Beeghly, 1990; Damon & Hart, 1988; Kopp & Brownell, 1991; Neisser, 1993; Parker, Mitchell, & Boccia, 1994; Rochat, 2001) with a general consensus having formed about two important issues: (1) at birth infants are probably unaware of their separateness from the environment and acquire this awareness following a gradual process of individuation which likely begins at birth (Butterworth, 1995; Meltzoff, 1990; Neisser, 1993), and (2) there exist at least two fundamental but interrelated aspects to the self, the "I," a subjective sense of the self as a thinker, knower, and causal agent, and the "me," an objective sense of the self with the unique and recognizable features and characteristics that constitute one's self-concept (see Neisser, 1988 for an alternative perspective).

For the most part, empirical investigation of the self in infancy has focused on the objective self, or the self as object-of-experience (i.e., the "me") with a particular emphasis on the development of visual self-recognition indexed by infants' reactions to their images in mirrors, photos, and videos (for a review see Howe & Courage, 1997). What these studies have shown is that: (a) from 3 months of age infants are both attentive and positive toward their mirror images and that within several months can discriminate their facial features from those of another infant; (b) by about 8 months of age infants are aware of the contingency cues provided by the tandem movement of the mirror image with themselves, can use these cues for play and imitation, and know something of the reflective properties of mirrors, turning to locate objects and people that they see reflected (but see Mitchell, 1993); and (c) by about 18 months infants show full self-recognition of a mirror image as their own and will touch their own noses rather than that of the mirror image after a spot of rouge has been covertly applied to the nose. Coincident with this mark-directed behavior, infants begin to show self-consciousness (shy smiling, gaze aversion, and self touching) when confronted with their images, and by about 22 months of age will correctly label the image. Collectively, these behaviors provide a consistent picture of an infant who recognizes the mirror (or video) image as "me." Moreover, there is evidence to suggest that these early developing components of objective self-awareness emerge in a systematic order within individuals over the second year of life — first physical self-recognition and self-consciousness, then linguistic self-description, and finally more complex emotional (e.g., Lewis & Ramsay, 1998) and empathic (e.g., Lewis, 1994) responses associated with self-evaluation.

According to some accounts, the self develops in a sudden, apparently discontinuous manner late in the second year of life (e.g., Kagan, 1998). However, according to others, there is considerable development of the self prior to mirror self-recognition that serves as a foundation for the emergence of the conceptual (or cognitive) self (for a review, see Rochat, 2001). For these latter theorists, prior to the explicit recognition of the self as "me", there is an "I" that has been actively developing since birth. Empirical work on the self as subject-of-experience (the "I") has been slow to accrue in part due to difficulties in operationalizing what is meant by "I." It is only in recent years that researchers have devised a variety of self-involvement-in-action tasks (i.e., those in which the infant recognizes the outcome as a result of their own participation) that help articulate what is meant by "I" (Bullock & Lutkenhaus, 1990; Meltzoff, 1990; Pipp, Fischer, & Jennings, 1987). In advance of this research has been considerable theoretical speculation concerning the nature of the infant's sense of self-as-subject-of-experience before the onset of (cognitive) self recognition and that this latter achievement has its nascent roots in processes of sensory perception (e.g., Gibson, 1995), self-control (e.g., Butterworth, 1990; Neisser, 1993; Rochat, 2001), and imitation (Meltzoff, 1990) in the early weeks and months of life.

Current theories of the early development of the self (the "I") vary in their emphasis on perceptual, social, and affective factors in structuring the "presymbolic" self (for reviews, see Cicchetti & Beeghly, 1990; Kopp & Brownell, 1991; Neisser, 1993; Rochat, 2001). As an example, one of the most comprehensive treatments has been provided by Neisser (1988, 1995) who proposed a cognitive analysis of the self based on the varieties of information available to infants, each of which specifies a different "type" of self. Of particular relevance to infancy are the *ecological* self, an awareness of where one is, what one is doing, and what one has done that is rooted in perceptual processes (Gibson, 1995) and the *interpersonal* self, an awareness of social affordances based on interactions with others. The foundations of a rudimentary interpersonal self in the early months can be indexed by an infant's imitation of facial expressions (Meltzoff & Moore, 1994), protoconversations (Bateson, 1975), and affective exchanges with caretakers (Stern, 1985, 1993). A third aspect of the self-as-I (although not perceived directly by the child) is the *conceptual* self that enables infants to begin to take themselves as objects of thought. The ability to think about oneself as the subject of experience probably begins to emerge with the realization that one is the object of another person's attention, an achievement unlikely to appear before the end of the first year. At this time, shared attention to objects and events becomes a common mode of parent–child interaction (Tomasello, 1993; Tomasello, Kruger, & Ratner, 1993), an activity that serves to foster the infant's early understanding of what other people are attending to or talking about — the object of attention sometimes being the child themselves. This sense of self is still immature and implicit as it does not require the explicit or conscious idea of "me."

Although it is possible that the "I" and the "me" develop in tandem and have been functioning in parallel, it is also a possibility that the cognitive self emerges in the second year of life as a consequence of the "I" that has been developing since birth. In fact, Rochat (2001) argues that the conceptual self as measured by mirror self-recognition arises as a direct consequence of the development of the "I." In particular, this emergence of the "me" may occur because of infants' "ability to contemplate and repeat actions in order to explore their consequences, beyond the immediate, embodied sense of the self infants experience from birth in their interaction with physical objects and people" (pp. 26–27). It is this objectification of the self that Rochat (2001) argues leads to mirror self-recognition.

Part of the uncertainty about the emergence of these two aspects of the self stems from the active debate about what mirror self-recognition actually means. Several arguments have been raised in this regard. One concerns the prerequisite cognitive-developmental achievements in addition to self-awareness that mediate (or mask) successful task performance. For example, it has been argued that mirror self-recognition is a complex intellectual problem that not only requires recognition of one's facial features, but also cognitive achievements such as visual-proprioceptive matching, Stage 6 object permanence, deferred imitation, and knowledge of the reflective properties of mirrors (for a discussion see Butterworth, 1995; Mitchell, 1993). Immaturity in any of these component skills might obscure the expression of visual self-recognition. In a related argument Rochat (1995) contends that infants' objectification of the self as "me" emerges from the feedback provided by their actions on objects, and their social interactions with others in the early months of life. Thus, when infants confront their mirror image they show embarrassment and puzzlement because they are trying to come to terms with an image that specifies two things that are normally viewed as one — the (already present) self (perceived via the temporal contingency of visual-proprioceptive information) and someone else (an animated, differentiated, and externalized other person) who "looks and moves like" the self. Finally, Neisser (1995) has argued that failure to recognize one's mirror reflection prior to 18 months does not occur because of a lack of self-awareness but because the face has not yet become an important component of the "ecological" self (i.e., the individual situated in and acting upon the immediate physical environment). This argument is supported by research that shows that infants can discriminate between certain body parts as theirs or as belonging to another infant well before 18 months of age (e.g., Bahrick & Watson, 1985; Rochat & Morgan, 1995; Schmuckler, 1994).

In contrast, proponents of the idea that mirror self-recognition is a critical marker of the onset of the objective sense of self do acknowledge the plausibility of an earlier developing, subjective sense of self-awareness. However, they contend that this is a very different self from the one that emerges in the middle of the second year of life (for a discussion see Lewis, 1994, 1995). This latter sense of self involves a unique mental state, a "knower who knows," one with intentions (not merely intentionality), and which may well differentiate humans and a few nonhuman primates (chimpanzees; orangutans) from the rest of the animal kingdom (but see Mitchell, 1993). This self should not be confused nor equated with the subjective self, the "I" that originates in neonatal perceptual and motor processes, includes self-regulation and self-other differentiation, and directs much of our behavior but which is not a conscious, mental state. Moreover, although this subjective self provides a foundation for the objective self, it is not replaced by it in ontogeny, rather, the two continue to coexist. The failure to differentiate these two aspects of the self underlies some of the argument over the onset and measurement of the objective self. Once matters of definition are resolved, Lewis (1994) argues that the infant's self-referential touching before the mirror image is the measure that most clearly separates the two aspects of the self, and as such is the best single index of the construct of "me." Finally, convergent evidence for the validity of the mirror response is evident from three areas of coherence that are predicted by a theory of the idea of "me": the appearance of empathy; self-conscious emotions such as pride, shame, and guilt; and changes in certain mother-child interactive behaviors at the end of the second year (for a review, see Courage & Howe, 2002).

Although much debate exists concerning the nature of the content of the self that is now recognized in the mirror, most would agree that visual self-recognition is only one facet of the self-concept that emerges at this time, one that is relatively easy to operationalize for research with infants. The self-concept (and self-aware-ness) implies more than recognition of one's physical features and is a fundamental aspect of social cognitive development that, according to some, has roots in the early weeks of life and continues to evolve throughout childhood and adolescence (see Damon & Hart, 1988 for a review). For example, Povinelli, Landau, and Perilloux (1996) have suggested that mirror self-recognition may be only the first step toward the recognition of the objective self as "temporally extended" and continuing to exist over time. In a series of experiments they have shown that 2-year-old children who were able to recognize themselves immediately failed to do so after a brief delay and provision of noncontingent video or photo feedback of themselves. Not until children were 3 to 4 years old were they able to identify themselves after a delay. However, measurement and definitional issues continue to cloud the issue of the development of the self. Recent work by Suddendorf (1999) has shown that there are interpretative problems with these data. Specifically, children fail to understand certain aspects of the video-delay task and their poor performance on that task may mask preschoolers' understanding of the self extended in time.

There is also general agreement that the achievement of mirror self-recognition marks an important developmental milestone in the second year of life (Asendorpf & Baudonniere, 1993; Asendorpf, Warkentin, & Baudonniere, 1996; Butterworth, 1990; Kagan, 1981; Lewis, 1994; Meltzoff, 1990; Neisser, 1993; Rochat, 2001) and that a critical step is reached when children are able to represent themselves as an object of knowledge and imagination. Therefore, mark-directed behavior reflects more than self-recognition and may portend a more widespread transition in cognitive development late in the second year of life. Indeed, the achievement of self-recognition is paralleled by developments in object perma-nence (Bertenthal & Fischer, 1978), altruism (Johnson, 1983), empathy and self-evaluation (Kagan, 1981; Lewis, Sullivan, Stanger, & Weiss, 1989), synchronic imitation (Asendorpf & Baudonniere, 1993; Asendorpf et al., 1996), the language "explosion" (Bates, Bretherton, & Snyder, 1988), and pretend play (Lewis & Ramsay, 1998). As Butterworth (1995) noted, it may be that mirror self-recognition marks both an ontogenetic and phylogenetic boundary between primary and higher-order consciousness (also see Damasio, 1999).

In summary, contemporary theories of the development of the self are con-sistent in the position that important foundations of the development of the self-as-subject are evident in early infancy, perhaps from birth. Although the two aspects of the self-system develop in tandem over the first two years (but see Kagan, 1998), by the time the infant shows mirror self-recognition she or he already has a healthy self-awareness (see Butterworth, 1990). Although the issue of precisely how the various facets of the self become integrated into a full self system developmentally has not been completely explicated, but as the contributors to a special issue of *Developmental Review*, "Development of the Self" (Kopp & Brownell, 1991) concur, a significant shift in one's sense of self seems to occur at about 18 months of age. The achievement of this critical mass of awareness of, and knowledge about, the self serves to provide a new organizer and regulator of experience and, as I have argued elsewhere (Howe, 2000), the foundation of early autobiographical memory.

EARLY MEMORY

A number of reviews of the early memory (from birth through preschool years) literature have been published recently (e.g., Howe, 2000), so only a brief precis of this literature will be presented here. The literature on early memory development is replete with examples of the infants' proficiency in encoding, storing, and retrieving information. This evidence has been gathered with a variety of procedures, paradigms, and tasks designed to harness the enormous curiosity of the human infant whose responses are limited by perceptual, cognitive, and motor immaturities. For example, researchers exploiting infants' visual responsiveness and robust preference for novelty have used habituation, paired-comparison, and other familiarization procedures to show that even neonates can recognize patterns seen previously (for reviews, see Fagan, 1990; Rovee-Collier & Bhatt, 1993; Slater, 1995). Moreover, recognition is not limited to the visual modality but includes recognition of familiar haptic, auditory, and olfactory stimuli as well (e.g., see Catherwood, 1993; Cernoch & Porter, 1985; Swain, Zelazo, & Clifton, 1993). Although studies using habituation and novelty preference procedures attest to the readiness of the infant to begin processing information from its earliest days, these are not ideal for examining long-term retention (see Rovee-Collier & Bhatt, 1993; but see also Bahrick & Pickens, 1995; Courage & Howe, 1998, 2001; Courage, Howe, & Squires, 2004).

Over the past decade or so several arguably more appropriate procedures have been implemented. In perhaps the most comprehensive investigation of infants' long-term memory, Rovee-Collier and her colleagues employed a mobile conjugate reinforcement paradigm to identify the factors that affect 2- to 6-month-olds' immediate and long-term retention of an operant foot-kick response. They found that 6 month olds learned the basic contingency faster than 2- and 3-month-olds and that despite similar levels of performance at the end of acquisition, infant age and the length of the retention interval were positively correlated. A comparable train-moving task with an operant lever pull response designed for older infants (to 18 months) revealed a similar trend in memory acquisition and retention. Further, they found that as in research with older children and adults, retention was affected by factors such as amount and distribution of practice, the match between the proximal (mobile) and distal (context) cues present at acquisition and those at long-term retention, and exposure to reinstating or interfering stimuli following simple forgetting and acquisition, respectively (see Hartshorn et al., 1998; Rovee-Collier & Bhatt, 1993 for reviews). The operant conditioning paradigm has also been effectively used to explore neonates' ability to retain auditory information. DeCasper and his colleagues showed that newborn infants can recognize the prosodic characteristics of a prose passage heard in the last trimester of their prenatal life and have identified a number of variables that affect their recognition of auditory stimuli (DeCasper & Prescott, 1984; DeCasper & Spence, 1986, 1991; Spence & Freeman, 1996).

Infants' readiness to imitate motor activities performed by an adult model has provided another opportunity to examine the development of long-term retention. Meltzoff and Moore (1994) demonstrated that 6-week-olds will reproduce certain facial expressions and head movements modelled by an adult and will retain them over a 24-hour retention interval. Further advances in infants' recall of action sequences occur during the second half of the first postnatal year at which time 9-month-olds show deferred imitation of novel object-specific actions witnessed (but not performed) by them 24 hours earlier (Meltzoff, 1988). Older infants at 14 and 16 months retained multiple modelled acts across 2- and 4-month retention intervals, respectively (Meltzoff, 1995). A particular strength of Meltzoff's research is that the novel activities were modelled only briefly without verbal instruction and were not performed by the infants themselves prior to the retention test. As infants' imitation of the novel actions was based on the stored representation of what they had seen previously, they are assumed to index recall rather than simple recognition. Using a variation of this paradigm, Bauer and her colleagues employed elicited imitation to show that 11- to 24-month-olds represent order information in their recall of two- to five-component event sequences and that recall is facilitated and prolonged (to several hours in the youngest infants and up to 8 months in the older children) if the components of the events contain enabling relations, are familiar, and are accompanied by verbal cues at the retention test (see Bauer, 1996; Bauer, Wenner, Dropik, & Wewerka, 2000 for reviews).

In the most recent research using deferred imitation, Hayne and colleagues (Barr, Dowden, & Hayne, 1996; Collie & Hayne, 1999; Hayne, MacDonald, & Barr, 1997; Herbert & Hayne, 2000a, 2000b) investigated developmental changes in deferred imitation by 6- to 30-month-old infants and found that even the youngest infants showed evidence of deferred imitation on a series of as many as eight unique actions with various toy props following a 24-hour delay. However, significant developmental improvements were evident over the age range studied. Younger infants required more exposure to the target actions in order to exhibit deferred imitation, were less accurate in their imitation (i.e., produced fewer components), and generalized the modelled actions less readily to a new object at test than were older infants. In addition, the duration of the retention interval for imitation of 3-step sequences of modelled actions increased from 14 days for 18-month-olds up to 3 months for 24-month-olds (Herbert & Hayne, 2000b). Hayne and her colleagues attribute these developmental advances in deferred imitation over the first 2 years of life to an increase in "representational flexibility," an inherent characteristic of declarative memory processing that depends on maturing interactions between the hippocampus and association cortex as well as on experiences at encoding and test (e.g., see Hayne, Boniface, & Barr, 2000).

Finally, studies of young children's memory for both naturally occurring and contrived events that occurred during their infant and toddler years have shown that those events are retained and under certain conditions can persist for months or years, although with the passage of time recollection of these events becomes increasingly fragmentary. For example, McDonough and Mandler (1994) found some evidence of recall of single object-specific actions in groups of 2-year-olds who had participated in an experiment when they were 11 months old. However, a longitudinal study of infants' memories of a toy-play event experienced at home when they were 10 and 14 months old and in a laboratory setting when they were 32 and 60 months old, revealed progressively less recollection of the event over time (Myers, Perris, & Speaker, 1994). Similarly, Boyer, Barron, and Farrar (1994) failed to find evidence of recollection of a 9-action event sequence learned by 20-month-olds and tested after a 12- to 22-month delay. As well, in a recent investigation of children's memories for injuries requiring emergency room treatment, Howe, Courage, and Peterson (1994) reported that children who were younger than 2 years old expressed recollection of their accidents nonverbally after a 5-day retention interval, but demonstrated very little recall 6 months later.

Although there is no doubt that even during the first few days of life infants can encode, store, and retrieve a great deal of information about events in their world and can retain that information over relatively lengthy periods of time (e.g., Bauer, 1996; Howe & Courage, 1997; Rovee-Collier, 1997), there is considerable debate about the nature of these early memories. Because infants of this age do not possess language with which to report on the contents of memory, it has not been easy to determine whether these memories are declarative (i.e., memory based on conscious recollection; e.g., showing explicit recognition or recall of people, places, dates, events) or nondeclarative (i.e., memory that does not require conscious recollection; e.g., habits, skills, priming, classical conditioning). For example, there has been considerable speculation in the cognitive neuroscience literature that the memory systems necessary for declarative memory do not come "on-line" until the latter half of the first year of life (e.g., C. A. Nelson, 1995). However, recent empirical evidence showing deferred imitation in 6-month-olds (Collie & Hayne, 1999) as well as a number of theoretical reviews of memory phenomena in the infant and adult literatures (e.g., Gerhardstein, Adler, & Rovee-Collier, 2000; Howe & Courage, 1997; Roediger, Rajaram, & Srinivas, 1990; Rovee-Collier, 1997) have provoked an active reevaluation of this hypothesis. As part of this debate more fundamental questions have arisen: for example, whether or not multiple memory systems exist at all. And, if so, whether they develop along serial or parallel developmental trajectories. And, finally, whether our standard tests and measures are sensitive enough to distinguish declarative from nondeclarative memories (e.g., Buchner & Wippich, 2000)? What we can conclude with confidence at this juncture is that by about 2 years of age, the earliest age that research places the onset of autobiographical memory, the development of both declarative and nondeclarative memory systems (if indeed such separate systems exist) are well underway. Moreover, although the neural substrates that subserve memory and other cognitive processes will continue to develop into adolescence, there is no evidence that any one particular development underlies the onset of autobiographical memory late in the second year of life. Given all of the evidence attesting to the continuity of memory development from infancy onward, it is more parsimonious to view memory as a unitary system, one that supports a variety of modes of remembering (e.g., Bauer, 1996; Howe, 2000).

Although there is considerable continuity in the development of memory processes, it is also the case that there are changes in these memory processes that permit children to have more durable and longer-lasting memories, ones whose representation becomes less perceptually and contextually bound (e.g., Hayne, Boniface, & Barr, 2000) and more flexible (e.g., Herbert & Hayne, 2000a; Howe, 2002). With development, infants and toddlers become more sensitive to the temporal/causal patterns in stimuli and can use these patterns to memorial advantage (e.g., Bauer et al., 2000). Indeed, by the beginning of their second year, toddlers can remember nonverbal event sequences for periods of over 6 months, with these intervals increasing with age (see Bauer et al., 2000; Howe, 2000). One of the factors that is universally acknowledged as aiding the development of long-term retention is the ability to organize information in storage in ways that promote the integrity of that information. As these organizational abilities develop, elements within a trace are more likely to have a high degree of internal cohesion and similarity whereas between traces the system must maintain maximal discrimina-bility and distinctiveness. The growth in our knowledge base, which begins fairly early in life, accomplishes both of these tasks. This includes knowledge (which need not be explicit) of how elements within an event are temporally and causally structured as well as how they are linked perceptually, associatively, and categor-ically. Advances in our ability to classify and categorize information affords us the opportunity to not only better understand the world we live in and events that occur in our lives, but also can beget more durable memories. Of particular interest in this chapter is how knowledge of ourselves early in life influences the longevity of memories for events that happened to us. It is this knowledge, I argue, that is critical not only to the longevity of personal memories but is itself critical to the onset of autobiographical memory.

WHEN SELF AND MEMORY MEET: THE EMERGENCE OF AUTOBIOGRAPHICAL MEMORY

Regardless of whether the self develops continuously from birth or emerges suddenly in the second year of life, the fact is that at about the age of 2 years the cognitive self, a new organizer of information and experiences, "comes of age" and facilitates the grouping and personalization of memories for events into what becomes autobiographical memory. Interestingly, this is consistent with the findings of several recent and well-controlled studies of the origin of autobiographical memory which place the lower limit of our earliest memories at about the age of 2 years (Eacott & Crawley, 1998; Usher & Neisser, 1993). Moreover, it is well documented that adults' recollections of childhood memories increase substantially in number from this age as well. We also know that a significant developmental advance in memory throughout childhood is the ability to maintain information in *storage*, not only information about autobiographical events but information in general (e.g., see Howe, 2000). To have a viable theory of autobiographical memory then, it is essential that we not only understand its origins but also the extent to which its basic processes are like (or perhaps unlike) those that drive memory functioning in general. In that regard, I have already pointed out that the basic encoding, storage, and retrieval processes needed to learn and retain information are intact very early in life (at least in rudimentary form) and that subsequent developments are mediated largely by ancillary changes in cognitive processes such as attention, strategy use, metamemory, and knowledge. As well, I have argued that many of the basic processes that drive memory are continuous across development, with one of the most pervasive being the ability to maintain information in storage over progressively longer intervals (Howe, 2000). With what we know about early developments in memory and about the emergence of the self in infancy, it remains only to ask what it is that makes memory autobiographical. What happens when memory and the self meet?

It is important to note at the beginning that although some of the key factors that contribute to memory development (e.g., changes in strategies, knowledge) are known, it is not clear from a basic-process perspective why such improvements occur. For example, although we know that strategic rehearsal can lead to better recall, it is not clear whether these effects arise because the stability of traces in storage increases, the ease of retrieving these traces increases, or both. Similarly, in order to discover what basic process or processes mediate these improvements in autobiographical retention, we must understand what processes are affected by the self in memory. A number of researchers who have addressed this issue have concluded that the self, like any other knowledge structure (e.g., see Bjorklund, 1987), can be used to interpret and organize incoming information (see Greenwald & Banaji, 1989; Klein & Kihlstrom, 1986). In a recent meta-analysis of studies of the self-reference effect in memory, Symons and Johnson (1997) concluded that the self is important not only because of its elaborative and organizational properties but also because it links encoding and test conditions, a phenomenon that facilitates access to memories (e.g., as in encoding-specificity theory, see Tulving, 1984). It is also significant that the self plays a prominent role in autobiographical recall, particularly at points in time where there are major transitions in the self. The view that the self behaves like any other organizational scheme in memory is consistent with the idea that autobiographical memory is functionally no different than any other "type" of memory.

Howe and Courage (1997; also see Howe, Courage, & Edison, 2003) have combined these ideas with the trace-integrity framework, a model that provides a quantitative and qualitative account of the development of long-term retention generally. Briefly, in this model storage and retrieval are processes lying on a single continuum and traces consist of collections of primitive elements (e.g., features). The key to initial acquisition is integrating features into a single, cohesive structure in memory. Across any retention interval, traces that are well integrated tend to disintegrate and their stability (both in terms of storage and retrieval) compromised. Here, the original memory trace begins to lose its cohesion and distinctiveness, and fades into the background noise of other memory traces. This conceptualization of how storage and retrieval processes operate in children's memory has gained broad acceptance and is generally consistent with other views of these processes in other recent models (e.g., see Howe, 2000; Howe & Courage, 1997; Schneider & Bjorklund, 1998).

The trace-integrity framework is important here because it (a) provides a general context (one that is common to all of long-term memory) in which to situate autobiographical memory and (b) explains the accumulation of autobiographical memories using a simple, basic process mechanism, namely, storage maintenance. By using the same mechanisms to explain autobiographical memory as those used to explain other memories and their development, we simplify and enhance our understanding of memory processes at both a very specific as well as a global level. To see how this synthesis is achieved, consider first how such a system might encode an event both before and after the emergence of the cognitive self. When sampling features from an ongoing event (or nominal stimulus), it is well known that interpretive or internal contextual features are included. It is also well known that only a subset of features that characterize an event (internal and external) are actually encoded and stored and that that subset is determined in a probabilistic fashion and is contingent on a number of factors (e.g., a feature's salience, the encoder's expectation, attentional factors). Reminiscent of stimulus sampling theory (e.g., see Hilgard & Bower, 1975; Neimark & Estes, 1967), then, the stored trace of encoded features (the functional stimulus) is extracted and consists of a subset of features from the event itself (the nominal situation) as well as interpretive elements.

Like other categories and concepts, it is not until the self becomes a viable cognitive entity with recognizable features that the encoding of such features into the functional memory trace becomes possible. Importantly, even when the self becomes viable and its features become *potentially samplable*, like other features in the nominal situation, there is no guarantee that they will be sampled. Indeed, like the features that comprise any memory trace, whether features about the self are sampled is determined probabilistically and is contingent on the same factors that control sampling probabilities for other features (e.g., salience, attention, the centrality of participation by the self in the event). These encoding fluctuations (also see Flexser & Tulving, 1978) may be used to explain the variability in the numbers of early autobiographical memories across individuals. As features get added to the self the likelihood that at least some self-features will be sampled and encoded in the functional trace for an event increases. Thus, although there is no chance of encoding self features prior to the emergence of a recognizable cognitive self, this does not mean that events cannot be remembered as events per se. Even when a viable cognitive self emerges, events can remain depersonalized if features of the self are not sampled and encoded in the stored trace. However, having a viable cognitive self does set the lower limit as to when autobiographical memories can be established; but this does not guarantee that such memories need be established at that age. As the number of features associated with the self increases, the corresponding likelihood of at least some of these features being sampled increases, with the result that memory for an event now becomes memory for an event that happened to me, a memory that, by definition, is now autobiographical. This, added to the growth in storage capacity, can account for the accumulation of autobiographical memories as we age in childhood.

What is the empirical evidence that backs up such claims? First, autobiographical memories do increase in both number and longevity in memory as childhood progresses (e.g., Wetzler & Sweeney, 1986). Second, a number of studies have shown that the best retained memories over the life span are those pertaining to the self, especially the self in times of transition (e.g., Conway, 1996). In particular, as the self goes through changes, events associated with those change points are well remembered (e.g., Csikszentmihalyi & Beattie, 1979). Although such findings highlight the importance of changes in the self in autobiographical memories, such transitions also represent unique occurrences in one's life, an idea that squares well with other findings showing that the uniqueness of an event is one of the best overall predictors of autobiographical recall (Betz & Skowkronski, 1997; Brewer, 1988; Linton, 1979). Thus, it is clear that events about the self, particularly those that are personally consequential, transition defining, or otherwise distinctive, are best remembered autobiographically.

INDIVIDUAL DIFFERENCES

As already mentioned, when adults are asked to recall their earliest experiences there is considerable individual variability in the age from which they can date their first autobiographical memory (e.g., Eacott & Crawley, 1998; Usher & Neisser, 1993). One reason for this may simply be that there are individual differences in forgetting rates. A more attractive possibility from my perspective is that these differences are related to individual differences in the age of onset of the cognitive self or perhaps individual differences in the propensity to encode self-relevant features into memory traces for early events. Although this second possibility has already been discussed, it is also important to note that there are substantial individual differences in the age of onset of mark-directed behavior in the second year of life (Bertenthal & Fischer, 1978; Lewis & Brooks-Gunn, 1979; Lewis, Brooks-Gunn, & Jaskir, 1985; Schneider-Rosen & Cicchetti, 1984, 1991). For example, research on mirror self-recognition has shown that whereas about 25% of 15- to 18-month-old infants showed mark-directed behavior to the red spots on their noses, others did not show self-recognition until the end of the second year, at which time about 75% showed mark-directed behavior.

These individual differences in the age of *onset* of visual self-recognition have not been fully explored, although the weight of the available evidence to date indicates that they may have their origins in maturational rather than social or experiential factors. For example, Lewis and Brooks-Gunn (1979) reported that neither the child's sex, maternal education, family socioeconomic status, birth order, or number of siblings were related to onset of self-recognition. Likewise, Cicchetti and his colleagues (Cicchetti & Beeghly, 1987; Cicchetti & Carlson, 1989; Kaufman & Cicchetti, 1989; Schneider-Rosen & Cicchetti, 1984, 1991) have found that maltreated infants whose abnormal caretaking environments are associated with delays or deviations in their emotional development as it relates to the self are also not delayed in the onset of visual self-recognition. In contrast, infants who have delayed maturation (e.g., Down syndrome, familial mental retardation, autism) do show delays in visual self-recognition (Cicchetti, 1991; Hill & Tomlin, 1981; Loveland, 1987, 1993; Mans, Cicchetti, & Sroufe, 1978; Schneider-Rosen & Cicchetti, 1991; Spiker & Ricks, 1984), although they usually succeed at the self-recognition task if and when they reach a mental age comparable to that of nondelayed infants who succeed at the task. Thus, the near universal appearance of visual self-recognition among infants who have attained the maturational prerequisites supports the hypothesis that its emergence is not influenced by variations in social or childcare experiences in any obvious way (but see Lewis, Brooks-Gunn, & Jaskir, 1985). Consistent with Kagan's (1981, 1994) work and the evidence just reviewed, more recent data demonstrate a link between the onset of the self and constitutional factors such as stress reactivity and temperament (DiBiase & Lewis, 1997; Lewis & Ramsay, 1997). For example, DiBiase and Lewis (1997) found that differences in temperament were related to variation in the age at which self-recognition emerged and that these same differences were predictive of when self-conscious emotions such as embarrassment begin to be expressed (see also Lewis, Sullivan, Stanger, & Weiss, 1989). Thus, infants with a difficult temperament at 5 months were more likely to show earlier self-recognition and embarrassment than were infants with an easy temperament. Using a longitudinal design, Lewis and Ramsay (1997) found that children with higher stress reactivity (measured both in terms of cortisol levels and behavioral responses to inoculations at 2, 4, 6, and 18 months) also had an earlier age of onset of self-recognition. Thus, self-recognition and self-conscious emotions such as embarrassment seem to be linked to a variety of constitutional factors, including temperament and stress reactivity. Specifically, a cognitive sense of self seems to emerge earlier for children who are classified as having a more difficult temperament or whose reactivity to stress is relatively high. Given this evidence then, it is perhaps logical to assume that individual differences in the onset of early autobiographical memories are related to these maturational, not social or experiential, factors associated with the emergence of the cognitive self.

I have argued here that differences in the onset of autobiographical memory in atypical populations may well be directly related to delays in the establishment of the cognitive self rather than to the child's chronological age. Importantly however, there is evidence that the mirror *behavior* of children with atypical cognitive development or those with adverse social environments is different from that of normally developing children. For example, normally developing children as well as those with maturational delays are generally quite positive in their responses to their self-images, even when a spot of rouge has been applied to their noses (Cicchetti, 1991; Lewis et al., 1989). However, children who have been maltreated show more neutral and negative behavior in response to their mirror images (Cicchetti, Beeghly, Carlson, & Toth, 1990), which raises the intriguing possibility that although social and experiential factors may not determine the *onset* of early autobiographical memory, they may contribute to the contents of these early memories.

WHEN SELF AND LANGUAGE MEET: SUBSEQUENT DEVELOPMENTS IN AUTOBIOGRAPHICAL MEMORY

As I have noted, once the cognitive self has emerged as a viable entity late in the second year of life, self features become available that serve to organize memories autobiographically. However, the mere availability of self features does not ensure that autobiographical memory is launched. As the previous section illustrates, there are a host of individual differences — cognitive, constitutional, and experiential — that singly and conjointly affect the subsequent development of autobiographical memory. Interestingly, many of these experiential factors directly or indirectly involve hypotheses about the development and deployment of language. What then is the role of language in autobiographical memory subsequent to the emergence of the cognitive self?

One prominent view has focused on the role of social interaction in the emergence of the autobiographical memory system (Fivush, Haden, & Reese, 1996; Fivush & Reese, 1992; Hudson, 1990; Nelson, 1993). In this view, autobiographical memory begins when children share their experiences with others linguistically. That is, as young children learn to talk about the past with adults, they begin to organize these events autobiographically in memory. Thus, the primary *function* of autobiographical memory is to develop a life history and to do that by telling others what one is like through narrating the events of the past. In this way, children learn both the form of reporting about past events and the social functions that talking about the past performs. It is important to note here that the functional aspects of memory should not be confused with its representational structure. In any event, research shows that at about 2.5 years most children begin to talk about specific events but that these early conversations are heavily "scaffolded" by adults (e.g., Hudson, 1990). By about 3 years, children assume more responsibility for talking about past events and begin to use the story or narrative form in these conversational interactions. However, although some of these advances begin to occur as early as 3 to 4 years of age, K. Nelson (1993) has maintained that "true" autobiographical memory is quite late to develop and may only be complete near the end of the preschool years. According to this sociolinguistic view, then, autobiographical memory is predicated on the development of rather sophisticated language-based representational skills, ones that do not emerge until children are about 5 or 6 years old. Once these skills are established, memories can be retained and organized around a life history, one that extends in time (see also Povinelli et al., 1996, 1999; Povinelli & Simon, 1998). As it is this "life history" element that makes a memory autobiographical, very young children's reports of personally experienced events are precluded, a determination that seems arbitrary at best.

Not surprisingly, this sociolinguistic perspective places considerable currency in children's conversations about the past, particularly with their parents (especially mothers). Research conducted within this framework reveals that individual differences in the way parents talk to their children about the past leads to individual differences in children's reporting of their own past experiences. In particular, two different parent conversational styles of talking with children have been identified. "High-elaborative" parents provide a large amount of detailed information about past events. They elaborate and expand on the child's partial recall, ask further questions to enhance event detail, and correct the child's memory if necessary. In contrast, "low-elaborative" parents tend to repeat their questions over and over in an attempt to get a specific answer from the child, switch topics more frequently, and do not seek elaborative detail from the child's report. Importantly, the high-elaborative style is associated with children's provision of more memory information, both concurrently and longitudinally (Haden, Haine, & Fivush, 1997; Reese, Haden, & Fivush, 1993). Although adult conversational style does appear to facilitate the richness and narrative organization of children's memory talk and in so doing plays an important role in children's developing ability to *report* autobiographical memories, it does not necessarily determine the *content* or *accuracy* of children's memory reports (see Fivush, 1994; Goodman, Quas, Batterman-Faunce, Riddlesberger, & Kuhn, 1994). In fact, reconstruction of events through conversations with others can lead to systematic distortions of memory details, ones that are congruent with the recaller's as well as the listener's current beliefs and expectations (e.g., Ross & Wilson, 2000). Thus, consistent with the well-replicated finding in-the-memory literature more generally, the strategy of verbal rehearsal can serve not only to reinforce and reinstate memories, but can also lead to a number of errors in recall.

From the sociolinguistic perspective then, parents are actively involved in teaching their children how to remember and also the techniques of sharing memories with others through narrative reports. On the broader scale in which culture is our teacher, recent research shows that like the individual differences in children's conversational styles and memory reports that correlate with parent talk, children in other cultures exposed to different conversational styles differ in memory reporting. For example, research shows that American mothers talk to their 3-year-olds about past events 3 times more often than Korean mothers. Further, American children talk about past events more than do Korean children and American adults report earlier autobiographical memories than do Korean adults (Han, Leichtman, & Wang, 1998; Mullen, 1994; Mullen & Yi, 1995). Similar relationships were found between age of earliest memory, culture, and conversational interactions in a comparison of Maori, Pakeha, and Asian adults living in New Zealand (MacDonald, Uesiliana, & Hayne, 2000).

Another view of the development of autobiographical memory in which language plays a more ancillary role is one in which children's own self-awareness or autonoetic consciousness is the critical necessary ingredient. Perner & Ruffman (1995) argue that autobiographical memory follows achievements in metacognition in which children begin to have recollective experiences of remembering (as opposed to simply knowing about) past events, experiences that are unlikely to occur before the age of 3 to 5 years. Like the sociolinguistic model, mother's elaborated talk about past episodes is thought to play a significant role in the evolution of autonoetic consciousness as well as in children's theory of the mind (see Perner & Ruffman, 1995). Although conscious awareness of oneself and one's experiences may be a component of episodic memory more generally, and may play a role in the accumulation of autobiographical memories throughout childhood, it does not appear to be necessary for the initial onset of autobiographical memory. That is, although the *experience* of remembering often accompanies autobiographical recall (e.g., see Conway, 1996), the existence of personalized memories is not contingent on such experiencing.

What these language-based theories of the development of autobiographical memory contribute to the debate is that the language environment of the child, be it familial or cultural, serves to teach children that reporting memories is important and that such reports have a particular narrative structure and a particular social and cognitive function. Further, and consistent with the mechanisms of storage maintenance that I have discussed, language can serve to strengthen the content of events to be preserved (or altered) over time. The importance of this role for language and language interactions in autobiographical memories is not a matter of debate. What is more controversial is the role of language in the initial onset of autobiographical memory. I have argued here and elsewhere (Howe, 2000; Howe & Courage, 1997; Howe et al., 2003) that it is negligible, and that what is critical is the onset of the cognitive self, and that alone. Once this has occurred, the foundation is laid and a variety of experiential factors (including language) and individual differences come into play to shape and mold our autobiographies and to permit us to reflect upon them.

Only recently has there been any empirical research that examined the role of the onset of the cognitive self and early language conjointly. In the first such study, Harley and Reese (1999) examined 58 mother-child dyads first when children were 19 months old, then at 25 months old, and finally at 32 months of age. Mother-child dyads were tested on a number of dimensions including language, self-recognition, deferred imitation, and memory conversation styles. For this latter measure, children's verbal memory and maternal reminiscing style (low or high elaboration) concerning real, one-time events in the past were evaluated at each interview. In order to evaluate the roles of self-recognition and maternal reminiscing styles in the development of children's talk about the past independent of children's language and nonverbal memory abilities, analyses were conducted on data in which variability in the language measure and nonverbal memory (deferred imitation measure) were removed using an analysis of covariance. The results showed that both self-recognition and maternal reminiscing style contributed independently to verbal memory with self-recognition emerging as a stronger predictor. In fact, memory appeared to be developing faster in early than in late self-recognizers. That is, self-recognition was a better predictor of later verbal memory especially for those children who were early self-recognizers. The authors concluded that their data provide the first direct empirical support for the argument that it is the advent of self-recognition that spells the end of infantile amnesia.

In an ongoing series of cross-sectional and longitudinal studies (see Howe et al., 2003), the conjoint development of the cognitive self, early memory, and early language are being examined in infants from 15 to 24 months of age. Infants' self-recognition, mirror knowledge, mirror experience, event memory, and language development were assessed with a series of standard tests and procedures. Preliminary findings indicate that children's memory performance on a toy-finding event when retention was tested at 3, 6, or 12 months after acquisitions was best predicted by their success on the mirror self-recognition task, with recognizers performing significantly better than the non-recognizers. This work supports the view espoused here that self-recognition, not language, is critical to very early memory for events. Consistent with this, preliminary findings from the longitudinal work indicates that all infants who achieved self-recognition were successful on the event memory task, independent of age. Among nonrecognizers, none recalled the location of the toy or were using self-referent pronouns. Clearly, there is a need for more research of this kind and there will be additional reports of data of this kind in the near future.

CONCLUSION

In summary, the data accumulated to date are consistent with the position that the emergence and subsequent development of autobiographical memory are governed by the discovery of the cognitive self and increases in the ability to maintain information in memory storage, respectively. Consistent with the function and development of other knowledge structures in memory, once infants acquire a cognitive sense of self, they possess a new organizer around which event memories can be personalized and "preserved" as autobiographical. Like other structures, categories, and concepts in memory, the cognitive sense of self first emerges and is represented and expressed nonverbally, only later to be articulated (but not determined), using language. Subsequent achievements in language can serve to strengthen (or possibly distort) personal memories through mechanisms such as rehearsal, reinstatement, or interference that also affect memory more generally. Verbally expressed memories related in conversation with others also serve a social function of creating a personal "life story" that defines for others who we are. Thus, it is my contention that the offset of infantile amnesia and the onset of autobiographical memory does not require the appearance of a separate memory system per se nor must it await the developments in language, autonoetic awareness, or metacognition that occur late in the preschool years. Rather, it is the natural consequence of young toddlers' more general tendency to develop nonverbal representational structures that describe the world around them (e.g., Karmiloff-Smith, 1992; Mandler, 1992).

Because this cognitive sense of self does not emerge until around 24 months, it is unlikely that personalized memories for experiences would be available before this age. Although this sets the lower limit for the formation of autobiographical memories, it does not guarantee that such memories will be formed at that age. Indeed, personalized memories may not be formed until sometime much later with the timing dependent on factors such as the number of features available for encoding and the distribution of sampling probabilities during encoding. The subsequent ability to retain more autobiographical information with age in childhood develops largely as a natural consequence of global improvements in children's general memory abilities, namely, the capacity to maintain information in storage over longer and longer intervals. Although a number of skills may be involved in, or at least correlated with, this improvement, including developments in language, strategies, knowledge, and gist extraction, the one common denominator to changes in children's retention over time is the basic ability of keeping information intact in storage.

So, what happens to event memories that are formed prior to the cognitive self? Although a discussion of the role of consciousness in memory is beyond the scope of this chapter, given our current understanding and the data gathered to date, it seems unlikely that these very early memories persist for a lifetime. One reason for this expectation is the fact that even under optimal conditions memories appear fragmentary and poorly organized when recalled. Few, if any, of these early memories become verbalizable (e.g., see Bauer, Kroupina, Schwade, Dropik, & Wewerka, 1998), even when based on traumatic events at the time they were encoded (Howe et al., 1994). Although the number of investigations is admittedly small and the evidence usually anecdotal, it is unlikely that without an organizer like the (cognitive) self, such events will persist unchanged in memory. Indeed, unless they have been recoded and reorganized within the framework of the cognitive self, making them distinctive and meaningful against the background of our other memories, it seems unlikely that they will remain intact in storage or to affect us even at the behavioral level. Just as our earlier concepts and categories become transformed and even supplanted by more mature forms of understanding, so too do our memories of early events. Because storage is dynamic and malleable in response to new experiences, it is extremely unlikely that what we remember of very early events, especially those not encoded with respect to the self, remains unaltered by the cumulative experiences of a lifetime.

ACKNOWLEDGMENTS

The author's work is supported by a grant from the Natural Sciences and Engineering Research Council of Canada. I thank Dr. Mary L. Courage for her comments on an earlier draft of this chapter. Correspondence should be addressed to Mark L. Howe, Department of Psychology, Lakehead University, 955 Oliver Road, Thunder Bay, Ontario, Canada P7B 5E1.

REFERENCES

Asendorpf, J., & Baudonniere, P.-M. (1993). Self-awareness and other awareness: Mirror self-recognition and synchronic imitation among unfamiliar peers. *Developmental Psychology, 29,* 88–95.

Asendorpf, J., Warkentin, V., & Baudonniere, P.-M. (1996). Self-awareness and other awareness II: Mirror self-recognition, social contingency awareness, and synchronic imitation. *Developmental Psychology, 32,* 313–321.

Bahrick, L., & Pickens, J. (1995). Infant memory for object motion across a period of three months: Implications for a four-phase attention function. *Journal of Experimental Child Psychology, 59,* 343–371.

Bahrick, L., & Watson, J. S. (1985). Detection of intermodal proprioceptive-visual contingency as a potential basis of self-perception in infancy. *Developmental Psychology, 21,* 963–973.

Barr, R., Dowden, A., & Hayne, H. (1996). Developmental changes in deferred imitation by 6- to 24-month-old infants. *Infant Behavior and Development, 19,* 159–170.

Bates, E. (1990). Language about me and you: Pronominal reference and the emerging concept of self. In D. Cicchetti & M. Beeghly (Eds.), *The self in transition: Infancy to childhood* (pp. 165–182). Chicago: University of Chicago Press.

Bates, E., Bretherton, I., & Snyder, L. (1988). *From first words to grammar: Individual differences and dissociable mechanisms.* Cambridge, England: Cambridge University Press.

Bateson, M.C. (1975). Mother-child exchanges: The epigenesis of conversational exchanges. In D. Aronson & R. W. Reiber (Eds.), *Annals of the New York Academy of Sciences: Vol. 263. Developmental psycholinguistics and communication disorders* (pp. 101–112). New York: New York Academy of Sciences.

Bauer, P. J. (1996). What do infants recall of their lives? Memory for specific events by one- and two-year-olds. *American Psychologist, 51,* 29–41.

Bauer, P. J., Kroupina, M. G., Schwade, J., Dropik, P., & Wewerka, S. (1998). If memory serves, will language? Later verbal accessibility of early memories. *Development and Psychopathology, 10,* 665–679.

Bauer, P. J., Wenner, J. A., Dropik, P. L., & Wewerka, S. S. (2000). Parameters of remembering and forgetting in the transition from infancy to early childhood. *Monographs of the Society for Research in Child Development* (Serial No. 263, No. 4).

Bertenthal, B. I., & Fischer, K. W. (1978). The development of self recognition in the infant. *Developmental Psychology, 14,* 44–50.

Betz, A. L., & Skowronski, J. J. (1997). Self-events and other-events: Temporal dating and event memory. *Memory & Cognition, 25,* 701–714.

Bjorklund, D. F. (1987). How age changes in knowledge base contribute to the development of organization in children's memory: An interpretative review. *Developmental Review, 7,* 93–130.

Bowlby, J. (1969). *Attachment and loss* (Vol. 1). New York: Basic Books.

Boyer, M. E., Barron, K. L., & Farrar, M. J. (1994). Three-year-olds remember a novel event from 20 months: Evidence for long-term memory in children? *Memory, 2,* 417–445.

Brewer, W. F. (1988). Memory for randomly sampled autobiographical events. In U. Neisser & E. Winograd (Eds.), *Remembering reconsidered: Ecological and traditional approaches to the study of memory* (pp. 21–90). New York: Cambridge University Press.

Buchner, A., & Wippich, W. (2000). On the reliability of implicit and explicit memory measures. *Cognitive Psychology, 40*, 227–259.

Bullock, M., & Lutkenhaus, P. (1990). Who am I? Self-understanding in toddlers. *Merrill-Palmer Quarterly, 36*, 217–238.

Butterworth, G. E. (1990). Self-perception in infancy. In D. Cicchetti & M. Beeghly (Eds.), *The self in transition: Infancy to childhood* (pp. 119–137). Chicago: University of Chicago Press.

Butterworth, G. E. (1995). The self as an object of consciousness in infancy. In P. Rochat (Ed.), *The self in infancy: Theory and research* (pp. 35–51). Amsterdam: Elsevier.

Catherwood, D. (1993). The robustness of infant haptic memory: Testing its capacity to withstand delay and haptic interference. *Child Development, 64*, 702–710.

Cernoch, J. M., & Porter, R. H. (1985). Recognition of maternal axillary odors by infants. *Child Development, 56*, 1593–1598.

Cicchetti, D. (1991). Fractures in the crystal: Developmental psychopathology and the emergence of the self. *Developmental Review, 11*, 271–287.

Cicchetti, D., & Beeghly, M. (1987). Symbolic development in maltreated youngsters: An organizational perspective. *New Directions for Child Development, 36*, 5–29.

Cicchetti, D., & Beeghly, M. (Eds.). (1990). *The self in transition: Infancy to childhood.* Chicago: University of Chicago Press.

Cicchetti, D., Beeghly, M., Carlson, V., & Toth, S. (1990). The emergence of the self in atypical populations. In D. Cicchetti & M. Beeghly (Eds.), *The self in transition: Infancy to childhood* (pp. 309–344). Chicago: University of Chicago Press.

Cicchetti, D., & Carlson, V. (1989). *Child maltreatment: Theory and research on the causes and consequences of child abuse and neglect.* New York: Cambridge University Press.

Collie, R., & Hayne, H. (1999). Deferred imitation by 6- and 9-month-old infants: More evidence for declarative memory. *Developmental Psychobiology, 35*, 83–90.

Conway, M. A. (1996). Autobiographical knowledge and autobiographical memories. In D. Rubin (Ed.), *Remembering our past: Studies in autobiographical memory* (pp. 67–93). New York: Cambridge University Press.

Conway, M. A., & Pleysell-Pearce, C. W. (2000). The construction of autobiographical memories in the self-memory system. *Psychological Review, 107*, 261–288.

Courage, M. L., & Howe, M. L. (1998). The ebb and flow of infants' attentional preferences: Evidence for long-term recognition memory in 3-month-olds. *Journal of Experimental Child Psychology, 70*, 26–53.

Courage, M. L., & Howe, M. L. (2001). Long-term retention in 3.5-month-olds: Familiarization time and individual differences in attentional style. *Journal of Experimental Child Psychology, 79*, 271–293.

Courage, M. L., & Howe, M. L. (2002). From infant to child: The dynamics of cognitive change in the second year of life. *Psychological Bulletin, 128*, 250–277.

Courage, M. L., Howe, M. L., & Squires, S. E. (2004). Individual differences in 3.5-month-olds' visual attention: What do they predict at 1 year? *Infant Behavior & Development, 27*, 19–30.

Csikszentmihalyi, M., & Beattie, O. (1979). Life themes: A theoretical and empirical exploration of their origins and effects. *Journal of Humanistic Psychology, 19*, 45–63.

Damasio, A. (1999). *The feeling of what happens: Body and emotion in the making of consciousness*. New York: Harcourt Brace & Company.

Damon, W., & Hart, D. (1988). *Self-understanding in childhood and adolescence*. Cambridge, England: Cambridge University Press.

Darwin, C. R. (1877). Biographical sketch of an infant mind. *Mind, 2*, 285–294.

DeCasper, A. J., & Prescott, P. A. (1984). Human newborns' perception of male voices: Preference, discrimination, and reinforcing value. *Developmental Psychobiology, 17*, 481–491.

DeCasper, A. J., & Spence, M. (1986). Prenatal maternal speech influences newborns' perception of speech sounds. *Infant Behavior and Development, 9*, 133–150.

DeCasper, A. J., & Spence, M. (1991). Auditory mediated behavior during the prenatal period: A cognitive view. In M. Weiss & P. Zelazo (Eds.), *Newborn attention: Biological constraints and the influence of experience* (pp. 142–176). Norwood, NJ: Ablex.

DiBiase, R., & Lewis, M. (1997). The relation between temperament and embarrassment. *Cognition and Emotion, 11*, 259–271.

Eacott, M. J., & Crawley, R. A. (1998). The offset of childhood amnesia: Memory for events that occurred before age 3. *Journal of Experimental Psychology: General, 127*, 22–33.

Fagan, J. (1990). The paired comparison paradigm and infant intelligence. In A. Diamond (Ed.), *Annals of the New York Academy of Science: Vol. 608. The development and neural basis of higher cognitive functions* (pp. 337–364). New York: New York Academy of Sciences.

Fivush, R. (1994). Young children's event recall: Are memories constructed through discourse? *Consciousness and Cognition, 3*, 356–373.

Fivush, R., Haden, C. A., & Reese, E. (1996). Remembering, recounting, and reminiscing: The development of autobiographical memory in social context. In D. Rubin (Ed.), *Remembering our past: Studies in autobiographical memory* (pp. 341–359). Cambridge, MA: Cambridge University Press..

Fivush, R., & Reese, E. (1992). The social construction of autobiographical memory. In M. A. Conway, D. C. Rubin, H. Spinnler, & W. A. Wagenaar (Eds.), *Theoretical perspectives on autobiographical memory* (pp. 115–132). Dordrecht, the Netherlands: Kluwer Academic.

Flexser, A. J., & Tulving, E. (1978). Retrieval independence of recognition and recall. *Psychological Review, 85*, 153–171.

Freud, S. (1959). Instincts and their vicissitudes. In E. Jones (Ed.), *Collected papers of Sigmund Freud* (pp. 317–385). New York: Basic Books.

Gerhardstein, P., Adler, S. A., & Rovee-Collier, C. (2000). A dissociation in infants' memory for stimulus size: Evidence for the early development of multiple memory systems. *Developmental Psychobiology, 36*, 123–135.

Gibson, E. J. (1995). Are we automata? In P. Rochat (Ed.), *The self in infancy: Theory and research* (pp. 3–15). Amsterdam: Elsevier.

Goldin-Meadow, S., Alibali, M. W., & Church, R. B. (1993). Transitions in concept acquisition: Using the hand to read the mind. *Psychological Review, 100*, 279–297.

Goodman, G. S., Quas, J. A., Batterman-Faunce, J. M., Riddlesberger, M. M., & Kuhn, J. (1994). Predictors of accurate and inaccurate memories of traumatic events experienced in childhood. *Consciousness and Cognition, 3*, 269–294.

Greenwald, A. G., & Banaji, M. R. (1989). The self as a memory system: Powerful but ordinary. *Journal of Personality and Social Psychology, 57*, 41–54.

Habermas, T., & Bluck, S. (2000). Getting a life: The emergence of the life story in adolescence. *Psychological Bulletin, 126,* 748–769.

Haden, C. A., Haine, R. A., & Fivush, R. (1997). Developing narrative structure in parent-child reminiscing across the preschool years. *Developmental Psychology, 33,* 295–307.

Han, J. J., Leichtman, M. D., & Wang, Q. (1998). Autobiographical memory in Korean, Chinese, and American children. *Developmental Psychology, 34,* 701–713.

Harley, K., & Reese, E. (1999). Origins of autobiographical memory. *Developmental Psychology, 35,* 1338–1348.

Hartshorn, K., Rovee-Collier, C., Gerhardstein, P., Bhatt, R. S., Wondolski, T., Klein, P., Gilch, J., Wurzel, N., & Campos-de-Carvalho, M. (1998). The ontogeny of learning and memory over the first year-and-a-half of life. *Developmental Psychobiology, 23,* 453–477.

Hayne, H., Boniface, J., & Barr, R. (2000). The development of declarative memory in human infants: Age-related changes in deferred imitation. *Behavioral Neuroscience, 114,* 77–83.

Hayne, H., MacDonald, S., & Barr, R. (1997). Developmental changes in the specificity of memory over the second year of life. *Infant Behavior and Development, 20,* 233–245.

Herbert, J., & Hayne, H. (2000a). Memory retrieval by 18–30-month-olds: Age-related changes in representational flexibility. *Developmental Psychology, 36,* 473–484.

Herbert, J., & Hayne, H. (2000b). The ontogeny of long-term retention during the second year of life. *Developmental Science, 3,* 50–56.

Hilgard, E. R., & Bower, G. H. (1975). *Theories of learning* (4th ed.). Englewood Cliffs, NJ: Prentice Hall.

Hill, S., & Tomlin, C. (1981). Self-recognition in retarded children. *Child Development, 52,* 145–150.

Howe, M. L. (2000). *The fate of early memories: Developmental science and the retention of childhood experiences.* Washington, D.C.: American Psychological Association.

Howe, M. L. (2002). The role of intentional forgetting in reducing children's retroactive interference. *Developmental Psychology, 38,* 3–14.

Howe, M. L. (2003). Memories from the cradle. *Current Directions in Psychological Science, 12,* 62–65.

Howe, M. L., & Courage, M. L. (1997). The emergence and early development of autobiographical memory. *Psychological Review, 104,* 499–523.

Howe, M. L., Courage, M. L., & Edison, S. C. (2003). When autobiographical memory begins. *Developmental Review, 23,* 471–494.

Howe, M. L., Courage, M. L., & Peterson, C. (1994). How can I remember when "I" wasn't there: Long-term retention of traumatic experiences and emergence of the cognitive self. *Consciousness and Cognition, 3,* 327–355.

Hudson, J. A. (1990). Constructive processing in children's event memory. *Developmental Psychology, 26,* 180–187.

James, W. (1890/1961). *The principles of psychology.* New York: Henry Holt.

Johnson, D. B. (1983). Self recognition in infants. *Infant Behavior and Development, 6,* 211–222.

Kagan, J. (1981). *The second year: The emergence of self awareness.* Cambridge, MA: Harvard University Press.

Kagan, J. (1994). *Galen's prophecy: Temperament in human nature.* New York: Basic Books.

Kagan, J. (1998). Is there a self in infancy? In M. Ferrari & R. Sternberg (Eds.), *Self awareness: Its nature and development*. New York: Guilford Press.

Karmiloff-Smith, A. (1992). *Beyond modularity: A developmental perspective on cognitive science*. Cambridge, MA: MIT Press.

Kaufman, J., & Cicchetti, D. (1989). Effects of maltreatment on school-aged children's socioemotional development: Assessments in a day-camp setting. *Developmental Psychology, 25*, 516–524.

Klein, S. B., & Kihlstrom, J. F. (1986). Elaboration, organization, and self-reference effects in memory. *Journal of Experimental Psychology: General, 115*, 26–38.

Kopp, C. B., & Brownell, C. A. (Eds.). (1991). The development of the self: The first three years [Special Issue]. *Developmental Review, 11(3)*.

Lewis, M. (1994). Myself and me. In S. Parker, R. Mitchell, & M. Boccia (Eds.), *Self awareness in animals and humans: Developmental perspectives* (pp. 20–34). Cambridge, MA: Cambridge University Press.

Lewis, M. (1995). Aspects of the self: From systems to ideas. In P. Rochat (Ed.), *The self in infancy: Theory and research* (pp. 95–115). Amsterdam: Elsevier.

Lewis, M., & Brooks-Gunn, J. (1979). *Social cognition and the acquisition of self*. New York: Plenum Press.

Lewis, M., Brooks-Gunn, J., & Jaskir, J. (1985). Individual differences in early visual self-recognition. *Developmental Psychology, 21*, 1181–1187.

Lewis, M., & Ramsay, D. S. (1997). Stress reactivity and self-recognition. *Child Development, 68*, 621–629.

Lewis, M., & Ramsay, D. S. (1998, April). *The onset of self-recognition and the emergence of self awareness*. Paper presented at the International Conference in Infant Studies, Atlanta, GA.

Lewis, M., Sullivan, M., Stanger, C., & Weiss, M. (1989). Self-development and self conscious emotions. *Child Development, 60*, 146–156.

Linton, M. (1979). Real-world memory after six years: An in vivo study of very long-term memory. In M. M. Gruneberg, P. E. Morris, & R. N. Sykes (Eds.), *Practical aspects of memory* (pp. 69–76). New York: Academic Press.

Loveland, K. (1987). Behavior of young children with Down syndrome before the mirror: Finding things reflected. *Child Development, 58*, 928–936.

Loveland, K. (1993). Autism, affordances, and the self. In U. Neisser (Ed.), *The perceived self* (pp. 237–253). New York: Cambridge University Press.

MacDonald, S., Uesiliana, K., & Hayne, H. (2000). Cross-cultural and gender differences in childhood amnesia. *Memory, 8*, 365–376.

Mandler, J. (1992). How to build a baby: II. Conceptual primitives. *Psychological Review, 99*, 587–604.

Mandler, J., & McDonough, L. (1993). Concept formation in infancy. *Cognitive Development, 8*, 291–318.

Mans, L., Cicchetti, D., & Sroufe, L. A. (1978). Mirror reaction of Down syndrome toddlers: Cognitive underpinnings of self recognition. *Child Development, 49*, 1247–1250.

Mazzoni, G. A. L., Loftus, E. F., & Kirsch, I. (2001). Changing beliefs about implausible autobiographical events: A little plausibility goes a long way. *Journal of Experimental Psychology: Applied, 7*, 51–59.

McDonough, L., & Mandler, J. M. (1994). Very long-term recall in infants: Infantile amnesia reconsidered. *Memory, 2*, 339–352.

Mead, G. H. (1934). *Mind, self, and society*. Chicago: University of Chicago Press.

Meltzoff, A. N. (1988). Infant imitation and memory: Nine-month-olds in immediate and deferred tests. *Child Development, 59,* 217–255.

Meltzoff, A. N. (1990). Toward a developmental cognitive science: The implications of cross-modal matching and imitation for the development of representation and memory in infants. In A. Diamond (Ed.), *The development and neural basis of higher cognitive functions* (Vol. 608, pp. 1–29). New York: New York Academy of Sciences.

Meltzoff, A. N. (1995). What infant memory tells us about infantile amnesia: Long-term recall and deferred imitation. *Journal of Experimental Child Psychology, 59,* 497–515.

Meltzoff, A. N., & Moore, M. K. (1994). Imitation, memory, and the representation of persons. *Infant Behavior and Development, 17,* 83–99.

Mitchell, R. W. (1993). Mental models of mirror self–recognition: Two theories. *New Ideas in Psychology, 11,* 295–325.

Mullen, M. K. (1994). Earliest recollections of childhood: A demographic analysis. *Cognition, 52,* 55–79.

Mullen, M. K., & Yi, S. (1995). The cultural context of talk about the past: Implications for the development of autobiographical memory. *Cognitive Development, 10,* 407–419.

Myers, N., Perris, E., & Speaker, C. (1994). Fifty months of memory: A longitudinal study in early childhood. *Memory, 2,* 383–415.

Neimark, E. D., & Estes, W. K. (1967). *Stimulus sampling theory.* San Francisco: Holden-Day.

Neisser, U. (1988). Five kinds of self knowledge. *Philosophical Psychology, 1,* 35–59.

Neisser, U. (Ed.). (1993). *The perceived self.* New York: Cambridge University Press.

Neisser, U. (1995). Criteria for an ecological self. In P. Rochat (Ed.), *The self in infancy: Theory and research* (pp. 17–33). Amsterdam: Elsevier.

Nelson, C. A. (1995). The ontogeny of human memory: A cognitive neuroscience perspective. *Developmental Psychology, 31,* 723–738.

Nelson, K. (1993). The psychological and social origins of autobiographical memory. *Psychological Science, 4,* 7–14.

Parker, S. T., Mitchell, R. W., & Boccia, M. L. (Eds.). (1994). *Self–awareness in animals and humans: Developmental perspectives.* Cambridge, MA: Cambridge University Press.

Perner, J., & Ruffman, T. (1995). Episodic memory and autonoetic consciousness: Developmental evidence and a theory of childhood amnesia. *Journal of Experimental Child Psychology, 59,* 516–548.

Piaget, J. (1954). *The construction of reality in the child.* New York: Basic Books.

Pipp, S., Fischer, K., & Jennings, S. (1987). Acquisition of self and mother knowledge in infancy. *Developmental Psychology, 23,* 86–96.

Povinelli, D. J., Landau, K. R., & Perilloux, H. K. (1996). Self-recognition in young children using delayed versus live feedback: Evidence of a developmental asynchrony. *Child Development, 67,* 1540–1554.

Povinelli, D., Landry, A. M., Theall, L. A., Clarke, B. R., & Castile, C. M. (1999). Development of young children's understanding that the recent past is causally bound to the present. *Developmental Psychology, 35,* 1426–1439.

Povinelli, D. J., & Simon, B. B. (1998). Young children's understanding of briefly versus extremely delayed images of the self: Emergence of the autobiographical stance. *Developmental Psychology, 34,* 188–194.

Reese, E., Haden, C. A., & Fivush, R. (1993). Mother-child conversations about the past: Relationships of style and memory over time. *Cognitive Development, 8,* 403–430.

Rochat, P. (1995). Early objectification of the self. In P. Rochat (Ed.), *The self in infancy: Theory and research* (pp. 53–71). Amsterdam: Elsevier.

Rochat, P. (2001). Origins of self-concept. In J. G. Bremner & A. Fogel (Eds.), *Blackwell handbook of infant development* (pp. 125–140). Oxford: Basil Blackwell.

Rochat, P., & Morgan, R. (1995). Spatial determinants in the perception of self-produced leg movements by 3- to 5-month-old infants. *Developmental Psychology, 31,* 626–636.

Roediger, H. L. III, Rajaram, S., & Srinivas, K. (1990). Specifying criteria for postulating memory systems. *Annals of the New York Academy of Sciences, 608,* 572–595.

Ross, M., & Wilson, A. E. (2000). Constructing and appraising past selves. In D. L. Schacter & E. Scarry (Eds.), *Memory, brain, and belief* (pp. 231–259). Cambridge, MA: Harvard University Press.

Rovee-Collier, C. (1997). Dissociations in infant memory: Rethinking the development of implicit and explicit memory. *Psychological Review, 104,* 467–498.

Rovee-Collier, C., & Bhatt, R. (1993). Evidence of long-term memory in infancy. *Annals of Child Development, 9,* 1–45.

Schmuckler, M. A. (1994, June). *Infants' visual-proprioceptive intermodal recognition.* Paper presented at the International Conference on Infant Studies, Paris, France.

Schneider, W., & Bjorklund, D. F. (1998). Memory. In W. Damon (Series Ed.) & D. Kuhn & R. S. Siegler (Vol. Eds.), *Handbook of child psychology: Vol. 2. Cognition, perception, and language* (5th ed.). New York: Wiley.

Schneider-Rosen, K., & Cicchetti, D. (1984). The relationship between affect and cognition in maltreated infants: Quality of attachment and the development of visual self-recognition. *Child Development, 55,* 648–658.

Schneider-Rosen, K., & Cicchetti, D. (1991). Early self-knowledge and emotional development: Visual self-recognition and affective reactions to mirror self-images in maltreated and non-maltreated infants. *Developmental Psychology, 27,* 471–478.

Slater, A. (1995). Visual perception and memory at birth. In C. Rovee-Collier & L. P. Lipsitt (Eds.), *Advances in infancy research, Vol. 9.* Norwood, NJ: Ablex.

Slobin, D. I. (1985). Crosslinguistic evidence for the language-making capacity. In D. I. Slobin (Ed.), *The crosslinguistic study of language acquisition* (pp. 1157–1256). Hillsdale, NJ: Erlbaum.

Spence, M. J., & Freeman, M. S. (1996). Newborn infants prefer the maternal low-pass filtered voice but not the maternal whispered voice. *Infant Behavior and Development, 19,* 199–212.

Spiker, D., & Ricks, M. (1984). Visual self-recognition in autistic children: Developmental relationships. *Child Development, 55,* 214–225.

Stern, D. N. (1985). *The interpersonal world of the infant.* New York: Basic Books.

Stern, D. N. (1993). The role of feelings for an interpersonal self. In U. Neisser (Ed.), *The perceived self* (pp. 205–215). New York: Cambridge University Press.

Suddendorf, T. (1999). Children's understanding of the relation between delayed video representation and current reality: A test for self-awareness? *Journal of Experimental Child Psychology, 72,* 157–176.

Swain, I., Zelazo, P., & Clifton, R. (1993). Newborn infants' memory for speech sounds retained over 24 hours. *Developmental Psychology, 29,* 312–323.

Symons, C. S., & Johnson, B. T. (1997). The self-reference effect in memory: A meta-analysis. *Psychological Bulletin, 121,* 371–394.

Tomasello, M. (1993). On the interpersonal origins of self-concept. In U. Neisser (Ed.), *The perceived self* (pp. 174–184). New York: Cambridge University Press.

Tomasello, M., Kruger, A. C., & Ratner, H. H. (1993). Cultural learning. *Behavioral and Brain Sciences, 16,* 495–552.

Tulving, E. (1984). Precis of elements of episodic memory. *Behavioral and Brain Sciences, 7,* 223–238.

Usher, J. A., & Neisser, U. (1993). Childhood amnesia and the beginnings of memory for four early life events. *Journal of Experimental Psychology: General, 122,* 155–165.

Wetzler, S. E., & Sweeney, J. A. (1986). Childhood amnesia: An empirical demonstration. In D. C. Rubin (Ed.), *Autobiographical memory* (pp. 191–201). New York: Cambridge University Press.

2

NARRATIVE CONCEPTIONS OF THE SELF AND MEMORY

4

The Silenced Self: Constructing Self from Memories Spoken and Unspoken

ROBYN FIVUSH
Emory University

A fundamental assumption in psychology is that our autobiographical memories and our self-concept are linked; autobiographical memory is the story of our life, the way that we construct a coherent narrative that describes and explains who we are (Bruner, 1987; Fivush, 1988; McAdams, 1992, 1996). A more controversial but widely accepted assumption is that individual autobiographies are, at least partly, socially constructed (Fivush, 1994; Gergen, 1994; Nelson, 1993). It is as we share our personal stories with others that they take on coherence and meaning and become part of our individual life story. Through reminiscing about our past with others we come to reconstruct and redefine both our experiences and ourselves. But what of experiences that we do not talk about? How do we integrate experiences of which we cannot speak? and What do these experiences mean for our evolving self-concept? As Jean Braham (1995) has argued, "We see the past . . . in something of the same way we see a Henry Moore sculpture. The 'holes' define the 'shape.' What is left repressed, or what cannot be uttered, is often as significant to the whole shape of the life as what is said" (p. 37).

In this chapter, I approach autobiographical memory from the feminist perspective of "voice" and "silence" (Belenky, Clinchy, Goldberger, & Tarule, 1986). Essentially, voice refers to the idea that some truths, or some versions of truth are privileged over others. These versions are the accepted canonical versions of events, whether they be historical or personal. Those who are given voice are given authority to tell the story from their perspective. In this way, voice is a form of power. However, it is also the case that who has voice changes with changing historical, social, and political contexts, as can be seen in the changing versions of history that include or exclude specific groups of people or specific historical events.

In the realm of personal memory, voice and silence are concepts that can help us understand the ways that individual lives are shaped by larger cultural frameworks (Fivush, 2000). Some versions of autobiographies are more acceptable than others; some parts of what we remember can be voiced whereas other parts may be silenced. Moreover, personal memory can be silenced in multiple ways at multiple levels. In the first part of this chapter, I discuss one way culture and gender shape autobiography by defining appropriate and inappropriate aspects of emotional experience, and I develop the idea of a gendered "emotional self-concept." I then turn to memory of trauma, which is almost always silenced in our culture. I use data from an intensive interview study of women who were sexually abused in childhood to argue that the way that trauma is voiced or silenced impacts the ability to develop an integrated sense of self. In conclusion, I return to a theoretical discussion of voice and silence, and to a discussion of how and why it matters what we can and cannot say about our past.

CULTURE AND GENDER AS VOICED AND SILENCED

Each culture defines the canonical shape of an individual life. In modern Western cultures, we construct an autobiography in which the self is an active agent, the protagonist of a life that centers on individual choices and decisions. In contrast, in Eastern cultures, the self is construed as part of the community; autobiography reflects the role of the individual within group life, a part of community values and morals (Oyserman & Markus, 1993). Recent cross-cultural research on autobiographical memory has demonstrated that these cultural forms are indeed reflected in individual life stories. Adults from Western cultures talk more about their past experiences, claim to have more memories and earlier memories of their childhood, and focus more on the self when narrating the past than do adults from Eastern cultures (see Leichtman, Wang, & Pillemer, 2003, for a review).

These patterns are clearly socialized; Western parents talk more about the past with their young preschool children, talk in more vivid and detailed ways about the past, and focus on the child as an active agent to a greater extent than do Asian parents. In contrast, Asian parents focus more on the child's role in the group and on violation of norms than do Western parents (Leichtman, Wang, & Pillemer, 2003; Mullen & Yi, 1995). By school age, Western children tell more richly detailed stories of the self in the past than do Asian children (Han, Leichtman & Wang, 1998). These patterns support the idea that the ways that cultures define selves privilege particular forms of personal memory over others; some stories are given voice and others are silenced. In Western cultures, voiced autobiographies focus on self and agency; in Eastern cultures, voiced autobiographies focus on community and relationships. Thus, certain aspects of experiences are foregrounded or backgrounded depending on the cultural norms in which we are socialized.

Obviously, culture is not monolithic, and versions of truth may differ for different groups within the culture. Gender is a prime example of a dimension along which voice and versions of truth may differ. The roles that women and men play within any given culture are prescribed and these cultural prescriptions help shape autobiography (see Fivush, 2000, for theoretical arguments). While there are certain basic similarities in the ways that women and men view their lives, there are also critical differences. In Western cultures, adult women tell longer, more detailed, and more vivid stories of their past than adult men. Women also talk more about people and relationships, and about emotions than adult men (Davis, 1990; Friedman & Pines, 1991). These differences reflect gendered cultural frameworks for understanding self and other that influence the kind of information women and men are more likely to focus on in constructing their life stories.[1] Because women are stereotypically the primary caregivers of children and the keepers of family history, they are focused on emotional aspects of experience that serve to regulate relationships (e.g., Chodorow, 1978; Gilligan, 1982; Ross & Holmberg, 1990). The focus on emotion is consistent with the larger cultural stereotypes of women being more emotional than men (Basow, 1992), and reflect the realities of women's lived experience in which they claim to experience emotions more frequently and more intensely than do men (see Fischer, 2000, for an overview). Again, similar to cross-cultural differences in autobiographical memory, these adult gender differences within Western culture can be seen as emerging from gendered patterns of socialization in which certain aspects of emotional experience are allowed to be voiced, and other aspects of emotional experience are silenced.

Voicing and Silencing Emotion

My colleagues and I have been examining the gendered socialization of autobiographical memory for the past several years and have documented two related ways that parents reminisce about past events differently with their preschool sons and daughters. First, parents focus more on emotional aspects of the past with daughters than with sons (Adams, Kuebli, Boyle, & Fivush, 1995; Fivush, 1995, 1989, 1991; Fivush, Brotman, Buckner, & Goodman, 2000; Kuebli & Fivush, 1992), and second, parents focus more on relationships and the emotional aspects of relationships with daughters and more on autonomy with sons (Buckner & Fivush, 2000; Fivush 1993; see Fivush, 1998, and Fivush & Buckner, 2003, for reviews). Across several studies, we have documented that both mothers and fathers mention and elaborate on emotions more frequently with daughters than with sons, they mention a wider variety of emotions with daughters than with sons, and they are more likely to discuss and resolve negative emotions with daughters than with sons. These patterns are especially pronounced when reminiscing about sad experiences (Fivush & Buckner, 2000). Importantly, these differences in parental talk begin early in the preschool years, well before there are any differences in the ways that girls and boys are talking about emotional experience.

That parents are so clearly discussing past emotions differently with their preschool daughters versus their preschool sons implies that parents are helping their young children to foreground or background particular kinds of emotional experiences into their evolving autobiographical memories. Moreover, they are doing so during a critical developmental period during which a stable self-concept is being formed (Lewis, 1992). Gender differences in emotional socialization are illustrated in the following excerpts from conversations between parents and their 4-year-old children (from Fivush et al., 2000). The first excerpt is a mother and daughter talking about a time the child felt sad:

MOTHER: I remember when you were sad. You were sad when Malika had to leave on Saturday, weren't you?

CHILD: Uh huh.

MOTHER: You were very sad. And what happened? Why did you feel sad?

CHILD: Because Malika, Malika say, was having (Unin.).

MOTHER: Yes.

CHILD: And then she stood up on my bed and it was my bedroom. She's not allowed to sleep there.

MOTHER: Is that why you were sad?

CHILD: Yeah. Now it makes me happy. I also, it makes me sad. But Malika just left.

MOTHER: Uh huh.

CHILD: And then I cried.

MOTHER: And you cried because? . . .

CHILD: Malika left.

MOTHER: Because Malika left? And did that make you sad?

CHILD: And then I cried [makes *aaahhhh* sounds] like that. I cried and cried and cried and cried.

MOTHER: I know. I know. I thought you were sad because Malika left. I didn't know you were also sad because Malika slept in your bed.

Clearly, this conversation is centered on the experience of the emotion of sadness. The conversation begins with framing the event as one during which the child felt sad, and both mother and daughter emphasize the causes and the experience of the emotion itself. Note also that the cause of sadness is the child's friend; emotions are explicitly placed in a social-relational context. Contrast this with the following excerpt of a father and his 4-year-old son, also talking about a time the child felt sad:

FATHER: Do you remember last night when you took your juice upstairs?

CHILD: Uh huh.

FATHER: What did you do with the juice? When you were going up the steps?

CHILD: I spilled it.

FATHER: You spilled it? Did you get upset?

CHILD: Uh huh. I was just sad.

FATHER: You were sad? What did you do?

CHILD: Went downstairs.

FATHER: Yeah, what did you do when you came downstairs?

CHILD: Get some more.

[Ten conversational exchanges about the child getting soda.]

FATHER: You came down. What did you tell me?

CHILD: That I spilled it.

FATHER: Yeah, what kind of face did you have?

CHILD: A sad face.

FATHER: A sad face.

CHILD: Uh huh.

FATHER: What did we do?

CHILD: Clean it up.

Here the conversation focuses on the activities and events comprising the experience; although sadness is mentioned, it is not the center of attention or discussion.

Moreover, the cause of sadness is a behavioral mishap; other people are simply not interweaved into the emotional experience.

These excerpts highlight the ways that emotions are an integral part of reminiscing in parent-daughter dyads but are not integral to parent-son reminiscing. By focusing more on the emotional aspects of their experiences with girls, parents may be teaching their daughters that this is an important and valuable aspect of their experiences, worth thinking about and reporting to others. Parents also reminisce more about people and relationships with daughters than with sons. Both mothers and fathers place emotional experiences in a more social and relational context with daughters than with sons, and place emotional events in a more autonomous context with sons than with daughters. For example, when reminiscing about sadness with daughters, parents focus on events such as not being able to play with a friend, someone being ill, or a parent leaving. With sons, reminiscing about sadness focuses on losing or breaking a favorite toy or the child not being able to do what he wants (Buckner & Fivush, 2000; Fivush, 1989, 1991). By placing emotions in a more social-relational context with daughters than with sons, parents may be teaching daughters that emotions are part of the glue that holds families and communities together.

Importantly, the ways that parents reminisce with their young children influence how children come to tell their own life stories. Although there are few differences in autobiographical recall between girls and boys early in the preschool years, by the end of the preschool years, girls are using more emotional language in their personal narratives (Kuebli, Butler, & Fivush, 1995; Reese, Haden, & Fivush, 1996) and are talking more about people and relationships than are boys (Buckner & Fivush, 1998, 2000). These patterns suggest that young children are learning to foreground and/or background emotional and relational aspects of their past experiences through conversing about these experiences with their parents.

Emotional Self-Concept

In addition to learning which particular aspects of past experience are important and appropriate to report and share with others, preschoolers are learning how to understand and present themselves in these early parent-guided conversations. At least part of children's developing self-concept is formed in social interaction with others who help provide an evaluative and interpretive framework for understanding past experiences. Through participating in parent-child reminiscing, children come to understand who they are in relation to other people and in relation to their past. By differentially discussing emotional aspects of past experiences with girls and boys, parents are helping their children learn gendered ways of being in the world. By focusing on emotional experience, on the causes and expression of emotions, and on the ways that other people are a context for experiencing emotion parents are helping girls form an emotionally rich self-concept. For girls, past experiences are imbued with emotions of both self and other. Moreover, girls are learning that emotions are ways of connecting with others. In thinking about one's own life history, it is replete with shared emotional experiences. In essence, for females, emotions are given voice. In contrast, for males, emotions are silenced. Past experiences are stripped of much of their emotional content. Emotions are internal and autonomous; they do not connect self to others. In thinking about one's life history, emotional experiences are sparse and isolating.

Clearly we must be careful about drawing gender differences too broadly. There is a great deal of variability within gender groups as well as between the genders. Just as culture is not monolithic, neither is gender. Just as there are differences within cultures, there are differences within genders. Rather than conceptualizing gender as an essential categorical difference (e.g., Gilligan, 1982), it may make more sense to conceptualize gender as a set of learned activities (Deaux & Major, 1987; Fivush, 1998; Fivush & Buckner, 2003). Gender may be best understood as skilled practice, similar to recent conceptualizations of culture (Rogoff, 1990).

Because males and females are more likely to find themselves in certain situations and engaged in certain activities they are more likely to learn certain skills and certain ways of acting in the world. Because parent-daughter reminiscing is replete with emotional language, females may come to learn how to express their emotional experiences more directly and in more nuanced ways than do males. They may also learn to value these aspects of experience more than males and to value sharing these experiences with others. This is not to argue that males are not able to experience, share, and value their emotions, but rather that it is more difficult for them as they are not as practiced in the requisite skills. In this sense, the argument is that females have an emotional self-concept in which emotional experience and expression is highly valued and easily shared, whereas males have an emotional self-concept in which emotions are internal, autonomous, and not as easily expressed. Thus it is not a matter of ability but of style. Still, these differences in style have implications for the ways that males and females may feel more or less comfortable in presenting themselves and sharing their lives with others.

Context Effects

Given this perspective, we also need to consider context effects in the autobiographical expression of self and emotion. While there may be enduring individual differences in how one constructs a sense of one's emotional self based on gender and early parent-guided reminiscing, it must also be the case that the ways that particular emotional experiences will be expressed will be a function of the specific context in which one is sharing one's life stories (Fivush & Buckner, 2003). Autobiographical memory is always selective. We do not recall everything that happens to us, nor do we choose to report everything we recall. Moreover, some aspects of what we choose to tell may be a function of enduring individual preferences, but some may be a function of our conversational partner (see Pasupathi, 2001, for a theoretical overview). Listeners can influence speakers' stories in various ways. In moment-to-moment interaction, listeners who are engaged and involved in listening to narratives allow speakers to tell longer, more coherent, and more detailed stories, while disengaged or distracted listeners lead to shorter, more disorganized, and more disfluent narratives (Pasupathi, Stallworth, & Murdoch, 1998).

In terms of the emotional aspects of our personal experiences, although it is the case that males do not discuss emotional experience as much as females do in general (Brody & Hall, 1993), it is also the case that under some circumstances, males talk about emotions as much as females. In particular, males are more likely to self-disclose emotional experiences with a female conversational partner (Aukett, Ritchie, & Mill, 1988), and discuss emotions as much as females do with intimate partners and therapists (Snell, Miller, Belk, Garcia-Falconi, & Hernandez-Sanchez, 1989). These patterns support the previous argument that emotional understanding and expression are partly a matter of style rather than ability. With certain conversational partners, males can be as emotionally expressive as females. Note, however, that these partners tend to be attuned to emotion, that is, females and therapists. Thus these partners may provide a more attentive and engaged audience allowing males to express emotional experience that might be difficult with a less engaged partner, that is, another male.

We can further speculate that over time, if certain stories or parts of stories are consistently responded to in one way or the other, these stories will either be reinforced or drop out of the individuals' repertoire of personal stories. In this way, how listeners respond to individuals' disclosure of personal narratives may come to have a cumulative effect on which personal stories become an active part of one's autobiography (see Pasupathi, 2001, for related arguments). Moreover, early parent-guided conversations about past emotions may be particularly formative because when children are younger they may be more vulnerable to the way that others construct experience for them. Thus the cultural, developmental, and contextual levels of voice and silence are dialectically related, such that culture prescribes a certain form and content to a canonical life story, and this prescription is communicated in numerous specific interactions in which a listener's reactions and responses help shape the individual's evolving life story. For females, overall, the life story is emotionally richer and denser than it is for males.

Thus far, I have discussed the ways that a universal aspect of all experience, emotion, may be given voice or silenced depending on one's gender. But what of entire events that are not allowed to be spoken of? Certainly in our culture, trauma is one such category of events. This may be especially true for victims of childhood sexual abuse. Indeed, until the 1970s it was assumed that childhood sexual abuse, and especially familial abuse, was extremely rare, yet more recent surveys have confirmed that as many as 20 to 25% of females experience sexual abuse during childhood and as many as 10% experience abuse by a family member (Edwards, Fivush, Anda, Felitti, & Nordenberg, 2001; Finkelhor, Hotaling, Lewis, & Smith, 1990). This is a category of events that is silenced in the most basic terms. Not only are individual stories not heard, but the culture as a whole has also conspired to erase these kinds of experiences from our cultural landscape of possible experiences. How do adult survivors of childhood sexual abuse come to remember or forget these experiences? What implications does this have for their self-concept?

Silencing of Childhood Sexual Abuse

With the political changes accompanying the second wave of the women's move-ment, sexual abuse against women has come into national focus (Enns, McNeilly, Corkery, & Gilbert, 1995). In addition to documenting the extent of these expe-riences, researchers have turned to examining more basic questions about the long-term effects of experiencing abuse. Here I focus on two aspects of this question relevant for this chapter: What do women remember about their abusive experiences and how might these memories affect their self-concept?

Memory of childhood sexual abuse has become quite controversial, especially surrounding the issue of recovered memories (see Conway, 1997, and Pezdek & Banks, 1996, for full discussions). Whereas many clinicians have described the subjective experiences of their clients who suddenly recall years of abuse after a period of amnesia, many researchers have argued that this kind of forgetting and recovery of memory is not cognitively possible. The nuances of this controversy are well beyond the scope of this chapter, but let me just note here that there is increasing evidence for the occurrence of recovered memories (Schooler, 2001), and that recovered memories are just as likely to be accurate as continuous memories of abuse (e.g., Brewin & Andrews, 1998). Moreover, there is growing evidence of specific cognitive mechanisms that can be easily demonstrated in a controlled laboratory setting that might explain the cognitive underpinnings of this phenomenon (Anderson & Green, 2001). Regardless of the ultimate fate of this controversy, what is clear is that the subjective experience of recovering memories is very real at least for some proportion of women who were sexually abused in childhood.

In order to explore the phenomenon of memory for childhood sexual abuse and relations to self-concept in more depth, Valerie Edwards and I (Fivush & Edwards, in press) conducted an interview study with 12 women ranging in age from 21 to 72 who had been severely sexually abused by a family member during their childhood. We were interested in exploring several questions. First, how do women describe their subjective experiences of remembering and forgetting abuse over time? Second, how do women actually narrate their experiences of abuse? Third, how do women describe their experiences of self and how does this relate to their memory of their abusive experiences? As just discussed, traumatic events, especially abuse, may be silenced both by others and by the self as too dangerous to even think about. For children experiencing abuse by a loved and trusted adult, trying to integrate the abusive experience with attachment and relationship needs may lead to a deep sense of emotional betrayal, and this betrayal may create an untenable psychological state (Freyd, 1996). Thus, an adaptive response may very well be to push these experiences from mind, to simply not think about them, and in this way to silence oneself. Even when children try to tell about their abusive experiences to other trusted adults, they are often not believed (Butler, 1999); indeed they are often accused of lying for their own purposes. This kind of reaction to disclosure would certainly fall into the category of silencing. Thus both the women themselves and those to whom they may have disclosed often conspire together to silence these experiences.

In terms of memory and self, we assumed that women who claimed they had never forgotten that they had been abused, and had continuous memories of their abusive experiences, would be able to narrate these experiences more coherently and in more detail than women who had recovered memories of abuse. We further speculated that women who had continuous memories of abuse would have a more integrated self-concept than women with recovered memories. Because recovered memories are associated with dissociative tendencies, we reasoned that recovered memories would also be associated with a more fragmented sense of self.

All of the women in our sample were abused by a family member; three by a father, one by a stepfather, three by a grandparent, three by a brother and two by an uncle. The beginning of the abuse ranged from preschool to preteen, all women experienced penetration and all but two experienced abuse over a period of several years. Nine had also experienced physical abuse during childhood and seven had experienced additional sexual assault as an adult. Thus this was a severely abused population. None of the women had recovered memories of abuse while in therapy although all of the women had been in therapy at some point during their lives.

Women were interviewed individually, and were asked to recall their abusive experiences, as well as a series of questions about their remembering and forgetting of these experiences over time. These were relatively open-ended interviews; although there was a standard set of questions, the interviewer allowed each woman to discuss her experiences as she chose, for as long as she chose, and followed up on what each woman disclosed in conversationally appropriate ways. Interviews lasted between 1 and 2 hours.

We first examined the women's subjective experiences of remembering and forgetting the abuse. Half of the women claimed that they had never forgotten their experiences. Three of these women claimed that they recalled the abuse in clear and consistent detail all their lives, while three claimed they had always remembered the events but the details came and went over time. Illustrative statements from the interviews are shown in Table 4.1; as can be seen from their statements, these women believed they had continuous memories of their abusive experiences. In contrast, six women claimed there was a period when they did not recall their abuse at all. As shown in Table 4.1, these women have the experience of a time when they totally forgot they had been abused, and then subsequently recalled these experiences. However, the subjective experience of forgetting and recovery is much more complex. Although these six women clearly claimed that they had forgotten their abuse and subsequently remembered it, at other points in the interview, they expressed more confusion. For example, participant #12 reported "I would totally forget about it" and "I forgot about it for quite a while," but later in the interview said, "It was never totally forgotten." Similarly, participant #3 described a flashback experience in which she suddenly remembered having been abused as a child, yet later said, "I don't think I ever forgot it." In some very real

TABLE 4.1. Subjective Memory Experiences

Participant	Statement of memory
	Group IA: Continuous memory, same detail
5	"I certainly never forgot it."
7	"There's not a time I've ever forgotten."
11	"I remembered it all along."
	Group IB: Continuous memory, differing detail
1	". . . a lot of this has resurfaced."
7	"I don't remember a lot of the details. . . . I fight to remember things."
10	"Since I've started talking about it, I've remembered more."
	Group II: Recovered memory
2	". . . when it came out all of a sudden, I just started crying."
3	"Basically my (memory) was one flashback that happened 12 years ago."
4	"I had just completely forgotten."
6	"It's resurfaced twice that I know of or that I remember . . . sometimes I wouldn't remember it for years."
9	"I lost memory . . . until I was in my 20s and it all came to me it seemed in kind of a rush."
12	"I would totally forget about it . . . in my early 20s I became aware."

sense, these women expressed remembering and not remembering, forgetting and not forgetting simultaneously.

Women's subjective experience of remembering and forgetting abuse was related to their ability to narrate their abusive experiences. All of the women were able to provide many details of what happened to them, but there were substantial differences in their ability to construct a coherent account of what occurred. Women were classified as providing a coherent or an incoherent narrative of their abuse. For example, one woman, when asked to talk about her experiences, began her narrative as follows:

My earliest memory that I can really identify as a specific instance was when I was about six, six or seven. And, uh, my family had gone to the Boys Scout Camp that my father was a Boy Scout executive and he had actually been the kingpin in getting this camp built. And at the end of the camping season, the Boy Scout leaders and their families had a little scouting experience, camping experience to use up all the staples and close the camp and so forth. And one day we took, there were a large group of us, a large group of parents and children that took a hike out in the shrub, umm, scrub brush. You don't get a lot of forest or anything in that part of the state that I was, uh, and, uh, the others went one way and my dad and I went another. And I remember we ended up lying down in the dirt. Actually I was afraid the ants would get on me, while he, uh, fondled me and had me fondle him. And I don't know whether that was the first incident but I remember that I think, because of the peculiar circumstances that surrounded it, the fact that we were out in brush country, and, uh, but from then on I can remember several things specifically.

This narrative was classified as coherent. This woman begins her narrative by placing the event in time and place, how old she was, where the incident took place and why they were there. She reports quite specific details about what occurred, what she was thinking at the time, and so on. She then goes on to narrate several more incidents in this very coherent manner. Contrast this with the following narrative of another woman, also abused by her father, also beginning at about age 6 (although she is not very clear about the age at which the abuse started):

> Well, I'm 48 now and probably when I was about 46, something like that, umm, and stuff I've been going through, umm, up until I was about 46, I remembered, umm, my dad, uh, when my mom was gone and all the other kids were gone, had me sleep in his room and wanted me to, I guess you'd say give him a hand job, or, sounds so funny. Um, anyways, so I was at that time, I was, I would take a wild guess, I don't know. Maybe 5 or 6 years old. And then, after I've been going through this stuff, it's like, uh, remembering all this stuff that was there that you just, I think you're lucky to block it out a lot of times but, uh, just as a baby, baby, I mean very small, I remember my dad, you know, molesting me. Uh, having intercourse with me and I was, I don't know, as far as I can remember, I get pieces that might have been earlier, but, uh, I don't know, as young as like 2–3 years old. So I'm not even sure if I've got all the pieces yet.

This excerpt is very hard to follow, and was classified as an incoherent narrative. It is not set in a specific time and place, the narrator moves back and forth in time, and presents specific events in a confused and confusing fashion. Although the listener has the overall sense of what happened, it is simply not a coherent presentation.

In total, six of the women were able to provide a coherent account of their abusive experiences and six were not. Intriguingly, five of the women with continuous memories gave coherent narratives and one gave an incoherent narrative, and five of the women with recovered memories gave an incoherent narrative and one gave a coherent narrative. Thus there is a close relation between the subjective experience of continuously remembering abusive experiences over time and being able to narrate these experiences coherently. Women who had the subjective experience of forgetting and remembering their experiences, on the other hand, were not able to provide a coherent narrative.

Although women were not directly asked about their experiences of self, all of the women spontaneously discussed how the abuse affected their self-concepts. Based on their statements, women could be categorized as expressing an integrated self-concept or a dissociated self-concept. Women who expressed a dissociated self-concept talked about splitting their mind from their body or splitting their memories of the abuse off from other memories of the self. Table 4.2 gives examples of statements from the five women who expressed a dissociative self-concept. As can be seen, these five women describe a sense of self as separate from their abusive experiences, as split off from themselves. The seven women who expressed an integrated self-concept not only never expressed any dissociative

TABLE 4.2. Statements about Self-Concept

Participant	Statement of self
	Self-as-dissociated
2	That was the very beginning of my learning how to take myself away from my body. I can be a watcher anytime I want to be. So they can't hurt me anymore. Nothing can hurt me anymore. It doesn't matter what happens to my body because they can't hurt me.
3	I heard about sexual abuse but I didn't really associate I with me. . . . It was like it went in and it went out and I didn't want to approach it.
4	It's still hard for me to accept . . . there are occasions, even, I guess it's called denial, even knowing all of it. Once in a while, I mean, it goes through my head, like, oh, you know I must be nuts or I'm making all this up. I mean fathers, how could they do this?
9	I don't go to that place in my head where I'm being abused.
10	And what I did with it was, I would totally forget about it. I mean I would internalize it and dissociate it basically. And so it was like it never happened.
	Self-as-integrated
1	I feel like I am getting more able to make decisions. . . . I feel like I must have some sort of survival skills.
5	I felt so alone and isolated . . . it certainly gave me very low self-esteem. I just felt that I was a rotten person because of these things that I had done. And, uh, that made me feel hopeless.
6	I think it's too much, you know, a part of me and who I am to ever actually forget it.
7	Finally growing old and learning to put things in perspective and put things in the past that belong in the past. Go for the future.
8	I had to figure out why it was so hard for me to trust. . . . And I think that's one of the things that's just part of me now.
11	I grew up through my teenage years thinking I was bad . . . that I had this hidden badness side to me, umm, and now, you know, I don't throw it away anymore.
12	I'm angry. I'm very angry. . . . But this is like 30, well a little less than 30, 25 years I'd say later, and you know, it's like I've gone through this and I'm trying to work it out.

tendencies during their interviews, they actively talked about how their very selves were defined by their experiences, as victims or survivors. Although not all of these women expressed a positive sense of self (in fact, three of them express a relatively negative sense of self as an angry or a bad person), it is still the case that they have not split themselves off from their abuse history.

Five of the seven women who expressed an integrated sense of self also claimed to have continuous memories, whereas two women with an integrated sense of self had recovered memories. On the other hand, four of the women who expressed a dissociated sense of self claimed recovered memories, and one claimed continuous memories. Again, there seems to be a relation between having an integrated sense of self and continuous memories of abuse.

Clearly, we need to be extremely cautious in drawing any conclusions from these interviews. It was a very small and a very targeted population. Moreover, we did not gather any independent evidence of these women's abuse histories, or of their memories of the abuse over time. We relied totally on what the women told us. We were interested more in describing what the subjective sense of remembering and forgetting abuse was for these women than whether their reports of remembering and forgetting over time were "accurate." Further, we did not have any independent measure of their self-concepts beyond the way that they spontaneously described themselves in these interviews. Still, the results are provocative. It seems that there are multiple outcomes for women experiencing horrendous abuse. Some of these women always recalled what happened, were able to tell coherent narratives about these events and seemed to be able to integrate their abusive experiences into their larger understanding of self. Other women seemed to have coped with their abuse by dissociating these memories from their other memories. This led to the sense of forgetting the abuse over time, and to a more dissociated sense of self as adults.

The pattern suggests that when traumatic experiences are silenced by being forced out of consciousness, there may be long lasting effects on the ability to construct a coherent life story that contributes to an integrated sense of self. Women who cope with childhood abuse through mechanisms of denial and dissociation seem to suffer greater threats to an integrated self-concept than women who do not use these coping strategies. At this point, it is unclear how to account for these individual differences in coping. One possibility suggested in the clinical literature is that children abused earlier in development, who have not yet had the opportunity to develop a more stable self-concept, will be more likely to use dissociation as a coping mechanism than older children (Enns et al., 1995). In our sample, four of the five women who evidenced dissociation were 5 years old or younger when their abuse began, while only two of the seven women who did not dissociate were this young. As already mentioned, developmental considerations are critical in evaluating emerging links between autobiographical memory and self-concept, and this pattern, while merely suggestive, affirms that this is an important dimension for further study.

VOICE, SILENCE, AND THE SELF-CONCEPT

In this chapter I have presented two lines of research that indicate that the ways in which experiences are given voice or are silenced have long lasting implications for our evolving self-concepts. In constructing our autobiographical life stories, we weave together a complex tapestry based on what happened and how it has come to be constructed in social reminiscing. How we think and talk about events as they are occurring, and in retrospect, will come to determine which aspects of experience are privileged over others. In this formulation, language is a critical tool for the construction of autobiographical memory. How we talk with other people and how we come to represent events for ourselves facilitates the ability to construct a coherent narrative account of what occurred and what it means in our evolving life stories.

Language is critical for two interrelated reasons. First, it is through language that we are able to share our past experiences with others. In the process of reminiscing, listeners provide feedback about appropriate and inappropriate communications; through the joint focus on particular aspects of experience, and the concomitant neglect of other aspects of experiences, we come to reinterpret and reevaluate the events of our lives. Moreover, early in development, children need help from adults to create coherent narratives of past events. In the absence of adult-guided reminiscing, young children may have difficulty creating and maintaining coherent memories of what occurred (Fivush, Pipe, Murachver, & Reese, 1997). However, this is a double-edged sword. In creating meaningful narratives, by definition some aspects of experience will be foregrounded and some will be backgrounded or even neglected. In this way, what is said, what is shared and what is jointly negotiated to be the "truth" comes to define what happened and how we feel about it. In the words of the novelist, Janet Fitch (1999), "That was the thing about words, they were clear and specific — but when you talked about feelings, words were too stiff, they were this and not that, they couldn't include all the meanings. In defining, they always left something out" (p. 265). By focusing on specific aspects of experience, and by necessity silencing other aspects of experience, language provides a filter through which we come to understand our lives and our selves.

Second, through talking about events with others, memories take on a canonical narrative form. Through the telling and retelling of what happened, memories become stories, and as we reinterpret and reevaluate these stories, they become stories about us. In the absence of the ability to talk about certain events, such as abuse, it may be difficult to create a meaningful account of what happened. In her memoirs of her childhood battle with cancer, Lucy Grealy (1994) writes, "It was as if the earth were without form until those words were uttered, until those sounds took on decisions, themes, motifs. . . . Language supplies us with ways to express ever subtler forms of meaning, but does that imply that language gives meanings, or robs us of it when we are at a loss to name things?" (pp. 43–44). In the absence of a meaningful organization through which to understand our experiences, we may not be able to integrate those experiences into our self-understanding. This, in turn, may lead to a fragmented sense of self, as in some of the abuse survivors discussed here, especially if the trauma occurs early in development before children have a stable self-concept or are able to construct a coherent narrative of a past event without adult guidance.

The arguments in this chapter are clearly speculative. The concepts of voice and silence provide a theoretical framework for thinking about the ways that autobiography is shaped both by what is spoken and what is unspoken. Voice and silence allow for a deeper analysis of the ways that culture, gender, and individual histories privilege some forms of knowing over others, some aspects of experience over others. Moreover, we need to consider how changing social and political contexts change what is allowed to be voiced and what is silenced. With the emergence of the second wave of the women's movement in the late 1960s and early 1970s, we also saw changes in cultural frameworks for understanding lives and selves in both of the domains discussed in this chapter. We have seen a loosening of cultural stereotypes about gender and emotions that surely play a role in how parents might socialize emotion differently with daughters and with sons. Similarly, issues of violence against women, including childhood sexual abuse, have been allowed to surface in this same time period. Thus we have seen the emergence of the ability to give voice to certain kinds of experience that had been historically silenced.

For obvious reasons, most of what we know about the structure and content of autobiographical memory relies on what is voiced. The challenge for future research is to develop methodologies that allow for an analysis of what is silenced. To truly understand the relation between autobiographical memory and self-concept, we must move beyond an analysis of what is spoken and begin to integrate the ways that self is also shaped by what must be left unsaid.

ENDNOTES

1. This is not to argue that all gender differences are culturally constructed. Gender differences may very well emerge from biological predispositions and evolutionary constraints. Rather the argument is that whatever gender differences may be biologically predisposed, the way in which they are canalized and shaped will be a matter of cultural constructions.

REFERENCES

Adams, S., Kuebli, J., Boyle, P., & Fivush, R. (1995). Gender differences in parent-child conversations about past emotions: A longitudinal investigation. *Sex Roles, 33,* 309–323.

Anderson, M. C., & Green, C. (2001). Suppressing unwanted memories by executive control. *Nature, 41,* 366–369.

Aukett, R., Ritchie, J., & Mill, K. (1988). Gender differences in friendship patterns. *Sex Roles, 19,* 57–66.

Basow, S. A. (1992). *Gender stereotypes and roles.* Belmont, CA: Brooks-Cole.

Belenky, M. F., Clinchy, B. M., Goldberger, N. R., & Tarule, J. M. (1986). *Women's ways of knowing: The development of self, voice and mind.* New York: Basic Books.

Braham, J. (1995). *Crucial conversations: Interpreting contemporary American literary autobiography of women.* New York: Teachers College Press.

Brewin, C. R., & Andrews, B. (1998). Recovered memories of trauma: Phenomenology and cognitive mechanisms. *Clinical Psychology Review, 18,* 949–970.

Brody, L. R., & Hall, J. A. (1993). Gender and emotion. In M. Lewis & J. M. Haviland (Eds.), *Handbook of emotions* (pp. 447–460). New York: Guilford Press.

Bruner, J. (1987). Life as narrative. *Social Research, 54,* 11–32.

Buckner, J. P., & Fivush, R. (2000). Gendered themes in reminiscing. *Memory, 8,* 401–412.

Buckner, J. P., & Fivush, R. (1998). Gender and self in children's autobiographical narratives. *Applied Cognitive Psychology, 12,* 407–429.

Butler, L. (1999, November). *Adult memories of childhood sexual abuse.* Paper presented at the meeting of the International Society for Traumatic Stress Studies, San Antonio, TX.

Chodorow, N. J. (1978). *The reproduction of mothering: Psychoanalysis and the socialization of gender.* Berkeley: University of California Press.

Conway, M. (Ed.). (1997). *True and false memories.* Oxford, England: Oxford University Press.

Cross, S. E., & Madson, L. (1997). Models of the self: Self-construals and gender. *Psychological Bulletin, 122,* 5–37.

Davis, P. J. (1990). Gender differences in autobiographical memories for childhood emotional experiences. *Journal of Personality and Social psychology, 76,* 498–510.

Deaux, K., & Major, B. (1987). Putting gender into context: An interactional model of gender-related behavior. *Psychological Review, 94,* 369–389.

Edwards, V. J., Fivush, R., Anda, R. F., Felitti, V. J., & Nordenberg, D. F. (2001). Autobiographical memory disturbances in childhood abuse survivors. *Journal of Aggression, Maltreatment and Trauma, 4,* 247–263.

Enns, C. Z., McNeilly, C. L., Corkery, J. M., & Gilbert, M. S. (1995). The debate about delayed memories of childhood sexual abuse: A feminist perspective. *The Counseling Psychologist, 23,* 181–279.

Finkelhor, D., Hotaling, G., Lewis, I. A., & Smith, C. (1990). Sexual abuse in a national survey of adult men and women: Prevalence, characteristics, and risk factors. *Child Abuse and Neglect, 14,* 19–28.

Fischer, A. H. (Ed.). (2000). *Gender and emotion: Social Psychological perspectives.* Cambridge, England: Cambridge University Press.

Fitch, J. (1999). *White oleander.* New York: Little, Brown and Company.

Fivush, R. (1988). The functions of event memory: Some comments on Nelson and Barsalou. In U. Neisser, & E. Winograd (Eds.), *Remembering reconsidered: Ecological and traditional approaches to memory* (pp. 277–282). New York: Cambridge University Press.

Fivush, R. (1989). Exploring sex differences in the emotional content of mother-child talk about the past. *Sex Roles, 20,* 675–691.

Fivush, R. (1991). Gender and emotion in mother-child conversations about the past. *Journal of Narrative and Life History, 1,* 325–341.

Fivush, R. (1993). Emotional content of parent-child conversations about the past. In C. A. Nelson (Ed.), *The Minnesota symposium on child psychology: Memory and affect in development* (pp. 39–77). Hillsdale, NJ: Erlbaum.

Fivush, R. (1994). Constructing narrative, emotion and self in parent-child conversations about the past. In U. Neisser & R. Fivush (Eds.), *The remembering self: Accuracy and construction in the life narrative* (pp. 136–157). New York: Cambridge University Press.

Fivush, R. (1998). Gendered narratives: Elaboration, structure and emotion in parent-child reminiscing across the preschool years. In C. P. Thompson, D. J. Herrmann, D. Bruce, J. D. Read, D. G. Payne, & M. P. Toglia (Eds.), *Autobiographical memory: Theoretical and applied perspectives* (pp. 79–104). Hillsdale, NJ: Erlbaum.

Fivush, R. (1998). Interest, gender and personal narrative: How children construct self-understanding. In A. Karp, A. Renninger, J. Baumeister, & L. Hoffman (Eds.), *Interest and gender in education* (pp. 58–73). Kiel, Germany: Institute for Science Education.

Fivush, R. (2000). Accuracy, authorship and voice: Feminist approaches to autobiographical memory. In P. Miller & E. Scholnick (Eds.), *Towards a feminist developmental psychology* (pp. 85–106). New York: Cambridge University Press.

Fivush, R., Brotman, M., Buckner, J. P., & Goodman, S. (2000). Gender differences in parent-child emotion narratives. *Sex Roles, 42, 233–254.*

Fivush, R., & Buckner, J. P. (2000). Gender, sadness and depression: Developmental and socio-cultural perspectives. In A. H. Fischer (Ed.), *Gender and emotion: Social psychological perspectives* (pp. 232–253). Cambridge, England: Cambridge University Press.

Fivush, R., & Buckner, J. P. (2003). Constructing gender and identity through aurtobiographical narratives. In R. Fivush & C. Haden (Eds.), *Autobiographical memory and the construction of a narrative self: Developmental and cultural perspectives* (pp. 140–168). Hillsdale, NJ: Erlbaum.

Fivush, R., & Edwards, V. (in press). Remembering and forgetting childhood sexual abuse. *Journal of Child Sexual Abuse.*

Fivush, R., Pipe, M.-E., Murachver, T., & Reese, E. (1997). Events spoken and unspoken: Implications of language and memory development for the recovered memory debate. In M. Conway (Ed.), *True and false memories* (pp. 34–62). Oxford, England: Oxford University Press.

Freyd, J. (1996). *Betrayal trauma: The logic of forgetting childhood abuse.* Cambridge, MA: Harvard University Press.

Friedman, A., & Pines, A. (1991). Sex differences in gender related childhood memories. *Sex Roles, 25, 25–32.*

Gergen, K. J. (1994). Mind, text and society: Self-memory in social context. In U. Neisser & R. Fivush (Eds.), *The remembering self: Construction and accuracy in the life narrative* (pp. 78–104). New York: Cambridge University Press.

Gilligan, C. (1982). *In a different voice: Psychological theory and women's development.* Cambridge, MA: Harvard University Press.

Grealy, L. (1994). *Autobiography of a face.* Boston: Houghton Mifflin.

Han, J. J., Leichtman, M. D., & Wang, Q. (1998). Autobiographical memory in Korean, Chinese, and American children. *Developmental Psychology, 34, 701–713.*

James, W. (1890). *The principles of psychology.* New York: Dover.

Kuebli, J., Butler, S., & Fivush, R. (1995). Mother-child talk about past events: Relations of maternal language and child gender over time. *Cognition and Emotion, 9, 265–293.*

Kuebli, J., & Fivush, R. (1992). Gender differences in parent-child conversations about past emotions. *Sex Roles, 12, 683–698.*

Leichtman, M., Wang, Q., & Pillemer, D. P. (2003). Cultural variations in interdependence and autobiographical memory: Lessons from Korea, China, India, and the United States. In R. Fivush & C. Haden (Eds.), *Autobiographical memory and the construction of a narrative self: Developmental and cultural perspectives* (pp. 73–98). Hillsdale, NJ: Erlbaum.

Lewis, M. (1992). The role of the self in social behavior. In F. S. Kessel, P. M. Cole, & D. L. Johnson (Eds.), *Self and consciousness: Multiple perspectives* (pp. 19–44). Hillsdale, NJ: Erlbaum.

McAdams, D. P. (1992). Unity and purpose in human lives: The emergence of identity as a life story. In R. A. Zucker, A. I. Rabin, J. Aronoff, & S. J. Frank (Eds.), *Personality structure in the life course* (pp. 323–375). New York: Springer.

McAdams, D. P. (1996). Narrating the self in adulthood. In J. E. Birren, G. M. Kenyon, J. Ruth, J. J. F. Schroots, & T. Svensson (Eds.), *Aging and biography: Explorations in adult development* (pp. 131–148). New York: Springer.

Mullen, M., & Yi, S. (1995). The cultural context of talk about the past: Implications for the development of autobiographical memory. *Cognitive Development, 10,* 407–419.

Nelson, K. (1993). The psychological and social origins of autobiographical memory. *Psychological Science, 1,* 1–8.

Oyserman, D., & Markus, H. (1993). The sociocultural self. In J. Suls (Ed.), *Psychological perspectives on the self: The self in social perspective* (Vol. 4; pp. 187–220). Hillsdale, NJ: Erlbaum.

Pasupathi, M. (2001). The social construction of the personal past and its implications for adult development. *Psychological Bulletin, 127,* 651–672.

Pasupathi, M., Stallworth, L. M., & Murdoch, K. (1998). How what we tell becomes what we know: Listener effects on speakers' long-term memory for events. *Discourse Processes, 26,* 1–25.

Pezdek, K., & Banks, W. (1996). *The recovered memory debate*. New York: Academic Press.

Reese, E., Haden, C., & Fivush, R. (1996). Mothers, fathers, daughters, sons: Gender differences in reminiscing. *Research on Language and Social Interaction, 29,* 27–56.

Rogoff, B. (1990). *Apprenticeship in thinking*. New York: Oxford University Press.

Ross, M., & Holmberg, D. (1990). Recounting the past: Gender differences in the recall of events in the history of a close relationship. In M. P. Zanna & J. M. Olson (Eds.), *The Ontario symposium: Vol. 6, Self-inference processes* (pp. 135–152). Hillsdale, NJ: Erlbaum.

Schooler, J. W. (2001). Discovering memories of abuse in the light of meta-awareness. *Journal of Aggression, Maltreatment and Trauma, 4,* 105–136.

Snell, W. E., Jr., Miller, R. S., Belk, S. S., Garcia-Falconi, R., & Hernandez-Sanchez, J. E. (1989). Men's and women's emotional self-disclosure: The impact of disclosure recipient, culture and the masculine role. *Sex Roles, 21,* 467–486.

5

The Redemptive Self: Narrative Identity in America Today

DAN P. McADAMS
Northwestern University

O ver the past 15 years, my students and I have explored the different ways that American adults construe their lives as stories — life narratives complete with settings, scenes, characters, plots, and themes. The guiding theoretical frame for these investigations is my *life-story theory of identity* (McAdams, 1985, 1993, 1996a). According to the life-story theory, people living in modern societies begin to put their lives together into internalized and evolving narratives of the self in late adolescence and young adulthood. The life stories they construct situate them within particular interpersonal, economic, ideological, and cultural niches in the adult world and provide their lives with some degree of unity and purpose. These stories continue to evolve across the adult life course, reflecting changing developmental agendas and a wide range of influences and factors in the social ecology of everyday life (Cohler, 1982; McAdams, 1996b). People's life stories are windows into human individuality and, along with personality traits and motivational concerns, life stories constitute important and ever-changing aspects of human personality (McAdams, 1995, 2001). In addition, life stories reflect the social and cultural worlds within which lives attain their existential meanings (Denzin, 1989; Shotter & Gergen, 1989). Therefore, life stories are as much about the social world as they are about the self (Holstein & Gubrium, 2000; Thorne, 2000).

Our research has focused on the life stories constructed by American adults. Every life story account we have observed, be it conveyed to us through interview or open-ended questionnaires, is unique, and therefore the quantitative and qualitative analyses we conduct on these protocols cannot do justice to the idiographic richness of each individual case. Nonetheless, we have found it scientifically useful to code and interpret life stories in terms of well-defined content themes, and to relate these themes to other aspects of human functioning displayed by our research subjects, such as psychological well-being, social motives, personality traits, occupational roles, and even demographic factors such as age and social class (e.g., McAdams, 1982; McAdams, Hoffman, Mansfield, & Day, 1996). In the current chapter, I describe a recent line of research in this regard that focuses on the themes of contamination and redemption in life stories. Supplemented by a reading of selected sociological and cultural-historical sources on conceptions of selfhood in America, our life-narrative studies point to the salience of a particular kind of narrative identity in contemporary America — what I will call the *redemptive self*. A key feature of redemptive life stories is the transformation of personal suffering into positive-affective life scenes that serve to redeem and justify one's life. The redemptive self is *not* a new personality type, but rather a characteristic narrative of selfhood that can be discerned in the life stories of many American adults today. Its emergence and proliferation recaptures classic themes of American selfhood that can be traced back hundreds of years as well as new features of social life characteristic of postmodernity.

THE PROBLEM OF CONTAMINATION

For Tanya Williams, a 41-year-old, African-American mother of four, the general arc of life is a contamination sequence (from McAdams & Bowman, 2001). Things begin well, but eventually they turn bad. In a 2-hour life-story interview, we asked Tanya to describe the single most wonderful moment in her life — a life-narrative high point. She described the birth of her first child. It was an experience of joy, wonder, and love. The baby was beautiful. Tanya was so happy to have a little girl to care for, now that she herself had turned 21 and was ready, she believed, to take on the responsibility of being a good mother. But as she looked back on the high point 20 years later, Tanya did not end her account of the scene with the baby's birth and the happiness she felt. Instead, she flashed forward 3 years to a kind of culmination of the sequence. The baby's father died, she reported. Three years after the birth, the father was found dead in a motel room, stabbed five times in the back. Note that the interviewer did not ask Tanya to tell the story in this way, to link in narrative the most emotionally positive moment in her life to a negative outcome. Tanya imposed the structure herself to convey a clear sequence: I became a mother, and then a widow.

In a contamination sequence, a very good or affectively positive life-narrative scene or chapter is followed by a very bad, affectively negative outcome (McAdams & Bowman, 2001). The bad ruins, spoils, sullies, contaminates the good that preceded it. Her childhood years were great, Tanya says. Her mother loved her; her sister and she stayed up late at night telling ghost stories; she learned to ride a bike. In Tanya's story, contamination began with puberty. In junior high school, she discovered she had a "mischievous streak," a trait she associated with her father. "They tended to tell me that I was like my father [then], which caused me a lot of problem." Puberty ushered in a dangerous chapter, as if the protagonist in her life story had no choice but to live out the traits that her father had given her. Around the time of puberty she began to drink. Soon she was using other drugs. By the time she was 15 years old, she had experimented with heroin. Still, eighth-grade graduation was a very nice memory. "That was something I achieved on my own, and I felt very proud." (To contaminate the sequence, she adds: "That was the last time I walked across the stage.")

What Tanya explicitly identifies as the low point in her life story does not occur until she was in her mid-30s. Trapped now in an abusive marriage, she took up romantically with a much younger man named Frank. Frank was a drug-dealer. Like her first husband, Frank, too, was killed, shot in a quarrel at a party. The lowest moment, though, occurs shortly before Frank actually died. As Tanya tells it, Frank was laid up in a hospital bed and Tanya, reluctantly, came to visit. Tanya had not thought that anybody knew about her sexual affair with Frank. But Frank's mother knew. Indeed, Frank's mother had found photographs that Frank had taken of Tanya — Tanya in *her* bed. "He had some pictures he had taken in my bed, satin sheets, and she [Frank's mother] got them blown up about as big as his window." Amazingly, Frank's mother pasted these enlarged photographs on the wall in Frank's hospital room. According to Tanya's account, Frank's mother hoped the photographs would "cheer him up" and presumably help stir him out of his coma. Frank never recovered, but the result of this bizarre sequence was that Tanya felt "stripped" and completely humiliated. All her friends, and presumably her husband, saw the pictures, or heard about them. Tanya's lover died, and, to make matters even worse, because of this she was exposed as an unfaithful wife.

Tanya's low-point scene is sequenced such that happiness leads to violence and humiliation. She was happy in the affair with Frank; Frank was shot; she was humiliated by the photographs. This is the same sequence that Tanya employed in a narrative account of an odd incident in childhood. She and her sister were happily playing outside. They were playing with frogs under an apple tree. A violent thunderstorm came in, and lightning struck the tree, splitting it in half. The children escaped injury, but as Tanya recalls it the lightning pulverized the frogs, turning "the frogs into slime." After relating this event in her interview, Tanya moves directly into an account of how the white kids in her neighborhood "used to tease us and call us crispy critters," presumably for the dark color of her and her siblings' skin. The sequence is thus complete: Happiness (playing with the frogs) is followed by violence (the thunderstorm) and humiliation (crispy critters). Like the frogs, Tanya has been burned to a crisp. She is black, but more importantly, as she repeats again and again in the interview, she is the "black sheep" in her family. What she sees as the beginning of the contamination — namely, puberty (and the love of "the streets" that puberty ushered in) — was like the lightning that burned her soul and made her bad. She cannot undo what her fiery biology has wrought. Instead, she is doomed to repeat the contamination sequence again and again. As a result, Tanya feels she can make no *progress* in her life. There is no forward, upward direction. "I'm 41 years old, but I still feel kind of lost. I know what to do when I get up everyday, but I don't really know where I am going."

Contamination sequences appear in many life stories, though rarely does the contamination theme come to dominate a story to the extent it does for the case of Tanya Williams. A man describes how wonderful his first marriage was, until one day when his wife tells him she wants a divorce. A woman remembers playing happily in a park as a young child, and then she realizes her parents are nowhere to be seen. A man tells of how exciting sex was before his marriage, but after the wedding his new wife is no longer interested. A woman receives a diamond ring, but the next day it is stolen from her home. In each case, the protagonist in the story experiences an initial state of goodness, happiness, satisfaction, joy, excitement, peace, closeness, intimacy, pride, status, or the like. But in each case, things turn bad.

Almost everybody can recall contamination events from the past. But people appear to differ with respect to just how many such sequences they can recall and the extent to which these sequences come to characterize their life stories (McAdams, Reynolds, Lewis, Patten, & Bowman, 2001). In the study that Tanya Williams participated in, we interviewed 74 adults between the ages of 35 and 65 years, approximately half who were African American and half white, half male and half female (McAdams et al., 2001). As part of a standard life-story interview (in McAdams, 1993), we asked them to describe in great detail eight key scenes in their life stories — discrete episodes from the past that stand out in memory as especially vivid or consequential. The eight discrete scenes were a life-story high point, low point, turning point, earliest memory, important childhood scene, important adolescent scene, important scene from adulthood, and one other scene that stands out in memory. Two independent coders, blind to identifying information on the subjects, scored each memory for the presence (score +1) or absence (score 0) of a contamination sequence. The results showed that those adults, like Tanya, who describe a greater number of contamination sequences in their life-narrative accounts tend to score significantly higher on a self-report measure of depression and lower on life-satisfaction, self-esteem, and sense of coherence. Midlife adults who are less happy, who report less self-esteem and life coherence, and who are more depressed are more likely to frame their life narratives in contamination terms, compared with adults who score higher on self-report measures of psychological well-being.

The results from correlational studies like McAdams and colleagues (2001) suggest a link between the quality of individuals' life stories and independent assessments of social and personal well-being. They support the general idea that a person's social and psychological situation in life is reflected in the kinds of themes that prevail in life narrative. But the results can be relatively open-ended. For example, the results leave open the question of causation. Does being relatively happy predispose one to recall fewer contamination sequences in life, or does recalling few such events lead to being happier? Furthermore, do some people recall fewer contamination sequences because they, in fact, have experienced fewer such events in their lives? Or is the difference simply due to their style or manner of recalling the past? To what extent are contamination memories veridical? These important questions, however, beg one even more basic question which should be addressed first. The most basic question in the research is this: Why examine life stories anyway?

LIFE STORIES AND THE DEVELOPMENT OF IDENTITY

The social sciences have witnessed an upsurge of interest in the study of life narratives, autobiographical stories, personal myths, and similar other concepts over the past two decades (Josselson & Lieblich, 1993; Josselson, Lieblich, & McAdams, 2003; McAdams, 1999, 2001). While investigators have worked from many different theoretical perspectives and have followed many different empirical agendas, a common rationale used for examining the stories people tell about their lives is that these stories speak directly to the issue of identity. My own work in this area is premised on this basic idea: *identity is itself a life story.*

Social scientists and laypersons alike commonly use the terms "self" and "identity" interchangeably. Following Erikson (1963), however, I employ a sharp distinction between the two. As William James (1892/1963) argued, the self may be viewed as both the subjective sense of "I" and the objective sense of "me." Accordingly, the "me" includes within it any and all things, features, and characteristics that the "I" may attribute to it — all that is me, all that is mine. By contrast, Erikson's conception of identity refers to a peculiar quality or flavoring of the self-as-me — a way that the I begins to arrange or configure the me in adolescence and young adulthood, when the standards for what constitutes an appropriate me change rather dramatically. It is at this time in the life course, Erikson maintained, that people *first* confront the problem of *identity versus role confusion*. In this, the fifth of Erikson's eight stages of life, people first explore ideological and occupational options available in society and experiment with a wide range of social roles, with the aim of eventually consolidating their beliefs and values into a personal ideology and making provisional commitments to life plans and projects that promise to situate them meaningfully into new societal niches (Marcia, 1980). It is during this developmental period, that people first seek to integrate their disparate roles, talents, proclivities, and social involvements into a patterned *configuration* of thought and activity that provides life with some semblance of psychosocial *unity and purpose* (Breger, 1974). That configuration is what identity is.

Employing Erikson's understanding of the term, then, identity is an integrative configuration of self-in-the-adult-world. This configuration integrates in two ways. First, in a synchronic sense, identity integrates the wide range of different, and likely conflicting, roles and relationships that characterize a given life in the here and now. "When I am with my father, I feel sullen and depressed; but when I talk with my friends, I feel a great surge of optimism and love for humankind." Identity needs to integrate these two things so that while they appear very different, they can be viewed as integral parts of the same self-configuration. Second, identity must integrate diachronically, that is, in time. "I used to love to play baseball, but now I want to be a cognitive psychologist." Or, "I was a born-again Christian, but these days I feel I am an agnostic." Identity needs to integrate these kinds of contrasts so that while self-elements are separated in time (and in content quality), they can be brought meaningfully together in a temporally organized whole. Put starkly, identity becomes a problem when the adolescent or young adult first realizes that he or she is, has been, and/or could be many different (and conflicting) things, and experiences a strong desire, encouraged by society, to be but *one* (large, integrated, and dynamic) thing. Young children have selves; they know who they are, and they can tell you. But they do not have identities, in Erikson's sense, in that they are not confronted with the problem of arranging the me into a unified and purposeful whole that specifies a meaningful niche in the emerging adult world (Arnett, 2000). Selves begin to take identity shape in late adolescence and young adulthood.

Why does identity wait so long? The reasons are both cultural and cognitive. In Western societies, we expect adolescents to begin the process of taking stock of the material, ideological, occupational, and interpersonal resources in their worlds, and taking stock of themselves, in order to find a reasonably good match between what a person can do and believe on the one hand and what adult society enables a person to do and believe on the other (McAdams, 1996a). Identity formation is considered an on-time developmental task for late adolescence and young adulthood (Cohler, 1982). Parents, high-school teachers, siblings, friends, college admissions counselors, the business world, the media, and many other aspects and agents of modern society explicitly and implicitly urge adolescents and young adults to "get a life" (Habermas & Bluck, 2000). It is time to begin to examine what society has to offer and, eventually, to make commitments, even if only temporary, to personalized niches in the adult world. This is to say that society and the young person are ready for the individual's identity explorations by the time he or she has reached late adolescence or young adulthood. Accordingly, Erikson (1959) wrote:

> The period can be viewed as a psychosocial moratorium during which the individual through free role experimentation may find a niche in some section of his society, a niche which is firmly defined and yet seems to be uniquely made for him. In finding it the young adult gains an assured sense of inner continuity and social sameness which will bridge what he was as a child and what he is about to become, and will reconcile his conception of himself and his community's recognition of him. (p. 111)

Although Erikson did not emphasize it, advances in cognitive development in the adolescent years are likely to be as important as any other forces in launching the identity project. Breger (1974) and Elkind (1981) argued that with the emergence of formal operations in adolescence, identity becomes an especially engaging abstraction for the abstract thinker: "[T]he idea of a unitary or whole self in which past memories of who one was, present experiences of who one is, and future expectations of who one will be, is the sort of abstraction that the child simply does not think about." But "with the emergence of formal operations in adolescence, wholeness, unity, and integration become introspectively real problems" (Breger, 1974, p. 330). The idea that one's life, as complex and dynamic as it increasingly appears to be, might be integrated into a meaningful and purposeful whole may represent, therefore, an especially appealing possibility to the now self-reflective young adult.

During this developmental period, people begin to put their lives together into self-defining stories. It is an internalized and evolving story of self that integrates the self synchronically and diachronically, explaining why it is that I am sullen with my father and euphoric with my friends and how it happened — step-by-step, scene-by-scene — that I went from being a born-again Christian who loved baseball to an agnostic cognitive psychologist. Only a story can accomplish the integrative psychosocial tasks the identity formation demands. In linking the selective reconstruction of the past with an imagined future, life stories begin, in late adolescence and young adulthood, to serve as new and powerful formats for arranging potentially discordant and unrelated aspects of selfhood into a purposeful psychosocial configuration.

Stories are fundamentally about the vicissitudes of human intention organized in time (Bruner, 1990; Ricoeur, 1984). In virtually all intelligible stories, humans or humanlike characters act to accomplish intentions, generating a sequence of actions and reactions extended as a plot in time (Mandler, 1984). Human intentionality is at the heart of narrative, and therefore the development of intentionality in humans is of prime importance in establishing the mental conditions necessary for life-story telling and story comprehension. Recent research with infants suggests that by the end of the first or early in the second year of life humans come to understand other persons as intentional agents (Tomasello, 2000). For example, 16-month-old infants will imitate complex behavioral sequences exhibited by other human beings only when those activities appear intentional. As Tomasello (2000) writes, "Young children do not just mimic the limb movements of other persons; rather, they attempt to reproduce other persons' intended, goal-directed actions in the world" (p. 38). With the emergence of what Dennett (1987) calls the *intentional stance*, children in the second year of life can experience the world from the subjective standpoint of an intentional, causal I, able now to assume the existential position of a motivated human subject who appropriates experience as his or her own (Kagan, 1994; McAdams, 1997). This existential I-ness is tacitly and immediately grasped in and through intentional action (Blasi, 1988).

In James's terms, with the consolidation of the existential I comes the eventual formulation of the me. In the second year of life, children begin to attribute various distinguishing characteristics to themselves, including their names, their favorite toys, their likes and dislikes, and so on. With the development of language, the self-as-object grows rapidly to encompass a wide range of things "about me" that can be verbally described. To be included in the mix eventually are memories of events in which the self was involved. According to Howe and Courage (1997), *autobiographical memory* emerges toward the end of the second year of life when children have consolidated a basic sense of I and reflexively begun to build up a rudimentary understanding of the me. Although infants can remember events (basic episodic memory) before this time, it is not until the end of the second year, Howe and Courage contend, that episodic memory becomes personalized and children begin to organize events they experience as "things that happened to me." From this point onward, the me expands to include autobiographical recollections, recalled as little stories about what has transpired in "my life."

Autobiographical memory emerges and develops in a social context (Nelson, 1988; Welch-Ross, 1995). Parents typically encourage children to talk about their personal experiences as soon as children are verbally able to do so (Fivush & Kuebli, 1997). Early on, parents may take the lead in stimulating the child's recollection and telling of the past by reminding the child of recent events, such as this morning's breakfast or yesterday's visit to the doctor. Taking advantage of this initial conversational scaffolding provided by adults, the young child soon begins to take more initiative in sharing personal events. By the age of 3, children are actively engaged in co-constructing their past experiences in conversations with adults. By the end of the preschool years, they are able to give a relatively coherent narrative account of the past. In conversations with adults about personal memories, young children become acquainted with the narrative structures through which people in their world typically discuss events. The sharing of personal experiences functions as a major mechanism of socialization (Miller, 1994) and helps to build an organized personal history from a growing base of autobiographical memories (Fivush, 1994).

As children move through elementary school, they come to narrate their own personal experiences in ways that conform to their implicit understandings of how good stories should be structured and what they should include. In this way, they imbue their experience with what Habermas and Bluck (2000) term *temporal coherence*. Before adolescence, however, temporal coherence applies mainly to single autobiographical events rather than to connections between different events. In elementary school, furthermore, children begin to internalize their culture's norms concerning what the story of an entire life should itself contain. As they learn, for example, that a telling of a single life typically begins with, say, an account of birth and typically includes, say, early experiences in the family, eventual emergence out of the family, geographical moves, and so on, they acquire an understanding of what Habermas and Bluck (2000) call *biographical coherence*. Cultural norms define conventional phases of the life course and suggest what kinds of narrative forms make sense in telling a life (Denzin, 1989). As children learn the culture's biographical conventions, they begin to see how single events in their own lives might be sequenced and linked to conform to the culture's concept of biography.

Still, it is not until adolescence, Habermas and Bluck contend, that individuals craft causal narratives to explain how different events are linked together in the context of a biography. *Causal coherence* is exhibited in the increasing effort across adolescence to provide narrative accounts of one's life that explain how one event caused, led to, transformed, or in some way is meaningfully related to other events in one's life. Traits, attitudes, beliefs, and preferences may now be explained in terms of the life events that may have caused them. An adolescent may, for example, explain why she rejects her parents' liberal political values, or why she feels shy around members of the opposite sex, or how it came to be that her junior year in high school represented a turning point in her understanding of herself in terms of personal experiences from the past that have been selected and, in many cases, reconstructed to make a coherent explanation. In what Habermas and Bluck term *thematic coherence*, furthermore, she may identify an overarching theme, value, or principle that integrates many different episodes in her life and conveys the gist of who she is and what her autobiography is all about. Studies reported by Habermas and Bluck suggest that causal and thematic coherence are rare in autobiographical accounts in early adolescence but increase substantially through the teenaged years and into young adulthood. By the time individuals have reached late adolescence and young adulthood, therefore, they are typically able and eager to construct stories about the past and about the self that exhibit temporal, biographical, causal, and thematic coherence. Autobiographical memory and narrative understanding now have developed to the level whereby they can be called into service in the making of identity.

AUTOBIOGRAPHICAL MEMORY AND THE SELF

An emerging theme in the study of memory for real-life and personal events is that autobiographical memory helps to locate and define the self within an ongoing life story that, simultaneously, is strongly oriented toward future goals (e.g., Pillemer, 1998; Schacter, 1996; Stein, Wade, & Liwag, 1997). For example, Conway and Pleydell-Pearce (2000) argue that a person's goals function as control processes in a self-memory system (SMS), modulating the construction of memories. Autobiographical memories are encoded and retrieved in ways that serve the goals of the current working self. As such, current goals influence how autobiographical information is absorbed and organized in the first place, and goals generate retrieval models to guide the search process later on.

In the SMS, personal goals are linked to an autobiographical knowledge base, which itself consists of information encoded at three levels of specificity: lifetime periods, general events, and event-specific knowledge (Conway & Pleydell-Pearce, 2000). Lifetime periods mark off relatively large chunks of autobiographical time, such as "my first marriage" and "Tanya's childhood, before puberty and the streets," and they correspond roughly to what I have designated as main *chapters* in a person's life story (McAdams, 1985). General events (e.g., "parties I attended in college," "fights Tanya had with men") and event-specific knowledge (e.g., "my father's funeral," "the birth of Tanya's first child") cover the same ground as Pillemer's (1998) *personal event memories* and what I have called *nuclear episodes* in the life story (McAdams, 1985). Indeed, the interview methodology that my colleagues and I employ in life-story research begins with accounts of life chapters, moves to accounts of particular episodes that stand out in bold print in the life story (nuclear episodes such as life-story high points, low points, and turning points), and moves eventually to accounts of future goals and plans. The life story is an integration of the reconstructed past, represented mainly as chapters and episodes, and the anticipated future, represented mainly as goals.

Some remembered episodes are more central to self-definition than are others. For example, Singer and Salovey (1993) have focused on *self-defining memories*, which they define as remembered episodes that are "vivid, affectively charged, repetitive, linked to other similar memories, and related to an important unresolved theme or enduring concern in an individual's life" (p. 13). It is these kinds of memories that occupy the most prominent positions within identity as a life story. In this regard, Robinson and Taylor (1998) make an important distinction between autobiographical memories and self-narratives. They point out that people remember many episodes in life that are mundane and appear to have little relevance to their self-concepts. Autobiographical memory, therefore, comprises a vast range of personal information and experience. Self-narratives, in contrast, "consist of a set of temporally and thematically organized salient experiences and concerns that constitute one's identity" (Robinson & Taylor, 1998, p. 126). Self-narratives include only a subset of the remembered events stored in autobiographical memory, Robinson and Taylor suggest, and, moreover, self-narratives may also include information that is not technically part of the autobiographical memory base. An example of the latter is the individual's imagined future — how I see myself in ten years, what events I believe I will experience one day, what I leave behind.

Nonetheless, there is significant overlap between the episodic knowledge that cognitive psychologists position within autobiographical memory and the lifetime periods, general events, and event-specific knowledge that go into the making of identity as a life story. Like many cognitive approaches to autobiographical memory, furthermore, the life-story theory of identity adopts a moderately reconstructive view of autobiographical recollections (e.g., Brewer, 1986; Ross, 1997). Personal goals and other concerns shape the encoding and recollection of self-defining memories and other important features of the life story. Reconstruction exerts a distorting effect, especially with regard to memories from long ago (Thompson, Skowronski, Larsen, & Betz, 1996). But for life stories the greatest degree of reconstruction may involve selection and interpretation, rather than outright distortion of the historical truth (Bluck & Levine, 1998). People select and interpret certain memories as self-defining, providing them with privileged status in the life story. Other potential candidates for such status are downgraded, relegated to the category of "oh yes, I remember that, but I don't think it is very important," or forgotten altogether. To a certain degree, then, *identity is a product of choice*. We choose the events we consider most important for defining who we are and providing our lives with some semblance of unity and purpose. And we endow them with symbolism, lessons learned, integrative themes, and other personal meanings that make sense to us in the present as we survey the past and anticipate the future.

The power of selection is apparent in the well-documented phenomenon of the memory bump (Fitzgerald, 1988; Rubin, Wetzler, & Nebes, 1986). People tend to recall a disproportionately large number of autobiographical events from the ages of approximately 15 to 25 years. There is some indication, furthermore, that episodic memories from this period are especially rich in emotional and motivational content (Thorne, 2000). Consistent with what the life-story theory of identity would predict, Fitzgerald (1988) and Conway and Pleydell-Pearce (2000) have argued that adults are wont to select events from this particular period in the life course because it is during adolescence and young adulthood that people are most preoccupied with forming their identities. It is indeed roughly during the period of the reminiscence bump that young people are first confronting the identity problem in modern society and actively formulating integrative life stories to address the psychosocial challenges they face. Consequently, they may be more likely to encode personal events occurring during these years as relevant to their psychosocial "goal" of formulating an identity. It may indeed be true, moreover, that the kinds of events that do tend to happen during this especially consequential period of the human life course are the kinds of autobiographical episodes that make for especially *good* stories (McAdams, 1993). In this regard, it should not be surprising that the "coming of age story" is such a staple in contemporary fiction and cinema and that the *myth of the hero* — the adventurous transition from young-adolescent innocence to full-fledged adulthood — is a timeless and universally celebrated mythic form (Campbell, 1949).

CULTURE AND NARRATIVE: THE REDEMPTIVE SELF

Life stories exist and are told within particular cultures. Each culture has its own traditions for what counts as a tellable story, a meaningful life (Rosenwald, 1992). Furthermore, life stories are gendered constructions that are also strongly influenced by class, ethnicity, religion, and other sociological and historical realities (Franz & Stewart, 1994). We cannot, therefore, hope to understand Tanya Williams's life story without knowing about the kinds of stories and life models that prevail in her world, as a 41-year-old black woman, now an unmarried mother of four living in urban America at the turn of the 21st century. From a life-story standpoint, lives are like evolving narrated texts, known and read as stories, framed through discourse, told in culture, and couched within a particular historical moment (Barresi & Juckes, 1997). To this effect, Cohler and Cole (1994) write:

> The life story is a narrative precisely because it represents a discourse of a particular kind, organized with a potential listener or reader in mind and with an intent, often implicit, to convince self and others of a particular plot or present ordering of experience rendered sensible within a particular culture. (p. 6)

A great deal has been written in recent years about differences in self-conceptions as they appear in the West (i.e., North America and Europe) and the East (i.e., Japan, Korea, China). It is argued that members of individualistic societies in the West hold to a view of self as individualized and agentic whereas collectivist Eastern cultures view the self as more interdependent and communal (Markus & Kitayama, 1991; Triandis, 1997). It should come as no surprise, therefore, that life stories told by Westerners reflect themes of autonomy and independence to a greater extent than life stories constructed by citizens of Japan and China, whose stories should emphasize the culturally valued motifs of interdependence and conformity to societal norms. In that our research has focused on American identities, the life stories we have examined over the past fifteen years doubtlessly reflect a Western conception of an autonomous and independent self.

But there appear to be other, more subtle themes apparent in many of the life stories we have analyzed, themes that also mark them as distinctively "American" in spirit and tone (McAdams, in press). Of special interest in this regard may be what is often perceived abroad as Americans' unbridled optimism. Cultural observers going back to Alexis de Tocqueville in the early nineteenth century have remarked on how Americans are wont to believe that things will often work out beautifully in the end, or if they do not work out perfectly, life will nonetheless show progress and people will continue to develop and grow and get further along over time. One American ideal has been to shed the trappings of the past and to move confidently forward in life, as the 18th- and 19th-century settlers moved westward to strike it rich, or at least to improve their lives. Indeed, some Americans still do move westward to improve their lives. Silicon Valley is a tremendous lure for some, and demographic trends suggest that people will continue to pour into California for at least another decade. But the movement of concern here is more psychological, and it is often revealed in stories of *overcoming* — overcoming trauma, for example, overcoming one's difficult beginnings, overcoming addiction. It is as if Americans must hold out hope that when it comes to their own lives there is always a chance for eventual *redemption*.

The theme of redemption is central to the life story of Jerome Johnson, a retired African-American police chief who spends a great deal of time and energy doing volunteer work with children and youth (from McAdams & Bowman, 2001). The turning point scene in Johnson's life story was a chance encounter with the Reverend Martin Luther King, Jr. in the mid-1960s. A year or two before he was assassinated, King came to a small city in the midwestern part of the United States to speak to civic and religious leaders and to rally citizens, black and white, for civil rights. Jerome Johnson was assigned to be King's bodyguard. Johnson was a black policeman in his early 30s, an ambitious man who had been a football star in high school and who had completed a tour of duty with the U.S. Air Force. Johnson dreamed of becoming a police chief. But he was frustrated. No black man had ever even been promoted to sergeant in that city, let alone been seriously considered for chief. Johnson's fellow officers counseled against taking the promotional exam. His friends told him that he should be satisfied with what he had. He was seriously considering quitting the force. "I was thinking of leaving the police force because I felt it was a hopeless thing that a black could ever be a police chief," Johnson said, in a life story interview conducted over 30 years later, in 1997. "But then my life turned around." Johnson explains:

It was at the time I was assigned to be the bodyguard for Dr. Martin Luther King. And he was here, I think maybe two, three days. And so I spent some time with him. . . . [On the last day] he was getting ready to leave, and he was standing in front of the hotel and waiting for transportation to take him to the airport. And we started talking, and I told him how frustrated I was about the fact that no black had ever been promoted [on the police force]. Maybe it's time to move on [I told him] because I didn't see there was anything that was gonna change at all. And he just said a couple of things, just very briefly he said, you know, he said, "Never give up." And that was basically the end of the conversation, and I thought about that before, but when he said it to me, and the way he said, "Keep the faith," you know, and "Never give up," you know, and "Never stop dreaming the dream," you know. And I held on to that, and I went on, and things changed. . . . He turned me around from walkin' out the door.

Notice the structure of Jerome Johnson's turning-point scene. The episode begins in hopelessness but the situation is transformed rather dramatically by a fortuitous meeting. In simple terms, there is a movement in the scene from a negative-affect situation to a very positive outcome — a redemptive sequence. Johnson did eventually take the exam. After many years he did become the first black chief on that force. Now in retirement, he tells a life story that is filled with redemptive scenes. In the worst days of the Great Depression, for example, his family had no money at Christmas time, but a neighbor stopped by and delivered a turkey and presents. At a high school basketball game, opposing players called Jerome a "nigger"; his mother ran home in tears, but Jerome said the event "toughened me up." Again and again in the story, the protagonist endures suffering at the beginning of a scene but is somehow rewarded at the end.

In a redemption sequence, a bad, affectively negative scene turns good, is salvaged, saved, redeemed by a positive outcome of some sort (McAdams, Diamond, de St. Aubin, & Mansfield, 1997). The positive transformation may be the result of the protagonist's striving to overcome, or it may simply be the result of luck, fate, God, or forces beyond the protagonist's immediate control. For example, a woman divorces her husband, but as a result she develops a closer relationship with her son. A young man is injured in a traffic accident, but in the hospital he has a great insight about his work, which eventuates in a major advance in his career. A man remarks that he was lonely as a child, but as a result of this experience he developed resilience and coping skills. A woman sinks into drug abuse, but she recovers with the help of her friends.

Redemption sequences come in many forms. In one study, we divided them into five types: sequences of sacrifice, recovery, growth, learning, and improvement (McAdams et al., 2001). But these groupings are somewhat arbitrary, and there would appear to be a plethora of contemporary discourses that people routinely draw upon to get across the idea of redemption. In the discourse of medicine, for example, people speak of healing, recovery, and achieving wellness. In the legal system, terms such as rehabilitation and restitution are invoked. Educators speak of learning, growth, development, and socialization. Contemporary American society is suffused with the rhetoric of psychotherapy, and today many laypeople speak knowingly of personal transformation and personal growth, fulfillment and self-actualization, individuation and reintegration, and the improvement, enlargement, perfection, and full expression of the self (Cushman, 1995), all variations on redemption sequences. The burgeoning popular literature on self-help offers a cornucopia of redemption stories as do contemporary talk shows on television and human-interest stories in the media. And of course the many discourses that may be grouped under the general category of American religion and spirituality invoke concepts such as sacrifice, atonement, enlightenment, transcendence, conversion, and so on — all ideas that find their way readily into personal stories that people tell to account for their own lives.

In our research, we have found that telling one's life in redemptive terms is positively associated with self-reported mental health. In the aforementioned study of 74 midlife adults who provided detailed accounts of eight key scenes in their life stories (McAdams et al., 2001), contamination sequences predicted low levels of self-report well-being in that sample, but the reverse was true for redemption. Adults whose life stories showed higher levels of redemption imagery tended to report higher levels of life satisfaction, self-esteem, and sense of life coherence, and lower levels of depression, compared to adults whose life stories contained less redemption imagery.

The findings were replicated in a second study of college students (McAdams et al., 2001). In this latter instance, 125 college students provided lengthy written accounts of ten important autobiographical scenes, including again life-story high points, low points, and turning points. The students also completed a short measure of life satisfaction and Ryff's (1989) 6-scale measure of psychological well-being, which gives scores on autonomy, environmental mastery, purpose in life, personal growth, quality of interpersonal relationships, and self-acceptance. Redemption sequences in written accounts were positively associated with five of the six indices of well-being in Ryff's measure, with the total index from Ryff, and with overall satisfaction with life on the short scale. Only the relation with Ryff's autonomy was nonsignificant. People who are more satisfied with their lives, be they students or midlife adults, tend to construct life-narrative accounts that accentuate the theme of personal redemption. It may indeed be the case that these people have actually had more experiences in their lives that objectively were redemptive, which perhaps has contributed over time to their well-being. It is also possible that their overall positive outlooks on life to begin with predispose them to see their past in redemptive terms, reflecting a cultural narrative that tends to be linked, in American society, to the good life. Most likely, both possibilities hold truth. Life stories reflect real lived experience; but as imaginative reconstructions of the past and anticipations of the future, life stories also reflect personal styles and biases in recollecting, anticipating, and narrating that experience.

It is important to note that the redemption theme in life stories is not itself reducible to the simpler idea of overall emotional positivity. To address the suggestion that redemption sequences are just "happy" stories and that people who tell happy stories will be happier, we coded the students' narrative accounts for the positivity of emotional tone (McAdams et al., 2001). The coding for positive emotionality turned out to be only slightly positively correlated with redemption imagery. Positive emotional tone in the stories did indeed predict life well-being at a statistically significant level, though the correlation was very modest in magnitude. In multiple regression procedures we found that redemption sequences significantly predicted self-report life satisfaction and total Ryff scale scores while emotional tone itself failed to account for a significant portion of the variance in these well-being assessments. It would appear, therefore, that claiming a life story contains a good deal of redemptive imagery is not the same thing as claiming that that story has an overall positive emotional tone. There are many kinds of happy stories; some of them may be redemptive. Furthermore, in the student study, it is the prevalence of redemptive imagery in the story, rather than the story's positive emotional tone, that significantly predicts self-report well-being.

Redemption often involves the sense of overcoming. "We shall overcome" was a great rallying cry of the American Civil Rights movement. The idea of redemption has always had an especially powerful meaning in the African-American community. The movement from slavery to emancipation may be the ultimate redemptive form. It is interesting to note, furthermore, that the same move is at the heart of Judeo-Christian religious traditions more generally, as in the book of Exodus for the Jews — God frees them from their Egyptian captors — and more symbolically perhaps in the New Testament, as Christ liberates people from their original sins, his death and rebirth suggesting a redemptive move that functions to redeem the world.

I recently completed a purely qualitative, in-depth analysis of life story interviews conducted with a group of 35 African-American adults, from which Tanya Williams and Jerome Johnson were chosen (McAdams, in press). Drawn from a large survey sample (Hart, McAdams, Hirsch, & Bauer, 2001), 21 of these 35 adults were chosen to be interviewed by virtue of their extremely high scores on self-report measures of what Erikson (1963) called *generativity*, and the other 14 subjects were chosen because they scored so low on generativity. Erikson described generativity as an adult's concern for and commitment to the well-being of the next generation, as evidenced in parenting, teaching, mentoring, and engaging in life activities aimed at leaving a positive legacy of the self for the future. According to Erikson, generativity is an especially salient psychosocial concern in the midlife years. Like any such concern, however, generativity shows substantial variability in the population (McAdams & de St. Aubin, 1998). Individual differences in generativity have been linked to a wide range of social behaviors, such as effective parenting styles and productive involvement in religious, community, and civic organizations (McAdams & de St. Aubin, 1998).

The goal of the qualitative study was to compare and contrast the life stories told by a small group of highly generative African-American adults to those told by less-generative African-American adults. How do people who have given over a considerable part of themselves to promoting the welfare of the next generation (highly generative adults) make sense of their own lives — past, present, and future? Among the 21 highly generative African-American adults we interviewed, redemption was an especially salient idea. For example, 13 of the 21 (61%)

described their single most important turning point scene in strikingly redemptive terms (as in the case of Jerome Johnson), whereas only 2 of the 14 turning point scenes (14%) described by the low generativity adults (of which Tanya Williams is a representative) showed redemption. The theme of redemption was so pervasive in some of the life stories of highly generative African-American adults that it occasionally served as something of a life credo. One highly generative black woman — a 45-year-old divorced mother of one, employed as a marketing research manager — concluded her interview by stating: "the negativeness and the badness of the things I had to overcome emotionally, you know, the dealing with the lies [of men] and the different things that he [her husband] said, um, it made me a better person, a stronger person; um, it sort of toughened me up." In her story, redemption came through hard-won struggles and considerable pain at the hands of abusive antagonists in her life. "That's not the way I would have chosen to get here, but it did force a lot of growth," she remarked. Her religious faith has promoted her movement forward: "salvation is what helps me grow and to rise above." Another highly generative woman — 61 years old, divorced, employed by the telephone company — concluded that "any person with a little knowledge can turn their life around." For a 62-year-old accountant, married with one grown child, life began (literally) as a kind of redemption scene: his birth was the result of his mother's being raped. What follows from childhood through midlife is one harrowing scene after another, culminating in the protagonist's recovery from a nearly fatal stab wound. "I was dead but the doctors brought me back alive." "My philosophy of life," he said, "has always been to be positive instead of negative on any circumstances you deal with." "If you go with positive ideas, you'll progress; if you get involved in the negative, you'll drown."

Findings from the qualitative study of life stories told by African-American adults are consistent with other studies showing that redemption sequences are associated with high levels of generativity. McAdams and colleagues (1997) examined the life stories of 40 highly generative adults, chosen from a pool of teachers and community volunteers, and 30 less generative adults who were matched on demographic characteristics. The highly generative adults showed higher scores on redemption imagery as coded in turning-point scenes, low-point scenes, and in life-story chapters compared to their less generative counterparts. Conversely, they showed fewer contamination sequences in life narrative accounts, compared to less generative adults.

The redemption theme may be part of a larger story about how the self engages the world in a progressive manner over time, a story that features a protagonist who continues to move forward in life with direction and purpose, even in the face of obstacles. Indeed, the obstacles are necessary for the story's upward thrust. There must be suffering if redemption is to occur. In McAdams and colleagues (1997) we identified a narrative prototype that more closely characterized the stories told by the 40 highly generative adults compared to the 30 less-generative adults. We called the prototype a *commitment story*. In the prototypical commitment story, the protagonist (1) enjoys an early family blessing or advantage, (2) is sensitized to others' suffering at an early age, (3) is guided by a clear and compelling personal ideology that remains stable over time, (4) transforms or redeems bad scenes into good outcomes (redemption sequences), and (5) sets goals for the future to benefit society and the next generation.

For a moment, imagine that you are the protagonist in this generic and idealized commitment story. The story begins with your receiving a lucky break, a special advantage, a family blessing. Maybe mom liked you best. Maybe you learn early on that you have a special talent. You are fortunate. But others are not. You witness suffering; you see and are affected by the misfortunes of others. (Highly generative adults were over four times more likely to recall spontaneously the suffering of others in childhood, compared to less generative adults.) By the time you are a teenager, you have a firm understanding of what is right and wrong in the world, a clear set of values, perhaps religiously based, perhaps not, that have guided your life to the present day. You have remained steadfast in those values, throughout the many changes in your life. Over time, bad things happen, but good outcomes have often been the result (the redemption sequence). As you look to the future today, you anticipate achieving goals that will both promote your own personal agenda and have a positive impact on your world.

The commitment story would appear to be an especially well-designed identity format for a generative life in contemporary America — a very good kind of narrative identity to have if you are a highly generative person (McAdams, in press). Believing that you are the fortunate protagonist, the chosen one, in the wake of others' suffering sets up a moral challenge, to be of good use to others, to feel that one is "called" to leave a positive legacy for generations to come. The protagonist of the commitment story makes strong generative commitments with the confidence that comes from knowing deep down what is good and right, and having known that same thing for a very long time. Especially powerful in the story is the redemption theme — when bad things turn good. Redemption sequences may sustain what Erikson once called the adult's "belief in the species" — a faith in the worthwhileness of human endeavors in the long run. Redemption sequences affirm the hope that suffering and hard work today will eventually be redeemed into good things in the future, perhaps for my children, and maybe for generations after that.

There are many ways to live, many kinds of life stories to tell, even among highly generative adults. But the commitment story — with its emphasis on being chosen early on, witnessing the suffering of those others not chosen, establishing clear values that remain stable over time, redeeming bad scenes into good outcomes, and optimistically construing the future in terms of progress and hope — recaptures a number of enduring ideas in American cultural history (e.g., Bellah, Madsen, Sullivan, Swidler, & Tipton, 1985; Cushman, 1995). It is worth considering the extent to which this kind of story resonates with the cultural narratives that Americans have traditionally held dear. John Winthrop and the pilgrims who settled Massachusetts in the 17th century explicitly described themselves as the chosen people of God, like the Old Testament Israelites, blessed with a special advantage, called to enact a morality tale in which redemption and progress — the Pilgrim's Progress — were to be the ultimate result. In his celebrated study of 19th-century American life, Tocqueville was impressed with how Americans unambivalently embraced the Enlightenment idea of progress and translated it into linear, goal-directed lives that were high on commitment and conviction but low on self-reflection. The commitment story speaks, on a personal level, to the American idea of manifest destiny, Westward expansion. In the New World, one could always move on, the folklore suggested, for redemption always lay 100 miles to the west.

American character may be less imperialistic today but perhaps no less redemptive and progressive in the way it is told in story, including the life stories of contemporary American adults. One can see similar patterns between the commitment stories told by highly generative adults and the kinds of stories of lives that enjoy increasing currency today in everyday discourse, in self-help books and advice manuals, among therapists and preachers, at AA meetings and town hall meetings (e.g., Maruna, 2001), in the stories politicians tell about their lives (think Ronald Reagan, Bill Clinton), and on television talk shows. It is a kind of narrative that is both steeped in American traditions and reflective of the post-modern sensibilities of the 21st century (Gergen, 1992). It is the story of the redemptive self. This kind of story trumps contamination by reframing it as the suffering that is necessary for redemption ultimately to occur. This is the kind of story that Tanya Williams longs for. "I am desperately seeking myself," she says. At the end of her interview, she asks the interviewer to offer her something in return for her story, something beyond the honorarium we pay our subjects, something like advice or a suggestion. Tanya calls it a "stepping stone." "Could you give me a stepping stone?" She asks for a lucky break, a turn of events, a piece of wisdom that might jumpstart a progressive process, that might provide her with the first *step* along the path to a better place. Tanya holds out hope for redemption. In that way, she hints at a narrative identity that resonates deeply with the American soul.

REFERENCES

Arnett, J. J. (2000). Emerging adulthood: A theory of development from the late teens through the twenties. *American Psychologist, 55*, 469–480.

Barresi, J., & Juckes, T. J. (1997). Personology and the narrative interpretation of lives. *Journal of Personality, 65*, 693–719.

Bellah, R. N., Madsen, K., Sullivan, W. M., Swidler, A., & Tipton, S. M. (1985). *Habits of the heart*. Berkeley, CA: University of California Press.

Blasi, A. (1988). Identity and the development of the self. In D. K. Lapsley & F. C. Power (Eds.), *Self, ego, identity: Integrative approaches* (pp. 226–242). New York: Springer-Verlag.

Bluck, S., & Levine, L. J. (1998). Reminscence as autobiographical memory: A catalyst for reminiscence theory development. *Ageing and Society, 18*, 185–208.

Breger, L. (1974). *From instinct to identity: The development of personality*. Englewood Cliffs, NJ: Prentice-Hall.

Brewer, W. F. (1986). What is autobiographical memory? In D. Rubin (Ed.), *Autobiographical memory* (pp. 25–49). New York: Cambridge University Press.

Bruner, J. S. (1990). *Acts of meaning.* Cambridge, MA: Harvard University Press.

Campbell, J. (1949). *The hero with a thousand faces.* New York: Bollingen Foundation.

Cohler, B. J. (1982). Personal narrative and the life course. In P. Baltes and O. G. Brim, Jr. (Eds.), *Life span development and behavior* (Vol. 4, pp. 205–241). New York: Academic Press.

Cohler, B. J., & Cole, T. R. (1994, June). *Studying older lives: Reciprocal acts of telling and listening.* Paper presented at the meeting of the Society for Personology, Ann Arbor, MI.

Conway, M. A., & Pleydell-Pearce, C. W. (2000). The construction of autobiographical memories in the self-memory system. *Psychological Review, 107,* 261–288.

Cushman, P. (1995). *Constructing the self, constructing America.* Reading, MA: Addison-Wesley.

Dennett, D. (1987). *The intentional stance.* Cambridge, MA.: The MIT Press.

Denzin, N. (1989). *Interpretive biography.* Newbury Park, CA: Sage.

Elkind, D. (1981). *Children and adolescents* (3rd Ed.). New York: Oxford University Press.

Erikson, E. H. (1959). Identity and the life cycle: Selected papers. *Psychological Issues, 1,* 5–165.

Erikson, E. H. (1963). *Childhood and society* (2nd Ed.). New York: Norton.

Fitzgerald, J. M. (1988). Vivid memories and the reminenscence phenomenon: The role of a self-narrative. *Human Development, 31,* 261–273.

Fivush, R. (1994). Constructing narrative, emotion, and self in parent-child conversations about the past. In U. Neisser & R. Fivush (Eds.), *The remembering self* (pp. 136–157). New York: Cambridge University Press.

Fivush, R., & Kuebli, J. (1997). Making everyday events emotional: The construal of emotion in parent-child conversations about the past. In N. L. Stein, P. A. Ornstein, B. Tversky, & C. Brainerd (Eds.), *Memory for everyday and emotional events* (pp. 239–266). Mahwah, NJ: Erlbaum.

Franz, C., & Stewart, A. J. (Eds.). (1994). *Women creating lives: Identities, resilience, and resistance.* Boulder, CO: Westview.

Gergen, K. J. (1992). *The saturated self: Dilemmas of identity in contemporary life.* New York: Basic Books.

Habermas, T., & Bluck, S. (2000). Getting a life: The emergence of the life story in adolescence. *Psychological Bulletin, 126,* 748–769.

Hart, H. M., McAdams, D. P., Hirsch, B. J., & Bauer, J. (2001). Generativity and social involvements among African Americans and white adults. *Journal of Research in Personality, 35,* 208–230.

Holstein, J. A., & Gubrium, J. F. (2000). *The self we live by: Narrative identity in a postmodern world.* New York: Oxford University Press.

Howe, M. L., & Courage, M. L. (1997). The emergence and early development of autobiographical memory. *Psychological Review, 104,* 499–523.

James, W. (1892/1963). *Psychology.* Greenwich, CT: Fawcett.

Josselson, R., & Lieblich, A. (Eds.). (1993). *The narrative study of lives* (Vol. 1). Thousand Oaks, CA: Sage.

Josselson, R., Lieblich, A., & McAdams, D. P. (Eds.). (2003). *Up close and personal: The teaching and learning of narrative research.* Washington, D.C.: American Psychological Association.

Kagan, J. (1994). *Galen's prophecy.* New York: Basic Books.

Mandler, J. M. (1984). *Stories, scripts, and scenes: Aspects of schema theory.* Hillsdale, NJ: Erlbaum.

Marcia, J. E. (1980). *Identity in adolescence.* In J. Adelson (Ed.), *Handbook of adolescent psychology* (pp. 159–187). New York: Wiley.

Markus, H., & Kitayama, S. (1991). Culture and the self: Implications for cognition, emotion, and motivation. *Psychological Review, 98,* 224–253.

Maruna, S. (2001). *Making good: How ex-convicts reform and rebuild their lives.* Washington, D.C.: American Psychological Association.

McAdams, D. P. (1982). Experiences of intimacy and power: Relationships between social motives and autobiographical memory. *Journal of Personality and Social Psychology, 42,* 292–302.

McAdams, D. P. (1985). *Power, intimacy, and the life story: Personological inquiries into identity.* New York: Guilford Press.

McAdams, D. P. (1993). *The stories we live by: Personal myths and the making of the self.* New York: William Morrow.

McAdams, D. P. (1995). What do we know when we know a person? *Journal of Personality, 63,* 365–396.

McAdams, D. P. (1996a). Personality, modernity, and the storied self: A contemporary framework for studying persons. *Psychological Inquiry, 7,* 295–321.

McAdams, D. P. (1996b). Narrating the self in adulthood. In J. Birren, G. Kenyon, J. E. Ruth, J. J. F. Shroots, & J. Svendson (Eds.), *Aging and biography: Explorations in adult development* (pp. 131–148). New York: Springer.

McAdams, D. P. (1997). The case for unity in the (post)modern self: A modest proposal. In R. Ashmore & L. Jussim (Eds.), *Self and identity: Fundamental issues* (pp. 46–78). New York: Oxford University Press.

McAdams, D. P. (1999). Personal narratives and the life story. In L. Pervin & O. John (Eds.), *Handbook of personality: Theory and research* (2nd ed., pp. 478–500). New York: Guilford Press.

McAdams, D. P. (2001). The psychology of life stories. *Review of General Psychology, 5,* 100–122.

McAdams, D. P. (in press). *The redemptive self: A narrative psychology of American identity. Stories Americans live by.* New York: Oxford University Press.

McAdams, D. P., & Bowman, P. J. (2001). Narrating life's turning points: Redemption and contamination. In D. P. McAdams, R. Josselson, & A. Lieblich (Eds.), *Turns in the road: Narrative studies of lives in transition* (pp. 3–34). Washington, D.C.: American Psychological Association.

McAdams, D. P., & de St. Aubin, E. (Eds.). (1998). *Generativity and adult development: How and why we care for the next generation.* Washington, D.C.: American Psychological Association.

McAdams, D. P., Diamond, A., de St. Aubin, E., & Mansfield, E. (1997). Stories of commitment: The psychosocial construction of generative lives. *Journal of Personality and Social Psychology, 72,* 678–694.

McAdams, D. P., Hoffman, B. J., Mansfield, E. D., & Day, R. (1996). Themes of agency and communion in significant autobiographical scenes. *Journal of Personality, 64,* 339–378.

McAdams, D. P., Reynolds, J., Lewis, M. L., Patten, A., & Bowman, P. T. (2001). When bad things turn good and good things turn bad: Sequences of redemption and contamination in life narrative, and their relation to psychosocial adaptation in midlife adults and in students. *Personality and Social Psychology Bulletin, 27,* 474–485.

Miller, P. J. (1994). Narrative practices: Their role in socialization and self-construction. In U. Neisser & R. Fivush (Eds.), *The remembering self* (pp. 158–179). New York: Oxford University Press.

Nelson, K. (1988). The ontogeny of memory for real events. In U. Neisser & E. Winograd (Eds.), *Remembering reconsidered* (pp. 244–276). New York: Cambridge University Press.

Pillemer, D. B. (1998). *Momentous events, vivid memories.* Cambridge, MA: Harvard University Press.

Ricoeur, P. (1984). *Time and narrative.* Chicago: University of Chicago Press.

Robinson, J. A., & Taylor, L. R. (1998). Autobiographical memory and self-narratives: A tale of two stories. In C. P. Thompson, D. J. Hermann, D. Bruce, J. D. Read, D. G. Payne, & M. P. Toglia (Eds.), *Autobiographical memory: Theoretical and applied perspectives* (pp. 125–143). Mahwah, NJ: Erlbaum.

Rosenwald, G. C. (1992). Conclusion: Reflections on narrative self-understanding. In G. C. Rosenwald & R. L. Ochberg (Eds.), *Storied lives: The cultural politics of self-understanding* (pp. 265–289). New Haven, CT: Yale University Press.

Ross, M. (1997). Validating memories. In N. L. Stein, P. A. Ornstein, B. Tversky, & C. Brainerd (Eds.), *Memory for everyday and emotional events* (pp. 49–81). Mahwah, NJ: Erlbaum.

Rubin, D. C., Wetzler, S. E., & Nebes, R. D. (1986). Autobiographical memory across the lifespan. In D. C. Rubin (Ed.), *Autobiographical memory.* New York: Cambridge University Press.

Ryff, C. D. (1989). Happiness is everything, or is it? Explorations in the meaning of psychological well-being. *Journal of Personality and Social Psychology, 57,* 1069–1081.

Schacter, D. L. (1996). *Searching for memory: The brain, the mind, and the past.* New York: Basic Books.

Shotter, J., & Gergen, K. J. (Eds.). (1989). *Texts of identity.* London: Sage.

Singer, J. A., & Salovey, P. (1993). *The remembered self.* New York: Free Press.

Stein, N. L., Wade, E., & Liwag, M. C. (1997). A theoretical approach to understanding and remembering emotional events. In N. L. Stein, P. A. Ornstein, B. Tversky, & C. Brainerd (Eds.), *Memory for everyday and emotional events* (pp. 15–47). Mahwah, NJ: Erlbaum.

Thompson, C. P., Skowronski, J. J., Larsen, S. F., & Betz, A. L. (Eds.). (1996). *Autobiographical memory: Remembering what and remembering when.* Mahwah, NJ: Erlbaum.

Thorne, A. (2000). Personal memory telling and personality development. *Personality and Social Psychology Review, 4,* 45–56.

Tomasello, M. (2000). Culture and cognitive development. *Current Directions in Psychological Science, 9,* 37–40.

Triandis, H. C. (1997). Cross-cultural perspectives on personality. In R. Hogan, J. Johnson, & S. Briggs (Eds.), *Handbook of personality psychology* (pp. 439–464). San Diego, CA: Academic Press.

Welch-Ross, M. K. (1995). An integrative model of the development of autobiographical memory. *Developmental Review, 15,* 338–365.

6

The Integrative Function of Narrative Processing: Autobiographical Memory, Self-Defining Memories, and the Life Story of Identity

JEFFERSON A. SINGER
Connecticut College

PAVEL BLAGOV
Emory University

*I*n the first author's psychotherapy practice, a man I will call James (not his actual name) came to see me on the advice of his former girlfriend. She had told him that he should pursue psychotherapy to work on his difficulty with expressing any vulnerability or sense of commitment in relationships. James explained to me that she was not the first woman to express this frustration with him. In fact he had developed a pattern of "shutting down" and withdrawing from intimacy in each successive long-term relationship that he had entered. As I took his history and learned more about him in the first weeks of our work together, it became clear that he had grown up in a family that was highly defended against emotion and intimate communication. His father had died when he was 6, and he had virtually no memories of his family mourning together. He described his mother and older sisters as doing their best to go on with their lives and hardly ever looking back to recognize or express their loss. He claimed that his father

117

was seldom mentioned in the family nor could he recall seeing his mother or sisters cry.

As we focused on his current problems with romantic relationships, and especially his passivity and inability to express his feelings, I raised the obvious connection to his family's stoic style of communication. At that moment he told me of a memory that suddenly came to him and, as he did, tears welled up in his eyes and then flowed freely as he described the memory's events.

One of his elementary school friends was having a hard time at home and happened to mention it to James. James, trying to show solidarity with his friend, agreed that the friend's father was being unfair. Suddenly, the friend turned on James and asked him how he would know since he didn't have a father. James was crushed, but said nothing. He went home that afternoon and kept the conversation to himself. That night he lay awake in his bed, sobbing over what his friend had said. His oldest sister must have heard him eventually and came into his room to check on him. She helped calm him down and he finally went to sleep. He recalled a mixture of gratitude for her comfort and embarrassment at his tears. The next day they did not speak of the episode.

In telling the memory to me, James attempted to minimize his current tears and to present the events in a slightly bemused tone. What was very apparent, however, was the power of this one specific memory to express major themes of James's identity. To show vulnerability and express sorrow were taboo behaviors, to acknowledge loss was to risk opening up a floodgate of pain that no one in the family felt equipped to endure. This brief narrative had become a touchstone experience in James's self-understanding, and more than any wordy interpretation could, it captured compactly and expressively his problem with the risks that intimate relationships demand. In subsequent weeks of therapy, James and I could make reference to this memory as a shorthand example of his fear of intimacy. In fact, the image of a boy hiding his tears in his darkened room became an extremely useful metaphor in our conversations.

James's boyhood memory of his friend's remark is what I have previously described as a "self-defining memory" (Singer, 1995; Singer & Moffitt, 1991–1992; Singer & Salovey, 1993). My interest in these affectively intense and vivid memories first emerged during my work on a study of the cardiovascular patterns of different affective states (Schwartz, Weinberger, & Singer, 1981). In this research, we asked individuals to recall a past event that evoked strong emotion in them and then to "re-live" this event in their minds. Though the ebb and flow of their systolic and diastolic blood pressures in response to these internal stimuli was a remarkable phenomenon, I found myself equally astonished by the participants' capacity to recall and become fully engrossed in their personal memories. I soon learned that I needed to have a box of tissues on hand for participants who received my request for sad memories. I also watched with a bit of concern as participants' necks reddened, jaws clenched, and fists balled up when they re-lived memories of anger and rage.

I came away from this research determined to gain a better understanding of why certain memories could have such an enduring and emotional hold over individuals. In time, I also began to wonder about the very nature of these memories: Where do they fit within the human information processing system? What are their structural features and organization? What role do they play in the overall personality and sense of identity that define us as unique individuals?

These questions have guided my research on self-defining memories in the two decades since. Self-defining memories have the following five characteristics:

1. Vivid
2. Affectively intense
3. Repetitively recalled
4. Linked to other similar memories
5. Focused on an enduring concern or unresolved conflict of the personality

Vividness and Affective Intensity

These memories have a strong sensory quality, usually visual, for the participants who recall them. When asking for vividness ratings on a 0–6 point scale, I have found that the mean value over numerous studies is at least 4.5 and often higher. Participants will describe the memory as having the quality of a "movie inside their heads" or a powerful evocative daydream. Similarly, individuals indicate that these memories have the power to affect them emotionally not just in the past, but also at the very moment of recollection. Ratings of specific emotions of happiness, anger, sadness, and pride often reach 5 and 6 on the previously mentioned rating scale.

Repetitively Recalled

Individuals return to these memories as touchstones in their lives; they are useful sources of information about what they want or don't want in their lives. They are commonly retrieved to serve as reference points to provide guidance or reinforcement with respect to specific current situations in the individuals' lives. In my discussions with numerous research participants and psychotherapy clients over the years, individuals will use the following language, "Whenever I am down, I will think of that memory of . . . and it will cheer me up" or "Before a big game [performance] [test] [meeting], I will recall that memory and it will make a big difference in my attitude." This same process can also work in a more negative direction as when individuals explain to me, "Every time I try to make peace with my dad, I can't help but recall my memories of the times he hurt me" or "Each time I try to overcome my fear, I remember the time that I . . . ."

Linked to Other Similar Intense Memories

This property consists of what Silvan Tomkins (1979) called "psychological magnification." With the exception of traumatic sudden events in one's life, usually the life events that become self-defining for the personality are ones that have been repeated over time with similar patterns and affective responses. An individual's sense of mastery or failure grows out of an accumulation of linked experiences that reinforce this self-perception. As Tomkins suggested, the repetition of events with similar outcomes and affective sequences magnifies their significance within the self and leads to the development of schemas based in these patterns. We may then tend to perceive new events through the lens of these schemas and create self-fulfilling interactions that further reinforce these "scripts" in our lives. Self-defining memories, to the extent that they capture characteristic and significant aspects of individuals' self-understanding, are likely to be connected to a network of related memories that share similar goals, concerns, outcomes, and affective responses.

Unresolved Conflicts or Enduring Concerns

Finally, self-defining memories connect to more than the transitory interests or activities of individuals. Given their enduring relevance and affective intensity for individuals, these memories reflect long-term and central areas of concern or conflict within the personality. These memories often touch on the timeless themes that shape individuals' unique sense of identity — conflicts with parents, love relationships lost or gained, sibling rivalries, personal failures or triumphs, moments of personal discovery or insight, moments of ethnic, racial or gender awareness, and so forth.

In order to test out these assumptions about the role of self-defining memories in personality, my colleagues and I developed a methodology for collecting self-defining memories and examining their relationships to both goals and affect (Moffitt & Singer, 1994; Singer, 1990; Singer & Moffitt, 1991–1992). We have also examined the role of self-defining memories, and autobiographical memories in general, in mood regulation and motivation (Josephson, Singer, & Salovey, 1996; Moffitt, Singer, Nelligan, Carlson, & Vyse, 1994). Through analysis of self-defining memories raised by clients during the course of psychotherapy, we have also explored their efficacy as a source of understanding and evocative communication between client and therapist (Singer, 2004; Singer & Blagov, 2004; Singer & Salovey, 1996; Singer & J. L. Singer, 1992, 1994).

In this book on advances in our understanding of the relationship of memory and self, we would like to return to my original questions about self-defining memories. How do certain memories, among the countless we experience in life, come to have an enduring and influential hold over us? What are the structural features and organization of these memories in a system of autobiographical memory? And what is the unique role of these memories in the individual personality? Why indeed does a memory bring tears to James's eyes, while simultaneously revealing core concerns of his sense of identity and capacity for intimacy?

Due to the exciting progress in the fields of cognitive and personality psychology, our ability to answer these questions has changed dramatically in the 20 years since these inquiries were first raised. Our goal in this chapter is to locate self-defining memories in two contemporary and complementary models of autobiographical memory and personality. To accomplish this task, we describe advances in current conceptions of personality and modes of information processing. Building on these ideas, we then explicate the relationship between a model of autobiographical memory and a model of personal identity.

Our governing thesis is that self-defining memories are a subset of "narrative processing," or storied thought (Singer & Bluck, 2001). Narrative processing has the capacity to integrate the cognitive, affective, and motivational subsystems of the personality in the service of unified functional goals. To elucidate the connection of narrative memories to specific goals of the personality, we draw on Conway and Pleydell-Pearce's (2000) model of autobiographical memory and the self. What distinguishes self-defining memories from other narrative memories, which are also linked to goals in the self-system, is the relationship of self-defining memories to goals that reflect central themes of identity within the personality. By "Identity," we mean the system of the personality that is responsible for creating an overall sense of coherence and meaning within the individual life. In the framework we describe, identity is synonymous with the autobiographical narrative individuals construct to weave together their past, present, and anticipated future into a unified whole (McAdams, 1985, 1990, 2001a).

Finally, individuals' capacity to use narrative processing to connect significant episodes from their past with an ongoing life story allows for the development of autobiographical reasoning, which Staudinger (2001) asserts is the foundation of wisdom about a given life and life in general. To trace the route a particular self-defining memory takes from recollection to the end point of life wisdom, we begin with a definition of personality.

PERSONALITY AS A SYSTEM

To define the unique contribution of self-defining memories to personality, we will first need a working conception of personality. In his summary of key issues in contemporary personality theory and research, Pervin (1999) contrasts approaches that emphasize personality processes or "parts" versus perspectives that take the "whole" of personality into account (p. 693). For example, Mischel and Shoda (1999) offer a representative definition of personality from a systems perspective. Personality consists of a set of psychological processes ". . . that are dynamically interconnected within an organized set of relationships, a unique network that functions as an organized whole that interacts with the social-psychological situations in which the system is activated and contextualized" (p. 199).

Systems perspectives on personality can vary in which aspects of systems interaction they emphasize; for example Magnusson (1999) is largely concerned with the person–environment interface, while Little (1999) targets purposeful action that is a major output of the personality system. Magnusson (1999, p. 220) also notes that systems approaches can ask questions about current functioning (synchronic perspective), the developmental history of the system in a given individual (diachronic perspective), or the development of the system across the whole species (evolutionary perspective).

In our analysis of self-defining memories, we will emphasize the interaction of intraindividual psychological processes from a current functioning or synchronic perspective. In applying a systems view of personality, we emphasize the following principles that apply to all working systems (Schwartz, 1990; von Bertalanffy, 1968). Every system contains a hierarchical structure that organizes its levels from most simple to most complex; complex functioning of the system depends upon the satisfactory functioning of each successive level of the system. Systems exist for functional purposes; a system has at least one dedicated goal toward which its effective functioning will carry it. To achieve this goal, the system integrates its various subsystems into united and synchronized responses that meet the demands of goal pursuit. All systems rely upon communication or feedback within and across the level of the system; this exchange of information allows for activation, termination, or maintenance of activity at each level. Positive feedback loops lead to the activation or acceleration of system activity; negative feedback loops indicate that current activity can be dampened or shut down. Finally, systems rely on an executive control function that converts the system's intended purpose into a sequence of information and action across the levels of the system; this executive control also continually evaluates the status of the system in its goal pursuit. One only needs to think about the integrated coordination of the various subsystems of an automobile to capture the complexity and elegance of a working system. Ignition, engine, cooling, and exhaust systems all combine in service of the steering and braking systems, which translate the complex symbolic intentions of the driver into the planful pursuit of travel to a particular destination.

These fundamental systems principles may be summarized as:

Integration of subsystems into a unified whole through feedback mechanisms
Hierarchical organization of subsystems
Dedication of the system toward a functional goal
Executive control system that monitors and evaluates the overall system's
  goal status

In applying a systems perspective to personality and the role of self-defining memories within the personality, we focus on the interaction of the three most directly relevant systems, cognition, affect, and motivation, leaving aside discussion of the psychophysiological and behavioral systems, which mediate the interaction of the person with internal or external physical cues. Our argument can be summarized in the following way. The role of the personality system within the individual is to achieve the coordinated integration of thoughts, feelings, and behaviors in the pursuit of goals that become active in given person–environmental interactions. The priorities assigned to the various goals that may be activated and that require responses from the personality system are ultimately dictated by the executive control system, which we submit is the role that *identity* plays in personality. McAdams (2001a) writes that identity performs the function of integrating the various aspects of the personality:

It brings together skills, values, goals and roles into a coherent whole. It brings together what the person can and wants to do with what opportunities and constraints for action exist in the social environment. It brings together aspects of the remembered past with the experienced present and anticipated future. (p. 643)

In the hierarchical organization of personality, self-defining memories are momentary expressions of identity that are activated in the service of its integrating function. The revival of a self-defining memory and its consideration in consciousness integrates the cognitive, affective, and motivational systems into a unified entity that allows the personality as a whole to focus on a specific functional priority, as determined by one's sense of identity.

The engine of integration that links memories and identity in this effective and focused way is a subsystem of the Cognitive System – what we call "narrative processing." Not only are self-defining memories critical narratives we recall about our lives, but also identity itself can be understood as an unfolding narrative or life story (McAdams, 1985, 1990, 1993, 2001b). Our capacity to translate information processed cognitively into "storied thought" is our means of linking specific past experiences to the enduring concerns of the overall personality system, as expressed through a sense of coherent and ongoing narrative identity. Although most autobiographical memories that remain with us take on a narrative form, it is the particular connection of self-defining memories to the most critical narrative themes of identity that differentiate them from other types of narrative memories. If narrative identity is the autobiographical text of an entire life, self-defining memories are uniquely eloquent passages that dramatize the major themes of the overarching narrative.

To understand how this last analogy actually works in the stream of conscious thought, it is necessary to examine the story-generating mode of information processing — narrative processing.

NARRATIVE PROCESSING IN THE PERSONALITY SYSTEM

The first three decades of the information-processing era in psychology, the 1950s–1970s, were dominated by what Bruner (1986) has called the "paradigmatic mode of thought." Paradigmatic thought seeks to create categories and identify abstract principles that underlie the entities to be classified. Pillemer (1998) offers this quote from Srull and Wyer (1990) as an example of the preference in psychology for abstract categorization,

Even undergraduates understand that the truly interesting question is how we ever come to represent abstractions from the particular world in which we live — to develop categories and impressions of *types* of people, *types* of situations and so on. (p. 166, cited in Pillemer, p. 5)

In contrast to this analytic and semantic mode, Bruner (1986), Polkinghorne (1988), and Sarbin (1986) have asserted their interest in a second distinct mode of thought, the *narrative mode*. Narrative thought organizes information not by abstract category or concept, but through the devices of story, including plot, intention, character, outcome, and theme. For example, if asked about the outcome of last fall's soccer season, a coach might reply that, "We were 6 and 6 with a young team and an inexperienced goalie." Alternatively, the coach might say, "In our last game, our young players finally came together as a team. They were down by a goal, but they rallied behind each other and finally pulled ahead. Our goalie, who was on a real learning curve this year, made a critical save and we managed to win, allowing us to make it to .500 for the season."

This second form of communication translates the same basic facts into a story, replete with plot twists, suspense, key characters, and an underlying moral or theme. This form of thought, what we call *narrative processing*, is not unique to the stories we tell each other in conversation or express in letters, diaries, and literature. Human beings employ narrative processing in their private thought about past experiences, daydreams, fantasies, and dreams (Singer & Bluck, 2001).

The importance of narrative in human thought has become a prominent theme in psychology in the last decade, though this emphasis can be traced back through the work of Tomkins (1979), Erikson (1959), Murray (1938), and Adler (1927) (for recent reviews on narrative approaches in personality, see McAdams, 1999, 2001b). Narrative processing vivifies ideas by linking cognitive material directly to the affect and motivation systems of the person. Once ideas are expressed in a storied form, they engage mental imagery, suspense, and a focus on goal-linked outcomes. The remembered story or the narrative fantasy is the closest we can come to engaging in an actual physical interaction without actually stepping forward and acting.

There is extraordinary evolutionary adaptive value to being able to "test the waters" psychologically before actually diving in and taking action. Human beings' capacity to listen to their own stories, as well as to share stories with others, must have marked a profound advance in our initial capacities to communicate to each other through language. We could not only say, "Be careful," to other people, but we could narrate a remembered encounter filled with imagery and emotion that would make our message even more convincing and compelling. It could tell us what was there, what form it took, what it made us feel like, and what we ought to do about it in the future. By engaging multiple systems of cognition, affect and motivation in the personality, narrative processing could direct attention and organize action in a way that allowed a more unified pursuit of specific goals to become active in consciousness.

To be even more precise, if we look at a contemporary definition of narrative offered by Gergen and Gergen (1988), we find embedded in this definition the three integrated systems of cognition, affect, and motivation. Narratives are based in the following criteria adapted from Gergen and Gergen (1988, pp. 19–22):

Establishment of a valued end point
Selection of events relevant to the goal state

Ordering of events
Establishing causal linkages
Demarcation signs

According to this definition, narrative processing harnesses the stream of consciousness and directs it to focus on a particular valued end. In establishing this end point, it selects a subset of relevant events that provide information about the status of an activated goal. This goal status (i.e., attained or not) triggers the quality and degree of affect experienced (e.g., triumphant joy, tragic loss, vengeful anger, etc.) The events that lead up to goal outcomes are placed in a temporal or sequential order that outlines a series of actions or activities that either enhance or obstruct attainment of the particular goal. By ordering events, inferences may be drawn about causal relationships of events within the narrative. Finally, narratives have beginnings, middles and ends; they thereby set parameters on the extent of goal pursuit, the duration of the affective experience and the distinctiveness of this particular narrative from others that might emerge in consciousness.

In this delineation of the specific properties of narrative processing, we can see how each subsystem of the personality is recruited to interact with the other subsystems.

In narrative processing of a past experience:

The cognitive system addresses the following questions,
    What is the content of the narrative?
    What is the structure or format of the narrative?

The affective system addresses the question,
    What feeling does this narrative evoke?

The motivational system addresses two distinct questions,
    What goals are active in the narrative?
    What function does this narrative serve for the person?

Over the years, our research on narrative memories has explored each of these five questions. In asking what a memory is about, we have relied on a variety of methods for coding the content of the memories (Singer, Sadler, & Musicant, 1995; Singer, Albert, Lally, Lizotte, Molina, & Scerzenie, 2000; for a recent content coding system, see Blagov & Singer, 2004; McLean & Thorne, 2001; Thorne, McLean, & Lawrence, 2004). These content coding procedures can divide memories by the connotative aspects of the memory (e.g., memories about sporting events, graduations, relationship issues, ethnic pride, etc.) or by denotative aspects (e.g., the coding of memories for underlying motives of intimacy, power, achievement, or generativity).

In asking about a memory's form, we have most often examined the degree of specificity present in a given memory narrative (Blagov & Singer, 2000, 2004; Moffitt et al., 1994; Singer & Moffitt, 1991–1992). According to well-established principles of human cognition, individuals tend to organize information according to increasing levels of abstraction or generality (see Gibson, 1979 for perceptual organization; Rosch, 1978 for concept formation; and Neisser, 1986, 1988 for memory organization). As discussed extensively in the work of Barsalou (1988) and Williams (1996; Williams & Broadbent, 1986), narrative memories can be evaluated for their reference to a unique event in time, an extended summary of several temporally linked events, or a generic amalgam of similar events repeated over discrete intervals of time.

Based on this research and our laboratory's earlier efforts to distinguish these different types of memory forms, we have recently developed a comprehensive manual for the categorization of narrative memory structure (Blagov & Singer, 2004; Singer & Blagov, 2000). Later in this chapter, we will report on some of our first research efforts to apply this scoring procedure to a sample of self-defining memories.

Most narrative memories, and especially self-defining memories, are hardly sterile communications about past events that inform us in a methodical manner about the content, time period, and location of previous experiences. To the contrary, they are affectively charged reconstructions of past events that have the power to shake our rational understanding of past experiences, bias our ongoing processing of information and intensify the importance of current events that bear similarities to the situations recollected in these memories. The affect system is clearly implicated in narrative memories and adds an evaluative dimension to every memory. Is the memory positive or negative (or both) in hedonic value and what is the intensity of the positive or negative affect associated with the memory? Of course, the particular affective value of a memory is not fixed; it can shift over time and vary depending on the situation in which it is recalled. Still, any full account of narrative memories must take into account their capacity to enlist strong responses from the affective system of the personality.

Finally, as with any aspect of thought or behavior generated by individuals, we can ask what purpose or function this particular product of thought, narrative memories, plays in the service of certain ends or active goals of the personality. The narrative in the memory highlights the status of a particular goal pursuit, which is the obvious plot engine that drives the particular story. In addition, Pillemer (1998, 2001), Staudinger (2001), and Habermas and Bluck (2000) have all written recently about the functional purposes served by recall of a particular memory. Pillemer (1992, 1998) has identified communicative functions related to rhetorical and persuasive devices in conversation, psychological functions that emphasize personal insight and mood regulation, and directive functions that highlight the use of memories as guides toward desired ends and away from unwanted outcomes. Staudinger (2001) perceives self-reflection about narrative memories as one form of autobiographical reasoning, which also includes life review in which individuals reflect about their lives as a whole, as opposed to about a specific self-defining memory.

Having established the integrative function that narrative processing performs for the overall personality in bringing together cognition, affect and motivation, we now turn to how one product of narrative processing, narrative memories, are retrieved from our overall autobiographical knowledge base. As we shall see, the key to retrieval of narrative memories from this base is their relationship to a hierarchy of goals in the personality.

NARRATIVE PROCESSING AND AUTOBIOGRAPHICAL MEMORY

It would appear that we have reached a reasonable answer to the question that began this chapter — Why do autobiographical memories have the power to move us to tears or laughter long after the originating events have passed and veridical details of the memory have faded? Autobiographical memories are a subset of narrative processing or storied thought that serves the particular function in consciousness of integrating the subsystems of personality to create an imagery-based approximation of goal pursuit preparatory to actual goal-directed behaviors. This linkage of an autobiographical knowledge base to the working goals of the self-system is in fact the fundamental premise of the landmark autobiographical memory model proposed by Conway and Pleydell-Pearce (2000) in a recent *Psychological Review* article.

Conway and Pleydell-Pearce propose an autobiographical knowledge base organized at three levels of specificity — event specific knowledge (sensory details, facts, and images), general events (categories of events linked across relatively brief time periods or organized by shared theme), and lifetime periods (large units of time in individuals' lives that reflect particular overarching goals and activities — e.g., early years of marriage, graduate school, or a period of financial hardship). In order to retrieve specific autobiographical memories, individuals must draw on the autobiographical knowledge indexed at these three levels and reconstruct the desired recollection. Conway and Pleydell-Pearce argue that the parameters for reconstruction and retrieval of these memories are set by the relevance of this autobiographical knowledge to goals activated within a working self-system. The working self-system, akin to working memory, is a temporarily activated self that consists of a particular hierarchy of goals. These goals then serve as retrieval cues for particular autobiographical memories. However, it is important to acknowledge the reciprocity of this memory-self relationship. Any particular hierarchy of goals activated within a working self will be limited by knowledge of previous experience with these goals and the outcomes that accrued.

Once memory-relevant goals are cued by internal or environmental stimuli, a search process for pertinent autobiographical knowledge is instantiated. Equally important for this self-memory model is that goal relevance also serves as a control process for terminating search activities. Once memories relevant to the activated goals are reconstructed and retrieved, a negative feedback mechanism in the working self shuts off the search process.

The working self-system and the autobiographical knowledge base are both components of an overarching self-memory system. This self-memory system encompasses the different subsystems of personality and putatively contains the ultimate hierarchy of long-term goals from which different working selves selectively draw their situationally contingent hierarchies. The self-memory system serves as the highest executive system of the personality and works to regulate affect and maintain relative equilibrium among the various subsystems of the person. Once a working self activates a goal-related search in the autobiographical knowledge base, the self-memory system guides the selection and elaboration of goal-relevant cues that access specific autobiographical memories, the evaluation of selected memories for goal compatibility, and the bringing forth of autobiographical knowledge into consciousness. The activation of particular memories is always weighed against the general needs of the overall self for affect regulation and maintenance of an acceptable self-concept. For example, as Conway and Pleydell-Pearce (2000, p. 268) note, when memories activated by a working self indicate a great discrepancy between the individual's resources and what is needed for goal attainment, the search process may be terminated to avoid intense disappointment or distress. Conway and Pleydell-Pearce write that the self-memory system draws on autobiographical knowledge to place ". . . consistency and plausibility constraints on what goals can be held by the working self" (p. 271). Additionally, the self-memory system must also respond to other processing demands that require attentional resources. Activation of a memory may be terminated when external stimuli require redirection of attention away from internal products of consciousness.

One question raised by the Conway and Pleydell-Pearce model is what might determine the particular importance of certain memories in the autobiographical knowledge base and of certain goals in any given working self. They present a few suggestions for consideration. Drawing on Higgins's (1987, 1989) self-discrepancy theory, they propose that individuals generate images of ideal, ought, and actual selves; goals and memories that most closely reflect the ought or ideal selves may be more affectively laden, as would be memories that most dramatically reflect discrepancies from these states. Although this explanation makes good sense, it takes us to a dead end in pursuit of our original question about why certain memories matter more than others. We are left to say only that individuals hold preferences for different self-images and that the value accorded to particular goals or memories are only a function of those preferences. Yet how do these preferences acquire their particular weight and importance to the self?

A second possibility and, what we find a more fruitful direction, is Conway and Pleydell-Pearce's suggestion that goals and memories in the self-memory system are particularly sensitive to developmental demands across the life span. At each stage of life, we are confronted with particular developmental challenges related to growth, autonomy, achievement, intimacy, generativity, acceptance of change, loss, and aging. These life milestones may indeed dictate dominant priorities within the self-memory system and encourage a reshuffling of goal-memory hierarchies. Conway and Pleydell-Pearce draw on this idea to account for phenomena like childhood amnesia and the reminiscence bump. With regard to childhood amnesia, the developmental priorities of adults are so massively discrepant from toddler and preschool children that there are virtually no relevant goal cues retained into adulthood that would allow us to reconstruct autobiographical knowledge from infancy. The result is a near total loss of specific memories from childhood.

The reminiscence bump is a widely noted cognitive phenomenon in which individuals older than 35 years tend to show better retention of memories from the period of 15 to 25 years old than any subsequent period with the exception of the most immediate years of recall (Rubin, Rahhal, & Poon, 1998; Rubin, Wetzler, & Nebes, 1986). Conway and Pleydell-Pearce (2000) suggest that the better retention for these adolescent and young adult memories is critically related to the individual's first consolidation of a sense of identity. This sense of identity incorporates enduring personal goals related to the major themes of achievement, power and intimacy that will dominate adult life (McAdams, 1985, 1990). Conway and Pleydell-Pearce also acknowledge adolescence as the point when individuals begin to organize autobiographical knowledge into a self-narrative that eventually becomes a life story account of personal identity (Habermas & Bluck, 2000; McAdams, 1990). The connection of particular memories from the reminiscence bump period to the origins of this overarching life story may give these memories a special prominence and enduring affective power in the self-memory system.

Although there may be a particular surge of memories from adolescence and young adulthood due to their linkage to identity formation, this developmental model clearly implies that other later memories linked to developmentally salient issues of later adulthood (e.g., parenthood, marital discord, career advancement, etc.) would also have the power to rise to the top of the self-memory hierarchy (for empirical support of this assertion, see Conway & Holmes, 2004).

One final point Conway and Pleydell-Pearce (2000) make with regard to this developmental argument is the influence of sociocultural and generational cohort effects. Certain memories may gain prominence in the self-memory system due to their connection to culturally significant events that coincide with individuals' own age cohort. For example, individuals who grew up in the 1960s may be more likely to retain memories of civil unrest or of confrontation with parents than individuals who grew up in the more complacent period of the 1980s. In a related vein, individuals who were raised in a more traditionally religious region of the United States, such as the Deep South, might place a more central importance on spiritual experiences than individuals raised in a more iconoclastic urban setting.

Having presented Conway and Pleydell-Pearce's model of autobiographical memory and the self, we can now return to an exploration of the particular power of self-defining memories in the personality. Narrative memories are linked to a hierarchy of goals within the self-memory system. This hierarchy of goals is in part determined by developmental and cultural factors related to the formation of a narrative identity that continues to evolve over the life span of the individual. We propose that self-defining memories are those memories that have the most relevance to the life story of identity fashioned by the individual. If this were the case, these memories would play a particularly important role in the self-memory system. They would be exactly those memories that make the most direct connection between the autobiographical knowledge base and the working self-system. Contained in their knowledge base would be both event specific detail and thematic commentary on the goal outcome for particularly critical questions of the life story ("What is it like to be loved?" "What happens to me when I take a risk in a career decision?" "How did I handle the death of a family member?").

NARRATIVE PROCESSING AND IDENTITY

To examine this proposed role for self-defining memories in the self-memory system, it would be useful to look more closely at a life story perspective on identity. Refined over the last two decades, McAdams's life story theory of identity (1985, 1987, 1990, 1993, 2001b) sees individuals as the authors of an elaborate and evolving autobiographical narrative that links together past, present and future aspects of the self, while providing a sense of purpose to thoughts and behaviors. Beginning in adolescence, we craft a personal story that identifies important archetypal characters, significant turning points, and imagined outcomes. This story, which we tell to ourselves and, in occasional intimate moments, to others, both links us to shared cultural values and differentiates us from every other person with whom we share the society. As McAdams suggests, our stories are not a result or by-product of our sense of identity, but rather the stories themselves constitute the primary means by which we express and understand who we are as individuals in a given epoch and society.

In his recent framework of personality, McAdams (1995, 1996) asserts that there are different levels by which we come to know a person and through which a person achieves self-knowledge. At the trait level, we learn about a person's decontextualized temperamental and behavioral tendencies. Trait measures, such as the Big Five (Costa & McCrae, 1992), offer a first pass at understanding a person and how they might behave across a variety of situations. However, this level of knowledge will be less effective in providing more specific information about how an individual will adapt to the demands of particular developmental, situational or role challenges, requirements, or both.

A characteristic adaptations level of understanding offers us an opportunity to evaluate individuals' social-cognitive responses to particular contextual presses. This level of personality analysis examines individuals' social motives (e.g., intimacy, power, achievement), coping styles (e.g., defensiveness, problem-focused behavior), goals (e.g., current concerns, personal strivings, life projects), and developmental responses (e.g., life tasks, ego identity styles, levels of generativity).

Finally, and most relevant to the present discussion, there is the Life Stories level of personality. At this level, research addresses the question of how individuals construct a sense of overall meaning and purpose from their life experiences. In effect, this level examines individuals' efforts to answer the questions, "Who am I?" and "What is the meaning I attribute to my life?" Although one could know a great deal about a person by identifying his or her temperamental or behavioral tendencies and their characteristic responses to particular situational and developmental demands, a full understanding of a person and his or her unique role in a given society would not seem possible without an examination of the personal narrative he or she offers to the world.

The life story expresses the individual's effort to step back from both goal pursuits and accumulated autobiographical knowledge and weave these two aspects of self-understanding into an overall coherent picture of the self. In other words, we are asserting that the self-memory system is not simply a mechanical regulatory system that measures self-goal discrepancies and automatically makes feedback adjustments. Building on Conway and Pleydell-Pearce's (2000) tentative linking of the self-memory system to the life story, we propose that the self-memory system is itself guided by an overarching life story narrative. Within this narrative, we define the balance in our lives between intimacy and power. We identify the archetypal individuals from our life who engender the strongest positive and negative affective reactions. We subscribe to an ideological setting that paints the overall tone of our stories as optimistic or pessimistic about the outcomes of our actions and surrounding events. We also come to identify particular episodes from our lives as eloquently expressive of what matters most to us in our personal stories. These episodes comprise our life turning points, peak and nadir experiences, and self-affirming incidents.

According to McAdams (1993), as our life stories evolve over a lifetime, we become increasingly concerned with the legacy that we will generate at our stories' appointed end. Individuals' stories turn to questions of lasting accomplishments, the impact they have had on offspring, and the contributions they have made to communities or institutions. These concerns often lead to a certain narrowing of focus in order to marshal energies toward a particular desired outcome. This more directed effort within the self-memory system might also account for the power of particular goals and memories that are relevant to these prominent generative concerns of the individual. Individuals can begin to define themselves by particular "central activities" of their lives (Fingarette, 1988; Singer, 1997, ch. 2), such as a specific occupation, parental role or community position. These overarching self-definitions tend to resonate across all other dimensions of individuals' lives, influencing their social relationships, leisure activities, and private thoughts. To understand the comprehensive power of these central activities, Fingarette suggests one perform the mental exercise of waking up one day with this central role vanished from one's life. How many other defining aspects of one's identity would be swept away by this sudden change? The reduction of side plots or digressions as the life story increases its focus may serve to intensify the power of particular narrative memories related to the central narrative.

THE RELATIONSHIP OF SELF-DEFINING MEMORIES TO NARRATIVE IDENTITY

By turning the diverse aspects of our personal experiences across the life span into a unified story, we repeat at a macro-level the same integrative activity achieved by the narrative processing of thoughts and images that emerge in the momentary stream of consciousness. That is, we link together the subsystems of personality — cognition, affect, and motivation and focus their organizing functions of categorization, evaluation, and goal selection in a concerted and directed fashion. This conception of identity as a life story, which in turn performs an executive control function in the system of personality, brings us to the conclusion of our quest for answers about self-defining memories. Self-defining memories retain their affective power over time due to their unique connection to the primary goals articulated by individuals' overarching life stories. Individuals' life stories are psychosocial constructions that respond to the developmental phases and cultural demands of a given life in a given societal epoch. As the goals salient in individuals' life stories shift over time, the relative power of self-defining memories to evoke feeling will also shift. Yet just as the characters of a fictional work retain a relative sameness and coherence over the course of the story, so too do actual persons stay true to certain defining concerns and interests. This consistency insures that certain self-defining memories will endure in meaning and affective intensity over a lifetime, despite developmental and cultural changes.

Regarding the structural features and organization of self-defining memories, we can conceptualize them as one form of narrative processing, the output of which is maintained and recollected from the autobiographical knowledge base, as guided by the goal hierarchies of shifting working selves. Self-defining memories may differ in specificity, depending on the extent of elaboration and search effort allocated by the self-memory system. Lack of specificity may reflect an attenuated connection to active goals or a more defensive avoidance in the interest of mood regulation and self-concept protection (for empirical support for this position, see Blagov & Singer, 2004). Finally, the unique role of self-defining memories would appear to be an efficient shorthand method of signaling to individuals the overarching themes of their larger life narrative. To use a crude analogy, they are the *Cliff Notes* of narrative identity.

Returning to the case study that began this chapter, in James's private sense of self, he has woven a life story of a boy overwhelmed with sadness who is not allowed to mourn, who fears that his own tears will drown him, and of a man who floats from relationship to relationship, withdrawing before the risk of loss could become palpable. In the self-defining memory he presented, he has captured his narrative identity's central conflict and desire — the recognition of loss, the pain of acknowledging it, and the wished-for comfort from a loved one. This memory belongs within the critical chapters of his life narrative and within the memory are this narrative's essential themes. The dynamic connection between the two is a function of the human information processing system's capacity to translate the events of our lives into a narrative structure that stores meaningful information both in memory and within the self.

AUTOBIOGRAPHICAL REASONING, SELF-DEFINING MEMORIES AND THE LIFE STORY

Before concluding, there is one final issue to consider — all narratives are implicitly dialogical (Hermans, 1996); they invoke a response from the self and others that have "read" or "listened' to them. Stories have audiences, real or imagined.

Unlike a mechanistic or thermostatic model of personality, any life story model of identity necessarily includes the concept of self-commentary and interpersonal response (Thorne, 2000). As creators of our life stories, we are also the audience and reviewer. Staudinger (2001) calls attention to the point that life reflection is more than simply reminiscence; it is reminiscence plus active analysis of the meanings extracted from a life review. In fact, Staudinger argues that a meaningful definition of "wisdom" is the capacity to reason about autobiographical experiences from one's life. She suggests that wise individuals do not simply re-live old memories, they use the memories for knowledge gathering ("epistemic function") and as catalysts for change ("emancipatory" function).

In addition to the narrative mode of processing, there is in fact a *paradigmatic* response that the self can make to the narratives it generates. In reviewing and then reacting to the stories they create, individuals turn their self-defining memories into exemplars of lessons to be learned and turning points to be highlighted. Put simply, one can ask what does my memory mean or what is the meaning of my life story? Such questions are the crux of Staudinger's life reflection and autobiographical reasoning. By making the connection of a narrative to an abstracted or ascribed meaning, individuals activate a positive feedback loop that promotes additional cognitive, motivational, and affective value of the memory to the self-memory system. The integrative meaning extracted from the memory offers further cognitive information beyond the experience of immediate memory recollection (i.e., how possible is goal attainment *of this type*?) and affective information (how does attainment *of this type* feel?). The combination of this knowledge may indeed motivate the individual more powerfully toward goal attainment, while the reinforcing role of memory insures its repeated revival into consciousness.

To examine this property of ascribed meaning in memory narratives, we have created a memory narrative scoring system that includes the identification of ascribed meanings in memory narratives (Blagov & Singer, 2004). We call these memory narratives with ascribed meaning statements, "integrative memories." We chose the term, "integrative," because the statements in these memories express linkages to other memories, overarching themes of identity, or both. Having developed our scoring system, we sought to demonstrate that individuals with optimal levels of life adjustment would display a tendency to report more self-defining memories with integrative statements contained within the narratives. To test this hypothesis, we asked 108 college student participants to fill out the Weinberger Adjustment Inventory — Short Form (WAI-SF, Weinberger, 1997) and to record 10 self-defining memories, using the standard self-defining memory request (Singer & Moffitt, 1991–1992). The WAI-SF measures effectiveness of social-emotional adjustment along two major factors: Distress and Self-Restraint. According to prior research with this scale, individuals who score in the moderate range tend to display the best life adjustment outcomes versus the low and high range self-restraint individuals.

The mean number of integrative self-defining memories for individuals with low, moderate, and high WAI-Restraint was compared with a Univariate ANOVA, which yielded a significant effect ($F (2, 100) = 4.03, p < 0.05$). Pairwise comparisons were consistent with the predicted pattern in the number of integrative memories for the moderate (M = 3.97) versus the low (M = 2.09, p = 0.006) and the high (M = 2.80, p = 0.083) self-restraint individuals. This finding offers valuable support for Staudinger's contentions about the connection between autobiographical reasoning and life effectiveness and wisdom.

To end this paper where we began, my goal in working with James is not simply to help him articulate his life story and to identify the most affectively evocative episodes from that story. Although the expression of his story, according to the theory we have presented, is, in and of itself, goal defining and motivating, this narrative demand for action and emotional response can be supplemented by paradigmatic insight and reasoning. As James reviews his story, he can begin to recognize the active role he plays as author. Having awoken his narrative muse, he can now ask how should this unfolding tale turn out? Through his work in therapy and increasing self-awareness, he may find the courage and inventiveness to write a different ending than he has seen before. If he takes the risk of intimacy and succeeds, both the content and the affective quality of the memories and the story that define him will inevitably change, as his life has already begun to change. The act of narrative processing, by engaging his thoughts, goals and emotions, has given him not only an opportunity to revive his past, but also offered him a tool of liberation to relinquish a story he no longer wants to tell, and to take his first steps toward a different and more satisfying self-defining story.

REFERENCES

Adler, A. (1927). *The practice and theory of individual psychology.* New York: Harcourt Brace World.

Barsalou, L. W. (1988). The content and organization of autobiographical memories. In U. Neisser & E. Winograd (Eds.), *Remembering reconsidered: Ecological and traditional approaches to the study of memory* (pp. 193–243). Cambridge, England: Cambridge University Press.

Blagov, P. S., & Singer, J. A. (2000, October). *Relationships between identity and social-emotional maturity: Self-defining memories, self-concept clarity, and self-restraint.* Paper presented at the meeting of the New England Psychological Association, Lewiston, ME.

Blagov, P. S., & Singer, J. A. (2004). Four empirically derived dimensions of self-defining autobiographical memories (structure, meaning, content, and affect) and their relationships to social-emotional maturity, distress, and repressive defensiveness. *Journal of Personality, 72,* 481–511.

Bruner, J. S. (1986). *Actual minds, possible worlds.* Cambridge, MA: Harvard University Press.

Conway, M. A., & Holmes, A. (2004). Psychosocial stages and the accessibility of autobiographical memories across the life cycle. *Journal of Personality, 72,* 481–511.

Conway, M. A., & Pleydell-Pearce, C. W. (2000). The construction of autobiographical memories in the self-memory system. *Psychological Review, 107,* 261–288.

Costa, P. T., & McCrae, R. R. (1992). *Professional manual for the Revised NEO Personality Inventory (NEO PI-R).* Odessa, FL: Psychological Assessment Resources.

Erikson, E. H. (1959). Identity and the life cycle: Selected papers. *Psychological Issues, 1,* 5–165.

Fingarette, H. (1988). *Heavy drinking: The myth of alcoholism as a disease.* Berkeley, CA: University of California Press.

Gergen, K., & Gergen, M. (1988). Narrative and the self as relationship. In L. Berkowitz (Ed.), *Advances in experimental social psychology* (Vol. 21, pp. 17–55). New York: Academic Press.

Gibson, J. J. (1979). *The senses considered as perceptual systems.* Boston: Houghton Mifflin.

Habermas, T., & Bluck, S. (2000). Getting a life: The emergence of the life story in adolescence. *Psychological Bulletin, 126,* 748–769.

Hermans, H. J. M. (1996). Voicing the self: From information processing to dialogical interchange. *Psychological Bulletin, 119,* 31–50.

Higgins, E. T. (1987). Self-discrepancy: A theory relating self and affect. *Psychological Review, 94,* 319–340.

Higgins, E. T. (1989). Continuities and discontinuities in self-regulatory and self-evaluating process: A developmental theory relating self and affect. *Journal of Personality, 57,* 407–444.

Josephson, B., Singer, J. A., & Salovey, P. (1996). Mood regulation and memory: Repairing sad moods with happy memories. *Cognition and Emotion, 10,* 437–444.

Little, B. R. (1999). Personality and motivation: Personal action and the conative evolution. In L. Pervin & O. John (Eds.), *Handbook of personality: Theory and research* (2nd ed., pp. 501–524). New York: Guilford Press.

Magnusson, D. (1999). Holistic interactionism: A perspective for research on personality development. In L. Pervin and O. John (Eds.), *Handbook of personality: Theory and research* (2nd ed., pp. 219–247). New York: Guilford Press.

McAdams, D. P. (1985). *Power, intimacy and the life story: Personological inquiries into identity.* New York: Guilford Press.

McAdams, D. P. (1987). A life-story model of identity. In R. Hogan & W. H. Jones (Eds.), *Perspectives in personality* (Vol. 2, pp. 15–50). Greenwich, CT: JAI Press.

McAdams, D. P. (1990). Unity and purpose in human lives: The emergence of identity as the life story. In A. I. Rabin, R. A. Zucker, R. A. Emmons, & S. Frank (Eds.), *Studying persons and lives* (pp. 148–200). New York: Springer.

McAdams, D. P. (1993). *The stories we live by: Personal myths and the making of the self.* New York: William Morrow.

McAdams, D. P. (1995). What do we know when we know a person? *Journal of Personality, 63,* 365–396.

McAdams, D. P. (1996). Personality, modernity and the storied self: A contemporary framework for studying persons. *Psychological Inquiry, 7,* 295–321.

McAdams, D. P. (1999). Personal narratives and the life story. In L. Pervin and O. John (Eds.), *Handbook of personality: Theory and research* (2nd ed., pp. 478–500). New York: Guilford Press.

McAdams, D. P. (2001a). *The person: An integrated introduction to personality psychology* (3rd ed.). Fort Worth, TX: Harcourt College.

McAdams, D. P. (2001b). The psychology of life stories. *Review of General Psychology, 5,* 100–122.

McAdams, D. P., Diamond, A., de St. Aubin, E., & Mansfield, E. (1997). Stories of commitment: The psychosocial constriction of generative lives. *Journal of Personality and Social Psychology, 72,* 678–694.

McAdams, D. P., Reynolds, J., Lewis, M. L., Patten, A. H., & Bowman, P. J. (2001). When bad things turn good and good things turn bad: Sequences of redemption and contamination in life narrative, and their relation to psychosocial adaptation in midlife adults and in students. *Personality and Social Psychology Bulletin, 27*, 474–485.

McLean, K. C., & Thorne, A. (2001). *Manual for coding meaning-making in self-defining memories.* Unpublished manuscript, University of California, Santa Cruz.

Mischel, W., & Shoda, Y. (1999). Integrating dispositions and processing dynamics within a unified theory of personality: The cognitive-affective personality system. In L. Pervin & O. John (Eds.), *Handbook of personality: Theory and research* (2nd ed., pp. 197–218). New York: Guilford Press.

Moffitt, K. H., & Singer, J. A. (1994). Continuity in the life story: Self-defining memories, affect, and approach/avoidance personal strivings. *Journal of Personality, 62*, 21–43.

Moffitt, K. H., Singer, J. A., Nelligan, D. W., Carlson, M. A., & Vyse, S. A. (1994). Depression and memory narrative type. *Journal of Abnormal Psychology, 103*, 581–583.

Murray, H. A. (1938). *Explorations in personality.* New York: Oxford University Press.

Neisser, U. (1986). Nested structure in autobiographical memory. In D. C. Rubin (Ed.), *Autobiographical memory* (pp. 71–81). New York: Cambridge University Press.

Neisser, U. (1988). What is ordinary memory the memory of? In U. Neisser & E. Winograd (Eds.), *Remembering reconsidered* (pp. 356–373). New York: Cambridge University Press.

Pervin, L. A. (1999). Epilogue: Constancy and change in personality theory and research. In L. Pervin and O. John (Eds.), *Handbook of personality: Theory and research* (2nd ed., pp. 689–704). New York: Guilford Press.

Pillemer, D. B. (1992). Remembering personal circumstances: A functional analysis. In E. Winograd & U. Neisser (Eds.), *Affect and accuracy in recall: Studies of "flashbulb" memories* (pp. 234–264). New York: Cambridge University Press.

Pillemer, D. B. (1998). *Momentous events, vivid memories.* Cambridge, MA: Harvard University Press.

Pillemer, D. B. (2001). Momentous events and the life story. *Review of General Psychology, 5*, 123–134.

Polkinghorne, D. (1988). *Narrative knowing and the human sciences.* Albany, NY: SUNY Press.

Rosch, E. (1978). Principles of categorization. In E. Rosch & B. B. Lloyd (Eds.), *Cognition and categorization* (pp. 29–47). Hillsdale, NJ: Erlbaum.

Rubin, D. C., Rahhal, T. A., & Poon, L. W. (1998). Things learned in early adulthood are remembered best. *Memory & Cognition, 26*, 3–19.

Rubin, D. C., Wetzler, S. E., & Nebes, R. D. (1986). Autobiographical memory across the lifespan. In D. C. Rubin (Ed.), *Autobiographical memory* (pp. 202–221). New York: Cambridge University Press.

Sarbin, T. (1986). The narrative as root metaphor for psychology. In T. Sarbin (Ed.), *Narrative psychology: The storied nature of human conduct* (pp. 3–21). New York: Praeger.

Schwartz, G. E. (1990). Psychobiology of repression and health: A systems approach. In J. L. Singer (Ed.), *Repression and dissociation* (pp. 405–434). Chicago: University of Chicago Press.

Schwartz, G. E., Weinberger, D. A., & Singer, J. A. (1981). Cardiovascular differentiation of happiness, sadness, anger, and fear following imagery and exercise. *Psychosomatic Medicine, 43*, 343–364.

Singer, J. A. (1990). Affective responses to autobiographical memories and their relationship to long-term goals. *Journal of Personality, 58*, 535–563.

Singer, J. A. (1995). Seeing one's self: Locating narrative memory in a framework of personality. *Journal of Personality, 63*, 429–457.

Singer, J. A. (1997). *Message in a bottle: Stories of men and addiction.* New York: Free Press.

Singer, J. A. (2004). A love story: The use of self-defining memories in couples therapy. In A. Lieblich, D. P. McAdams, & R. Josselson (Eds.), *Healing plots: The narrative basis of psychotherapy.* Washington, D.C.: American Psychological Association.

Singer, J. A., Albert, D., Lally, R., Lizotte, M., Molina, C., & Scerzenie, S. (2000). Gender and self-disclosure in self-defining memories. Agentic and communal themes. Unpublished manuscript, Department of Psychology, Connecticut College, New London, CT.

Singer, J. A., & Blagov, P. S. (2000, June). *Classification system and scoring manual for self-defining autobiographical memories.* Paper presented at the meeting of the Society for Applied Research on Memory and Cognition, Miami Beach, FL.

Singer, J. A., & Blagov, P. S. (2003). Self-defining memories, narrative identity, and psychotherapy: A conceptual model, empirical investigation, and case report. In L. E. Angus & J. McLeod (Eds.), *Handbook of narrative and psychotherapy: Practice, theory and research.* Thousand Oaks, CA: Sage.

Singer, J. A., & Bluck, S. (2001). New perspectives on autobiographical memory: The integration of narrative processing and autobiographical reasoning. *Review of General Psychology, 5*, 91–99.

Singer, J. A., & Moffitt, K. M. (1991–1992). An experimental investigation of generality and specificity in memory narratives. *Imagination, Cognition, and Personality, 10*, 235–258.

Singer, J. A., Sadler, I., & Musicant, J. (1995, July) *Personal and cultural implications of memories of racial/ethnic awareness and prejudice.* Presented at the Annual Meeting of the Society for Applied Research in Memory and Cognition, Vancouver, B.C., Canada.

Singer, J. A., & Salovey, P. (1993). *The remembered self: Emotion and memory in personality.* New York: The Free Press.

Singer, J. A., & Salovey, P. (1996). Motivated memory: Self-defining memories, goals, and affect regulation. In L. Martin, & A. Tesser (Eds.), *Striving and feeling.* New York: Erlbaum.

Singer, J. A., & Singer, J. L. (1992). Transference in psychotherapy and daily life: Implications of current memory and social cognition research. In J. W. Barron, M. N. Eagle, & D. L. Wolitzky (Eds.), *Interface of psychoanalysis and psychology* (pp. 516–538). Washington, D.C.: American Psychological Association.

Singer, J. A., & Singer, J. L. (1994). Social cognitive and narrative perspectives on transference. In J. M. Masling & R. R. Bornstein (Eds.), *Empirical perspectives on object relations* (pp. 157–194). Washington, D.C.: American Psychological Association.

Staudinger, U. M. (2001). Life reflection: A social-cognitive analysis of life review. *Review of General Psychology, 5*, 148–160.

Thorne, A. (2000). Personal memory telling and personality development. *Personality and Social Psychology Review, 4*, 45–56.

Thorne, A., McLean, K. C., & Lawrence, A. M. (2004). When remembering is not enough: Reflecting on self-defining memories in late adolescence. *Journal of Personality, 72*, 513–541.

Tomkins, S. S. (1979). Script theory: Differential magnification of affects. In H. E. Howe and R. A. Dienstbier (Eds.), *Nebraska symposium on motivation* (Vol. 26, pp. 201–236). Lincoln: University of Nebraska Press.

von Bertalanffy, L. (1968). *General systems theory.* New York: Braziller.

Weinberger, D. A. (1997). Distress and self-restraint as measures of adjustment across the life span: Confirmatory factor analyses in clinical and non-clinical samples. *Psychological Assessment, 9,* 132–135.

Williams, J. M. G. (1996). Depression and the specificity of autobiographical memory. In D. C. Rubin (Ed.), *Remembering our past: Studies in autobiographical memory* (pp. 244–267). Cambridge, England: Cambridge University Press.

Williams, J. M. G., & Broadbent, K. (1986). Autobiographical memory in suicide attempters. *Journal of Abnormal Psychology, 95,* 144–149.

3

THE SELF AND MEMORY FOR EMOTIONALLY VALENCED INFORMATION

7

How Emotional and Nonemotional Memories Define the Self

DENISE R. BEIKE
ERICA KLEINKNECHT
ERIN T. WIRTH-BEAUMONT
University of Arkansas

Poetry is the spontaneous overflow of powerful feelings: it takes its origin from emotion recollected in tranquillity.

—William Wordsworth

We must believe that "emotion recollected in tranquillity" is an inexact formula. . . . [E]xperiences are not "recollected" and they finally unite in an atmosphere which is "tranquil" only in that it is a passive attending upon the event.

—T. S. Eliot

Wordsworth and Eliot agreed that life experiences are an important part of the poetic process, but disagreed about the process by which these experiences were recollected and turned into poetry. Wordsworth concentrated on the process of recreating an emotional experience in words, so that the emotion could be fully reexperienced by the self or others. Eliot insisted instead that a "passive attending" should be the poet's objective. Elsewhere, he wrote that "poetry is not a turning loose of emotion, but an escape from emotion." We believe that the views of these writers on the proper place of emotion in poetry are analogous to two views in the literature on the nature of emotion in autobiographical memory. Some theories focus on memories that are highly emotional, those that inspire affective and even physiological reactions such as tears upon recollection. Other theories focus on the process of passive attending or escape

141

from emotion in memory. Dividing theories into two types admittedly obliterates important differences among theories of the same type, but we believe the distinction has heuristic value. We review some representative "Wordsworthian" theories, then some representative "Eliotic" theories. After our review of theories, we introduce our own theory, which contains elements of both types.

Only some of the theories we review make a clear distinction between the emotional quality of *memories* for life experiences and the emotional quality of the original *experiences* themselves. As researchers rarely know the actual details surrounding the original experiences reported by participants, the memory rather than the original experience must be our focus. Moreover, memory is crucial because experiences usually have long-term effects only indirectly through memory. For example, if George has a fender-bender, the experience may affect him directly for a short time (e.g., he may suffer whiplash, he will need to have his car repaired, and his insurance rates will increase temporarily). But once these "sequelae" (Wagenaar, 1986) of the experience have subsided, George's experience will affect him mainly through memory. Does he remember the accident as being his fault, or the other driver's? Does he continue to remember the accident at all, or is it one of the myriad daily experiences that are simply forgotten? Does he remember feeling pain, guilt, fear, or nothing at all? The implications of the final question for George's self-concept and his adjustment will be explored in this chapter.

THE WORDSWORTHIAN APPROACH TO EMOTION IN AUTOBIOGRAPHICAL MEMORY

Several prominent theories in autobiographical memory and personality characterize emotion as an integral part of memory for life experiences, and emotional memories in particular as integral to the self. Pillemer (1998), for example, wrote about a subtype of autobiographical memories he called *personal event memories.* Such "momentous" memories refer to specific events, are detailed, contain reference to sensory and phenomenal experience, and are believed to be true. They are virtually reexperienced upon recall, therefore leading to highly emotional, present-tense narrations and indeed emotional reactions (Pillemer, Desrochers, & Ebanks, 1998). Personal event memories provide an important directive function (Pillemer, 2003). They guide us in day-to-day decisions, representing the wisdom of experience, or "autobiographical intelligence" (Pillemer, 1998). The self is thereby strongly influenced by personal event memories.

Another example of a theory linking self, memory, and emotion is that of McAdams (1996, 2001). He has suggested that personality and identity be conceptualized not merely as a list of traits, but as a story told by the individual. This life story expresses themes that are of central importance to oneself, and provides the sense of coherence or purpose in life that is an essential component of selfhood. The life story or narrative has an overall emotional tone. It also encapsulates the person's primary motivations, what he or she wants and strives for in the present and future. Because of their close tie to current concerns and goals, autobiographical scenes are usually bound up with emotion. In fact, highly emotional autobiographical narratives (such as peak experiences and turning points) express themes and motives most clearly (McAdams, Hoffman, Mansfield, & Day, 1996).

Another Wordsworthian theory has been proposed by Singer (this volume; Singer & Salovey, 1993), who posits that a particular subtype of autobiographical memories, called *self-defining memories*, encapsulate our life story, enduring concerns, and unmet goals. Their highly emotional nature is a consequence of their close link with the self and its valued goals. Self-defining memories tend to arouse significant emotion upon recall. This emotion guides us as we strive to achieve unmet goals and act upon personal concerns (Emmons, 1989; Singer, 1990).

THE ELIOTIC APPROACH TO EMOTION IN AUTOBIOGRAPHICAL MEMORY

In contrast, other theories characterize memory for life experiences as having little emotion. William James succinctly describes one Eliotic aspect, the tendency to lose emotion from memory: "The revivability in memory of the emotions, like that of all the feeling of the lower senses, is very small. We can remember that we underwent grief or rapture, but not just how the grief or rapture felt" (1890/1981, p. 474). Indeed, recent research indicates that memory for emotional experience is quite poor. Emotionally arousing events themselves, and particularly their most important, central details, are well remembered (e.g., Christianson & Loftus, 1991). But studies of people's ability to remember what they felt and how intensely they felt it reveal a number of biases and inaccuracies. In fact, in 1996, Christianson and Safer stated that there were *no* published studies in which participants evinced accurate recall of their emotions.

Not only is emotion poorly recalled, but also there is a pattern to the forgetting of emotion, and a pattern to the reconstruction thereafter. The most commonly found pattern of forgetting has been termed *fading affect* (Thompson, 1998; Walker, Vogl, & Thompson, 1997). Freud was one of the first theorists to discuss fading affect. He contrasted abnormal processes such as repression or screen memories with a healthy memory process in which the emotional reaction to a memory fades with time: "A normal person," Freud claimed, "is . . . capable of dissipating the accompanying affect by means of association" (1893/1990, p. 27). On the other hand, pathological memories "have been preserved for a long time with wonderful freshness and with their perfect emotional tone" (p. 27). Freud believed it was maladaptive to let the feelings of the past pervade decisions in the present. Today, one might take an evolutionary perspective on the same issue. The present rather than the absent environment should generally motivate action. For this reason, conscious recollection is generally effortful so as to mark its products as past rather than present (Glenberg, 1997).

Fading affect is easiest to spot in studies using a diary methodology. Participants are asked to record daily experiences and their characteristics, including how strongly positively or negatively the event made them feel. After some weeks have passed, participants try to remember precisely how they had rated the event at the time it occurred. Participants recall their emotions as being less intense than they actually were. The effect is stronger for negative than positive affects, but it occurs for both types of affect as time passes (Thompson, 1998; Walker et al, 1997).

There is little agreement about the processes that result in fading affect. Thompson (1998) suggests the mobilization–minimization process as a candidate. Emotion (particularly negative emotion) is minimized over time by the cognitive system after the initial mobilization that takes place to deal with an important event (Taylor, 1991). Thompson notes that the minimization process may protect the self from the impact of negative events, and may also occur due to social pressures. Other theorists simply refer to a hedonic adaptation process (Diener, Suh, Lucas, & Smith, 1999; Frederick & Loewenstein, 1999), akin to the processes that cause the sensory system to reduce its sensitivity to the same input over time. For example, a scented candle produces a noticeable aroma for the first few minutes of exposure, but the fragrance becomes less detectable thereafter. As there is no change in the olfactory environment, response to the information ceases. Similarly, an emotionally arousing event may cause turmoil for hours or perhaps days afterward, but the emotional reaction fades as the event becomes part of the background rather than the focus of attention. Yet a third process is offered by other theorists. Christianson and Safer (1996) suggest that emotions are stored in a different fashion from other information in memory, implicitly rather than explicitly. M. A. Conway and Pleydell-Pearce (2000) cite brain imaging and neuropsychological evidence to support the contention that emotion is stored separately from the rest of the memory for the event.

Another theory places emotion not in implicit memory, but in a schematized form. While a memory is fresh, it is possible to recollect emotional experience and its intensity. As time passes, however, a perceiver comes to rely more and more on schemas about emotion as the source of information about what he or she (must have) felt (M. Robinson & Clore, 2002). Moving toward a more abstract notion of emotional experience seems to encapsulate the "passive attending" and "escape from emotion" that Eliot recommended to poets. Yet another possibility is offered by J. Robinson (1996), who suggests that emotions are cognitively controlled at recall by adopting an observer perspective rather than a field or actor perspective. Clearly, more research is needed to determine how much each of these processes contributes to the phenomena of emotional fading in memory and in hedonic experience.

Although fading of affect with time is the normative pattern, it does not describe the experience of all individuals (Lucas, Clark, Georgellis, & Diener, 2003). We believe this is true within individuals as well. Fading affect describes the memory for many, but not all, life experiences. Thus, each person has many memories in which affect has faded, and some in which affect is retained. We refer to the former as *closed* memories, and the latter as *open* memories. Closed memories are recollected with a sense of calm or resolution. They have gone through the process of emotion features becoming unbound from the event memory trace, as described by M. A. Conway and Pleydell-Pearce (2000). Rememberers are sensitive to the dissociation of emotion from the rest of the memory, we believe, and it is this property of the memory that produces the feeling of closure. The rememberer's subjective sense of closure originates from the quantity and vividness of affective information available upon recall.

The only studies investigating *subjective* fading of affect over time of which we are aware have been conducted in our lab. In four studies, participants were asked to indicate how intense their emotional reactions to a life event were at the time, versus how intense they were now upon recollection. These items are two among dozens on the Memory Characteristics Questionnaire (Johnson, Foley, Suengas, & Raye, 1988). A reanalysis of these four studies reveals people's awareness of (or at least belief in) fading affective experience for most of their memories. Only 29% of event memories were reported to retain the same level of affect at recall compared to when they originally happened, whereas 64% were reported to arouse less affect upon recall. Relevant to our theory, the self-reported fading in affect was associated with a sense that an experience was closed in all four studies (Beike & Wirth, 2001; Beike & Wirth-Beaumont, 2004).

OPEN VERSUS CLOSED MEMORIES

For the past several years, we have investigated the sources and consequences of this sense of closure in memory. In some studies, participants were provided with a definition of openness, closure, or both in memory. An open memory was defined as "poorly understood and not yet behind you" in some studies, or as "unfinished business" in other studies. A closed memory was defined as "well understood and behind you" in some studies, or as "a closed book" in other studies. The characteristics of each type of memory, and their differential impact upon recollection, were then measured. In other studies, participants brought to mind a memory of their choosing and its sense of closure was experimentally manipulated or simply measured, with correlates of memory closure measured as well. The basic hypothesis guiding the research program is that memories with an open feel contain more emotional detail. This greater detail has been operationalized in a number of converging ways, including the number of emotions listed as part of the memory, the intensity of emotional experience at retrieval, and the extent to which the memory is linked with the idea or concept of emotion (as opposed to being represented in a different organizational scheme, such as a life history structure; M. A. Conway & Bekerian, 1987; M. A. Conway & Pleydell-Pearce, 2000).

To summarize the results of these studies: (1) when asked to list various features present in open versus closed memories participants list a larger number of emotional details for open memories (Beike & Wirth-Beaumont, in press); (2) in contrast to the usual finding that emotion words make poor autobiographical memory cues (Conway & Bekerian, 1987; J. Robinson, 1976), open memories are readily primed by emotion concepts or words (Beike & Wirth-Beaumont, 2004);

and (3) regardless of their emotional tone, open memories arouse more agitated emotion upon recall than do closed memories (Beike & Wirth, 2000). Supporting our contention that a greater degree of emotion in the memory is suboptimal, we have demonstrated that altering the openness of an event memory increases the number of emotional and peripheral details reported, as well as increasing physical health complaints in the months that follow reporting of the event memory (Beike & Wirth-Beaumont, 2004, in press).

Three qualities that do *not* differentiate open from closed memories are theoretically important as well. First, open and closed memories are not simply memories of different types of experiences. Their parents' divorce, for example, has been reported to be an open memory by some participants and a closed memory by others. On average, the experiences underlying open memories are equally emotionally intense, equally important, and usually equally distant in time to the experiences underlying closed memories. We infer that thought processes following the event rather than the qualities of the original experience are paramount in producing memory closure. Second, analyses of the linguistic content of the narratives used to describe open and closed memories reveal no differences in the tendency to use emotion words in the description (Wirth, 2001), underscoring the distinction between a memory and a narrative report (J. Robinson & Taylor, 1998).

Third, and contrary to the views of M. A. Conway and Pleydell-Pearce (2000) and Singer and Salovey (1993), the greater emotional content of open memories does not appear to be a consequence of goal relevance or goal incompleteness. In a series of studies, we have found no differences between open and closed memories in terms of their tendency to bring to mind important or uncompleted goals (Beike, 2001). Note, however, that emotion may be aroused by goals without the goals themselves coming to the conscious mind (M. A. Conway & Pleydell-Pearce, 2000; Thorne, 1995). It is therefore possible that open memories retain their emotional content because they remain linked with ongoing goals, but that participants are unable to recognize or to articulate this linkage. We suspect that their relation to incomplete goals is only one of many possible reasons that memories may remain open, and therefore thoughts about goals will not characterize all open memories. What does characterize all open memories is a highly emotional representation (or reconstruction) and an emotional reaction evoked upon recall.

IMPLICATIONS FOR THE SELF

Before a discussion of the ways that emotional and unemotional memories influence the self, we first review the basic mechanisms that operate to link the self, memory, and emotion. M. A. Conway and Pleydell-Pearce (2000) propose a self-memory system (SMS), an executive function that shapes retrieval (or more accurately, construction) of recollected life experiences. The SMS contains two mutually interacting components: The working self, which is defined as the currently active set of goals the individual is pursuing, and the autobiographical knowledge base, which breaks down further into lifetime periods, general events, and event-specific knowledge. The two components constrain each other. Memories are retrieved in such a form that they represent current goals and concerns, and goals are based in large part on remembered past experiences.

To understand how memories may influence the self, consider the working self defined not just as current goals, but more inclusively as the momentary characterization of the self, or working self-concept (Markus & Wurf, 1987; see M. A. Conway & Pleydell-Pearce, 2000, footnote 2). The working self-concept is dynamic. Changes in the present environment or task lead to a momentary construal of the self that best suits the environment (Markus & Kunda, 1986; McGuire & McGuire, 1988). Despite this frequent change in people's self-concepts, however, people maintain a solid sense of continuity of the self (Gergen, 1982; Hoyle, Kernis, Leary, & Baldwin, 1999). This change/stability paradox is one of the thorniest dilemmas in the study of the self, and a number of different resolutions have been offered.

Gergen (1982) suggests three reasons why shifts in the momentary self-concept do not shake one's sense of stability of the self. One is that only peripheral or unimportant dimensions of the self shift, whereas central self-concepts remain stable. Thus, the sense of continuity or unity comes from that stable core. But Gergen criticizes this explanation as tautological: perhaps dimensions of the self that fail to change are merely perceived as central as a consequence of their stability. A second possible reason why frequent shifts do not disturb self-stability is that people are attracted to similar situations over time. Gergen argues that this view solves the dilemma for self-concept shifts that are based on situation changes, but it does not allow for self-concept shifts that have to do with internal changes.

The third possible reason the self-concept may shift without disturbing the sense of a stable self, and the one Gergen prefers, is a postmodern explanation: there is no reality to self-concepts. Instead, every action a person takes has whatever meaning he or she chooses from among the web of possible meanings agreed upon in the social world. Because words, feelings, and actions allow multiple interpretations, it is not difficult to maintain the sense of a coherent self despite constant change. The perceiver simply argues for a different meaning of any given behavior or thought that will restore the continuity of the self. For example, a person who believes herself to be a couch potato but who begins taking aerobics classes simply characterizes taking aerobics as a way to pass the time or to meet new people, rather than as exercise. The process Gergen describes seems akin to a dissonance reduction process, where the divergence between the stable self one believes in and the unstable self of reality is canceled out by fancy cognitive footwork. It echoes the earlier sentiments of Hume (1739/1979), who argued that our strong need for identity and stability in both the self and objects produces an illusion of stability, despite the fact that stability does not exist.

McAdams (1996), on the other hand, suggests a fourth possibility: There are two senses of the self in operation. Like James (1890/1981), McAdams distinguishes the "I" self from the "me" self. The I self is subjective, and it is omnipresent in thoughts (the "flow of consciousness"). Alongside this I self stands what James called the me self, or the self as object to be described. McAdams clarifies this distinction by positing that the I self is actually a process, whereas the me self is the product created by that I self. Because the me self is a construction and a story, it is expected to convey information about change. But an effective story that provides a sense of identity must integrate the changes that have occurred across time and situations. In this way, both change and stability are inherent to the self-concept.

We propose a similar distinction, but view the operation of the I and me self somewhat differently. Specifically, each embodies a different need. One need is for continuity in the self, which allows us to feel stable and to ward off anxiety (Swann, 1997). The other need is for constant fluctuation. People value their ability to demonstrate flexibility in their behavior (Sande, Goethals, & Radloff, 1988), sometimes even exaggerating the changes that have occurred in the self over time (M. Conway & Ross, 1984). To achieve these opposing goals, two senses of the self are maintained, I and me (cf. Hilgard, 1949). The me self looks to the situation to activate relevant self-knowledge. Meanwhile, the I self pursues its own ends, looking across situations and time for reassuring evidence of continuity. Consistent with a separate I and me, people are able to separate the amount of change they perceive from their sense that their selfhood has altered: An individual may say that she has changed tremendously over the years, and yet claim that she is still the same person, or vice versa (Lampinen, Odegard, & Leding, this volume). By operating separately, the me self can shift as much as necessary to allow fluid interaction with the environment while the I self remains largely untouched. This constant shifting of the me self without the I self taking notice, we believe, is the very process posited in the SMS theory.

Although the I and me self are separate, they are not mutually exclusive (as in Duval & Wicklund, 1972), nor does one control the other (as in McAdams, 1996). Rather, they peacefully coexist, each working on its own task without consulting the other. Sometimes, however, the I is forced to take notice of the ever-changing me self because the flow of the self-memory system is disrupted. The retrieval of a highly emotional memory presents the greatest risk of perturbing the I and me self. M. A. Conway and Pleydell-Pearce (2000) claim that "if intense emotions are (re)experienced . . . the current operation of the whole cognitive system could be disrupted" (p. 271). In their view, the problem is that "emotional memories could reinstate (past) signals for action" (p. 271), which would be maladaptive in the present environment. Despite the potential risks, the emotional compoment of autobiographical memories *can* sometimes be retrieved, in the case of open memories. The emotional spillover of the open memory causes *mood-induced self-focused attention* (Salovey, 1992), which occurs for both negative and positive mood states. This navel-gazing process breaks the normally seamless integration of self, memory, and environment, interrupting the I self and its executive functions.

The specific effects of recollecting an open memory on self-definition are twofold. First, the predicted shift of attentional focus should be apparent in a tendency to describe what is being observed, that is, the internal aspects of the self. Private feelings, thoughts, and experiences should dominate the me self, and make their way into a self-description taken at the time (e.g., Salovey, 1992). Second, the focus on the self will be uncomfortable (M. Conway, Giannopoulos, Csank, & Mendelson, 1993; Duval & Wicklund, 1972; Lyubomirsky & Nolen-Hoeksema, 1993). In fact, in the longer term, self-focused rumination is a risk factor for depression (Nolen-Hoeksema, 2000), and is associated with greater physiological reactivity and stress (Glynn, Christenfeld, & Gerin, 2002; Roger & Najarian, 1998). Over months or years, as people continue to remember an experience in an open fashion and ruminate on the self, psychological and physical health may suffer. Consistent with this logic, lingering openness in memory was a significant predictor of self-reported illness in a earlier study (Beike & Wirth-Beaumont, 2004).

When closed memories come to mind, on the other hand, the me self will simply shift to reflect relevant aspects of the external environment as it ordinarily does (Markus & Wurf, 1987). This shift will cause little disruption to the executive control functions in the SMS, because closure in memory allows the "passive attending" to the memory that Eliot valued so highly. The working self-concept will be defined in more externally focused ways. One's place in the world, in time, and in the web of social relationships is more likely to become part of the working self-concept, and therefore more likely to be mentioned in a self-description.

Our theory does not predict that the *themes* of either open or closed memories will be reflected directly in a self-description made afterward. Rather, the mere fact of recollecting any open, emotional memory interrupts the operation of the SMS, leading to self-analysis and lowered self-esteem. The mere fact of recollecting any closed, no-longer emotional memory allows the me self to be interwoven with the present environment, leading to a more externally defined self-concept. Whether the event memory brought to mind concerns the death of a loved one, winning an award, breaking a leg, or going on a date is irrelevant and may or may not appear in the description of the self. The emphasis on perspective rather than themes distinguishes our theory from others with which it shares some assumptions (e.g., McAdams, 1996; Pillemer, 1998; Singer & Blagov, this volume).

To investigate the differential relationship of open and closed memories to the self, we conducted two studies. In each study, participants were asked to bring to mind memories of life events, and to describe the self, evaluate the self, or both. The studies differed in the retrieval methodology used, the manner in which the self was described, and other procedural details, but the results are consistent both with each other and with our theory. To reiterate, open memories are predicted to disrupt the operation of the SMS, thereby causing an internally focused description of the self and a lowered sense of self-esteem. Closed memories are predicted to cause an externally focused description of the self with no impact on self-esteem.

Study 1: Open Memories Depress Self-Esteem

In the first study, we measured the correlation between openness in memory and self-esteem. To make sure the memories to be measured were as similar as possible, we chose a set of 10 events and asked participants which of these they had experienced and to bring the memories of any of these events to mind. Specifically, a questionnaire was administered to 520 male and female University of Arkansas students as part of a series of questionnaires given during the first week of class. First, they were asked to indicate which of 10 stressful life events they had ever experienced by checking "yes" for each. For each "yes" response, they were asked to rate the closure of their memory for the event on a 1 to 10 scale, and to give the month and year in which the event took place, so that mere time passage could be distinguished from memory closure. The 10 events were chosen because they are relatively common in college student populations. The events were death of a parent, death of a sibling, accident that led to your disability, fire that destroyed your home, rape, incest, robbery, abortion or miscarriage, trouble with the law, and being "dumped" by a relationship partner. The first six came from Janoff-Bulman (1989) and the remaining four from experience with commonly reported life events in this student population. In addition to the event checklist, the students filled out Janoff-Bulman's World Beliefs Scale (1989), which includes a measure of self-worth composed of items from the Rosenberg (1965) self-esteem scale.

Overall, 76% of the students had experienced at least 1 of the 10 stressful events. We examined the association between closure of the memory for these events and self-esteem. To do this, we first calculated for each participant in this subset the average closure of the memories for all events experienced. The average date was also calculated, and the total number of events determined. These three variables were used as predictors of self-esteem scores. A stepwise regression analysis was conducted, with the total number of events and the average date of occurrence entered in the first step, and the average closure score entered in the second step. The results were that, accounting for date and total number of events experienced, memory closure was positively associated with self-esteem, as predicted.

Moreover, memory closure seemed to have a recuperative effect. A median split of memory closure scores was used to delineate a high-closure and a low-closure group. These two groups were compared with those students who had not experienced any of the stressful events listed (a procedure similar to that used by Janoff-Bulman, 1989, 1992). Students with open memories for their experiences had lower self-esteem than the other two groups. Students who experienced stressful events but gained closure on the memories for them thus had self-esteem equivalent to that of students who had never experienced these events. That open memories disrupt the working self is therefore consistent with the results of Study 1.

However, Study 1 was correlational, so it is not possible to determine whether recollecting open memories depresses self-esteem, or whether those with low self-esteem have trouble gaining a sense of closure in memory. Moreover, despite the fact that the mere passage of time since the event did not account for the relationship, there could be a fourth, unmeasured factor that causes both open memories and low self-esteem. A second limitation of Study 1 was that only negative event memories were studied. It is possible that open memories depress self-esteem only if the content of the memories is negative. To address both concerns, an experimental study was conducted.

Study 2: Open Memories Channel Self-Definition toward Internal Elements

In Study 2, we tested the causal relationship between open memories and low self-esteem by manipulating the closure of a recollected memory and the positivity of self-aspects brought to mind. We added a self-description task so that the nature of the attributes used to describe the working self-concept could be analyzed. Ninety male and female participants completed the experiment. Forty-five of these participants first retrieved and briefly described an open or a closed pleasant or unpleasant event memory. The closure of the memory and pleasantness and date of the event were then measured. Afterward, participants completed a self-description task.

A brief set of instructions explained that participants were to list the important defining features or characteristics of the self as they see it today, then to go back and indicate the positivity of each feature. These self-ratings provided the basis for a measure of self-esteem, as people with higher self-esteem also consider themselves to have a greater number of positive attributes (e.g., Marsh, 1986; Showers, 1992). Participants then described the past self in the same manner. (Effects on the past self-description were similar to those on the present self, but weaker. For this reason, and because of its closer correspondence to the theoretical working self-concept, only results concerning the present self-description are presented.)

The other 45 participants began with a self-description task. They were asked to list some things that they especially liked (or disliked) about themselves, in both the past and the present. Liking for the self was then measured. Afterward, participants were asked to retrieve and briefly describe either an open or a closed memory (pleasantness was unspecified). The closure of the memory and the pleasantness and date of the event were then measured.

Two hypotheses were tested. The first hypothesis was that open memories would depress self-esteem as measured by the positivity of the self-descriptors chosen afterward. The alternative hypothesis was that describing the self in negative terms would both depress self-esteem (as measured by liking for the self) and cause the memory that was brought to mind later to feel more open. The second hypothesis concerned the content of event descriptions and self-descriptions. The verbal descriptions were transcribed and submitted to analysis by the Linguistic Inquiry and Word Count program (LIWC; Pennebaker & Francis, 1999), a program that calculates the proportion of words of various types that are used in a text sample. Three categories of word types were created from the LIWC output: internal-referent words (emotions, thoughts, and sensory words); external-referent words (social relationships and roles, words referring to occupations and leisure); and context words (words referring to time and place).

The second hypothesis was that self-descriptions following open memory recollection would contain more internal references and fewer external and context references than those following closed memory recollection. However, there should be no differences in the event descriptions themselves. Moreover, there should be no differences in these dimensions in the self-descriptions when they were generated first. Whether the memories generated after self-description would vary in internal, external, and context language is not specified in our theory, but we investigated these memory descriptions as well.

Initial analyses revealed that open and closed memories did not differ in rated pleasantness, but they did differ in how long ago they had taken place. Open memories were more recent, but only when memories were listed before the self-aspects. The date of the event was used as a covariate in all the remaining analyses. Manipulation checks revealed that both the memory closure and the positivity manipulations were effective.

To test the first hypothesis and its alternative, the proportion of positive self-descriptors of the total number listed (which did not differ by condition) was analyzed. Consistent with the first hypothesis, after open event memory recollection, 64% of the self-descriptors participants wrote were positive, and after closed memory recollection, 80% were positive. Contrary to the alternative hypothesis, the positivity of the self-aspects brought to mind did not influence the positivity of the memory brought to mind. That is, memory closure influenced the self, but the self did not influence memory closure.

To test the second hypothesis, the proportions of internal-referent, external-referent, and context words used in each verbal description (self and event memory) were analyzed. Relevant to the second hypothesis, the event memories were described similarly across all conditions, with 12% internal-referent, 15% external-referent, and 9% context words. But the self was described differently depending upon whether an open or a closed memory had just been retrieved. After an open memory, participants described the self with more internal-referent words, as predicted (35% after open, 27% after closed). After a closed memory, participants described the self with more external-referent and context words (18% external and 3% contextual after open, 24% external and 7% contextual after closed).

Prototypic examples of memory descriptions and the associated self-descriptions are provided to clarify how open and closed memories influenced the self. The participant's ratings of pleasantness (on a 1 to 7 scale) and memory closure (on a 1 to 10 scale) are given for each.

Open pleasant memory (pleasantness 7, closure 5). Relationship with a girl over the past year. We were really close, but felt obligated to break up because she's going to school in New York. I still use her as a watermark to compare other girls to and we joke about getting married on the phone. (*Self-description afterward:* Self-confident; selfish; loves frisbee; cunning; self-sufficient; controlled; long-haired; confused; student; lonely; level)

Open unpleasant memory (pleasantness 4, closure 3). Getting involved emotionally and physically with two very good friends. To this day I continue to deny ever being involved with one, while the other knows the truth. (*Self-description afterward:* Outgoing; determined; love sex; patient; enthusiastic; little too hyper; love music; love women; love sports; hard worker; caring; understanding; forgiving; lonely; falls in love too fast; blessed; shy)

Closed pleasant memory (pleasantness 7, closure 10). The first night that I met my girlfriend of almost three years. It was at a football game on Halloween night and all I could think about was whether I should go talk to her or not. Finally, one of my friends made me and we spent the rest of the night getting to know each other. It was a great night. (*Self-description afterward:* Excited; student; outgoing; tall; healthy; athletic; roller blading; basketball; tennis; studies; stressful; knowledgeable; girlfriend of three years; in love; marriage soon; computers; programming)

Closed unpleasant memory (pleasantness 2, closure 8). When my friend got hit by a drunk driver. She survived the crash, but was in a coma for two and a half weeks and they didn't know if she would. She did end up having some brain damage. (*Self-description afterward:* Short; musical; student; college; shy; aunt; in band; loves pets; quiet; sister; daughter; Christian; friend)

Notice that the two open memory descriptions lead to self-descriptions that mention a large number of internal states ("confused," "lonely," "love frisbee" in the shorter description; "love women," "caring," "understanding" and most of the other descriptors in the more detailed description) while providing relatively few descriptors of the person's external world ("long-haired" and "student" are the only two given in the first; "hard worker" the only external descriptor in the second). The two closed memory descriptions are followed by self-descriptions that reveal less about the private internal world of the person ("excited," "stressful," and "in love" are the only internal descriptors provided in the first self-description; "shy" the only internal descriptor in the second) and more about social roles and activities ("student," plus discussion of a girlfriend, major, activities, and plans for the future are all contained in the first; the second contains "student" and references to activities, plus a plethora of social roles—aunt, sister, daughter, Christian, friend). As predicted, then, bringing to mind an open memory caused participants to take a more introspective, ruminative view of the self, and lowered their self-esteem, without necessarily reflecting the themes present in the recollected experience.

Study 2 (Continued): Comparison to Self-Defining Memories

In addition to linguistic analyses of the memory descriptions provided in this study, we also conducted structural analyses. If open memories are truly more emotional, they might also be more likely to be self-defining memories. We were able to compare some properties of open and closed memories to the properties of self-defining memories investigated by Singer and Salovey (1993). Self-defining memories are highly emotional, vivid, and tied to other memories; deal with enduring concerns or unresolved conflicts; and frequently recur in memory. In experiments, self-defining memories as compared to "the first memory that comes into your mind" are described in a more generic way and in a more integrative way (i.e., mentioning self-discovery or understanding), although not in a more emotionally intense way (Singer & Moffitt, 1991–1992). We used Singer and Blagov's (2000) event memory coding system to assign a code to each of the 90 memory descriptions given in this study. Three dimensions were coded: structure, which refers to whether a single event or a summary of repeated events is described; integrative meaning, which refers to whether a lesson or unifying theme is explicitly mentioned; and valence, which refers to the positivity of the description as a whole.

Analyses of these ratings revealed that (a) open memories were described in a slightly more summarized way than closed memories; (b) open memory descriptions were less likely to be integrative than closed memories (although the majority of memories were nonintegrative in both conditions); and (c) open memory descriptions were more negative in content than closed memories (despite the fact that participants themselves did not rate the experiences underlying open memories as more unpleasant). Relative to closed memories, then, open memories share with self-defining memories the characteristic of being described in a summarized rather than a specific way. But open memories differ from self-defining memories in that they tend to contain references to more unpleasant properties of events. It is unclear whether open memories relate to enduring concerns, because they were rarely described in an integrative way. We conclude that open memories and self-defining memories overlap only to a degree. Open memories include both self-defining memories that are particularly worrisome to the perceiver, and other autobiographical memories that retain their emotionality despite the fact that they do not express central motives of the personality.

Open memories do, therefore, influence the self, but closed memories do as well. How and why both influence the me self is further clarified by a study conducted by Beike & Wirth-Beaumont (2004). We used a Crovitz cue-word methodology to learn which cues would preferentially access open memories and which would access closed memories. We predicted, and found, that emotion words ("happy") cued open memories, and life chapter words ("high school") cued closed memories. In other words, closed memories have a clearer place in M. A. Conway and Pleydell-Pearce's (2000) three-level hierarchy of event knowledge. Closed memories in Study 2 were more specific in terms of the experience they reported, but we believe that they are more abstract than open memories in another way. Closed memories have found their place in the extended timeline (Barsalou, 1988) or life history structure (M. A. Conway & Pleydell-Pearce, 2000) that characterizes autobiographical memory. Seen from this perspective, a memory can be passively attended without significantly disrupting the operation of the SMS.

CONCLUSIONS

M. A. Conway (1990) charged that "[t]he intersection of self, emotion, and memory in cognition undoubtedly represents one of the key areas in which psychology must advance if the discipline as a whole is to progress" (p. 104). Much progress has been made since that time, by M. A. Conway and his collaborators, contributors to this volume, and researchers cited throughout it. One common approach to understanding this critical intersection is the Wordsworthian approach. Wordsworthian theories place central importance on unifying themes that are embedded in both the memory and the self-concept, and on the affect that arises as a consequence of goals that are linked to memories. Many of these theories refer to narrative properties of the event memory — its place in the narrative, or its narrative form (verb tenses, emotion, etc.), are often analyzed. Vivid, momentous, self-defining, or nuclear episode memories have priveleged places in this narrative in the Wordsworthian view. They arouse significant emotion, and thereby link the past with the present and future.

We believe these Wordsworthian theories are concerned with a type of event memory that is the exception rather than the rule. A few event memories do retain and arouse emotion, but these open memories cause a reflexive, inward-looking stance on the self, which is inherently painful. It might be argued that such a focus is ultimately productive or therapeutic, yet we have never found this in our research. Health and self-esteem problems are associated with open memories, both retrospectively and prospectively. This pattern is consistent with the dysphoria usually associated with self-focused rumination (Nolen-Hoeksema, 2000) and self-focused attention in general (M. Conway et al., 1993; Mor & Winquist, 2002). This ruminative stance is the result of the I self taking notice of potentially dysfunctional changes in the me self, those that do not correspond to the immediate environment.

Meshing with the environment is promoted by closed or unemotional memories. Eliotic theorists investigate how most memories lose their emotion, both in the memory itself and in their impact upon the person remembering. The typical event memory does not contain much information about emotion, but it still may influence the me self when brought to mind. Closed memories influence thoughts about the self and the world in general. They cause us to look outside the claustrophobic internal world for our sense of self, and to set the self in a social and temporal context. Their contextual nature makes closed memories an especially appropriate source of information for life choices. These memories may be a better source of autobiographical intelligence (Pillemer, 1998) than are highly emotional memories, because closed memories are seen with a more objective eye. As Marigold Linton found in a study of her own memories, the original report of a memory becomes unrecognizable as we learn more with time (Linton, 1982). The emotion experienced at the time of the event fades from memory, and the meaning assigned to the event changes with the accumulated wisdom of experience.

To conclude, highly emotional memories — whether they are called personal, nuclear, or self-defining — do transfix and transform us. But their number must be kept quite small to allow the SMS to function, so they are the exception rather than the rule. We hope to stimulate more research attention toward the less glamorous, more common memories that enable the SMS to function most adaptively, the closed memories. Despite the fact that the emotional component has been stored elsewhere or has faded with time, closed memories also influence the self. They enhance the coordination of the me self with the environment, and they allow the I self to look for evidence of continuity across these changes. In addition, closed memories point up one of the yet-unresolved dilemmas in autobiographical memory: Where does the emotion in memory go? Several candidate processes for the separation of emotion from memory have been proposed, but no consensus has emerged. If the process underlying fading affect is better understood, it may be fruitfully applied to improve health and self-esteem among those with lingering open memories.

REFERENCES

Barsalou, L. W. (1988). The content and organization of autobiographical memories. In U. Neisser & E. Winograd (Eds.), *Remembering reconsidered* (pp. 193–243). New York: Cambridge University Press.

Beike, D. R. (2001). Evaluations of the impact of open and closed memories. Unpublished raw data.

Beike, D. R., & Wirth, E. T. (2000). Affective consequences of recalling open versus closed memories. Unpublished raw data.

Beike, D. R., & Wirth-Beaumont, E. T. (2001). Subjective characteristics of memories. Unpublished raw data.

Beike, D. R., & Wirth-Beaumont, E. T. (2004). *Memory closure, motivation, and health.* Unpublished manuscript.

Beike, D. R., & Wirth-Beaumont, E. T. (in press). *Psychological closure as a memory phenomenon.*

Christianson, S., & Loftus, E. F. (1991). Remembering emotional events: The fate of detailed information. *Cognition and Emotion, 5,* 81–108.

Christianson, S., & Safer, M. A. (1996). Emotional events and emotions in autobiographical memories. In D. C. Rubin (Ed.), *Remembering our past: Studies in autobiographical memory* (pp. 218–243). Cambridge, England: Cambridge University Press.

Conway, M., Giannopoulos, C., Csank, P., & Mendelson, M. (1993). Dysphoria and specificity in self-focused attention. *Personality and Social Psychology Bulletin, 19,* 265–268.

Conway, M., & Ross, M. (1984). Getting what you want by revising what you had. *Journal of Personality and Social Psychology, 47,* 738–748.

Conway, M. A. (1990). *Autobiographical memory: An introduction.* Philadelphia, PA: Open University Press.

Conway, M. A., & Bekerian, D. A. (1987). Organization in autobiographical memory. *Memory and Cognition, 15,* 119–132.

Conway, M. A., & Pleydell-Pearce, C. W. (2000). The construction of autobiographical memories in the self-memory system. *Psychological Review, 107,* 261–288.

Crovitz, H. F., & Schiffman, H. (1974). Frequency of episodic memories as a function of their age. *Bulletin of the Psychonomic Society, 4,* 517–518.

Diener, E., Suh, E. M., Lucas, R. E., & Smith, H. L. (1999). Subjective well-being: Three decades of progress. *Psychological Bulletin, 125*(2), 276–302.

Duval, S., & Wicklund, R. (1972). *A theory of objective self-awareness.* New York: Academic Press.

Emmons, R. A. (1989). The personal striving approach to personality. In L. A. Pervin (Ed.), *Goal concepts in personality and social psychology* (pp. 87–126). Hillsdale, NJ: Erlbaum.

Frederick, F., & Loewenstein, G. (1999). Hedonic adaptation. In D. Kahneman, E. Diener, & N. Schwarz (Eds.), *Well-being: The foundations of hedonic psychology* (pp. 302–329). New York: Russell Sage Foundation.

Freud, S. (1983/1990). *Selected papers on hysteria*. In M. J. Adler (Ed.), *The major works of Sigmund Freud*. Chicago: Encyclopaedia Britannica, Inc.

Gergen, K. J. (1982). From self to science: What is there to know? In J. Suls (Ed.), *Psychological perspectives on the self* (Vol. 1, pp. 127–149). Hillsdale, NJ: Erlbaum.

Glenberg, A. M. (1997). What memory is for. *Behavioral and Brain Sciences, 20,* 1–55.

Glynn, L. M., Christenfeld, N., & Gerin, W. (2002). The role of rumination in recovery from reactivity: Cardiovascular consequences of emotional states. *Psychosomatic Medicine, 64,* 714–726.

Hilgard, E. R. (1949). Human motives and the concept of self. *American Psychologist, 4,* 374–382.

Hoyle, R. H., Kernis, M. H., Leary, M. R., & Baldwin, M. W. (1999). *Selfhood: Identity, esteem, regulation.* Boulder, CO: Westview Press.

Hume, D. (1739/1979). A treatise of human nature, Volume 1. In R. I. Watson (Ed.), *Basic writings in the history of psychology.* New York: Oxford University Press.

James, W. (1890/1981). *Principles of psychology* (2 vols.). In F. Burkhardt (Ed.), *The works of William James.* Cambridge, MA: Harvard University Press.

Janoff-Bulman, R. (1989). Assumptive worlds and the stress of traumatic events: Applications of the schema construct. *Social Cognition, 7,* 113–136.

Janoff-Bulman, R. (1992). *Shattered assumptions: Towards a new psychology of trauma.* New York: Free Press.

Johnson, M. K., Foley, M. A., Suengas, A. G., & Raye, C. L. (1988). Phenomenal characteristics of memories for perceived and imagined events. *Journal of Experimental Psychology: General, 117,* 371–376.

Linton, M. (1982). Transformations of memory in everyday life. In U. Neisser (Ed.), *Memory observed: Remembering in natural contexts* (pp. 77–92). San Francisco: W. H. Freeman and Company.

Lucas, R. E., Clark, A. E., Georgellis, Y., & Diener, E. (2003). Reexamining adaptation and the set point model of happiness: Reactions to changes in marital status. *Journal of Personality and Social Psychology, 84,* 527–539.

Lyubomirsky, S., & Nolen-Hoeksema, S. (1993). Self-perpetuating properties of dysphoric rumination. *Journal of Personality and Social Psychology, 65,* 339–349.

Markus, H., & Kunda, Z. (1986). Stability and malleability of the self-concept. *Journal of Personality and Social Psychology, 51,* 858–866.

Markus, H., & Wurf, E. (1987). The dynamic self-concept: A social psychological perspective. *Annual Review of Psychology, 38,* 299–337.

Marsh, H. W. (1986). Global self-esteem: Its relation to specific facets of self-concept and their importance. *Journal of Personality and Social Psychology, 51,* 1224–1236.

McAdams, D. P. (1996). Personality, modernity, and the storied self: A contemporary framework for studying persons. *Psychological Inquiry, 7,* 295–321.

McAdams, D. P. (2001). The psychology of life stories. *Review of General Psychology, 5,* 100–122.

McAdams, D. P., Hoffman, B. J., Mansfield, E. D., & Day, R. (1996). Themes of agency and communion in significant autobiographical scenes. *Journal of Personality, 64,* 339–377.

McGuire, W. J., & McGuire, C. V. (1988). Content and process in the experience of self. In L. Berkowitz (Ed.), *Advances in experimental social psychology* (Vol. 21, pp. 97–144). New York: Academic Press.

Mor, N., & Winquist, J. (2002). Self-focused attention and negative affect: A meta-analysis. *Psychological Bulletin, 128,* 638–662.

Nolen-Hoeksema, S. (2000). The role of rumination in depressive disorders and mixed anxiety/depressive symptoms. *Journal of Abnormal Psychology, 109,* 504–511.

Odegard, T. N., & Lampinen, J. M. (in press). Memory conjunction errors for autobiographical events: More than just familiarity. *Memory.*

Pennebaker, J. W., & Francis, M. E. (1999). *Linguistic Inquiry and Word Count (LIWC): A computer-based text analysis program.* Mahwah, NJ: Erlbaum.

Pillemer, D. B. (1998). *Momentous events, vivid memories.* Cambridge, MA: Harvard University Press.

Pillemer, D. B. (2001). Momentous events and the life story. *Review of General Psychology, 5,* 123–134.

Pillemer, D. B. (2003). Directive functions of autobiographical memory: The guiding power of the specific episode. *Memory, 11,* 193–202.

Pillemer, D. B., Desrochers, A. B., & Ebanks, C. M. (1998). Remembering the past in the present: Verb tense shifts in autobiographical memory narratives. In C.P. Thompson, D. J. Herrmann, D. Bruce, J. D. Read, D. G. Payne, & M. P. Toglia (Eds.), *Autobiographical memory: Theoretical and applied perspectives* (pp. 145–162). Mahwah, NJ: Erlbaum.

Robinson, J. A. (1976). Sampling autobiographical memory. *Cognitive Psychology, 8,* 578–595.

Robinson, J. A. (1996). Perspective, meaning, and remembering. In D. C. Rubin (Ed.), *Remembering our past: Studies in autobiographical memory* (pp. 199–217). Cambridge, England: Cambridge University Press.

Robinson, J. A., & Taylor, L. R. (1998). Autobiographical memory and self-narratives: A tale of two stories. In C.P. Thompson, D. J. Herrmann, D. Bruce, J. D. Read, D. G. Payne, & M. P. Toglia (Eds.), *Autobiographical memory: Theoretical and applied perspectives* (pp. 125–143). Mahwah, NJ: Erlbaum.

Robinson, M. D., & Clore, G. L. (2002). Belief and feeling: Evidence for an accessibility model of emotional self-report. *Psychological Bulletin, 128,* 934–960.

Roger, D., & Najarian, B. (1998). The relationship between emotional rumination and cortisol secretion under stress. *Personality and Individual Differences, 24,* 531–538.

Rosenberg, M. (1965). *Society and the adolescent self-image.* Princeton, NJ: Princeton University Press.

Salovey, P. (1992). Mood-induced self-focused attention. *Journal of Personality and Social Psychology, 62,* 699–707.

Sande, G. N., Goethals, G. R., & Radloff, C. E. (1988). Perceiving one's own traits and others': The multifaceted self. *Journal of Personality and Social Psychology, 54,* 13–20.

Showers, C. (1992). Compartmentalization of positive and negative self-knowledge: Keeping bad apples out of the bunch. *Journal of Personality and Social Psychology, 62,* 1036–1049.

Singer, J. A. (1990). Affective responses to autobiographical memories and their relationship to long-term goals. *Journal of Personality, 58*, 535–563.

Singer, J. A., & Blagov, P. A. (2000, October). *Classification system and scoring manual for self-defining autobiographical memories*. Paper presented at the annual meeting of the Society for Applied Research in Memory and Cognition, Miami Beach, FL.

Singer, J. A., & Moffitt, K. H. (1991–1992). An experimental investigation of specificity and generality in memory narratives. *Imagination, Cognition, and Personality, 11*, 233–257.

Singer, J. A., & Salovey, P. (1993). *The remembered self: Emotion and memory in personality.* New York: Free Press.

Swann, W. B., Jr. (1997). The trouble with change: Self-verification and allegiance to the self. *Psychological Science, 8*, 177–180.

Taylor, S. E. (1991). Asymmetrical effects of positive and negative events: The mobilization-minimization hypothesis. *Psychological Bulletin, 110*, 67–85.

Thompson, C. P. (1998). The bounty of everyday memory. In C. P. Thompson, D. J. Herrmann, D. Bruce, J. D. Read, D. G. Payne, & M. P. Toglia (Eds.), *Autobiographical memory: Theoretical and applied perspectives* (pp. 29–43). Mahwah, NJ: Erlbaum.

Thorne, A. (1995). Developmental truths in memories of childhood and adolescence. *Journal of Personality, 63*, 138–163.

Wagenaar, W. A. (1986). My memory: A study of autobiographical memory over six years. *Cognitive Psychology, 18*, 225–252.

Walker, W. R., Vogl, R. J., & Thompson, C. P. (1997). Autobiographical memory: Unpleasantness fades faster than pleasantness over time. *Applied Cognitive Psychology, 11*, 399–413.

Wirth, E. T. (2001) *Linking event closure theory and the health benefits of self-disclosure through writing*. Unpublished master's thesis, University of Arkansas, Fayetteville, AR.

8

Self-Protective Memory

CONSTANTINE SEDIKIDES
University of Southampton

JEFFREY D. GREEN
Soka University

BRAD PINTER
University of Washington

A fundamental issue in the behavioral, educational, and social sciences concerns the intrapersonal and interpersonal struggle with the question "who am I?" This issue is reflected in such research themes as self definition, identity seeking, self-knowledge, search for identity, self seeking, identity quest, symbolic self-completion, and self-interpretation. For the purposes of this chapter, we will adopt the term self-definition, given that this term has enjoyed widespread use in social and personality psychology as of late.

What do people want to know about themselves? What information are they likely to endorse or reject? For exactly what sort of self-definition do people strive and what kind of self-knowledge will they store in their memory? Epistemic and pragmatic reasons suggest that people strive, or at least should strive, for a self-definition that is accurate, balanced, and truthful. Epistemic reasons date back to ancient Greek philosophers. Socrates, for example, advocated the pursuit of accurate self-knowledge (*gnothi seauton*) as the highest human virtue and value. Socrates prescribed self-scrutiny as the method to achieve truthful knowledge about the self, and he also guarded against the uncritical endorsement of desirable information. Importantly, the search for an accurate self-definition has pragmatic benefits. Such a definition informs and guides the individual in selecting environments that match her or his abilities, including appropriate positions in professional and social hierarchies. Hence, in the long run, an accurate self-definition facilitates planning, contributes to goal success, and enhances personal and social well-being (Strube, 1990; Strube, Yost, & Bailey, 1992; Trope, 1986).

Alternatively, people may eschew information accuracy and truthfulness when such information is at the expense of self-positivity, as other Greek philosophers have maintained (e.g., Epicurus). People may pursue a self-definition that is positive and flattering and may protect this self-definition against threatening infiltrators (e.g., negative feedback, unsupportive others, evaluative contexts). There are epistemic reasons for positivity strivings. Most people think favorably of themselves (Kendall, Howard, & Hays, 1989; Schwartz, 1986). Hence, positive feedback solidifies the internal consistency of the self-concept (Swann, 1987), thus circumventing internal turbulence and turmoil. Pragmatic reasons for the pursuit of desirable feedback also abound. A positive self-definition infuses the individual with optimism, feelings of efficacy, and the motivation to plan and engage in decisive action (Taylor, Lerner, Sherman, Sage, & McDowell, 2003; Updegraff & Taylor, 2000). As Cairns (1990) put it, self-definitions ". . . do not always have to be veridical in order to be functional. . . . Even if one is sick and anxious and poor, there should be reason to get up in the morning" (p. 77).

Recently, we have initiated a program of research with the purpose to test these two broad theoretical frameworks. We have treated memory for self-relevant feedback as a proxy for self-definition and, more specifically, for the struggle to achieve self-definition. In this chapter, we will articulate two theoretical models derived from the above frameworks, will present the results of several experiments testing these competing models, and will discuss implications for future research while placing our findings in the context of the broader literature on memory and the self.

Before the exposition of the theoretical models, however, we will articulate both the specific questions that guided our investigation, and we will explicate our experimental paradigm. We were concerned with three general issues. First, we wanted to know how people cope with feedback that is negative or inconsistent with their self-definition. In particular, how do people process information that is evaluatively inconsistent (i.e., contains both positive and negative behaviors which people are ostensibly likely to enact)? Will they remember negative information better than positive information? Second, we wanted to know whether people process negative or inconsistent feedback differently when it is directed to the self as opposed to an acquaintance (hypothetically named "Chris"). In particular, will they remember negative feedback better or worse than positive feedback depending on whether the feedback describes the self versus Chris? Third, we wanted to know whether structural features of the feedback make a difference in the way it is processed. More specifically, is feedback remembered differently when it conveys information about one's central versus peripheral self-aspects? People are highly certain they possess central self-aspects and also regard these aspects as highly self-descriptive and important. In contrast, people are less certain about possessing peripheral self-aspects and also consider these aspects moderate-to-low in self-descriptiveness and importance (Sedikides, 1993, 1995).

We designed our experimental paradigm with an eye toward addressing the above questions. In all our experiments, participants received feedback in the form of behaviors that were evaluatively inconsistent with regard to each of four personality trait dimensions. That is, the feedback included both positive and negative behaviors for each trait dimension. Additionally, the feedback referred either to the self or Chris. Finally, the feedback was relevant both to central and peripheral self-aspects.

In all, eight behaviors exemplified each of two central and two peripheral trait dimensions. Specifically, eight behaviors exemplified the central trait dimension of trustworthy–untrustworthy (e.g., "would keep secrets when asked to," "would often lie to his or her parents") and another eight behaviors exemplified the central trait dimension of kind–unkind (e.g., "would help a handicapped neighbor paint his or her house," "would make fun of others because of their looks"). Furthermore, eight behaviors exemplified the peripheral trait dimension of modest-immodest (e.g., "would never openly brag about his or her accomplishments," "would show off in front of others") and another eight behaviors exemplified the peripheral trait dimension of uncomplaining–complaining (e.g., "would minimize bad experiences when telling about them," "would constantly talk about how much stuff there is to be done") (Sedikides & Green, 2000, Appendix A). Note that the centrality and peripherality of both the traits and the behaviors were determined through extensive pretesting. When participants finished processing the feedback, they were asked to free recall it.

It is worth pointing out that the experimental task has an important processing implication: It would be extraordinarily difficult for participants to process the self-referent behaviors in the same manner as the Chris-referent behaviors. Let us clarify why we think so. Imagine that you receive feedback to the effect that you are the kind of person who would often lie to your parents. No doubt, you would think spontaneously whether you lied to your parents in the past or are likely to lie to them in the future. You would dig deep into your self-knowledge in answering the question. This is a form of information processing that Klein and Loftus (1988) termed *elaboration* (i.e., thinking about the behaviors in relation to prior knowledge). Alternatively, imagine receiving feedback that Chris is the kind of person who would often lie to his or her parents. In this case, you will likely attempt to comprehend this feedback in terms of generic social knowledge: you will try to determine whether Chris would enact such a behavior on the basis of other information concurrently available about Chris. Klein and Loftus (1988) labeled this type of information processing *organization* (i.e., thinking about the behaviors in relation to one another). In summary, elaborative processing is more likely to be instigated in the case of self-referent feedback, whereas organizational processing is more likely to be instigated in the case of other-referent feedback.

Still, though, some interesting questions arise. How do elaborative and organizational processes operate in the context of the current experimental paradigm? What are the memorial consequences of elaborative and organizational processing? What are the implications of elaborative and organizational processing for self-knowledge and self-definition? Below, we will discuss theoretical formulations that address these questions.

THEORETICAL MODELS ON THE RELATION BETWEEN SELF AND MEMORY

Two theoretical models speak to the relation between self and memory: the inconsistency-negativity resolution model and the inconsistency-negativity neglect model.

The Inconsistency-Negativity Resolution Model

The inconsistency-negativity resolution model (resolution model, for short) is based on proposals that depict people as striving for an accurate, balanced, and truthful self-definition (e.g., Festinger, 1954; Jahoda, 1958; Kelley, 1967; Kruglanski, 1990; Trope, 1986). According to the resolution model, people are motivated to reduce uncertainty about themselves and to find out what kind of person they truly are. When people receive inconsistent feedback, they will attempt to resolve the inconsistency even when such an attempt risks an outcome that has unfavorable implications for their self-definition.

The resolution model posits that inconsistent (i.e., negative, particularly central) feedback about the self will have a processing advantage over other types of feedback (e.g., positive, particularly central), because participants encode inconsistent information more deeply. That is, participants compare and integrate new inconsistent behaviors with stored self-knowledge (*elaboration*). Hence, inconsistent information is linked via multiple associative pathways to stored information. In turn, these pathways facilitate retrieval of the information (Srull & Wyer, 1989). Additionally, the resolution model posits that inconsistent feedback about another person will also be recalled better (Skowronski & Carlston, 1989), although, in this instance, deep processing and associative pathways will result from interbehavior comparisons (*organization*) and attributional processes (Hastie, 1984).

We will proceed with a more detailed description of the resolution model. As mentioned above, behavioral feedback can refer either to the self or Chris. When receiving positive feedback that pertains to central aspects of the self (e.g., "would keep secrets when asked to," "would help a handicapped neighbor paint his or her house"), participants will accept the consistency between feedback and self-knowledge at face value and thus cease processing. Positive feedback is consistent with the self, given that most people's self-definitions are positive (Kendall et al., 1989; Schwartz, 1986). However, when receiving negative feedback about central facets of the self (e.g., "would often lie to his or her parents," "would make fun of others because of their looks"), participants will notice the inconsistency between the feedback and their self-definition and will attempt to resolve it by processing the feedback information deeply (i.e., relating it to self-knowledge). The result will be higher recall for negative central than positive central information.

Importantly, the model also predicts that negative central information that refers to the self will be recalled better than negative central information that refers to Chris, because the former is more inconsistent with self-knowledge than the latter. Finally, the above patterns will hold for central information but not for peripheral information, because the latter will be processed in a shallow manner and thus be recalled poorly regardless of whether it is negative (e.g., "would show off in front of others," "would constantly talk about how much stuff there is to be done") or positive (e.g., "would never openly brag about his or her accomplishments," "would minimize bad experiences when telling about them") and regardless of whether it refers to the self or Chris.

The Inconsistency-Negativity Neglect Model

The inconsistency-negativity neglect model (neglect model, for short) is based on proposals that depict people as striving for a positive self-definition or the avoidance of a negative self-definition; such strivings occur often at the expense of accuracy and truthfulness (Campbell & Sedikides, 1999; Dunning, 1993; Greenberg, Solomon, & Pyszczynski, 1997; Taylor & Brown, 1988; Tesser, 2001). According to the model, people are motivated to neglect the processing of feedback that threatens their self-definition. The more threatening the feedback is, the more likely people are to neglect it (Greenwald, 1981; Holmes, 1970), in the interest of a stable and coherent, albeit positively skewed, self-definition (Beike & Landoll, 2000; Greenwald, 1980; Vallacher & Nowak, 2000).

In particular, the neglect model posits that feedback threatening to the self (i.e., negative central information) will have a processing *dis*advantage over non-threatening feedback (i.e., positive central information). Hence, processing of self-threatening feedback will be terminated early on, resulting in poor recall. However, this relative pattern will not hold in the case in which the negative central feedback refers to Chris: such feedback will have lost much of its threat potential and thus will be processed shallowly.

Next, we will proceed with a more detailed description of the neglect model. When the self-referent behavioral feedback is positive and central (i.e., highly consistent with self-knowledge, and, hence, nonthreatening), participants will process relatively deeply by connecting the behaviors to prior self-knowledge. However, in the case of negative and central self-referent feedback, a clear and present danger exists: participants will regard such feedback as inconsistent with self-knowledge and, thus, threatening. It follows that participants will terminate further processing of these behaviors. As a result, negative central behaviors will be recalled more poorly than positive central behaviors. Furthermore, negative central behaviors referring to the self will be recalled more poorly than negative central behaviors referring to Chris, because the former pose a stronger threat than the latter. However, peripheral behaviors will not be recalled differently, regardless of whether they are negative or positive and whether they refer to the self or Chris: such behaviors are simply not threatening.

EMPIRICAL FINDINGS

Having laid out the rationale and predictions behind the resolution and neglect models, we will proceed with the exposition of our empirical work. The purpose of our initial experiment (Sedikides & Green, 2000, Experiment 1) was to determine the viability of the models by pitting one against the other. Participants took an ostensibly reputable and widely used personality inventory. They were informed that the inventory was rather unique in providing respondents with concrete (i.e., behavioral) feedback. In actuality, the inventory was fabricated (although perceived as valid, according to manipulation checks), and the feedback consisted of the prepared 32 behaviors. As already mentioned, half of these behaviors pertained to central and half to peripheral behaviors, whereas half of the behaviors were positive and half negative. Additionally, half of the participants learned that *they* were likely to enact these behaviors, whereas the remaining half of the participants learned that *Chris* was likely to enact these behaviors. Following the administration of feedback, participants engaged in a distractor exercise. Subsequently, they were given a surprise recall test: they were instructed to recall all behavioral feedback that they received.

The recall findings confirmed the neglect model at the expense of the resolution model. When the feedback referred to the self, participants recalled fewer negative central than positive central behaviors. Moreover, participants recalled fewer negative central behaviors when the feedback referred to the self rather than Chris. (As expected, no recall differences were obtained in the case of peripheral feedback.) Clearly, participants did not allocate processing resources to the pursuit of inconsistent and negative, albeit potentially informative, feedback. Instead, participants neglected information that posed a threat to the positivity and integrity of the self. Participants strove for the preservation or formation of a positive self-definition.

Our preliminary foray into the processes that people deploy to maintain or achieve self-definition led us to the conclusion that people are concerned with assuaging imminent threat rather than welcoming potential accuracy. They are trying to barricade under self-protection rather than venture the unknowns of self-accuracy. In a subsequent experiment (Sedikides & Green, 2000, Experiment 2), we set to test some boundaries of this self-defensive information processing mode. How rigid is self-defensiveness? What if the feedback is not presented to participants under the veneer of a valid personality inventory, but rather as completely imaginary and fictitious? Surely, participants would not be threatened by make-believe information about themselves, would they?

We instructed participants in the self-referent condition to "consider the following description of yourself. Think of the description as being based on actual knowledge of people who know you well. Think of the description as real." We instructed participants in the other-referent condition to "consider the description of a person named Chris. Think of the description as being based on actual knowledge of people who know Chris well. Think of the description as real."

Otherwise, we followed a procedure and design identical to those of the previous experiment.

The findings fully replicated the results of Experiment 1, thus bolstering the neglect model. Participants who engaged in self-referent processing recalled fewer negative central than positive central behaviors. Additionally, participants in the self-referent condition recalled fewer negative central behaviors compared to participants in the Chris-referent condition. (No recall differences emerged in the case of peripheral behaviors.)

So far, in two experiments, we obtained strong support for the neglect model. People are highly motivated to protect the self against threat, even when this threat is hypothetical and seemingly inconsequential. Self-protection appears to be a rather crude and unwieldy mechanism, with seemingly no solid boundaries. The task of self-definition protection is of paramount importance to participants.

Nevertheless, important questions about the neglect model are left unanswered. One such question pertains to information diagnosticity. In the above-mentioned experiments, behavioral feedback was high in diagnosticity: All behaviors were good indicators of the relevant trait. Stated somewhat differently, the behaviors provided credible testimony as to whether a person who enacted them had or did not have the underlying personality trait. For example, a person who keeps secrets is trustworthy, whereas a person who lies to her or his parents is untrustworthy. We opted for the exclusive use of high diagnosticity behaviors, because of our intention to operationalize the construct of psychological threat in a valid way. In particular, we considered high diagnosticity and negative behaviors as especially potent in evoking psychological threat: After all, being informed that you are the kind of person who is not trusted by your employer is not particularly comforting.

The neglect model postulates that recall of negative central feedback referring to the self will be poor when the feedback is diagnostic or threatening. This effect, though, will be canceled out when the feedback is undiagnostic or nonthreatening. We designed an experiment to test directly this tenet of the model (Green & Sedikides, 2004). We used the 32 high diagnosticity behaviors of previous experiments (i.e., Sedikides & Green, 2000, Experiments 1–2), and generated a new set of 32 low diagnosticity behaviors. As before, eight low diagnosticity behaviors exemplified the central trait dimension of trustworthy–untrustworthy (e.g., "would promptly pick up a friend at the agreed-upon time," "would use the toothpaste of a roommate without asking"), and another eight low diagnosticity behaviors exemplified the central trait dimension of kind–unkind (e.g., "would oil a squeaky door in the dorm hallway," "would return a greeting when a stranger says hello on the street"). Also, eight low diagnosticity behaviors exemplified the peripheral trait dimension of modest–immodest (e.g., "would not overemphasize strong points on a graduate school application," "would become rowdy when his or her favorite team wins"), and another eight behaviors exemplified the peripheral trait dimension of uncomplaining-complaining (e.g., "would not send back restaurant food that was slightly overcooked," "would complain about extremely cold or wet weather") (Green & Sedikides, 2004, Appendix). Diagnosticity was manipulated on a between-participants basis. Note that the diagnosticity level of the behaviors was determined through pretesting. The procedure, otherwise, was identical to Experiment 2 of Sedikides and Green (2000). That is, the procedure involved hypothetical feedback.

The findings were fully supportive of the neglect model. Participants recalled fewer negative central self-referent behaviors than positive central self-referent behaviors. Additionally, they recalled fewer negative central behaviors when these behaviors were self-referent than Chris-referent. Interestingly, however, these patterns were obtained *only* when the feedback was diagnostic. In the case of undiagnostic feedback, no differential recall emerged as a function of referent (i.e., self vs. Chris) or information valence (i.e., positive vs. negative behaviors). (As in previous research, no recall differences were found in the case of peripheral feedback.)

The experiment reported above (i.e., Green & Sedikides, 2004) established that threatening behaviors are recalled poorly compared to nonthreatening behaviors. This finding confirms a key tenet of the neglect model: it is threat that underlies low recall of negative, central, and self-referent feedback. Still, however, there is another crucial postulate of the model that needs to be put to empirical scrutiny. This is the postulate that threatening information is processed shallowly.

The neglect model posits that participants allocate minimal processing resources (e.g., time) to negative central self-referent (i.e., threatening) behaviors relative to either positive central self-referent behaviors or negative central Chris-referent behaviors. Minimal processing time, then, is a key determinant of poor recall. Sedikides and Green (2000, Experiment 3) tested this proposition. The experiment exclusively used high diagnosticity behaviors and manipulated the presentation duration of the behaviors. The logic of the experimental design was as follows. If reduced behavior processing time is a determinant of poor recall of negative central self-referent behaviors, then an experimental intervention that limits severely the presentation duration for *all* behaviors would result in poor recall for *all* behaviors, not just negative central self-referent ones.

The procedure was similar to that of Sedikides and Green (2000, Experiment 2), with an important exception. Although in this previous experiment the behaviors were blocked by trait on the same page of the booklet, in this new experiment the behaviors were presented one at a time on a computer screen. Also, the design was similar to that of Sedikides and Green (2000, Experiment 2), with one critical addition: the behavior presentation duration variable. For half of the participants, the behaviors were presented for 8 seconds each (*ample duration* condition). This condition replicated the previously reported experiments. For the other half of the participants, however, the behaviors were presented for 2 seconds each (*limited duration* condition). We arrived at these duration intervals through pretesting.

The prior results were replicated in the *ample duration* condition. Participants who received self-referent feedback recalled fewer negative central behaviors than either those receiving Chris-referent feedback or those receiving positive self-referent feedback. Importantly, these patterns were eliminated in the *limited duration* condition. Here, no significant recall differences were found. These results lend support to a crucial proposition of the neglect model. Feedback that is threatening (i.e., negative central and directed to the self) is recalled poorly because, at least in part, such feedback is allotted minimal processing time. (As in all previous experiments, recall for peripheral behaviors did not vary significantly between experimental conditions.)

Why is threatening feedback allotted minimal processing time? Self-other differences in behavioral expectancies may constitute a reason. In particular, people may expect for the self, but not an acquaintance, to enact highly positive behaviors and to shy away from highly negative behaviors (cf. Gilbert & Gill, 2000; Mischel, Ebbesen, & Zeiss, 1976). If so, negative central self-referent behaviors are recalled poorly not because they pose a threat to the self but rather because they do not fit with participants' expectancies.

We tested empirically this possibility (Sedikides & Green, 2004, Experiment 1). All participants received hypothetical behavioral feedback. However, the referent of the feedback differed. A quarter of participants received feedback about themselves, whereas another quarter of participants received feedback about Chris. These two conditions were identical to those of all of our prior experiments. We introduced two other conditions. The third quarter of participants received feedback referring to a person who had been described to them in glowing terms (Chris/glowing). Specifically, Chris/glowing was described as exceedingly trustworthy, kind, modest, and uncomplaining. Hence, participants had formed highly positive expectancies about Chris/glowing before processing the feedback information. The final quarter of participants received feedback referring to a close friend; naturally, participants had highly positive expectancies about their friends. In fact, extensive pretesting revealed that participants held the most positive expectancies for Chris/glowing, regarding him or her as least likely to enact (central and peripheral) negative behaviors and as most likely to enact (central and peripheral) positive behaviors. Expectancies for close friend and self did not differ significantly, and they were both more positive than expectancies for Chris.

If expectancies alone were a sufficient reason for the phenomenon of neglect, then neglect would be more strongly manifested in the case of Chris/glowing rather than self, and neglect would be manifested to an equal degree for close friend and self. This is not, however, what the evidence arbitrated. Participants displayed the highest level of neglect (i.e., poorest recall for negative and central behaviors) in the self-referent condition, followed by the friend-referent condition and by the Chris/glowing and Chris conditions. Clearly, there is more to the phenomenon of neglect than expectancies. It appears to be something beyond inconsistency that threatens the self.

We wondered whether this "something" might be information valence. Are participants threatened by information inconsistency or rather information valence? Are participants intolerant of inconsistency per se or rather negativity? In our previous work, we confounded information inconsistency with information valence: behaviors consistent with self-knowledge were positive, whereas behaviors inconsistent with self-knowledge were negative. To remedy this problem, we designed an experiment that disentangled information inconsistency from information valence (Sedikides & Green, 2004, Experiment 2). This experiment had the potential to uncover the primary determinant of neglect.

The experiment tested participants whose central self-conceptions were either positive (as was mostly the case in the previous experiments) or negative. As an example, participants with positive self-conceptions regarded the traits trustworthy and kind as self-descriptive, whereas participants with negative self-conceptions regarded the traits untrustworthy and unkind as self-descriptive. To be more specific, we conducted a pilot study with the objective of identifying participants with positive versus negative self-views. Based on their self-descriptiveness ratings, we invited back to the laboratory only those participants with highly positive or highly negative self-views. We provided these participants with behavioral feedback and then gave them a surprise recall task.

Interestingly, both participants with positive self-views *and* those with negative self-views displayed the lowest level of recall for the negative self-referent behaviors. Stated somewhat differently, both participants who considered the traits trustworthy and kind as self-descriptive *as well as* participants who considered the traits untrustworthy and unkind as self-descriptive manifested the lowest recall for untrustworthy and unkind behaviors. Information valence (i.e., negativity) is the primary determinant of neglect. Participants are threatened by self-referent information that is negative, not by self-referent information that is inconsistent.

IMPLICATIONS

The road to self-definition is motivated. The exact nature of this motivation has been debated for at least three thousand years. In the rather venerable tradition of experimental social psychology, we attempted to distil this accumulated philosophical wisdom into two testable theoretical models: the resolution model and the neglect model. The former model postulates deeper processing and predicts superior recall of feedback that threatens cherished aspects of self-knowledge. The latter model postulates shallow processing and predicts inferior recall of self-threatening feedback.

Using a personality feedback and a hypothetical feedback paradigm, we rendered empirical substance to the neglect model. Participants recalled threatening information about the self poorly. In fact, they recalled self-threatening information more poorly compared to either nonthreatening information about the self or threatening information about another person. We termed this phenomenon "neglect" and, given its implicit and unintentional nature, we regarded it as a defensive mechanism functioning to stabilize and consolidate a positive self-definition. (For a discussion of classification criteria for defense mechanisms, see Cramer, 1998, 2000, 2001.)

What are the determinants of neglect? In another empirical investigation, we established that a reason for the phenomenon of neglect is decreased allocation of processing resources to the threatening information: as predicted by the inconsistency-negativity neglect model, participants allocated limited processing time to self-threatening feedback. In still another empirical investigation, we ruled out self-other asymmetries in expectancies as an explanation for neglect. Neglect is not necessarily due to the violation of highly positive behavioral expectancies for the self relative to others.

We believe that our most definitive empirical finding involved pinning down the phenomenon of neglect to information valence. A core determinant of neglect is feedback negativity. Participants process shallowly and recall poorly threatening feedback because this feedback is negative, not because the feedback is inconsistent with self-knowledge. Memory serves the function of shielding a positive self-definition from negativity.

The identification of feedback negativity as the primary determinant of neglect is in line with research on autobiographical memory. People remember poorly unpleasant as opposed to pleasant life events (Skowronski, Betz, Thompson, & Shannon, 1991; Walker, Skowronski, & Thompson, 2003). Autobiographical memory, however, is influenced by meta-cognitive beliefs. People's current theories of themselves influence recall for past self-attributes (Conway & Ross, 1984; Ross, 1989; Ross & Buehler, 2001). Given that, for the most part, people harbor overblown evaluations of themselves (Brown & Dutton, 1995; Sedikides, 1993; Sedikides & Strube, 1997), they will remember their past as more positive (or less negative) than it really is. A reason for biased autobiographical recall is that affect linked to unpleasant events fades faster than affect linked to pleasant events (Walker et al., 2003). Another reason is the selective accessibility of autobiographical memories (Sanitioso, Kunda, & Fong, 1990). Self-enhancing or self-protective motivation leads to an autobiographical search for motive-consistent evidence. This search, reinforced through social rehearsal (Walker et al., 2003) is bound to lead to a positive self-inference (Kunda, 1987; Kunda & Sanitioso, 1989; Sanitioso et al., 1990).

Our experimental paradigm differed in an important way from autobiographical memory research. We were concerned with the on-line processing of a concrete and experimentally provided array of self-relevant information rather than the reconstruction of pleasant or unpleasant subjective life events. Thus, in our research, we exerted tight control over the to-be-remembered material (Banaji & Crowder, 1989). In so doing, our experimental paradigm complements nicely autobiographical memory research. In particular, our findings offer another compelling explanation for the well-established pattern of relatively poor autobiographical memory for unpleasant events: Such events are remembered poorly because they are processed in a shallow processing at the time of their occurrence.

Our investigation is also relevant to a highly nuanced debate, the consistency-positivity debate (e.g., Sedikides & Strube, 1997; Swann, Rentfrow, & Guinn, 2002). Does the human perceiver strive for information that is consistent with self-knowledge or for information that is positive? Are people concerned with a consistent or a positive self-definition? To recast the debate terms in terms of our current experimental paradigm, what type of self-relevant information will people remember poorly — information that is inconsistent with self-knowledge or information that is negative? Our findings (i.e., Sedikides & Green, 2004, Experiment 2) provide an unequivocal answer to this last question. People remember poorly negative information, regardless of whether this information is consistent or inconsistent with self-knowledge. (For a conceptual replication, see Sedikides, 1993, Experiment 4.) It is the avoidance of negativity rather than the avoidance of inconsistency that motivates more strongly self-definitional strivings.

What are the physiological and neuropsychological bases of neglect? Evidence supports the notion that the left hemisphere is implicated in self-defensive processing. Greater EEG activity in the left hemisphere is associated with defensive processing of opposing argumentation (Cacioppo, Petty, & Quintanar, 1982) and, more generally, with a repressive cognitive style (Tomarken & Davidson, 1994). Additionally, when left hemispheric activation is induced, recall of unpleasant information (Drake, 1991) as well as selective discounting of truthful information (Drake, 1993) become more prevalent. It follows from the research that the left hemisphere will be more potently implicated in the phenomenon of neglect.

Although we consider neglect a fundamental and general self-defensive process, we wish to acknowledge our exclusive reliance on a single memorial measure, namely free recall. Research using additional assessments, such as recognition memory (Mischel et al., 1976; Story, 1998; Tafarodi, Tam, & Milne, 2001), will need to test the external validity of our findings and conclusions. In a related vein, it is worth exploring the limitations of our free recall-based experimental paradigm. We wondered whether the functionality of the feedback places boundaries on neglect. For example, when threatening or critical feedback comes from a close other (e.g., romantic partner, friend), it cannot be easily neglected. This is because the future of the relationship depends on how the individual responds to criticism and also because the individual anticipates continuing interactions with the feedback-giver and hence is likely to feel accountable for the manner in which criticism is handled. Consequently, the individual may become self-aware of his or her inadequacies, take a long-term view toward self-improvement and relationship-improvement, and pour cognitive resources into processing and hence remembering the critical feedback better (Duval & Silvia, 2002; Sedikides, Herbst, Hardin, & Dardis, 2002).

Past research is consistent with the hypothesis that relationship closeness curtails self-enhancement. In particular, participants are less likely to manifest the self-serving bias (i.e., taking credit for success but displacing responsibility for failure) when they work interdependently with a close other as opposed to a stranger (Sedikides, Campbell, Reeder, & Elliot, 2002). Will relationship closeness curtail self-protection as well? We conducted an experiment to find out if the source of feedback attenuates, eliminates, or even reverses neglect (Pinter, Green, & Sedikides, 2004). We followed the same basic method, procedure, and design as in the previous experiments, but made one critical addition: half of the participants were instructed to imagine that the source of the feedback was an acquaintance, whereas the remaining half imagined that the source of the feedback was a close friend. The phenomenon of neglect was replicated but was unqualified by source of feedback. That is, participants recalled poorly self-threatening information (compared either to non self-threatening information or Chris-threatening information) regardless of whether the source of feedback was a stranger or a close other.

The lack of evidence for the neglect-constraining role of close relationships may have to do with a weakness in our manipulation: the presence of the close other was imagined rather than real. Although imagination instructions are sufficient to produce powerful statistical effects, as much of the current research has demonstrated, we will need to replicate the Pinter and colleagues' (2004) study with a more realistic procedure. As part of such a procedure, participants will report to the laboratory with a close other (friend or romantic partner). The members of the dyad will be tested in separate rooms but they will be mildly deceived into believing that the source of the behavioral feedback is the close other (cf. Sedikides et al., 2002). For example, they will be told that their close companion was presented with an extensive list of behaviors and was instructed to select those 32 behaviors that best described them.

We are also in the process of exploring another potential qualifier of neglect, trait modifiability. Past research has shown that participants reduce their self-enhancement tendencies when they evaluate themselves on traits they perceive as modifiable compared to traits they perceive as unmodifiable (Alicke, 1985; Dunning, 1995). The explanation for this finding is that unmodifiable traits leave participants with no option but to self-defend; on the other hand, modifiable traits afford participants the option of working harder toward improvement (Dweck, 1999; Sedikides, 1999; Sedikides & Strube, 1997). To extrapolate, it is likely that participants will display exaggerated neglect when they regard the behavioral feedback as unmodifiable, but will manifest reduced or no neglect when they consider the behavioral feedback as modifiable. Along with trait modifiability, self-affirmation is also likely to yield a reduction or elimination of neglect. A substantial bolstering of one's self-worth can form such a self-protective buffer that the impact of central, negative, self-referent feedback is rather negligible (Sherman & Cohen, 2002).

The role of individual differences is also worth considering. Two highly relevant variables are self-esteem and narcissism. Recent research has shown that high self-esteem individuals and narcissists are easily threatened compared to their counterparts (Baumeister, Smart, & Boden, 1996; Brown, Farnham, & Cook, 2002; Heatherton & Vohs, 2000; Sedikides, Campbell, Reeder, Elliot, & Gregg, 2002). Other research has reported that, following threat, high self-esteem individuals and narcissists solicit competency feedback, whereas low self-esteem individuals and non-narcissists seek out interpersonal feedback (Campbell, Rudich, & Sedikides, 2002; Vohs & Heatherton, 2001). Based on these research findings, we venture to hypothesize that, compared to their counterparts, individuals high in self-esteem and narcissism (1) will manifest more neglect (a rather counterintuitive hypothesis) and, in particular, (2) will display more neglect when the behavioral feedback pertains to the competency rather than the interpersonal dimension. Other individual difference variables, such as repressive coping (Newman & McKinney, 2002) and self-doubt (Herman, Leonardelli, & Arkin, 2002) are also promising and worthy of empirical attention.

Finally, the phenomenon of neglect may be qualified by a broader dimension, cultural context. Although it has been proposed (Heine, Lehman, Markus, & Kitayama, 1999) that members of Eastern cultures (e.g., East Asia) are less likely to self-enhance than members of Western cultures (e.g., North America), this proposal has been challenged recently with the counterargument that members of both Eastern and Western cultures self-enhance on personally important attributes: Easterners self-enhance on interdependent attributes (e.g., loyal), whereas Westerners self-enhance on independent attributes (e.g., leader) (Sedikides, Gaertner, & Toguchi, 2003). More relevant to the point, members of Eastern culture are relatively more likely to engage in self-protective information processing (Elliot, Chirkov, Kim, & Sheldon, 2001). It would be interesting, then, to explore whether Easterners display higher levels of neglect than Westerners.

CONCLUDING NOTES

How does the individual connect with the social environment? This question has been pondered by several towering figures in the social sciences, such as Cooley (1902), Mead (1934), Durkheim (1950), and Weber (1964). We propose that self-definitional strivings represent an important connectional mechanism, if not the ultimate glue. Indeed, self-definition is a pivotal task not only in late childhood and adolescence (Damon, 1983; Damon & Hart, 1986), but throughout the life course (Breytspraak, 1984; Roberts, Caspi, & Moffitt, 2001). Self-definition is also a dynamic and contextually dependent process (Brewer & Roccas, 2001; Onorato & Turner, 2001; Spears, 2001). A critical assumption underlying our program of research is that core elements of the self-definition processes can be captured and distilled in the laboratory. In several experiments, we obtained support for the notion that, at least in early adulthood, people process information selectively and strategically in order to shield off the self from negative information.

The avoidance of negativity is extraordinarily powerful. We have been impressed by the robustness of the phenomenon of neglect and regard it as a Nietzschean case of memory yielding to pride. People are so hypersensitive to threat potential that they will even neglect self-threatening feedback that is fictitious and seemingly harmless. They are so intolerant to negativity that they will neglect it regardless of whether it is consistent or inconsistent with self-knowledge. And they will mobilize recall in the service of the implicit goal of deflecting negativity and stabilizing a positive self-definition.

REFERENCES

Alicke, M. D. (1985). Global self-evaluation as determined by the desirability and controllability of trait adjectives. *Journal of Personality and Social Psychology, 49,* 1621–1630.

Banaji, M. R., & Crowder, R. G. (1989). The bankruptcy of everyday memory. *American Psychologist, 44,* 1185–1193.

Baumeister, R. F. (1998). The self. In D. T. Gilbert, S. T. Fiske, & G. Lindzey (Eds.), *The handbook of social psychology* (Vol. 1, pp. 680–740). New York: Oxford University Press.

Baumeister, R. F., Smart, L., & Boden, J. M. (1996). Relation of threatened egotism to violence and aggression: The dark side of high self-esteem. *Psychological Review, 103,* 5–33.

Beike, D. R., & Landoll, S. L. (2000). Striving for a consistent life story: Cognitive reactions to autobiographical memories. *Social Cognition, 18,* 292–318.

Brewer, M. B., & Roccas, S. (2001). Individual values, social identity, and optimal distinctiveness. In C. Sedikides & M. F. Brewer (Eds.), *Individual self, relational self, collective self* (pp. 219–237). Philadelphia, PA: Psychology Press.

Breytspraak, L. (1984). *The development of self in later life.* Boston: Little, Brown.

Brown, J. D., & Dutton, K. A. (1995). Truth and consequences: The costs and benefits of accurate self-knowledge. *Personality and Social Psychology Bulletin, 21,* 1288–1296.

Brown, J. D., Farnham, S. D., & Cook, K. E. (2002). Emotional responses to changing feedback: Is it better to have won and lost than never to have won at all? *Journal of Personality, 70,* 127–141.

Cacioppo, J. T., Petty, R. E., & Quintanar, L. R. (1982). Individual differences in relative hemispheric alpha abundance and cognitive responses to persuasive communications. *Journal of Personality and Social Psychology, 43,* 623–636.

Cairns, R. B. (1990). Developmental epistemology and self-knowledge: Towards a reinterpretation of self-esteem. In G. Greenberg & E. Tobach (Eds.), *Theories of the evolution of knowing: The T. C. Schneirla conference series* (Vol. 4, pp. 69–86). Hillsdale, NJ: Erlbaum.

Campbell, W. K., Rudich, E., & Sedikides, C. (2002). Narcissism, self-esteem, and the positivity of self-views: Two portraits of self-love. *Personality and Social Psychology Bulletin, 28,* 358–368.

Campbell, W. K., & Sedikides, C. (1999). Self-threat magnifies the self-serving bias: A meta-analytic integration. *Review of General Psychology, 3,* 23–43.

Conway, M., & Ross, M. (1984). Getting what you want by revising what you had. *Journal of Personality and Social Psychology, 47,* 738–748.

Cooley, C. H. (1902). *Human nature and the social order.* New York: Scribner's.

Cramer, P. (1998). Coping and defense mechanisms: What's the difference? *Journal of Personality, 66,* 233–247.

Cramer, P. (2000). Defense mechanisms in psychology today: Further processes for adaptation. *American Psychologist, 56,* 761–762.

Cramer, P. (2001). The unconscious status of defense mechanisms. *American Psychologist, 56,* 762–763.

Damon, W. (1983). *Social and personality development: Infancy through adolescence.* New York: Norton.

Damon, W., & Hart, D. (1986). Stability and change in children's self-understanding. *Social Cognition, 4,* 102–118.

Drake, R. A. (1991). Processing persuasive arguments: Recall and recognition as a function of agreement and manipulated activation asymmetry. *Brain and Cognition, 15,* 83–94.

Drake, R. A. (1993). Processing persuasive arguments: 2. Discounting of truth and relevance as a function of agreement and manipulated activation asymmetry. *Journal of Research in Personality, 27,* 184–196.

Dunning, D. (1993). Words to live by: The self and definitions of social concepts and categories. In J. Suls (Ed.), *Psychological perspectives on the self* (Vol. 4, pp. 99–126). Hillsdale, NJ: Erlbaum.

Dunning, D. (1995). Trait importance and modifiability as factors influencing self-assessment and self-enhancement motives. *Personality and Social Psychology Bulletin, 21,* 1297–1306.

Durkheim, E. (1950). *The rule of sociological method.* New York: Free Press.

Duval, T. S., & Silvia, P. J. (2002). Self-awareness, probability of improvement, and the self-serving bias. *Journal of Personality and Social Psychology, 82,* 49–61.

Dweck, C. S. (1999). *Self theories: Their role in motivation, personality, and development.* Philadelphia, PA: Psychology Press.

Elliot, A. J., Chirkov, V. I., Kim, Y., & Sheldon, K. M. (2001). A cross-cultural analysis of avoidance (relative to approach) personal goals. *Psychological Science, 12,* 505–510.

Festinger, L. (1954). A theory of social comparison processes. *Human Relations, 2,* 117–140.

Gilbert, D. T., & Gill, M. J. (2000). The momentary realist. *Psychological Science, 11,* 394–398.

Green, J. A., & Sedikides, C. (2004). Retrieval selectivity in the processing of self-referent information: Testing the boundaries of self-protection. *Self and Identity, 3,* 69–80.

Greenberg, J., Solomon, S., & Pyszczynski, T. (1997). Terror management theory of self-esteem and cultural worldviews: Empirical assessments and cultural refinements. In M. Zanna (Ed.), *Advances in experimental social psychology* (Vol. 29, pp. 61–139). San Diego, CA: Academic Press.

Greenwald, A. G. (1980). The totalitarian ego: Fabrication and revision of personal history. *American Psychologist, 35,* 603–618.

Greenwald, A. G. (1981). Self and memory: In G. H. Bower (Ed.), *The psychology of learning and motivation* (Vol. 15, pp. 201–236). Orlando, FL: Academic Press.

Hastie, R. (1984). Causes and effects of causal attribution. *Journal of Personality and Social Psychology, 46,* 44–56.

Heatherton, T. F., & Vohs, K. D. (2000). Interpersonal evaluations following threats to self: Role of self-esteem. *Journal of Personality and Social Psychology, 78,* 725–736.

Heine, S. J., Lehman, D. R., Markus, H. R., & Kitayama, S. (1999). Is there a universal need for positive self-regard? *Psychological Review, 106,* 766–794.

Herman, A. D., Leonardelli, G. J., & Arkin, R. M. (2002). Self-doubt and self-esteem: A threat from within. *Personality and Social Psychology Bulletin, 28,* 395–408.

Holmes, D. S. (1970). Differential change in affective intensity and the forgetting of unpleasant personal experiences. *Journal of Personality and Social Psychology, 15,* 234–239.

Jahoda, M. (1958). *Current conceptions of positive mental health.* New York: Basic Books.

Kelley, H. H. (1967). Attribution theory in social psychology. In D. Levine (Ed.), *Nebraska symposium on motivation* (pp. 192–238). Lincoln: University of Nebraska Press.

Kendall, P, C., Howard, B. L., & Hays, R. C. (1989). Self-referent speech and psychopathology: The balance of positive and negative thinking. *Cognitive Therapy and Research, 13,* 583–598.

Klein, S. B., & Loftus, J. (1988). The nature of self-referent encoding: The contributions of elaborative and organizational process. *Journal of Personality and Social Psychology, 55,* 5–11.

Kruglanski, A. W. (1990). Motivations for judging and knowing: Implications for causal attribution. In E. T. Higgins & R. M. Sorrentino (Eds.), *Handbook of motivation and cognition* (Vol. 2, pp. 333–368). New York: Guilford Press.

Kunda, Z. (1987). Motivation and inference: Self-serving generation and evaluation of evidence. *Journal of Personality and Social Psychology, 53,* 636–647.

Kunda, Z., & Sanitioso, R. (1989). Motivated changes in the self-concept. *Journal of Experimental Social Psychology, 25,* 272–285.

Mead, G. H. (1934). *Mind, self, and society.* Chicago: University of Chicago Press.

Mischel, W., Ebbesen, E. B., & Zeiss, A. M. (1976). Determinants of selective memory about the self. *Journal of Consulting and Clinical Psychology, 44,* 92–103.

Newman, L. S., & McKinney, L. C. (2002). Repressive coping and threat-avoidance: An idiographic Stroop study. *Personality and Social Psychology Bulletin, 28,* 409–422.

Onorato, R. S., & Turner, J. C. (2001). The "I," the "Me," and the "Us": The psychological group and self-concept maintenance and change. In C. Sedikides & M. F. Brewer (Eds.), *Individual self, relational self, collective self* (pp. 219–237). Philadelphia, PA: Psychology Press.

Pinter, B. T., Green, J. D., & Sedikides, C. (2002). *Does relationship closeness attenuate neglect?* Unpublished data, The Pennsylvania State University — Altoona College.

Roberts, B. W., Caspi, A., & Moffitt, T. E. (2001). The kids are alright: Growth and stability in personality development from adolescence to adulthood. *Journal of Personality and Social Psychology, 81,* 670–683.

Ross, M. (1989). Relation of implicit theories to the construction of personal histories. *Psychological Review, 96,* 341–357.

Ross, M., & Buehler, R. (2001). Identity through time: Constructing personal pasts and futures. In A. Tesser & N. Schwarz (Eds.), *Blackwell handbook of social psychology: Intraindividual processes* (pp. 518–544). Oxford, England: Blackwell Publishers.

Sanitioso, R., Kunda, Z., & Fong, G. T. (1990). Motivated recruitment of autobiographical memories. *Journal of Personality and Social Psychology, 59,* 229–241.

Schwartz, R. M. (1986). The internal dialogue: On the asymmetry between positive and negative coping thoughts. *Cognitive Therapy and Research, 10,* 591–605.

Sedikides, C. (1993). Assessment, enhancement, and verification determinants of the self-evaluation process. *Journal of Personality and Social Psychology, 65,* 317–338.

Sedikides, C. (1995). Central and peripheral self-conceptions are differentially influenced by mood: Tests of the differential sensitivity hypothesis. *Journal of Personality and Social Psychology, 69,* 759–777.

Sedikides, C. (1999). A multiplicity of motives: The case of self-improvement. *Psychological Inquiry, 9,* 64–65.

Sedikides, C., Campbell, W. K., Reeder, G., & Elliot, A. J. (2002). The self in relationships: Whether, how, and when close others put the self "in its place." In W. Stroebe & M. Hewstone (Eds.), *European review of social psychology* (pp. 237–265). New York: Wiley.

Sedikides, C., Campbell, W. K., Reeder, G., Elliot, A. J., & Gregg, A. P. (2002). Do others bring out the worst in narcissists? The "Others Exist for Me" illusion. In Y. Kashima, M. Foddy, & M. Platow (Eds.), *Self and identity: Personal, social, and symbolic* (pp. 103–123). Mahwah, NJ: Erlbaum.

Sedikides, C., Gaertner, L., & Toguchi, Y. (2003). Pancultural self-enhancement. *Journal of Personality and Social Psychology, 84,* 60–79.

Sedikides, C., & Green, J. D. (2000). On the self-protective nature of inconsistency/negativity management: Using the person memory paradigm to examine self-referent memory. *Journal of Personality and Social Psychology, 79,* 906–922.

Sedikides, C., & Green, J. D. (2004). What I don't recall can't hurt me: Information negativity versus information inconsistency as determinants of memorial self defense. *Social Cognition, 22,* 4–29.

Sedikides, C., Herbst, K. C., Hardin, D. P., & Dardis, G. J. (2002). Accountability as a deterrent to self-enhancement: The search for mechanisms. *Journal of Personality and Social Psychology, 83,* 592–605.

Sedikides, C., & Strube, M. J. (1997). Self-evaluation: To thine own self be good, to thine own self be sure, to thine own self be true, and to thine own self be better. In M. P. Zanna (Ed.), *Advances in experimental social psychology, 29,* 209–269.

Sherman, D. K., & Cohen, G. L. (2002). Accepting threatening information: Self–affirmation and the reduction of defensive biases. *Current Directions in Psychological Science, 11,* 119–123.

Skowronski, J. J., Betz, A. L., Thompson, C. P., & Shannon, L. (1991). Social memory in everyday life: Recall of self-events and other-events. *Journal of Personality and Social Psychology, 60,* 831–843.

Skowronski, J. J., & Carlston, D. E. (1989). Negativity and extremity biases in impression formation: A review of explanations. *Psychological Bulletin, 105,* 131–142.

Spears, R. (2001). The interaction between the individual and the collective self: Self-categorization in context. In C. Sedikides & M. F. Brewer (Eds.), *Individual self, relational self, collective self* (pp. 219–237). Philadelphia, PA: Psychology Press.

Srull, T. K., & Wyer, R. S., Jr. (1989). Person memory and judgment. *Psychological Review, 96,* 58–83.

Story, A. (1998). Self-esteem and memory for favorable and unfavorable personality feedback. *Personality and Social Psychology Bulletin, 24,* 51–64.

Strube, M. J. (1990). In search of self: Balancing the good and the true. *Personality and Social Psychology Bulletin, 16,* 699–704.

Strube, M. J., Yost, J. H., & Bailey, J. R. (1992). William James and contemporary research on the self: The influence of pragmatism, reality, and truth. In M. E. Donnelley (Ed.), *Reinterpreting the legacy of William James* (pp. 189–207). Washington, D.C.: American Psychological Association.

Swann, W. B., Jr. (1987). Identity negotiation: Where two roads meet. *Journal of Personality and Social Psychology, 53,* 1038–1051.

Swann, W. B., Jr., Rentfrow, P. J., & Guinn, J. S. (2002). Self-verification: The search for coherence. In M. R. Leary & J. P. Tangney (Eds.), *Handbook of self and identity* (pp. 367–383). New York: Guilford Press.

Tafarodi, R. W., Tam, J., & Milne, A. B. (2001). Selective memory and the persistence of paradoxical self-esteem. *Personality and Social Psychology Bulletin, 27,* 1179–1189.

Taylor, S. E., & Brown, J. D. (1988). Illusion and well-being: A social psychological perspective on mental health. *Psychological Bulletin, 103,* 193–210.

Taylor, S. E., Lerner, J. S., Sherman, D. K., Sage, R. M., & McDowell, N. K. (2003). Portrait of the self-enhancer: Well adjusted and well liked or maladjusted and friendless? *Journal of Personality and Social Psychology, 84,* 165–176.

Tesser, A. (2001). On the plasticity of self-defense. *Current Directions in Psychological Science, 10,* 66–69.

Tomarken, A. J., & Davidson, R. J. (1994). Frontal brain activity in repressors and nonrepressors. *Journal of Abnormal Psychology, 103,* 339–349.

Trope, Y. (1986). Self-enhancement and self-assessment in achievement behavior. In R. M. Sorrentino & E. T. Higgins (Eds.), *Handbook of motivation and cognition: Foundations of social behavior* (Vol. 1, pp. 350–378). New York: Guilford Press.

Turner, J. C., Oakes, P. J., Haslam, S. A., & McGarty, C. (1994). Self and collective: Cognition and social context. *Personality and Social Psychology Bulletin, 20,* 454–463.

Updegraff, J. A., & Taylor, S. E. (2000). From vulnerability to growth: The positive and negative effects of stressful life events. In J. Harvey & E. Miller (Eds.), *Loss and trauma: General and close relationship perspectives* (pp. 3–28). Philadelphia, PA: Brunner-Routledge.

Vallacher, R. R., & Nowak, A. (2000). Landscapes of self-reflection: Mapping the peaks and valleys of personal assessment. In A. Tesser, R. B. Felson, & J. M. Suls (Eds.), *Psychological perspectives on self and identity* (pp. 35–65). Washington, D.C.: American Psychological Association.

Vohs, K. D., & Heatherton, T. F. (2001). Self-esteem and threats to self: Implications for self-construals and interpersonal perceptions. *Journal of Personality and Social Psychology, 81,* 1103–1118.

Walker, W. R., Skowronski, J. J., & Thompson, C. P. (2003). Life is pleasant — and memory helps to keep it that way! *Review of General Psychology, 4,* 203–210.

Weber, M. (1964). *Basic concepts in sociology.* New York: Citadel Press.

4

THE SELF
AND MEMORY
ACROSS TIME

9

Who Was I When That Happened? The Timekeeping Self in Autobiographical Memory

JOHN J. SKOWRONSKI
Northern Illinois University

W. RICHARD WALKER
Winston-Salem State University

ANDREW L. BETZ
Progressive Insurance

*P*sychology has long been concerned with the sources of self-knowledge. Although some self-knowledge takes the form of stored self-inferences, other self-knowledge involves memory for individual events (Klein, 2001; Klein, Babey, & Sherman, 1997; Klein, Chan, & Loftus, 1999). Much of the research exploring memory for self-events has focused on the content of such stored memories. This focus is entirely appropriate: after all, the content of those memories may provide substantial grist for the self-inference mill (see Sedikides & Skowronski, 1995), regardless of whether inferences are made when events occur or when events are retrieved. However, in our view, a third important component of self-knowledge is temporal knowledge. That is, the self not only contains a sense of what a person is right now, but it also conveys a sense of growth, development, and change. Are you the same person today that you were yesterday? Are you the same person that you were last week, last month, or last year? Are you the same person today that you were before the terrorist destruction of the World Trade Center? These questions would not easily be answerable without knowledge of *when* events happened.

In order to create and maintain this sense of continuity and change, the self must be able to project itself through time with a fair degree of accuracy. We think that this ability is highly functional: events in the recent past are more likely to be applicable to a person's current situation than older events. This temporal projection ability might also be useful in predicting the future: in prospective tasks, the self must be able to anticipate possible future events in order to make appropriate plans. This capability of projecting the self forward in time might also allow a person to better consider the possible consequences of his or her intended actions.

The functionality of temporal knowledge is also highlighted if one attempts to imagine what life would be like if one had perfect recall for the content of all the events that happened in one's life, but no sense of when the events occurred. It seems obvious that a person who had no access to temporal knowledge would likely have a difficult time functioning. Such a person would also likely have a difficult time developing and managing a self-concept. Larsen, Thompson, and Hansen (1996) neatly captured the interrelations between temporal knowledge, adaptive functioning and the self when they wrote: "Indeed, a person whose past was lacking temporal organization could not have the awareness of a history, of a course of development that is a defining part of the experience of a self; she/he would not only be a disorderly person, but a severely disordered personality" (p. 129). A loss of the ability to remember the times at which events occurred is, indeed, an indicator of psychological dysfunctions, including those resulting from closed-head injuries, alcohol-related dementia (Meudell, Mayes, Ostergaard, & Pickering, 1985; Shimamura, Janowsky, & Squire, 1990), and Alzheimer's disease (Madsen & Kesner, 1995).

We know from past research that a person's ability to place events in time is derived from many different memory-based sources, such as time cues that are retrieved with event memories or the accessibility of memory traces. People can also use external cues, records, or devices to locate events in time (e.g., a review of a calendar stored in one's Palm Pilot). However, building on the thinking of Larsen and colleagues (1996), we argue in this chapter that another source of temporal knowledge is derived from the self. We propose that a person's self-concept is inexorably linked to the ability to gauge the passage of time, an idea that we term the *timekeeping self*.

Our reasoning is straightforward. As people experience new events, their self-concept is altered. We postulate that the ability to place events in time is related to changes in the self that occur as a result of such events. These changes, as reflected in the timekeeping self, can serve as the source of a rough guess about an event's age when other strategies or external aids might fail to provide cues to that age. However, when other temporal information sources are available, this guess can be augmented by, supplanted by, or combined with the application of knowledge derived from these additional sources. Hence, we think that relating an event to the self may often contribute a "base estimate" to the age of an event, an estimate that can be further altered by access to other cues available in memory.

Our ideas about the timekeeping self will be in a clearer focus if they are presented in the context of other research and theory that has pursued sources of temporal knowledge. In the next sections of this chapter we present a brief review of some of the existing theory and research.

EXISTING THEORETICAL IDEAS EXPLAINING MEMORY FOR TIME

There are a number of theoretical ideas that attempt to explain how people know when an event occurred. In recent years at least one conclusion has consistently emerged from the diverse body of research that has been stimulated by these theoretical ideas: rarely does exact temporal information (often called a temporal tag) accompany an event memory. Instead, in most instances, the time at which an event occurred must be *reconstructed* from a variety of clues that an individual has at his or her disposal (for reviews, see Friedman, 1993; Larsen et al., 1996).

For example, one of the classic signatures of reconstructive processing is the presence of systematic biases in recall. Such biases emerge frequently in studies of temporal memory. These biases, several of which are discussed in more detail later in this chapter, include: (1) the day-of-week effect in dating errors (guessing that an event occurred on the correct day of the week, but placing the event in the wrong week); (2) the effects of boundaries on forward and backward telescoping biases (these biases are defined as underestimation and overestimation of an event's age, respectively); (3) the effects of memory clarity and memory accessibility on forward telescoping; and (4) output biases in which temporal estimates are rounded to prototypic values (an event that is 26 days old is said to be "about a month" old). Yet other temporal reconstruction errors are described elsewhere in this volume. For example, Ross's chapter discusses how people's estimates of event age are biased by the self-protective and self-enhancing motives of the self.

Before reviewing some of the theories relevant to temporal reconstruction, we should say at the outset that, in our view, none of the theories that have attempted to explain how temporal information is reconstructed and how such biases are produced provides a complete explanation. Instead, we believe that the mental structures and processes that are involved in reconstructing an event's age will vary, depending on such things as: (1) the cues that are available when temporal reconstructions are concocted, (2) the way that people are asked to report their temporal reconstructions (age, exact date), and (3) the amount of precision that is required in the temporal reconstructions. Research findings are consistent with this pluralistic view. For example, people who are attempting to reconstruct event dates report using a variety of cues and strategies to reconstruct those dates (Betz & Skowronski, 1997; Skowronski, Betz, Thompson, & Larsen, 1995; Thompson, Gibbons, Vogl, & Walker, 1997; Thompson, Skowronski, & Betz, 1993).

Associative linkage or order code models (see Kemp, 1999; McElree & Dosher, 1993; Underwood, 1977) suggest that event ages can be derived from associative links among events. This idea is consistent with results provided by Anderson and Conway (1993), who found that the details of autobiographical events were recalled more easily when they were ordered from beginning to end rather than using another recall strategy (e.g., try recalling the most important detail first). The formation of such ordered associations among events might be prompted by repeated event comparisons. For example, Barry Bonds's major-league home run record might often be compared to the record held by the prior record-holder, Mark McGuire. Such comparisons may also be prompted or reinforced by the narratives produced during social interactions, such as describing to a friend how a recently completed vacation was better than the previous one (Guenther & Linton, 1975; Schank & Abelson, 1995). Alternatively, such linkages might be produced by the vagaries of memory: as one event spontaneously reminds one of an earlier event, the link between the two events would be accompanied by knowledge of which event came first (e.g., meeting a new graduate student for the first time might remind one of a similar meeting that happened with a student last year; see N. R. Brown & Schopflocher, 1998a,b; Winograd & Soloway, 1985). In addition, associative linkages can exist because of knowledge structures, such as scripts, that provide expectations about event sequences (Schank & Abelson, 1977). When memory is vague, these scripts can be the source of reasonable guesses about probable event orders. In addition, these scripts can prompt people to extensively process relations between events that violate the script so that temporal information related to the script-violating events are well recalled (e.g., "There was this one time, though, when the waiter did not bring us the wine until we had all finished our meal"; see Reiser, Black, & Abelson, 1985). Additional temporal information might come from "counting links." That is, when events are chained or sequenced, one might be able to get a sense of how much time passed between two events by counting the number of events that intervene between the two events of interest.

Sometimes the associations that aid temporal memory are not between events themselves, but are between events and higher-order categories that can be arrayed to provide a sense of temporal order. For example, imagine that a person takes a trip on which she first flew to Chicago and then to St. Louis. The Chicago events might all be organized around a "Chicago" node in the mental representation while the St. Louis events might all be organized around a "St. Louis" node. Hence, if one remembers that a particular event occurred while one was in Chicago, then it must have occurred in the first part of the trip. When outlining a model of order judgment known as perturbation theory, Estes (see Estes, 1972, 1987) suggested that this type of organizational structure exists in people's short-term memory for event orders in serial lists. Nairne (1991) extended perturbation theory to long-term memory, which presumably includes autobiographical memory. Recent hierarchical models of the structure of autobiographical memory, including those in which events can be linked to life periods or themes (e.g., when I was a sophomore in college), can be viewed as a variant of the mental structures that are fundamental to perturbation models (Conway & Bekerian, 1987; Conway & Pleydell-Pearce, 2000; Conway & Rubin, 1993).

Perturbation-style models are intriguing because they can conceivably explain numerous effects that appear in the temporal judgment literature. For example, perturbation models predict that people may be more likely to confuse the order of events that are linked to the same node in memory than events that are linked to different nodes. This can occur even when the events linked to two different nodes occurred more closely to each other in real time than events linked to the same node. For example, assume that on my vacation I visited Brookfield Zoo on Monday, U.S. Cellular Field on Saturday, and the Gateway Arch on Sunday. Perturbation models predict that I could be more likely to confuse the order of the two Chicago events (the visits to Brookfield Zoo and U.S. Cellular Field) than the order of the two events that occurred on consecutive days but in different cities (U.S. Cellular Field and Gateway Arch). This increased confusion can occur despite the fact that it is usually easier to make order judgments of events that are widely separated in time (in this case, Monday and Saturday) than events that are temporally proximate (e.g., Saturday and Sunday). Variants of this finding have emerged in laboratory research examining recall of positions in serial lists (Nairne, 1991), as well as in autobiographical memory studies examining recall for real-world event orders (Fuhrman & Wyer, 1988; Skowronski, Betz, & Walker, 2003; Skowronski, Walker, & Betz, 2003).

Another potential source of information about the age of an event comes from *inferences derived from the characteristics of the event memory trace*. Events that: (1) are easily accessible, (2) have a memory trace that is strong, or (3) contain clear and vivid sensory details, tend to be viewed as occurring more recently than events that are less accessible or that do not contain clear and vivid details (for an early example of such ideas, see Hinrichs, 1970). Although data pertaining to these mechanisms are not overwhelmingly powerful, there is some research suggesting that they do, indeed, affect temporal reconstructions. For example, accessible memories sometimes show evidence of forward telescoping (i.e., they are judged to have occurred more recently than their actual date of occurrence; Bradburn, Rips, & Shevell, 1987). Similar forward telescoping results from memories that are particularly clear and vivid (N. R. Brown, Rips, & Shevell, 1985).

The *content of memory* can also aid temporal estimation by providing a number of different memory cues that are related to the time at which an event occurred. These content cues can be used in conjunction with generalized real-world knowledge about time to generate temporal estimates. For example, recalling that it was blisteringly hot while playing a softball game might lead a person to guess that an event occurred during the summer months. Various forms of self-knowledge might also enter into these content-based reconstructions. For example, if a person recalls that he or she slipped and broke their hip one night while going to psychology class, the person might be willing to guess that the event occurred on a Monday (the only night of the class) during the winter months of the Autumn term (the term when he or she took the class). If temporal reconstructions depend on temporal cues embedded in event memories, one would expect that as memory fades, the accuracy of these reconstructions should decrease. In fact, this relation has already been observed in event dating research (see Thompson, Skowronski, Larsen, & Betz, 1996; Betz & Skowronski, 1997).

METHODS OF EXPLORING MEMORY FOR TIME: EXAMINING DIFFERENT ELEMENTS OF RECONSTRUCTION

The reconstructive nature of temporal knowledge is also emphasized by research results suggesting that error patterns in temporal reconstructions are affected by assessment method. These method effects are quite understandable from a reconstructive point of view: different assessment methods provide different clues that can be used in the reconstruction of temporal knowledge. For example, one common method simply asks people to *report the age of an event* (Huttenlocher, Hedges, & Bradburn, 1990; Huttenlocher, Hedges, & Prohaska, 1988, 1992; Linton, 1975). Such age estimates are affected by output distortions, such as rounding. Rounding reflects at least two tendencies: the tendency to use "prototypical" values (e.g., 5 days, 10 days, 20 days) in preference to nonprototypical values and the tendency to use values that are meaningful given the temporal patterns that characterize our calendars (7 days, 30 days). These open-ended event age estimates are also affected by the boundary values that encompass the time period during which an event is thought to have occurred. Forward telescoping (the tendency to perceive events as younger than they actually are) is one consequence of the presence of such boundaries. For example, if an event is known to have occurred after one left college, the tendency would be to displace the date of that event forward from the lower bound set by the college exit date (i.e., the event would be estimated as occurring more recently than its actual date of occurrence; see Figure 9.1).

Forward telescoping is also observed in results obtained from calendar-aided dating studies. In experiments using this method, participants are given a calendar, blank except for month and day-of-week information, and are asked to *indicate the exact date* on which events occurred. Data collected using this technique suggest that forward telescoping may occur only for events near the lower (older) bound of an interval. For events near an upper (recent) bound, backward telescoping (judging an event to be older than it actually is) may occur (Skowronski et al., 1995; Thompson, Skowronski, & Lee, 1988; see Figure 9.1). In addition, participants who date events using this method evince systematic day-of-the-week errors. That is, as first noted in a study by Skowronski, Betz, Thompson, and Shannon (1991), people often misdate an event by multiples of a week (e.g., a person may know that an event occurred on a Monday but may select the wrong Monday in reconstructing the event date; see Figure 9.2). Analyses of these day-of-week errors further suggest that people have their week segmented into two or more components, such as weekdays and weekends. Errors tend to be more likely within

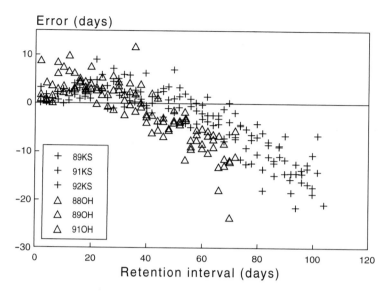

FIGURE 9.1. The relation between retention interval and signed dating error illustrating both forward telescoping (negative error bias for older events) and backward telescoping (positive error bias for recent events) across multiple data sets (from Thompson et al., 1996).

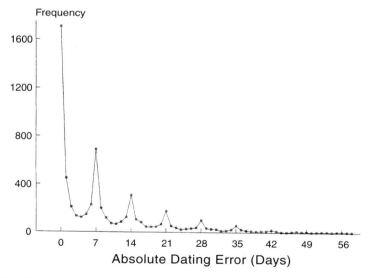

FIGURE 9.2. The relation between error magnitude and error frequency illustrating the tendency to make day-of-week errors (from Skowronski et al., 1991).

TABLE 9.1. Confusion Matrix for Days of the Week Calculated from Event Dates Provided for Self Events and Other-Person Events in a Calendar-Aided Dating Paradigm

	Actual Day of Week on Which Event Occurred						
	Sunday	Monday	Tuesday	Wednesday	Thursday	Friday	Saturday
	Self Events						
Sunday	38.1	6.0	3.4	4.2	2.0	2.6	6.8
Monday	6.7	22.9	17.2	12.5	8.9	5.8	3.4
Tuesday	4.9	16.0	24.7	14.9	16.6	8.5	5.1
Wednesday	8.1	25.6	21.8	31.5	26.7	14.3	7.1
Thursday	5.3	14.8	22.6	19.9	27.1	12.5	9.7
Friday	9.9	9.5	8.8	10.4	11.7	37.5	24.0
Saturday	26.9	5.2	1.6	6.6	6.8	18.8	43.9
	Other-Person's Events						
Sunday	26.5	7.5	3.4	3.4	5.0	5.9	10.5
Monday	7.6	16.3	15.9	13.6	10.0	10.3	5.9
Tuesday	5.8	20.3	20.9	19.3	13.1	10.3	3.2
Wednesday	12.5	23.0	19.7	25.2	21.2	14.3	10.4
Thursday	13.5	9.7	19.7	20.9	24.0	11.8	3.7
Friday	9.9	14.0	12.6	12.8	17.2	34.3	25.0
Saturday	24.2	9.2	8.0	4.7	9.5	13.2	41.4

Note: Columns are actual days of week, rows are reported days of week, and entries are probabilities for each reported day within each actual day. Adapted from Betz & Skowronski, 1997.

one of these components than between them (Betz & Skowronski, 1997). Furthermore, errors may be more frequent in one direction (e.g., mistaking a Saturday event for a Sunday event) than in the opposite direction (e.g., mistaking a Sunday event for a Saturday event; see Table 9.1). However, the presence of such day-of-week errors seems to be strongly technique dependent: Recent evidence suggests that these day-of-week errors are less likely to emerge in studies that do not use external aids, such as calendars, or in studies that obtain open-ended age estimates (Gibbons & Thompson, 2001; also see Prohaska, N. R. Brown, & Belli, 1998).

Other evidence for the reconstructive nature of temporal memory comes from participants' own self-reports. Participants in some of the calendar-aided dating studies were asked to indicate the various cues and strategies that they used to reconstruct the dates of events. Exact date recall was unusual. More often, participants reconstructed event dates and they used a multiplicity of strategies and cues in doing so (Betz & Skowronski, 1997; Thompson et al., 1993). Furthermore, the effectiveness of the strategies varied: some yielded more accurate date estimates than others. Finally, participants were aware of the fact that different strategies and cues were associated with different levels of reconstruction accuracy (see Table 9.2).

TABLE 9.2. Reports of Information Use in Event Dating by Retention Interval: Usage Rate (in %), Error Magnitude (in days), and Exact Dating Accuracy (in %) for Events up to 2.5 Years Old

		Retention Interval		
		Recent	Intermediate	Old
Exact Date Known	% Used	20.58	6.65	3.16
	Error Magnitude	6.82	8.91	61.38
	% Exactly Correct	87.32	88.09	71.67
Used Reference Event	% Used	18.55	15.91	8.95
	Error Magnitude	4.26	20.88	50.63
	% Exactly Correct	40.62	28.36	25.29
Knew General Reference Period	% Used	37.10	57.80	55.89
	Error Magnitude	15.78	28.24	56.99
	% Exactly Correct	26.56	11.37	8.38
Estimated # Intervening Events	% Used	.29	0	.53
	Error Magnitude	63.00	—	46.60
	% Exactly Correct	0	—	10.00
Used Memory Clarity to Estimate	% Used	7.54	2.45	6.16
	Error Magnitude	18.15	53.62	130.38
	% Exactly Correct	38.46	16.13	2.56
Used Prototypic Information	% Used	8.99	3.80	2.79
	Error Magnitude	28.32	11.17	75.81
	% Exactly Correct	35.48	31.25	32.07
Guess	% Used	4.64	11.96	20.68
	Error Magnitude	81.63	85.13	135.74
	% Exactly Correct	6.25	1.99	1.53
Other	% Used	2.32	1.43	1.84
	Error Magnitude	1.88	108.00	83.31
	% Exactly Correct	62.50	5.56	5.71

Note: Recent events are defined as those that are less than 3 months old, intermediate events are events that are between 3 months and 1 year old, and old events are those that are older than one year. Adapted from Skowronski et al., 1995.

A third approach to assessing temporal knowledge involves people's *memories for event sequences or event orders*. For example, one of the frequently discussed effects in the autobiographical memory literature involves the use of "temporal landmarks" in event dating. These temporal landmarks typically have a huge impact on our lives and hence, they make it easy to parse life into the period of time before the landmark event and the period of time after the landmark event. Typical landmarks include graduations, floods, moves to new locales, and wedding days (see Loftus & Marburger, 1983; Shum 1998). Although such landmarks can enhance dating accuracy, they can also produce systematic errors. For example, error patterns suggest that people sometimes use the beginning point of an event sequence as a "date anchor" and date other events relative to that anchor. If the anchor is dated incorrectly, all of the events in a sequence evince the same dating error. For example, the first day of one's vacation is misdated by a week and the dates of other vacation days are estimated relative to that first day, then all of the vacation events will be erroneously dated by seven days (Betz & Skowronski, 1997).

Data from other studies suggest that the use of relational judgment strategies might not be limited to event pairs in which one of the events is a temporal landmark. Even when dating the relatively mundane events of day-to-day life, people sometimes report that they attempt to date some events by using a relational strategy (Thompson et al., 1993). The use of such a strategy is also suggested by the research on self-narratives conducted by Singer, McAdams, and Fivush that is presented in their chapters in this volume. Narratives often have a temporal structure. That is, narratives often have a beginning, a middle, and an end, and important points about change and growth in the narrative are conveyed by comparing some element of one's state at an earlier point in the narrative to one's state at a later point in the narrative.

Two approaches have dominated the study of memory for event orders. One approach is derived largely from laboratory research on serial list learning. In this research participants are asked to learn a list and then later attempt to recall the list in exact order. The percentage of items correctly recalled at each serial position is assessed. These studies typically obtain bowed serial position curves in which positional recall is better for items that are early and late in the list than for items that are midlist (e.g., Healy, 1974). However, this kind of "exact position" scoring provides only a partial picture of people's event-ordering abilities. Such scoring ignores the fact that some events might be misplaced by a number of positions while others might be misplaced by only a few positions. It also ignores other error patterns in the data, such as the possibility that there might be "error runs" in which a series of events might be off by the same positional value (e.g., a sequence of items that are all listed as occurring two items too early; see Betz & Skowronski, 1997). In addition, this "exact position" scoring might be overtly misleading. Two participants may show equal positional error frequency, but one participant might be wildly wrong in his or her erroneous positional placements while the other participant's placements might be very close to the actual serial positions of the items in the list. Only recently have researchers devised a seemingly valid scheme for using both error frequency and error magnitude in scoring the overall accuracy of entire recall sequences (Burt, Kemp, Grady, & Conway, 2000).

One way to simplify the scoring problem is to repeatedly and randomly select two events from an event sequence and obtain judgments of the order in which two events occurred, a technique known as the judgment-of-recency (JOR) paradigm. Much of the research using this paradigm has been conducted using artificial stimulus lists and relatively short timeframes (see G. D. A. Brown, Preece, & Hulme, 2000; Guttentag & Carroll, 1997; Hacker, 1980). Only a few studies, including some of our own recent efforts, have tried to use this paradigm to explore

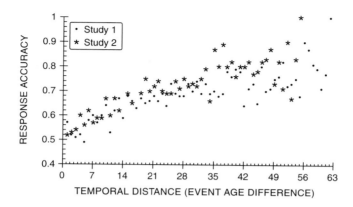

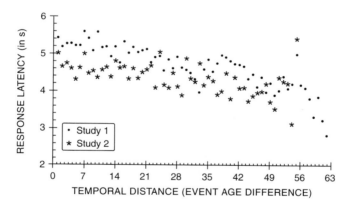

FIGURE 9.3. An illustration of the symbolic temporal distance effect in both error frequency and response time in two studies examining paired recency judgments of autobiographical events (from Skowronski et al., 2003b).

long-term autobiographical temporal memory (Fuhrman & Wyer, 1988; Skowronski et al., 2003a,b; Underwood, 1977). These studies demonstrate that order judgments are easier when the events are widely separated in time than when they are not, an outcome known as the symbolic temporal distance effect. An example of this effect is presented in Figure 9.3 (Skowronski et al., 2003b, Experiment 1). The data depicted in that figure were obtained from recency judgments of pairs of everyday events that occurred during the course of an academic quarter. The data clearly show a symbolic temporal distance effect: Events that were widely

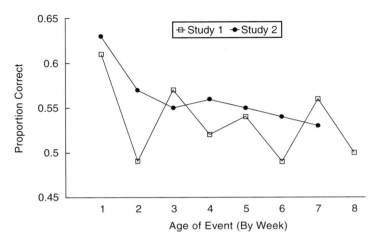

FIGURE 9.4. The decrease in accuracy of judgments-of-recency across retention lag (excluding the first week of the study) for all judged event pairs separated by between 1 to 7 days across two studies (data from Skowronski et al., 2003b).

separated in time were easier to judge (higher accuracy, more quickly judged) than events that were temporally proximate. A second effect that is typically observed in people's judgments of recency is an age effect. That is, temporal order judgments are easier when the youngest of the events in the pair is relatively recent than when the youngest event in the pair is relatively old. A third effect that emerges in JOR experiments is that the symbolic temporal distance effect varies with event age. That is, when events are relatively young, a small age difference between events is associated with relative ease in judgments (higher accuracy). As the events become increasingly old, that same small difference is associated with increasing judgment difficulty as reflected in lower judgment accuracy (see Figure 9.4).

However, the symbolic temporal distance effect is also related to factors other than the age of the events that are involved in the judgment. For example, Fuhrman and Wyer (1988) and Skowronski et al. (2003a) showed that it is easier to judge the order of autobiographical events that occurred in different temporal categories (e.g., high school versus college) than events that occurred within the same temporal category (e.g., two high school events). This outcome is consistent with the predictions of those models suggesting that temporal knowledge about events is at least partially reconstructed from the higher-order categories to which behaviors are linked (e.g., perturbation theory and Conway's model of temporal organization in memory). It follows that remembering that the senior prom is a high school event and that flunking calculus is a college event provide an easy way to order those events (high school comes before college — at least for most of us).

A VIEW OF THE DATA FROM ANOTHER ANGLE: SOME SURPRISING STABILITIES IN TEMPORAL MEMORY

The multiplicity of estimation strategies and the systematic errors that are exhibited in the various tasks exploring memory for time might lead one to conclude that temporal memory is a highly unstable and unpredictable phenomenon. However, at least some of the data from our studies show considerable regularities in the temporal reconstructions that are provided by our participants. For example, consider the relation between event age and the magnitude of dating error associated with the event. The decrease in dating accuracy with time can be highly systematic and bears considerable resemblance to Weber's psychophysical law that the error of a judgment is a constant proportion of the magnitude of the property being judged. In his calendar-aided dating studies Thompson (1982) estimated that dating error increases by about 1 day of error with the passage of each additional week of time. This relation has held up remarkably well in a number of calendar-aided event dating studies (see Figures 9.5 and 9.6), even in those studies using time intervals as long as 6 years (see Rubin & Baddeley, 1989; Skowronski et al., 1995; Thompson et al., 1996). Moreover, these data suggest a degree of accuracy in event dating, even while, at the same time, events are showing evidence of systematic reconstructive biases.

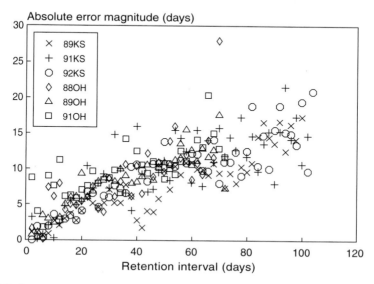

FIGURE 9.5. The relatively constant increase in error magnitude with increasing event age in a number of data sets in which the events dated were 9 to 15 weeks old (from Thompson et al., 1996).

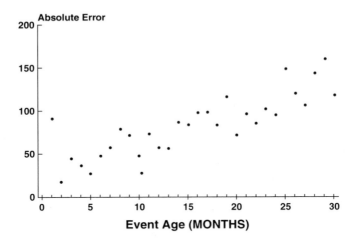

FIGURE 9.6. The relatively constant increase in error magnitude with increasing event age in a data set in which the events dated were up to 2.5 years old (from Skowronski et al., 1995).

We believe that such data lead to an important insight: though temporal reconstruction might be subject to various reconstructive biases, there often seems to be a "core of temporal truth" in those reconstructions. On the whole, events that are recent are generally estimated to be younger, while events that are old are generally estimated to be older. We do not believe that this effect (which we term the *temporal stability effect*) is due to artifacts such as the regression to the mean or the averaging of errors across people. Instead, people do often seem to have a basic sense of whether an event is "old" or "recent," and many of the reconstructive biases that have been documented may occur when people try to go beyond this general sense of event age to more precisely determine the exact age of a given event.

Another indication of this temporal stability effect comes from the judgment of recency data. As noted earlier in this chapter, it is easier to report the order of two events when the events are widely separated in time than when the events are temporally proximal. However, if temporal memory is solely determined by the reconstructive processes that we have described so far, why should such a temporal distance effect emerge? After all, memory traces for old events should be hard to access and the content of those traces should be degraded. If memory for even one of the events in a pair is poor, and if temporal estimations are derived solely from memory content, then one would expect there to be a great amount of uncertainty in the temporal placement of the poorly recalled event. Hence, event pairs in which one of the events was recalled poorly, as might occur when an event was very old, should be time-consuming and difficult, even when the

other memory in the pair is well recalled (as when one event is very young). Instead, order judgments in which a large span of time passes between two events are quite easy: They are responded to quickly and accurately.

Hierarchical theories, such as perturbation theory or views of autobiographical memory in which events are organized into various life periods or themes (Conway & Rubin, 1993), can seemingly account for some of these findings reasonably well. To the extent that event orders can be judged by simply accessing lifetime categories that are linked to the events, such as "childhood" versus "adulthood," temporal judgments can be made rapidly. Because the events involved are linked to high-level nodes, accessing these linkages obviates the need to spend time accessing the events in detail: remembering the high-level theme is enough to produce a fast and accurate judgment. On the other hand, judgments involving temporally proximate events likely necessitate deeper probes into the hierarchy. To make an ordering decision about an event that occurred in freshman year of high school and one that occurred in sophomore year, one must progress downward from a higher-order node such as "teenage years" into the various subcategories that comprise those years or even into event-specific knowledge. These are represented at a lower level in the memory network and take longer to access and compare.

Although theories that postulate this type of a memory network structure might explain why it takes longer to access event memories that are linked to these subcategories, they do not easily explain why judgments are made more quickly and accurately when events are widely separated within a given level of the network. For example, consider the high school years. In these hierarchical schemes, why should it be easier to judge two events that occurred at widely different times within the freshman year than two events that occurred in temporal proximity to each other?

One possible answer to this question is that the freshman year itself is parsed into subcategories, and that each of these subcategories is parsed into sub-sub-categories, and so on. However, this logic rapidly becomes cumbersome: pushed to its limit, each life event would inhabit its own temporal category. That seems no different from the idea of temporal tagging. An additional difficulty concerns the multiple reorganizations of the mental hierarchy that seemingly are necessary with development. That is, how does an event get recategorized from "yesterday's event" to "last week's event" to "last winter's event" to "last year's event?" Doubtless some recategorization and rearrangement of the category hierarchy can occur as a result of mental processes (e.g., rumination) and social interactions with others, but these clearly cannot be the whole story. For this kind of a hierarchical memory scheme to work, such recategorizations need to occur continuously. These recategorizations would seem to require a tremendous amount of cognitive work — much more cognitive work than we suspect is actually expended on such activity. So why does the temporal distance effect obtain, even for events that may inhabit the same level of the memory hierarchy?

AN ARGUMENT FOR THE TIMEKEEPING SELF
IN AUTOBIOGRAPHICAL MEMORY

One answer to this question might be that the self serves as a source of *implicit* knowledge about the time at which an event occurred. Glenberg, Bradley, Kraus, and Renzaglia (1983) suggested that temporal reconstructions can be based on the extent to which the contextual information encoded at information exposure overlaps with the current context. It seems plausible that the "state of the self" can serve as a learning context in the same way that elements of the environment can serve as a context. Hence, when an individual retrieves an event, the self-context associated with that memory may also be activated. A comparison of the activated self-context accompanying event recall with the status of the current self-concept can provide a rough sense of the age of the event, independently of event content. To the extent that the self-contexts are similar, the memory will be judged as recent. To the extent that the self-contexts are substantially different, the memory will be judged as old. Similarly, a comparison of the relative discrepancies between each of two events and the current self (as might occur in the JOR task) can provide clues to the relative ages of the two events.

What is this "self-context?" Here, we are influenced by recent connectionist theorizing about memory storage (Conway & Pleydell-Pearce, 2000; Smith & DeCoster, 2000). In the connectionist view, information is stored as a pattern of connection weights that link the processing units comprising the network. As information is learned, the pattern of weights across the network shifts. These shifts tend to be larger in the early stages of network learning; the network tends to be less responsive to new information as the network "ages" (e.g., gets more experience). To recall information, a stimulus (such as a memory cue) helps to drive the connection weights back into the original pattern that was present at initial event learning.

We propose that the self, broadly construed, is represented as a pattern of connection weights in the mental network, and that this pattern serves as a part of the learning context for an event. Later, when the event is remembered, that event memory can serve to activate the learning context, which includes the connection weight pattern that represents the self at the time the information was learned. The timekeeping self is reflected in the comparison between the current self-pattern and the self-pattern that is associated with the recalled event. To get a rough sense of the age of the event, then, a person needs only to compare the current self-pattern to the pattern activated at event recall: the bigger the difference, the older the event feels. This timekeeping self provides only a general sense of temporal location and does not preclude the use of other temporal information in temporal reconstructions. Temporal information obtained from already discussed sources, such as information contained in the memory trace and recalled event orders, may often serve to sharpen the broad temporal information that may be provided by the timekeeping self. In our view, temporal information derived from the timekeeping self is just one of many sources of temporal information that an individual may have at his or her disposal.

That the self can serve as an implicit timekeeper for autobiographical memories makes intuitive sense. For example, consider a thought experiment in which one has access to a list of events from a person's lifetime. Imagine that these events were presented to the person in a random order, one at a time. The respondent's task in the experiment is to make a speeded response to the event, classifying it as "old" or "recent." What result might emerge from such an experiment? We would predict that one would obtain a prototypicality curve: recent events would be judged quickly and accurately, old events would be judged quickly and accurately, and events of middling age would be judged more slowly (and variably). In other domains of research, the presence of such a prototypicality curve is thought to indicate comparison of stimulus features to a cognitive representation that serves as a comparison standard for the judgment. Applying this to our thought experiment, one might ask how the concept of "now" is represented and which characteristics of an autobiographical memory are compared to "now." In our view, one simple but powerful explanation for the probable emergence of prototypicality effects is comparison of the "self as I was then" to "the self as I am now."

Our argument for an implicit component to temporal memory is not new. Other theories have similarly suggested that implicit characteristics of memory, such as memory accessibility, can affect temporal judgment (see G. D. A. Brown et al., 2000; N. R. Brown, 1990; N. R. Brown et al., 1985). Our perusal of the literature suggests that such implicit effects are weak, but this weakness might be a partial function of many of the methodologies that have been used to study temporal memory. For example, our own calendar-aided event dating studies present numerous dating cues and seemingly demand a high level of precision in temporal estimation by asking for an exact date for an event. In such studies the cognitive effort that is activated in response to task demands might overwhelm feelings of event age. However, when cognitive effort is futile, the timekeeping self idea suggests that people will still have a general sense of when an event occurred. Suggestive evidence on this point can be observed in the "Guess" data in Table 9.2. Even though people's event dates were highly inaccurate when they reported that they guessed at an event's date, these guesses were still more accurate for events that were recent than events that were old. If people were indeed randomly guessing at an event's date, this should not be the case — the average error should be the same for young, middling, and old events.

However, other methodologies might be better suited to the study of the implicit effects of the timekeeper self on temporal reconstructions. The "how old does the event feel" question used by Wilson and Ross (2001) may be a good prototype for such effects. Similarly, because it demands only a judgment of event order, the JOR paradigm might similarly be a good vehicle for studying such implicit effects (for a similar idea, see Fernandez & Glenberg, 1985).

POSSIBLE EMPIRICAL IMPLICATIONS
OF THE TIMEKEEPING SELF

The notion of the timekeeping self leads to several testable hypotheses. For example, temporarily driving the current self toward the self-state that represented the self during learning of an autobiographical event ought to make the event seem younger. This could seemingly be done in various ways. For example, one might expect that manipulating emotional states might sometimes affect temporal judgments. That is, if one initially learned an event when one was feeling depressed, that event may seem to be younger if one is driven into a depressed state prior to recalling the event. In fact, Wilson and Ross (2001) have already obtained data that can be construed as supporting this conjecture. They found that negative events "feel older" than positive events. One possible interpretation of this outcome is that positive events are congruent with the positive current self-concept that people typically have of themselves, and hence, seem to be younger than negative events. A similar effect might derive from events that one has brought to psychological closure in one's life rather than events that are psychologically "open" (Beike & Landoll, 2000; see chapter by Beike, this volume). Psychologically closed events have been put into one's past; open events have not. Recall of psychologically open events should be associated with a recall context that is more similar to the current self than recall of psychologically closed events. Hence, those open events should seem younger.

A similar effect might be produced as a result of shifts in the self concept induced by reminiscing. This is an idea derived from the musings of Hall (1899), who suggested that reminiscing about events makes those events seem as if they had occurred relatively recently. We might account for such an effect by suggesting that reminiscences may temporarily cause a shift in the current self-concept, driving it into a state that was more similar to the self concept that was present during the events that are the focus of the reminiscence (e.g., thinking of the game-winning home run that one hit may make one feel more like an athlete). After this shift occurs, events that are congruent with this new self-concept might be estimated to have occurred more recently than events that are inconsistent with this new self-concept.

The role of the timekeeping self in temporal reconstruction might also be examined by looking at the dating errors made for events that vary in the extent to which those events match the "current self." For example, one might expect that events that are rated as reflecting a high degree of similarity to the current self might be those that would be subject to forward telescoping biases in event dating; events with low current self-similarity might be less subject to those biases, or might even show backward telescoping.

Another line of exploration might compare the temporal judgments of adults who have experienced rapid and profound life changes to the temporal judgments of those who have not. For example, consider a recently divorced individual who also experienced a job change that required a move to a new city. To that person, an event that occurred a year ago might seem like it occurred in the distant past.

More generally, we would predict that those with the greatest life changes have the greatest change in the self-state, so that events that occurred prior to the instability should seem older than equivalently aged events for individuals whose lives were relatively stable. A similar study could investigate different age segments. Imagine asking preteens and college students to make order judgments of events that occurred in the last two years. One might expect that the self-concept of preteens is changing rapidly with respect to the self-concept of adults (see Mortimer, Finch, & Kumka, 1982; Sedikides & Strube, 1997). If temporal judgment is related to the rate of change of the self-concept, then the symbolic temporal distance effect should be stronger in preteens than in college students.

Rapidly changing self-concepts may also affect the spontaneous creation and use of temporal landmarks. Temporal landmarks tend to form when events are both experienced for the first time and have personal significance (Robinson, 1992; Shum, 1998). Of course, many such "first time" events are widely recognized in society, such as having sex for the first time or leaving for college. Such temporal landmarks tend to remain personally significant throughout our lives. Yet consider the possibility that individuals with rapidly changing self-concepts may spontaneously form other, person-specific landmarks. Because these person-specific landmarks receive less validation from society, their personal significance may depend almost entirely on the current self-concept. As a result, the significance of a person-specific temporal landmark may change as the self-concept changes. One implication of this line of reasoning is that the current self might impact temporal judgment because of the effect that the self has on the continuing selection and use of temporal landmarks. This effect can seemingly occur in at least two different ways.

The first of these concerns the loss of temporal landmarks already formed. With sufficient change in the self-concept, person-specific temporal landmarks that may once have been important may fall out of use entirely. Consider the case of young schoolchildren for whom promotion to a higher grade is arguably a landmark event: being promoted from first to second grade (and its accompanying move to the upstairs classrooms) might have seemed to be tremendously important when it happened. However, as our self-concept changes, the significance of that landmark diminishes substantially: in adulthood the transition from first to second grade, once such an important landmark, hardly seems like a landmark at all. As a second, more idiosyncratic, example, consider a person who undergoes an occupation change. While pursuing an academic career, that person's first publication might seem like a landmark event. However, after moving to the business world that publication might no longer serve a landmark function.

The second implication concerns the retrospective creation of temporal landmarks as the self evolves. Autobiographical events often change in their perceived significance in light of new life experiences. In the movie *When Harry Met Sally* (Reiner & Ephron, 1989), two college students met while sharing a cross-country drive during which they alienate each other. Years later, the two reunited, became friends, and eventually fell in love. After the romantic relationship developed, the two characters changed their perception of that initial meeting. That is, an event that was, for a long time, probably ill-remembered and infrequently rehearsed suddenly became personally significant and was ascribed to "fate." Most studies of temporal landmarks have focused on events that were obviously landmarks when they occurred; no one, to our knowledge, has explored the implications of such retrospectively created landmarks for temporal knowledge. Whether such retrospectively created landmarks have the same effects on temporal judgment as other types of landmarks remains an open question.

The timekeeping self may also have some implications for other aspects of cognition. For example, consider long-term prospective memory. Many people devise "life plans" that center around professional and personal goals: For example, an ambitious young psychologist might want to have 20 or more publications by the time the person reaches 40 years of age. How long will it really take to achieve those 20 publications? From one point of view, such thinking represents a projection of the timekeeping self into the future. One might hypothesize that individuals whose lives have been relatively stable across time might make very different projections than those who have experienced considerable life instability or change.

CONCLUDING THOUGHTS

We emphasize that the self-based timekeeping mechanism that we propose in this chapter is not "temporal tagging": temporal information is not "stamped in" with the event. Instead, the time at which an event occurred must be inferred from a comparison between the remembered context self and the present self. Furthermore, even if new data support the notion that the self serves as an implicit timekeeper, it is certainly not the only mechanism that affects our knowledge of when events happened. Temporal knowledge is retrieved and reconstructed in a variety of ways from a variety of sources in a variety of circumstances. The idea of a self-based implicit timekeeper is just another source of information for such reconstructions.

Moreover, we do not believe that the self context will always be useful as a rough guide to event age. Certainly, when events occur repeatedly there will be some uncertainty as to which of the multiple events is being cued, so the proper self-context for the event will be unclear.

Nonetheless, we believe that a self-based implicit comparison mechanism can help people to know that an event is "old" or "recent" without having much access to event detail. This mechanism leads to the prediction of new phenomena that have not yet been explored in the temporal judgment literature. In future research we will be pursuing such possibilities. We will also be pursuing other cognitive and social mechanisms that allow us to know when events occurred, and the order in which those events occurred, both in our own lives and in the lives of others.

Finally, we began this chapter by asking readers to imagine how the self would be disrupted if individuals were unable to locate autobiographical events in time. In making that argument, we noted that individuals with several psychological disorders often evince deficits in temporal judgment and event ordering. Because many of these deficits also accompany disruption of the sense of self, it is tempting to conclude that such cases constitute proof that the disruption of the self is caused by the inability to locate events in time. However, the implications of the argument that we pursue in this chapter suggest that the loss of a sense of self might be a cause of the inability to locate events in time, not a consequence of that inability. Nonetheless, regardless of the direction of causality, we think that there is good reason to consider the possibility that there is a link between the ability to temporally locate events in one's life and the self concept. It may be the case that one cannot functionally exist without the other.

ENDNOTES

1. Of course, this statement is not intended to refer to those studies that have used a variant of the JOR paradigm as an aid to the diagnosis of psychopathology (e.g., Madsen & Kesner, 1995; Meudell et al., 1985; Shimamura et al., 1990).

REFERENCES

Anderson, S. J., & Conway, M. A. (1993). Investigating the structure of autobiographical memories. *Journal of Experimental Psychology: Learning, Memory, & Cognition, 19,* 1178–1196.

Beike, D. R., & Landoll, S. L. (2000). Striving for a consistent life story: Cognitive reactions to autobiographical memories. *Social Cognition, 18,* 292–318.

Betz, A. L., & Skowronski, J. J. (1997). Self-events and other-events: Temporal dating and event memory. *Memory & Cognition, 25,* 701–714.

Bradburn, N. M., Rips, L. J., & Shevell, S. K. (1987). Answering autobiographical questions: The impact of memory and inference on surveys. *Science, 236,* 158–161.

Brown, G. D. A., Preece, T., & Hulme, C. (2000). Oscillator-based memory for serial order. *Psychological Review, 107,* 127–181.

Brown, N. R. (1990). Organization of public events in long-term memory. *Journal of Experimental Psychology: General, 119,* 297–314.

Brown, N. R., Rips, L. J., & Shevell, S. K. (1985). The subjective dates of natural events in very-long-term memory. *Cognitive Psychology, 17,* 139–177.

Brown, N. R., & Schopflocher, D. (1998a). Event clusters: An organization of personal events in autobiographical memory. *Psychological Science, 9,* 470–475.

Brown, N. R., & Schopflocher, D. (1998b). Event cueing, event clusters, and the temporal distribution of autobiographical memories. *Applied Cognitive Psychology, 12,* 305–319.

Burt, C. D. B., Kemp, S., Grady, J. M., & Conway, M. A. (2000). Ordering autobiographical experiences. *Memory, 8,* 323–332.

Conway, M. A., & Bekerian, D. A. (1987) Organization in autobiographical memory. *Memory & Cognition, 15,* 119–132.

Conway, M. A., & Pleydell-Pearce, C. W. (2000). The construction of autobiographical memories in the self-memory system. *Psychological Review, 107,* 261–288.

Conway, M. A., & Rubin, D. C. (1993). The structure of autobiographical memory. In A. E. Collins, S. E. Gathercole, M. A. Conway, & P. E. M. Morris (Eds.), *Theories of memory* (pp. 103–137). Hillsdale, NJ: Erlbaum.

Estes, W. K. (1972). An associative basis for coding and organization in memory. In A. W. Melton & E. Martin (Eds.), *Coding processes in human memory* (pp. 161–190). Washington, D.C.: Winston.

Estes, W. K. (1987). One hundred years of memory theory. In D. S. Gorfein & R. R. Hoffman (Eds.), *Memory and learning: The Ebbinghaus Centennial Conference* (pp. 11–33). Hillsdale, NJ: Erlbaum.

Fernandez, A., & Glenberg, A. M. (1985). Changing environmental context does not reliably affect memory. *Memory & Cognition, 13,* 333–345.

Friedman, W. J. (1993). Memory for the time of past events. *Psychological Bulletin, 113,* 44–66.

Fuhrman, R. W., & Wyer, R. S., Jr. (1988). Event memory: Temporal-order judgments of personal life experiences. *Journal of Personality & Social Psychology, 54,* 365–384.

Gibbons, J. A. & Thompson, C. P. (2001). Using a calendar in event dating. *Journal of Applied Cognitive Psychology, 15,* 33–44.

Glenberg, A. G., Bradley, M. M., Kraus, T. A., & Renzaglia, G. J. (1983). Studies of the long-term recency effect: Support for the contextually guided retrieval hypothesis. *Journal of Experimental Psychology: Learning, Memory & Cognition, 9,* 231–255.

Guenther, R. K., & Linton, M. (1975). Mechanisms of temporal coding. *Journal of Experimental Psychology: Human Learning & Memory, 1,* 182–187.

Guttentag, R. E., & Carroll, D. (1997). Recency judgments as a function of word frequency: A framing effect and frequency misattributions. *Psychonomic Bulletin & Review, 4,* 411–415.

Hacker, M.J. (1980). Speed and accuracy of recency judgments for events in short-term memory. *Journal of Experimental Psychology: Human Learning & Memory, 6,* 651–675.

Hall, G. S. (1899). Note on early memories. *Pedagogical Seminary, 6,* 485–512.

Healy, A. F. (1974). Separating item from order information in short-term memory. *Journal of Verbal Learning & Verbal Behavior, 13,* 644–655.

Hinrichs, J. V. (1970). A two-process memory-strength theory for judgment of recency. *Psychological Review, 77,* 223–233.

Huttenlocher, J., Hedges, L. V., & Bradburn, N. M. (1990). Reports of elapsed time: Bounding and rounding processes in estimation. *Journal of Experimental Psychology: Learning, Memory, & Cognition, 16,* 196–213.

Huttenlocher, J., Hedges, L. V., & Prohaska, V. (1988). Hierarchical organization in ordered domains: Estimating the dates of events. *Psychological Review, 95,* 471–484.

Huttenlocher, J., Hedges, L. V., & Prohaska, V. (1992) Memory for day of the week: A 5 + 2 day cycle. *Journal of Experimental Psychology: General, 121,* 313–325.

Kemp, S. (1999). An associative theory of estimating past dates and past prices. *Psychonomic Bulletin and Review, 6,* 41–56.

Klein, S. B. (2001) A self to remember: A cognitive neuropsychological perspective on how self creates memory and memory creates self. In C. Sedikides & M. B. Brewer (Eds.), *Individual self, relational self, collective self* (pp. 25–46). Philadelphia, PA: Psychology Press.

Klein, S. B., Babey, S. H. & Sherman, J. W. (1997). The functional independence of trait and behavioral self-knowledge: Methodological considerations and new empirical findings. *Social Cognition, 15,* 183–203.

Klein, S. B, Chan, R. L., & Loftus, J. (1999). Independence of episodic and semantic self-knowledge: The case from autism. *Social Cognition, 17*, 413–436.

Larsen, S. F., Thompson, C. P., & Hansen, T. (1996). Time in autobiographical memory. In D. C. Rubin (Ed.), *Remembering our past: Studies in autobiographical memory* (pp. 129–156). New York: Cambridge University Press.

Linton, M. (1975). Memory for real-world events. In D. A. Norman & D. E. Rumelhart (Eds.), *Explorations in cognition* (pp. 376–404). San Francisco: Freeman.

Loftus, E. F., & Marburger, W. (1983). Since the eruption of Mt. St. Helens, has anyone beaten you up? Improving the accuracy of retrospective reports with landmark events. *Memory & Cognition, 11*, 114–120.

Madsen, J., & Kesner, R. P. (1995). The temporal-distance effect in subjects with dementia of the Alzheimer type. *Alzheimer Disease and Associated Disorders, 2*, 94–100.

Meudell, P. R., Mayes, A. R., Ostergaard, A., & Pickering, A. (1985). Recency and frequency judgments in alcoholic amnesiacs and normal people with poor memory. *Cortex, 21*, 487–511.

McElree, B., & Dosher, B. A. (1993). Serial retrieval processes in the recovery of order information. *Journal of Experimental Psychology: General, 122*, 291–315.

Mortimer, J. T., Finch, M. D., & Kumka, D. (1982). Persistence and change in development: The multidimensional self-concept. In P. B. Baltes & O. G. Brim, Jr. (Eds.), *Life-span development and behavior* (Vol. 4, pp. 263–312). New York: Academic Press.

Nairne, J. S. (1991). Positional uncertainty in long-term memory. *Memory & Cognition, 19*, 332–340.

Prohaska, V., Brown, N. R., Belli, R. F. (1998). Forward telescoping: The question matters. *Memory, 6*, 455–465.

Reiner, R. (Director) & Ephron, N. (Writer). (1989). *When Harry met Sally* [Motion picture]. United States: Columbia Pictures.

Reiser, B. J., Black, B. J., & Abelson, R. P. (1985). Knowledge structures in the organization and retrieval of autobiographical memories. *Cognitive Psychology, 17*, 89–137.

Robinson, J. A. (1992). First experience memories: Contexts and functions in personal histories. In M. A. Conway, D. C. Rubin, H. Spinnler, & W. A. Wagenaar (Eds.), *Theoretical perspectives on autobiographical memory* (pp. 223–239). Dordrecht, the Netherlands: Kluwer Academic Press.

Rubin, D. C., & Baddeley, A. D. (1989). Telescoping is not time compression: A model of the dating of autobiographical events. *Memory & Cognition, 17*, 653–661.

Schank, R. C., & Abelson, R. P. (1995). Knowledge and memory: The real story. In R. S. Wyer, Jr. (Ed.), *Advances in social cognition* (Vol. 8, pp. 1–85). Hillsdale, NJ: Erlbaum.

Schank, R. C., & Abelson, R. P. (1977). *Scripts, plans, goals and understanding: An inquiry into human knowledge structures*. Hillsdale, NJ: Erlbaum.

Sedikides, C. & Skowronski, J. J. (1995). On the sources of self-knowledge: The perceived primacy of self-reflection. *Journal of Social & Clinical Psychology, 14*, 244–270.

Sedikides, C., & Strube, M. J. (1997). Self-evaluation: To thine own self be good, to thine own self be sure, to thine own self be true, and to thine own self be better. In M. P. Zanna (Ed.), *Advances in Experimental Social Psychology* (Vol. 29, pp. 209–269). New York: Academic Press.

Shimamura, A. P., Janowsky, J. S., & Squire, L. R. (1990). Memory for the temporal order of events in patients with frontal lobe lesions and amnesiac patients. *Neuropsychologia, 28*, 803–813.

Shum, M. S. (1998). The role of temporal landmarks in autobiographical memory processes. *Psychological Bulletin, 124*, 423–442.

Skowronski, J. J., Betz, A. L., & Walker, W. R. (2003a). *Ordering our world II: Temporal themes affect JOR judgments about autobiographical events.* Manuscript in preparation.

Skowronski, J. J., Betz, A. L., Thompson, C. P., & Larsen, S. (1995). Long-term performance in autobiographical event dating: Patterns of accuracy and error across a two-and-a-half year time span. In A. F. Healy & L. E. Bourne (Eds.), *Learning and memory of knowledge and skills: Durability and specificity* (pp. 206–233). Thousand Oaks, CA: Sage.

Skowronski, J. J., Betz, A. L., Thompson, C. P., & Shannon, L. (1991). Social memory in everyday life: The recall of self-events and other-events. *Journal of Personality and Social Psychology, 60,* 831–843.

Skowronski, J. J., Walker, W. R., & Betz, A. L. (2003b). Ordering our world: An examination of time in autobiographical memory. *Memory, 11,* 247–260.

Smith, E. R., & DeCoster, J. (2000). Dual-process models in social and cognitive psychology: Conceptual integration and links to underlying memory systems. *Personality & Social Psychology Review, 4,* 108–131.

Thompson, C. P. (1982). Memory for unique personal events: The roommate study. *Memory & Cognition, 10,* 324–332.

Thompson, C. P., Gibbons, J. A., Vogl, R. J., & Walker, W. R. (1997). Autobiographical memory: Individual differences in using episodic and schematic information. In D. G. Payne and F. G. Conrad (Eds.), *Intersections in basic and applied memory research* (pp. 193–213). Mahwah, NJ: Erlbaum.

Thompson, C. P., Skowronski, J. J., Larsen, S., & Betz, A. L. (1996). *Autobiographical memory: Remembering what and remembering when.* Hillsdale, NJ: Erlbaum.

Thompson, C. P., Skowronski, J. J., & Betz, A. L. (1993). The use of partial temporal information in dating personal events. *Memory & Cognition, 21,* 352–360.

Thompson, C. P., Skowronski, J. J., & Lee, D. J. (1988). Telescoping in dating naturally occurring events. *Memory & Cognition, 16,* 461–468.

Underwood, B. J. (1977). *Temporal codes for memories: Issues and problems.* Hillsdale, NJ: Erlbaum.

Winograd, E., & Soloway, R. M. (1985). Reminding as a basis for temporal judgments. *Journal of Experimental Psychology: Learning, Memory, & Cognition, 11,* 262–271.

Wilson, A. E., & Ross, M. (2001). From chump to champ: People's appraisals of their earlier and present selves. *Journal of Personality & Social Psychology, 80,* 572–584.

10

Autobiographical Memory and Self-Assessment

JESSICA J. CAMERON
University of Manitoba

ANNE E. WILSON
Wilfrid Laurier University

MICHAEL ROSS
University of Waterloo

*I*n a well-known analogy, Neisser (1967) compared the act of remembering to the paleontologist's task of reconstructing a dinosaur from a few pieces of bone. The paleontologist's reconstruction is guided by the fossil remains, as well as by his or her current understanding of biology and dinosaurs. The same remains might have yielded a quite different reconstruction 100 years earlier, because of shifts in scientific knowledge. Similarly, people reconstruct and interpret episodes from their pasts by using the bits and pieces they retrieve from memory together with their current knowledge and understanding of themselves and their social world. When relevant knowledge and understanding changes with time, so too might memory even if the information retrieved remains constant.

Professional historians show a similar propensity to use the present to reconstruct the past. The term "presentism" (Butterfield, 1965; Hull, 1979) is associated with the tendency to recreate and interpret history on the basis of current ideas and values, rather than from the knowledge and values of the period. Presentism also involves an inclination to write on the side of the victor (e.g., histories of the colonization of North America are typically presented from the perspective of Europeans rather than aboriginals, Richter, 2001) and to produce a story that justifies and glorifies the present. Various authors have noted the perils of presentism and admonished historians to understand the past on its own terms (e.g., Butterfield, 1965).

In the current chapter we document the role of presentism in people's autobiographical memories. We propose that past selves and episodes are constructed, in part, on the basis of present understandings and with the goal of producing an account that justifies and enhances the present self. Although we suggest that memory is influenced by present knowledge and motivations, we do not argue that memory is necessarily erroneous. Like paleontologists and historians, rememberers can be accurate or inaccurate in their inferences. Moreover, episodes are often sufficiently complex that any number of different perspectives are equally (in)accurate. However, we are not so much concerned with the validity of memory as we are with its relation to self-identity.

Psychologists have long recognized the intimate and reciprocal association between autobiographical memory and self-identity (e.g., James, 1890/1950; Singer & Salovey, 1993). For example, Klein (2001) noted that the self is a product of an individual's personal memories (e.g., Bruner, 1994), while at the same time, a sense of a temporally extended self is a logical prerequisite of autobiographical memory (e.g., Nelson, 1988, 1997). The reciprocal nature of memory is again illustrated when a lack of self-identity (due either to developmental stage or pathology) appears to disrupt memory and in turn, memory deficits (e.g., amnesia, Alzheimer's dementia) disturb one's sense of self (Klein, 2001).

REMEMBERING AND SELF-REGARD

We, too, assume reciprocity between autobiographical memory and personal identity: people fashion identities that fit their memories and memories that fit their identities. In Western cultures at least, a favorable self-evaluation seems to be an important aspect of self-identity. People tend to think that they are better than others (and better than others think they are) on many skills and attributes (Baumeister, 1998; Taylor & Brown, 1988). Such glowing self-appraisals reflect a motivation to think favorably about the self (Baumeister, 1998; Taylor & Brown, 1988; Wilson & Ross, 2000). However, people are not at liberty to conclude whatever they want, simply because they wish it were so (Kunda, 1990). Instead, individuals conduct a motivated search for evidence that supports their preferences. Of course, not all evidence is created equal; people appear to be quite comfortable taking some poetic license in their selection and interpretation of relevant "facts."

Individuals can potentially derive their self-appraisals from a variety of sources, including social comparisons, feedback from others, memories of personal experiences, and comparisons with past, future, and possible selves (Sedikides & Skowronski, 1995; Taylor, Neter & Wayment, 1995). Wilson and Ross (2000, 2001a) have suggested that, despite the multiplicity of possible sources of information, people may rely heavily on their personal memories in fashioning a self-appraisal.

Why might individuals prefer the past to other potential sources of information? The personal past may represent a particularly flattering, risk-free source of information, especially for young adults. When people seek self-appraisal evidence from other sources (e.g., social comparisons, feedback from others, contrasts to possible selves) they may discover some favorable information, but they may also come face-to-face with their shortcomings. Consider for example the possible pitfalls of social comparisons. In many settings, most people cannot help but notice at least some other individuals who are better looking, wittier, more sophisticated, more successful, wealthier, and so forth. In contrast, people may exert greater control over the specific episodes they select from their autobiographical memories and their reconstruction. They can interpret and evaluate earlier occurrences in self-serving ways. Because the past is ephemeral (and memory is often private), there may be no compelling check on the validity of the memories. Thus, people may find it particularly safe and effective to search the past for evidence that supports their preferred views of themselves.

Wilson and Ross (2000) obtained evidence of the self-enhancing value of the past as a source of self-appraisal information. University students described themselves on an anonymous and confidential questionnaire, and the comparisons they made to past selves (temporal comparisons) and to other people (social comparisons) were identified and coded. Across several studies, temporal comparisons were more likely to be in a self-enhancing downward direction (aspects of present self better than comparable aspects of past self) than in an upward direction (past self superior to present). In contrast, social comparisons were equally as likely to be upward (self inferiority to others) as downward (self as superior to others). In subsequent research Wilson and Ross demonstrated that people are especially inclined to invoke temporal comparisons when they are motivated by self-enhancement concerns and social comparisons when they are more concerned with accurate self-evaluation. In this study, participants reconstructed both social and temporal comparisons from their autobiographical memories, and both types of comparisons were influenced by present goals. Apparently, though, respondents were able to retrieve more flattering temporal than social comparisons, likely due to their greater freedom in interpreting their personal past than their standing relative to others. Next we examine evidence of a presentism bias in people's reconstructions of past selves.

MALLEABILITY OF MEMORIES

...the past is being continually re-made, reconstructed in the interests of the present.

—Fredric Bartlett, 1932

Researchers have repeatedly found evidence for presentism in personal recall. For example, current characteristics, knowledge, emotions, attitudes, goals, and implicit theories of stability and change can influence how individuals recall their pasts (Bartlett, 1932; Fischhoff & Beyth, 1975; Greenwald, 1980; Mead, 1929/1964; Ross, 1989; Ross & Buehler, 1994; Schacter, 1996; Singer & Salovey, 1993; Wilson & Ross, 2001a). For example, Fischhoff and Beyth (1975) demonstrated a hindsight bias: people's knowledge of the outcome of an event caused them to revise their memories of how they expected the episode to happen. Along the same lines, several researchers reported that people who experience a change in attitudes exaggerate the consistency between their new opinions and their earlier beliefs and behaviors (e.g., Bem & McConnell, 1971; Goethals & Reckman, 1973; Ross, McFarland, & Fletcher, 1981). For example, McFarland and Ross (1987) examined dating partners' evaluations of their relationships over time. People who fell more in love after their initial evaluations retrospectively exaggerated the intensity of earlier reports of love; those whose affection waned underestimated their original reports of caring for their partners. Finally, Lewinsohn and Rosenbaum (1987) linked current affect to adults' retrospective evaluations of childhood experiences. Individuals prone to depression recalled more unpleasant childhoods when they were currently depressed than when they were happier.

Greenwald (1980) and Ross (1989; Ross & Buehler, 2001) reviewed the existing research showing that people's current knowledge, beliefs, and affect can bias their recollections. They concluded that personal historians, like their academic counterparts, are highly susceptible to a presentism bias. This bias has two major implications for self-identity. First by remembering past actions and opinions as consistent with their current beliefs, people can derive support and justification for their present viewpoints and affect. Second by exaggerating consistency, people can perceive the self as coherent and stable over time. There is some evidence that perceptions of personal stability are positively associated with emotional and psychological well-being (Keyes, 2000; Keyes & Ryff, 2000) and that perceiving inconsistency within the self is associated with tension and discomfort (Festinger, 1957).

Although individuals often exaggerate their stability over time, they sometimes overestimate the degree to which they have changed. Ross (1989) proposed that an illusion of change occurs when people expect change to occur when little or no change actually took place. For example, people engaging in self-help programs (e.g., diets, assertiveness training programs, study skills courses) typically expect to improve. Unfortunately, most programs are remarkably unsuccessful, even though they often have many loyal adherents (Ross & Conway, 1986). Why do people continue to believe in the usefulness of ineffectual programs? Conway and Ross (1984) proposed that a memory bias might foster an illusion of change. They found that repeated assessments revealed little improvement in skills or grades as a function of participation in a study skills program. However, after taking the program, participants remembered their preprogram study skills as being worse than they had indicated initially. By retrospectively disparaging their earlier skills, participants could claim improvement and confirm their belief in the effectiveness of the program.

Another theory of change that seems resistant to contrary evidence concerns the effects of the menstrual cycle on women's psychological and physical well-being. Assessments across the menstrual cycle indicate that the changes that do occur are much smaller than most women (and men) presume (McFarland, Ross, & DeCourville, 1989). McFarland and her associates implicated memory in the maintenance of women's false beliefs. Some women inadvertently bias their recall so as to support their theories of extreme menstrual distress. When they are not menstruating, these women retrospectively overestimate the actual impact of their previous menstrual periods.

Greenwald (1980) described illusions of change as a "special case" (p. 608) and less probable than a tendency to perceive personal consistency when recalling the past. Ross (1989) similarly suggested that perceptions of consistency predominate because people actually are quite stable over time. In contrast, recent research on temporal self-appraisal theory (Ross & Wilson, 2000, 2002; Wilson & Ross, 2001a) suggests that the perception of personal change may be far more common than these authors previously proposed.

Temporal Self-Appraisal Theory

Temporal self-appraisal theory is based, in part, on an analogy between temporal and social comparisons. Ross and Wilson (2000, 2002; Wilson & Ross, 2000, 2001a) consider past selves to be similar to an interconnected chain of different individuals who vary in closeness and relative position (inferior/superior) to the current self. If past selves are in some ways akin to other people, then social comparison theory and research should help explain temporal comparisons (Albert, 1977). Tesser and his colleagues conducted research on social comparisons that is particularly relevant to the concerns addressed in the present paper (Tesser, 1980, 1988; Tesser & Campbell, 1982, 1983; Tesser & Paulhus, 1983). Proposing that individuals are motivated to protect their self-esteem, these researchers investigated how individuals maintain a favorable self-image when confronted with others who are superior in some way. Tesser and his associates identified two key determinants of the impact of social comparison: the personal importance or self-relevance of the comparison dimension and the individual's closeness to the comparison target. When another person achieves in a domain that is unimportant to the self, increased closeness to that successful individual allows people to bask in the reflected glory of the successful individual (e.g., Cialdini, Borden, Thorne, Walker, Freeman, & Sloan, 1976). Conversely, when a close other outperforms the self in a personally important domain, the inferiority of one's own performance will be highlighted and self-regard may suffer (i.e., contrast effect). Tesser and his colleagues suggest that people employ three main psychological mechanisms to avoid damage to their self-regard when an intimate other succeeds on a self-relevant dimension. Individuals can maintain their self-regard by diminishing their closeness to the successful individual, by deemphasizing the personal importance of the dimension, and by diminishing the magnitude of the other person's achievement (Tesser, 1988).

In their work on temporal self-appraisal, Ross and Wilson (2000; Wilson & Ross, 2001a) examined variables similar to those studied by Tesser and his colleagues. Like Tesser, Ross and Wilson assume that individuals are motivated by a desire to maintain positive self-regard. For Ross and Wilson, however, the "others" in question are past selves rather than other people. Note that Ross and Wilson's focus on past selves deviates somewhat from many autobiographical memory researchers' focus on more specific personal episodes. However, we suggest that the effects of recalling a general past self or a specific event will be quite comparable, insofar as the recalled event has implications for personal identity. Ross and Wilson predict that the closeness and relative inferiority or superiority of the past self (or a personally relevant past event) combine with the importance of the target attribute to determine the impact of a temporal comparison on current identity. While Tesser demonstrated that for social comparisons, personal importance determines the direction of impact (whether contrast or basking in reflected glory will occur) and closeness determines intensity (close others have greater impact than distant ones); Ross and Wilson suggest that for temporal comparisons, closeness to past selves determines the direction of comparison whereas importance determines the intensity. Recent, or close, successes and failures continue to have implications for the current self: the greater the recent success, the better one feels about the current self; the greater the failure the worse one feels. Conversely, more distant glories or shortcomings may no longer have the power to directly bolster or blemish the current self. However, just because these distant outcomes no longer have a direct impact does not mean they have no impact on current self-regard. Distant, inferior former selves may act as downward comparisons against which people can measure their current accomplishments (Wills, 1981; Wilson & Ross, 2000; 2001a). Consequently, people may actually be motivated to derogate remote former selves. This contrast is flattering to the current self and creates a desirable impression of improvement over time. Finally, because important attributes should have a greater overall impact on self-regard, the predicted pattern should be strongest for highly valued attributes: individuals should be particularly critical of distant selves and approving of recent former selves when evaluating their most personally important qualities.

Although the closeness of past episodes is an important variable in temporal self-appraisal theory, the focus is on subjective rather than actual temporal closeness. Psychologists and philosophers have long noted that the subjective experience of time is affected by a variety of factors and is sometimes independent of actual time (e.g., Block, 1989; Brown, Rips & Shevell, 1985; James, 1890/1950; Ross & Wilson, 2002). Temporal self-appraisal predicts that when people *feel* close to a past self, its successes and failures psychologically belong to the present, regardless of their actual temporal distance. Conversely when people feel distant from a past self, they can dissociate themselves from its experiences and outcomes, regardless of actual temporal distance.

In the set of temporal-self appraisal theory hypotheses presented previously, closeness, valence of the past self, and importance serve as independent variables. However, Ross and Wilson (2000; Wilson & Ross, 2000, 2001a) also include each of these dimensions as dependent variables. According to the theory, people can maintain favorable self-regard by perceiving failures as farther away than equally distant successes, by criticizing distant selves and praising recent ones, and by valuing current strengths and deemphasizing the importance of current weaknesses. Next we review evidence regarding each of these variables in temporal self-appraisal theory.

Retrospective Appraisals: Derogating and Enhancing Past Selves

Wilson and Ross (2001a) tested temporal self-appraisal theory's prediction that people would derogate a relatively distant past self. In one study, university students described themselves in their own words, at the current time and at a more distant time, age 16. Participants' descriptions of their current selves contained more favorable and fewer unfavorable statements than did their descriptions of their earlier selves. In subsequent studies, Wilson and Ross (2001a) obtained similar results when they asked participants to evaluate their current and past selves on a list of positive and negative attributes and when the participants were middle-aged rather than young adults. In all of these studies, participants were asked to evaluate themselves relative to same-aged peers. Although participants rated themselves as superior to their peers at each point in time, they viewed their relative preeminence as increasing markedly as they aged. In other words, the advantage of self over the average person is greater at the current time than it is retrospectively at earlier periods.

According to temporal self-appraisal theory, the former selves that people downplay today would once have been praised as highly as the current self is now. However, perhaps the participants really were more inferior in the past and their retrospective evaluations accurately reflect change. Indeed, Roberts, Caspi, and Moffitt (2001) found that although the majority of the attributes of adolescents and young adults remain stable over time, change is mostly in a positive direction. Although Wilson and Ross (2001a) do not dispute the possibility of actual improvement, they propose that retrospective evaluations reflect more improvement than would be observed contemporaneously over time. To examine this prediction directly, they conducted a longitudinal study (Wilson & Ross, 2001a, Study 3).

During the first few weeks of the academic term (September), university students rated their current selves relative to their same-aged peers on a variety of traits (e.g., social skills, self-confidence, self-motivation, and maturity). Two months later (November), participants completed the same questionnaire, again rating their current selves relative to peers. In both cases, the current self was defined within the past two weeks. After rating their current selves during the November session, participants were asked to think back to the first few weeks of the term, and to rate themselves as they recalled being at that time in the past, again relative to their same-aged peers at the time. Although 2 months of an academic term is a short period of actual time, it can seem like a long time in the life of a university student. Consequently, Wilson and Ross expected to find some evidence of retrospective derogation.

Looking first at participants' ratings of their current selves in September and November, participants' contemporaneous evaluations did not evidence any improvement over the 2-month period. In fact, their self-assessments declined marginally over time. Interestingly, their retrospective ratings reflected neither decline nor constancy. Instead, when participants were asked, in November, to think back to their September selves, they retrospectively rated their former selves as inferior to their current selves, and as worse than they had rated themselves originally in September. By retrospectively criticizing past selves, participants created an illusion of self-improvement in the face of marginal decline. Notably, Wilson and Ross' study, spanning only 2 months, replicates earlier findings of Woodruff and Birren (1972) which spanned a much longer period. These researchers located a subset of individuals who had completed a test of personal and social adjustment 25 years earlier, and asked them to complete the test as they were now and as they thought they would have responded at the time of the original testing. Participants displayed remarkable stability over a quarter century; their current scores did not differ systematically from earlier results. However, when participants completed the measure in retrospect, they rated their former selves as significantly less well adjusted than they indicated currently or had reported originally.

In a final study, Wilson and Ross (2001a) tested the prediction that psychologically distant past selves should be criticized to a greater extent than psychologically close past selves, even if "real" calendar time remains constant. In addition, Wilson and Ross examined participants' appraisals of their most and least valued attributes. According to the theory of temporal self-appraisal, individuals should evaluate themselves favorably on important traits in the subjectively recent past because this evaluation reflects directly on the current self. On the other hand, people should evaluate their subjectively distant pasts negatively on important attributes to highlight improvement on attributes that matter most to them. The same pattern should not be evident for unimportant attributes as these traits have less impact on self-regard.

All participants first rated their current selves, relative to same-aged peers on a set of attributes. Next, they indicated which attributes in the list were most and least important to them. Finally, they retrospectively appraised their past selves at the beginning of the academic term, 2 months earlier. To create differences in the subjective experience of time, Wilson and Ross depicted the beginning of the academic term as either recent ("think of a point in time in the recent past, the beginning of this term") or distant ("think all the way back to the beginning of this term").

As predicted, the subjective representation of time influenced participants' self-appraisals. When the beginning of the term was portrayed as recent, participants rated their former selves just as favorably as their current selves. However, when a different group of participants was asked to think "way back" to that same point in time, they were significantly less impressed with their earlier selves. As well, participants were particularly critical of distant selves and favorable toward recent selves on attributes that they considered to be important. Because the actual passage of time does not vary between conditions and assignment to condition is random, the "distant" group could not actually have improved more than the "recent" group. Thus, such perceptions of improvement appear to be motivated by a desire to feel good about the present.

Research by other investigators provides further evidence that perceptions of self-improvement may be illusory and motivated by a desire to reach preferred conclusions about the self and one's circumstances. McFarland and Alvaro (2000) suggested that people should be particularly motivated to perceive personal improvement after experiencing a threat to self such as a traumatic life event. All participants in their studies were asked to reflect on a traumatic life event that had occurred to them in the past and were asked to evaluate their present selves. The threatening episode was rendered either salient or nonsalient to participants before they made their appraisals. Those for whom the event was salient were significantly more critical of their earlier selves (and thus presumably saw more improvement in themselves). In addition, those who thought about more severely threatening events derogated their present selves to a greater extent than did those who considered milder negative incidents, providing further evidence for the role of motivation. In addition, other researchers have demonstrated that people who rate their current selves more favorably than former selves tend to be more satisfied with their present state of affairs (Fleeson & Baltes, 1998). Overall, research suggests that people derogate past selves to maintain or enhance their current self-regard.

When do people hesitate to derogate even distant selves? People may depreciate former selves when doing so allows them to perceive self-improvement. Individuals should be reluctant to criticize even a remote self if they see its defects as potentially staining the present self. Whether people perceive defects as enduring or not depends, in part, on their personal implicit theories concerning the mutability of traits. People view some of their characteristics as readily changeable and others as stable over time (Dweck & Leggett, 1988). Consequently, they should be hesitant to criticize even subjectively distant past selves on attributes that they perceive to be important and unchangeable. Additionally, even when they believe an attribute is changeable, people will not be inclined to derogate past selves that are psychologically irrelevant to the present self. Ross and Wilson (2002) propose a latitude of temporal comparison: people judge some recent and distant past selves to be sufficiently similar to the current self to serve as relevant objects of comparison on a specific attribute, whereas they regard other past selves as too dissimilar to serve as pertinent comparisons. Outside the latitude of comparison, temporal self-appraisal predictions should not apply. For example, a 40-year-old woman may take pleasure in the sense of improvement derived from disparaging her social skills when she was 25. She is unlikely, however, to obtain any satisfaction from disparaging her social skills when she was 10 years old.

People may not only fail to disparage subjectively distant past selves — they may actually exaggerate their merits. Casual observation suggests that some middle-aged individuals enjoy telling overblown stories of earlier athletic triumphs and past romances. We suggest that people might be especially inclined to enhance distant selves on attributes that were once personally important, but that are now less significant determinants of self-regard. For example, individuals who have retired or changed careers may look back on their successes of their former careers happily. Because the domain was more important in the past than the present, these individuals may be able to "bask in the reflected glory" (Cialdini et al., 1976) of former careers without being threatened by the possibility that they have deteriorated. In contrast, when people perceive decline on an attribute that remains currently important, highlighting past accomplishments should make present achievements pale by comparison. Individuals without jobs who focus on their earlier periods of employment report increased depression and lower self-esteem than those who focus on other sources of self-appraisal information (Sheeran, Abrams, & Orbell, 1995). Presumably, they are unable to derive pleasure from their former achievements, because the attribute on which they declined remains important to them.

SUBJECTIVE TEMPORAL DISTANCE: FEELING CLOSE OR FAR FROM THE PAST

According to temporal self-appraisal theory, people adjust their subjective distance from past outcomes to maintain favorable self-regard. Ross and Wilson (2002) tested this prediction by asking people how close or far away they felt from past events or selves that could potentially have favorable or unfavorable implications for their current self-regard. In their first study, Ross and Wilson asked university students to evaluate their degree of social success in high school and to indicate how distant they felt from high school. Participants indicated subjective distance by placing a mark on a line with endpoints such as: "feel very close to my past self" and "feel very distant from my past self." Participants reported feeling farther away from socially unsuccessful selves than from equally distant socially successful selves, even after controlling for the actual temporal distance since graduating. Ross and Wilson replicated this pattern in a second study, in which they randomly assigned participants to report either their best or their worst grade from the previous term. Controlling for actual distance, participants felt farther away from the course in which they performed poorly than from the course in which they performed well.

These results support the prediction that people feel farther away from events that have negative implications for their self regard than from equally distant positive events. According to temporal self-appraisal theory, people show this pattern of distancing because they are motivated to maintain current self-regard. To examine the motivational account, Ross and Wilson (2002, Study 3) asked participants to report their subjective distance from positive and negative events that either happened to themselves or to an acquaintance. Participants were randomly assigned to describe a proud or an embarrassing incident that happened either to them or to an acquaintance. After describing the incident, participants indicated their feelings of subjective temporal distance from the target incident. If participants engage in motivated distancing, they should feel farther from events that embarrassed them personally than from events that made them feel proud.

Additionally, they should not report any difference in the subjective distance of proud and embarrassing events that happen to acquaintances. The results supported the motivational hypothesis: participants reported feeling closer to their own proud events than to their equally distant embarrassing events; in contrast, they felt equivalently far from proud and embarrassing events that happened to their acquaintances.

Individual differences in the motivation to self-enhance provide another way to test the motivational interpretation of the asymmetry in the distancing positive and negative events. Individuals with high self-esteem (HSEs) are generally more inclined to counter threats to their self-regard than are those with lower self-esteem (LSEs; Baumeister, 1998; Blaine & Crocker, 1993; Mussweiler, Gabriel, & Bodenhausen, 2000). For example, in comparison to LSEs, HSEs are more skilled at interpreting and recalling negative feedback in a self-protective manner (e.g., Aspinwall & Taylor, 1993; Brown, Collins, & Schmidt, 1988; Brown & Dutton, 1995; Brown & Mankowski, 1993; Crocker, Thompson, McGraw, & Ingerman, 1987; Reis, Gerrard, & Gibbons, 1993; Schlenker, Weigold, & Hallam,1990). HSEs are also more likely than LSEs to take greater personal responsibility for success than for failure (Blaine & Crocker, 1993) and to dwell on their strengths rather than weaknesses following disappointments (Brown & Smart, 1991; Dodgson & Wood, 1998; Steele, Spencer, & Lynch, 1993). Mussweiler and colleagues (2000) reported findings that are particularly pertinent to current concerns. Relative to LSEs, HSEs are more inclined to ward off a threatening *social* comparison by dissociating themselves from the comparison individual. Along the same lines, Ross and Wilson (2002) predicted that HSEs would be more likely than LSEs to feel subjectively distant from former selves and outcomes that could have negative implications for their present self-worth and close to selves and outcomes with favorable implications.

Ross and Wilson (2002) measured participants' self-esteem in each of their studies. As predicted, HSEs were consistently more likely than LSEs to show a relation between subjective distance and the valence of an outcome. For example, HSEs felt farther away from their worst than from their best course, but LSEs reported feeling equally distant from the two courses. Moreover, HSEs felt closer to proud events that happened to them rather than to their acquaintances and tended to feel farther away from embarrassing events that occurred to them rather than their acquaintances. In contrast, LSEs felt equally distant from their own and their acquaintances' events, and showed no evidence of a valence-based asymmetry in subjective distance for either target person. The self-esteem findings provide further support for a motivational interpretation of the asymmetry in subjective distancing.

It is important to note that the logic of this research on subjective distancing assumes that measures of actual and subjective distance are at best imperfectly related. Measures of subjective time can be affected by a host of factors (e.g., Block, 1989; Brown, Rips, & Shevell, 1985; James, 1890/1950) other than actual time. Across a large number of studies, Ross and Wilson find a generally significant but low to moderate relation between subjective and actual time when individuals recall valenced personal episodes. On average, the correlation between the two time measures is about 0.25 in these studies. Interestingly, the association between the two measures seems to be considerably higher when the memories concern episodes occurring to other people (Ross & Wilson, 2002). In this case, actual time seems to be the critical determinant of subjective time, whereas for the self, actual time is only one of several factors (e.g., self-esteem, event valence) contributing to the subjective experience of time.

Finally, note that subjective measures of time have nothing to do with the accuracy of temporal judgments. The subjective assessment indicates how far away an episode feels, not how far away it is. Differences in subjective time estimates occur even when individuals are fully aware of when an episode actually happened (Ross & Wilson, 2002).

How the Past Influences the Present

We have shown that people's memories of their personal pasts are malleable and may be influenced by self-motives. Next, we examine the other side of the bidirectional relation between autobiographical memory and self-identity. We have assumed that people's memory revisions and distancing maneuvers alter the impact of past selves and outcomes on current self-regard. In particular, past selves that are perceived as temporally recent should be experienced as part of the current self. Consequently, the outcomes obtained by subjectively recent selves should have a direct impact on present self-evaluations. On the other hand, past selves regarded as distant should be seen as detached from the current self. The actions/evaluations of a distant self should not directly impact the current self.

To directly test these predictions, Wilson (2000) first induced participants to feel subjectively close to or distant from positive or negative past selves (e.g., socially successful or unsuccessful high school selves). She then examined the impact of remembering these earlier selves on evaluations of the current self. She altered participants' feelings of subjective distance by changing representations of spatial distance on a timeline. Students were randomly assigned to complete a timeline spanning many years (e.g., Birth to Today) or only the fairly recent past (e.g., Age 16 to Today). They were instructed to locate and mark the "target" event (e.g., last semester of high school) on the timeline. As Figure 10.1 illustrates, people should place a target event (in this case, their last semester of high school) closer to "today" when the timeline spans many years as opposed to a briefer time span. This manipulation of spatial distance altered people's reports of subjective distance from the target event: they felt closer to events that were spatially closer to the present.

Wilson (2000; Wilson & Ross, 2001b) found that the manipulation of subjective distance had the predicted impact on people's evaluations of their current selves. Students who were induced to feel close to negative earlier episodes (including social inadequacies, low grades, and interpersonal transgressions) evaluated their current selves and circumstances less favorably than those induced to feel distant from similar shortcomings. In contrast, participants encouraged to regard earlier

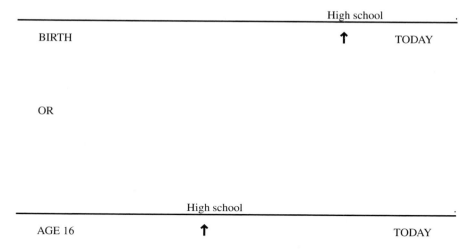

FIGURE 10.1. Timeline Manipulation of Spatial Distance. *Note:* The Birth to Today timeline makes high school seem subjectively more recent than the Age 16 to Today timeline.

successes as subjectively recent appraised their current selves more favorably than those who were persuaded to see the same former achievements as remote.

Wilson's (2000; Wilson & Ross, 2001b) findings support temporal self-appraisal theory's proposition that self-enhancement goals can be served by recollecting the past in specific ways. The remembered past can influence people's current views of themselves, but *how* they remember (whether the past feels close or far) matters as much as *what* they remember (whether the past is positive or negative).

BEYOND THE SELF: TEMPORAL APPRAISALS IN CLOSE RELATIONSHIPS

Temporal self-appraisal theory can be extended to the temporal assessments of any event, person, relationship, or even object, as long as it is experienced as part of the self or has implications for self-identity and self-regard (Ross & Wilson, 2000). Close relationships are often likely to fit this criterion (e.g., Aron, Aron, Tudor & Nelson, 1991). Consequently, we would expect that the same processes outlined in the temporal self-appraisal theory would occur for romantic relationships. Indeed, previous research indicates that intimates recall their relationship as improving even when contemporaneous ratings suggest otherwise (Karney & Coombs, 2000; Karney & Frye, 2002; Sprecher, 1999). Thus, the illusory improvement evident in recollections of past selves also occurs in memories of relationship histories. As well, Cameron, Ross, and Holmes (2002) recently examined how recollections of a past dispute affect temporal appraisals of individuals and their relationships. Specifically, these researchers investigated memories of improvement since the occurrence of a relationship transgression. They hypothesized that perpetrators of a transgression would maintain positive self-regard and their sense of security in their romantic relationships by claiming improvement in themselves and their relationship since the time of the transgression. In this way, perpetrators can dissociate themselves from their misdeeds and deny lasting damage to the relationships. Cameron and colleagues hypothesized that victims of the transgression would be less motivated to perceive improvement in the transgressor or the relationships over the same time interval, because the wrongdoing did not have implications for their own character or self-view.

Cameron and her associates invited exclusively dating couples to participate in their study. One member of each couple was randomly assigned by the flip of a coin to be the perpetrator and the other to be the victim (the terms perpetrator and victim were not used in the study). Couples jointly nominated a past incident in which the partner randomly assigned to be the "perpetrator" had upset or annoyed his or her partner. After selecting an event, partners completed a questionnaire anonymously and confidentially. As predicted, perpetrators perceived more improvement in themselves and their relationships since the time of the transgression than did their victims. Interestingly, perpetrators also reported more favorable expectations for the future of their relationship than did victims. Evidently, perceiving improvement enabled perpetrators to feel secure in their relationships and hope for their future. The intriguing aspect of these data is that participants were randomly assigned to roles. Presumably those assigned to the victim role would have been more optimistic about the future of their relationships if they had been reminded of their own misdeeds.

Additional research by Karney and Frye (2002) has also demonstrated that couples may be motivated to engage in retrospective devaluation to counter insecurities about their relationships. They conducted a prospective and retrospective analysis of married couples' satisfaction with their relationships. Satisfaction declined over time, but, in retrospect, participants remembered recent improvements that were not evident from contemporaneous reports. Importantly, recollections of improvement predicted partners' optimism about the future of their relationships, whereas absolute level of satisfaction did not. Again, perceiving improvement in an intimate relationship enables individuals to feel hopeful for the future of their relationships, even in the face of evidence to the contrary.

LOOKING FORWARD: COMPARISONS TO THE FUTURE SELF

Although we have focused primarily on the relations between past and present selves, recent evidence suggests parallel associations between present and future selves. Lawford, Wilson and Buehler (2002) found that people rate themselves more favorably in the future than they do in the present on a host of attributes. Evidently, the perception of improvement between the past and the present extends into the future (see also Brickman, Coates, & Janoff-Bulman, 1978; Robinson & Ryff, 1999). In addition, Lawford and colleagues found when participants were induced to feel subjectively *closer* to a point in the future, they rated their future selves even more favorably than they did when they regarded the same time period as more remote. At first blush, this finding might seem counterintuitive, given that one might expect that people would like to expect continual improvement far into the future. Indeed, Lawford and her colleagues suggest that unlike people's perceptions of the distant past, people will be disinclined to deprecate even a remote future self, because they expect to become that self someday. However, subjectively close and distant future selves differ psychologically, in that the near future (like the recent past) can be included in present identity. Thus, having great expectations for a subjectively close future self can provide immediate benefits for current self-regard, motivating individuals to sing the glories of the future just around the corner. On the other hand, favorable forecasts for a distant future self have mixed implications for the current self — one might look forward to someday reaping those benefits, but at the same time the present may pale in comparison.

Finally, Wilson (2002) found that the asymmetry in the subjective distance of negative and positive past events has a parallel pattern for future events. University students read a bogus passage describing former students' experiences with graduation. In the positive condition, university graduation was portrayed as a joyful event, associated with feelings of accomplishment, promise, and wealth. In the negative condition, graduation was depicted as a difficult and uncertain time, marred by sadness at leaving friends, questions about job prospects, and new financial responsibilities. Participants were then asked to indicate how far they felt from graduation. Participants with HSE reported feeling significantly more distant from graduation when they anticipated an unpleasant experience than when they looked forward to its benefits. LSEs, in contrast, viewed the two experiences as equally distant. Once again, then, HSEs appear to capitalize on information that should enhance current self-regard by pulling it closer, and reduce the threat of negative information by keeping it psychologically at bay.

SUMMARY

We reviewed evidence documenting a presentism bias in autobiographical memory. People reconstruct and interpret their personal histories on the basis of current knowledge and motives. We focused primarily on the retrospective biases that serve to sustain and enhance present self-regard. From the perspective of temporal self-appraisal theory, we explored the reciprocal connections between the past and the present that serve these self-enhancing motives. People can affirm their current self-regard by praising subjectively near and disparaging more distant past selves. Similarly, people push former episodes with unfavorable implications for their self-regard into the subjectively distant past and keep favorable episodes temporally close. Such temporal adjustments affect people's assessments of their current selves: individuals feel better about their present selves when they view unfavorable outcomes as distant and positive ones as close.

Perhaps another way of considering the presentism bias, in light of the current findings, is to ask: What do people include in their psychological present? James (1890/1950) describes the experienced, or "specious" present as more than an instant of time, but rather deriving itself from the recent past and near future. Indeed, the present is "no knife-edge, but a saddle-back, with a certain breadth of its own on which we sit perched, and from which we look in two directions into time" (p. 605). According to temporal self-appraisal theory, we create our psychological present by selecting the elements of the past and the future to be included in current identity, and by constructing our more extended histories in a way that reinforces our desired view of the present. Not only does our presentism bias influence what we recall and predict about our own attributes, but it also extends to our views of close relationships through time, and conceivably should apply to any event, association, or object that has direct implications for our personal identity. In short, we are motivated historians, with a stake in telling our life stories in a manner that glorifies the present and assures us that the best is yet to come.

REFERENCES

Albert, S. (1977). Temporal comparison theory. *Psychological Review, 84,* 485–503.

Aron, A., Aron, E. N., Tudor, M., & Nelson, G. (1991). Close relationships as including other in the self. *Journal of Personality and Social Psychology, 60,* 241–253.

Aspinwall, L. G., & Taylor, S. E. (1993). Effects of social comparison direction, threat, and self-esteem on affect, self-evaluation, and expected success. *Journal of Personality and Social Psychology, 64,* 708–722.

Bartlett, F. C. (1932). *Remembering.* Oxford, England: University Press.

Baumeister, R. F. (1998). The self. In D. T. Gilbert, S. T. Fiske, & G. Lindzey (Eds.), *Handbook of social psychology* (4th ed., pp. 680–740). New York: McGraw-Hill.

Bem, D. J., & McConnell, H. K. (1971). Testing the self-perception explanation of dissonance phenomena: On the salience of premanipulation attitudes. *Journal of Personality and Social Psychology, 14,* 23–31.

Blaine, B., & Crocker, J. (1993). Self-esteem and self-serving biases in reactions to positive and negative events. In R. Baumeister (Ed.), *Self-esteem: The puzzle of low self-regard* (pp. 55–85). New York: Plenum.

Block, R. A. (1989). Experiencing and remembering time: Affordances, context, and cognition. In I. Levin & D. Zakay (Eds.), *Time and human cognition: A life-span perspective* (pp. 333–364). Amsterdam: Elsevier Science Publishers.

Brickman, P., Coates, D., & Janoff-Bulman, R. (1978). Lottery winners and accident victims: Is happiness relative? *Journal of Personality and Social Psychology, 36,* 917–927.

Brown, J. D., Collins, R. L., & Schmidt, G. W. (1988). Self-esteem and direct versus indirect forms of self-enhancement. *Journal of Personality and Social Psychology, 55,* 445–453.

Brown, J. D., & Dutton, K. A. (1995). The thrill of victory, the complexity of defeat: Self-esteem and people's emotional reactions to success and failure. *Journal of Personality and Social Psychology, 68,* 712–722.

Brown, J. D., & Mankowski, T. (1993). Self-esteem, mood, and self-evaluation: Changes in mood and the way you see you. *Journal of Personality and Social Psychology, 64*, 421–430.

Brown, J. D., & Smart, A. (1991). The self and social conduct: Linking self-representations to prosocial behavior. *Journal of Personality and Social Psychology, 60*, 368–375.

Brown, N. R., Rips, L. J., & Shevell, S. K. (1985). The subjective dates of natural events in very-long-term memory. *Cognitive Psychology, 17*, 139–177.

Bruner, J. (1994). The "remembered self." In U. Neisser & R. Fivush (Eds.), *The remembering self: Construction and accuracy in the self narrative* (pp. 41–54). Emory Symposia in Cognition 6. New York: Cambridge University Press.

Butterfield, H. (1965). *The Whig interpretation of history.* New York: W. W. Norton.

Cameron, J. J., Ross, M., & Holmes. J. G. (2002). Loving the one you hurt: Positive effects of recounting a transgression against an intimate partner. *Journal of Experimental Social Psychology, 38*, 307–314.

Cialdini, R. B., Borden, R. J., Thorne, A., Walker, M. R., Freeman, S., & Sloan, L. R. (1976). Basking in reflected glory: Three (football) field studies. *Journal of Personality and Social Psychology, 39*, 406–415.

Conway, M., & Ross, M. (1984). Getting what you want by revising what you had. *Journal of Personality and Social Psychology, 47*, 738–748.

Crocker, J., Thompson, L., McGraw, K., & Ingerman, C. (1987). Downward comparison, prejudice, and evaluation of others: Effects of self-esteem and threat. *Journal of Personality and Social Psychology, 52*, 907–916.

Dodgson, P. G., & Wood, J. V. (1998). Self-esteem and the cognitive accessibility of strengths and weaknesses after failure. *Journal of Personality and Social Psychology, 75*, 178–197.

Dweck, C. S., & Leggett, E. L. (1988). A social-cognitive approach to motivation and personality. *Psychological Review, 95*, 256–273.

Festinger, L. (1957). *A theory of cognitive dissonance.* Stanford, CA: Stanford University Press.

Fischhoff, B., & Beyth, R. (1975). "I knew it would happen": Remembered probabilities of once-future things. *Organizational Behavior & Human Decision Processes, 13*, 1–16.

Fleeson, W., & Baltes, P. (1998) Beyond present-day personality assessment: An encouraging exploration of the measurement properties and predictive power of subjective lifetime personality. *Journal of Research in Personality, 32*, 411–430.

Goethals, G. B., & Reckman, R. F. (1973). The perception of consistency in attitudes. *Journal of Experimental Social Psychology, 9*, 419–423.

Greenwald, A. G. (1980). The totalitarian ego: Fabrication and revision of personal history. *American Psychologist, 35*, 603–618.

Hull, D. L. (1979). In defense of presentism. *History and Theory, 18*, 1–5.

James, W. (1890/1950). *Principles of psychology.* New York: Dover.

Karney, B. R., & Coombs, R. H. (2000). Memory bias in long-term close relationships: Consistency or improvement? *Personality and Social Psychology Bulletin, 26*, 959–970.

Karney, B. R., & Frye, N. E. (2002). "But we've been getting better lately": Comparing prospective and retrospective views of relationship development. *Journal of Personality & Social Psychology, 82*, 222–238.

Keyes, C. L. M. (2000). Subjective change and its consequences for emotional well-being. *Motivation & Emotion, 24*, 67–84.

Keyes, C. L. M., & Ryff, C. D. (2000). Subjective change and mental health: A self-concept theory. *Social Psychology Quarterly, 63,* 264–279.

Klein, S. B. (2001). A self to remember: A cognitive neuropsychological perspective on how self creates memory and memory creates self. In C. Sedikides & M. B. Brewer (Eds.), *Individual self, relational self, collective self* (pp. 25–46). Philadelphia, PA: Psychology Press.

Kunda, Z. (1990). The case for motivated reasoning. *Psychological Bulletin, 108,* 480–498.

Lawford, H., Wilson, A. E., & Buehler, R. (2002, June). *The effect of perceived temporal distance on future predictions.* Paper presented at the Canadian Psychology Association Annual Convention, Vancouver, B.C., Canada.

Lewinsohn, P. M., & Rosenbaum, M. (1987). Recall of parental behavior by acute depressives, remitted depressives, and nondepressives. *Journal of Personality & Social Psychology, 52,* 611–619.

McFarland, D., & Alvaro, C. (2000). The impact of motivation on temporal comparisons: Coping with traumatic events by perceiving personal growth. *Journal of Personality and Social Psychology, 79,* 327–343.

McFarland, C., & Ross, M. (1987). The relation between current impressions and memories of self and dating partners. *Personality and Social Psychology Bulletin, 13,* 228–238.

McFarland, C., Ross, M., & DeCourville, N. (1989). Women's theories of menstruation and biases in recall of menstrual symptoms. *Journal of Personality and Social Psychology, 57,* 522–531.

Mead, G. H. (1929/1964). The nature of the past. In J. J. Cross (Ed.), *Essays in honor of John Dewey* (pp. 235–242). New York: Henry Holt & Co.

Mussweiler, T., Gabriel, S., & Bodenhausen, G. V. (2000). Shifting social identities as a strategy for deflecting threatening social comparisons. *Journal of Personality and Social Psychology, 79,* 398–409.

Neisser, U. (1967). *Cognitive Psychology.* East Norwalk, CT: Appleton Century Crofts.

Nelson, K. (1988). The ontogeny of memory for real events. In U. Neisser, & E. Winograd (Eds.), *Remembering reconsidered: Ecological and traditional approaches to the study of memory* (pp. 244–276). Emory Symposia in Cognition 2. New York: Cambridge University Press.

Nelson, K. (1997). Finding one's self in time. In J. L. Snodgrass & R. L. Thompson (Eds.), *The self across psychology: Self-recognition, self-awareness, and the self concept* (pp. 103–116). New York: New York Academy of Sciences.

Reis, T. J., Gerrard, M., & Gibbons, F. X. (1993). Social comparisons and the pill: Reactions to upward and downward comparisons of contraceptive behavior. *Personality and Social Psychology Bulletin, 19,* 13–20.

Richter, D. (2001). *Facing east from Indian country.* Cambridge, MA: Harvard University Press.

Roberts, B. W., Caspi, A., & Moffitt, T. E. (2001). The kids are alright: Growth and stability in personality development from adolescence to adulthood. *Journal of Personality and Social Psychology, 81,* 670–683.

Robinson, M. D., & Ryff, C. D. (1999). The role of self-deception in perceptions of past, present, and future happiness. *Personality and Social Psychology Bulletin, 25,* 595–606.

Ross, M. (1989). The relation of implicit theories to the construction of personal histories. *Psychological Review, 96,* 341–357.

Ross, M., & Buehler, R. (1994). Creative remembering. In U. Neisser & R. Fivush (Eds.), *The remembering self: Construction and accuracy in the self-narrative* (pp. 205–235). Emory Symposia in Cognition 6. New York: Cambridge University Press.

Ross, M., & Buehler, R. (2001). Identity through time: Constructing personal pasts and futures. In A. Tesser & N. Schwarz (Eds.), *Blackwell handbook in social psychology, Vol. 1: Intraindividual processes* (pp. 518–544). Oxford: Blackwell.

Ross, M., & Conway, M. (1986). Remembering one's own past: The construction of personal histories. In R. M. Sorrentino & E. T. Higgins (Eds.), *The handbook of motivation and cognition: Foundations of social behavior.* New York: Guilford Press.

Ross, M., McFarland, C., & Fletcher, G. J. (1981). The effect of attitude on the recall of personal histories. *Journal of Personality & Social Psychology, 40,* 627–634.

Ross, M., & Wilson, A. E. (2000). Constructing and appraising past selves. In D. L. Schacter & E. Scarry (Eds.), *Memory, brain, and belief* (pp. 231–258). Cambridge, MA: Harvard University Press.

Ross, M., & Wilson, A. E. (2002). It feels like yesterday: Self-esteem, valence of personal past experiences, and judgments of subjective distance. *Journal of Personality and Social Psychology, 82,* 792–803.

Schacter, D. L. (1996). *Searching for memory: The brain, the mind, and the past.* New York: Basic Books.

Schlenker, B. R., Weigold, M. F., & Hallam, J. R. (1990). Self-serving attributions in social context: Effects of self-esteem and social pressure. *Journal of Personality and Social Psychology, 58,* 855–863.

Sedikides, C., & Skowronski, J. J. (1995). On the sources of self-knowledge: The perceived primacy of self-reflection. *Journal of Social & Clinical Psychology, 14,* 224–270.

Sheeran, P., Abrams, D., & Orbell, S. (1995). Unemployment, self-esteem, and depression: A social comparison theory approach. *Basic and Applied Social Psychology, 17,* 65–82.

Singer, J. A., & Salovey, P. (1993). *The remembered self: Emotion and memory in personality.* New York: Free Press.

Sprecher, S. (1999). "Love you more today than yesterday": Romantic partners' perceptions of changes in love and related affect over time. *Journal of Personality and Social Psychology, 76,* 46–53.

Steele, C. M., Spencer, S. J., & Lynch, M. (1993). Self-image resilience and dissonance: The role of affirmational resources. *Journal of Personality and Social Psychology, 64,* 885–896.

Taylor, S. E., & Brown, J. D. (1988). Illusion and well-being: A social psychological perspective on mental health. *Psychological Bulletin, 103,* 193–210.

Taylor, S. E., Neter, E., & Wayment, H. A. (1995). Self-evaluation processes. *Personality & Social Psychology Bulletin, 21,* 1278–1287.

Tesser, A. (1980). Self-esteem maintenance in family dynamics. *Journal of Personality and Social Psychology, 39,* 77–91.

Tesser, A. (1988). Toward a self-evaluation maintenance model of social behavior. In L. Berkowitz (Ed.), *Advances in experimental social psychology* (Vol. 21, pp. 181–227). New York: Academic Press.

Tesser, A., & Campbell, J. (1982). Self-evaluation maintenance and the perception of friends and strangers. *Journal of Personality, 59,* 261–279.

Tesser, A., & Campbell, J. (1983). Self-definition and self-evaluation maintenance. In J. Suls & A. G. Greenwald (Eds.), *Psychological perspectives on the self* (Vol. 2, pp. 1–31). Hillsdale, NJ: Erlbaum.

Tesser, A., & Paulhus, D. (1983). The definition of self: Private and public self-evaluation maintenance strategies. *Journal of Personality and Social Psychology, 44,* 672–682.

Wills, T. A. (1981). Downward comparison principles in social psychology. *Psychological Bulletin, 90,* 245–271.

Wilson, A. E. (2000). *How do people's perceptions of their former selves affect their current self-appraisals?* Unpublished doctoral dissertation, University of Waterloo.

Wilson, A. E. (2002). Perceived distance from favorable and unfavorable expected future outcomes. Unpublished raw data, Wilfrid Laurier University.

Wilson, A. E., & Ross, M. (2000). The frequency of temporal-self and social comparisons in people's personal appraisal. *Journal of Personality and Social Psychology, 78,* 928–942.

Wilson, A. E., & Ross, M. (2001a). From chump to champ: People's appraisals of their earlier and current selves. *Journal of Personality and Social Psychology, 80,* 572–584.

Wilson, A. E., & Ross, M. (2001b, February). *How do perceptions of former selves affect current self-appraisals?* Paper presented at the Society for Personality and Social Psychology Convention, San Antonio, TX.

Woodruff, D. S., & Birren, J. E. (1972). Age changes and cohort difference in personality. *Developmental Psychology, 6,* 252–259.

11

Diachronic Disunity

JAMES M. LAMPINEN
TIMOTHY N. ODEGARD
JULIANA K. LEDING
University of Arkansas

"I'd become a different person since I'd written [my early songs] and, frankly, they mystified me."

— Bob Dylan

PERSISTENCE CONDITIONS OF PHYSICAL OBJECTS

How is it that things can change and yet retain their identities? This is a classic problem in the history of philosophy. The ancient Greek philosopher Heraclitus (trans 2001) asked us to consider the example of a river. The substance that makes up the river, the actual water molecules, are constantly changing as the water flows from the river and into the sea. The substance of the river is never the same from one moment to the next, and yet it is the same river. What gives the river its identity despite the fact that none of the actual physical stuff that makes up the river is the same?

Or consider the classic thought experiment known as the *Ship of Theseus* (e.g. Garrett, 1985; Plutarch, trans. 1992, lines 45–120; Rea, 1995; Scaltsas, 1980; Wiggins, 1967). Imagine you are the owner of a large wooden ship. One day as you are inspecting the deck of your ship, you notice an old rotten board. You grab your tools, remove the board and replace it with a new one. Are you now the owner of a new ship? Most people would say, "No, of course not." Although you replaced a part of the ship, the ship is still the same ship. But what if the next day you replace another board? Do you now have a new ship? Most people would still say, "No, the ship is still the same ship." But what if over the course of many years board after board is replaced until a day arrives in which none of the boards making up the ship are the same as the original? The ship is made up of entirely new components. Is it the same ship? What if instead of doing it over many years you did it in a day? What if you were to take all the old discarded boards and use them to create a new ship that is exactly the same shape as the old one? Which ship is the old ship and which ship is the new ship?

These riddles invite us to consider the persistence conditions for physical objects (Burke, 1994; Haslanger, 1989; Merricks, 1999; Zimmerman, 1996). In what ways can you change an object and still have it be the same object? Consider water. You can take a gallon of water and you can freeze it. Most people would say it is still water, although in a frozen state. You can boil the water. Most people would say the gas molecules now zipping about in the steam cloud are still molecules of water. You can take the gallon of water and pour it over your best friend's head. The water would still be water (although your friend may no longer be your friend). You can pour food coloring into the water. It would still be water. The gallon of water you have can go through countless and diverse transformations and still retain its identity as water.

But now imagine that you take the gallon of water and add an additional atom of oxygen to each water molecule. Would it still be water? Of course, the answer is "No." You would no longer have water. You would have hydrogen peroxide. What if you ripped apart the hydrogen and oxygen atoms that make up the water molecule? Would it still be water? No. There are things you can do to water through which its identity will persist and there are things you can do to water through which its identity will cease to persist. Things can change, sometimes dramatically, and still have the same identity.

PERSONAL IDENTITY

Personal identity presents similar problems (Olson, 2002). None of us is exactly the same as we were when we were children. None of us is exactly the same as we were when we were college sophomores. None of us is exactly the same as we were even a year ago. We have changed in both profound and superficial ways. Waistlines have gotten thicker. Hairlines have gotten thinner. Some of us have mellowed, while others have gotten more extreme in our views. And knowledge. We have all learned so much. We have had experiences of great joy and great sadness. We have experienced love, friendship, grief, anger, betrayal, pride, and a host of adult emotions that have a depth that we never experienced as children. We have learned from our honest critics and endured the betrayal of our false friends, as Emerson is often quoted as saying.[1] And yet for most of us, despite the sometimes dramatic changes we have gone through, we still see ourselves as the same people, the same selves, the same people we have always been. How could this be? How can one change so much and still retain the same identity?

There are at least two candidate explanations that seem plausible to us as accounts of the continuity of the self. We believe that the first account captures the spirit of what many of the contributors to this volume believe. The self is unified across time because we are motivated and able to create a story, a narrative, that ties different aspects of the self together over time. The self is unified through memory and the process of narrative reconstruction. The *self* according to Daniel Dennett (1992) is a "center of narrative gravity." We create in the words of Dan McAdams (1993) "personal myths." "Ordinary everyday memories," according to Barclay and DeCooke (1988), are "[s]ome of the things of which selves are made."

The relationship between narrative and the self has been emphasized by many of the contributors to this volume and so we will not belabor the substantial evidence for the relationship (e.g. Brewer, 1986; Fivush, 1991, 1994; McAdams, 1993, this volume; Neisser, 1988). Let us just say that it indeed seems compelling that narrative, by providing a story connecting the disparate episodes of our lives, helps to unify our sense of self. A sense of personal continuity is more likely to exist when people must know who they were, who they are, and the developmental trajectory that connects the two. And it is an essential characteristic of narrative that it provides just that connectivity (Habermas & Bluck, 2000). Yet, with all the strengths of the narrative account, there seems to us to be something missing in it. The account is not wrong and yet we believe it is incomplete (see also Neisser, 1994).

While a graduate student, one of us (JML) had the experience of attending a colloquium on autobiographical memory. After the talk, a member of the audience asked the speaker the following question. Imagine there was a patient suffering from a dense retrograde amnesia. Imagine further, that before the accident that had caused this memory loss, the patient had written a detailed and complete autobiography. Imagine this autobiography was more detailed than any autobiography ever before written. Imagine it was the most detailed autobiography that can be conceived of. If the patient committed the autobiography to memory, would they be cured? Would the patient then have autobiographical memories? Would their original sense of identity suddenly be restored? Our intuitions are that the answer to all of these questions is "No." We would say no despite the fact that the patient would now have a detailed narrative account of their life, despite the fact that they would have a full and detailed life story. Because no matter how detailed, no matter how rich the narrative structure, they would never truly own these stories that they've memorized. The stories would be about them and yet, in a way, not about them. These memories would not be experienced with the unique first person experiential perspective that would make them their own.

This thought experiment suggests that while narrative structure may help one experience the self in a continuous fashion (although see Strawson, in press), it does not provide the sufficient conditions needed to do so. The element that seems to be missing from the narrative account is what philosophers call *phenomenology*. The study of phenomenology springs from an understanding that there is such a thing as a first person perspective in addition to the third person perspective typically studied by experimental psychologists. The philosopher Thomas Nagel (1974) asked us to imagine what it would be like to be a bat. Bats, as we all know, have only weak eyesight but can navigate quite well by means of sonar. What would it be like to have sonar? It is, of course, possible to answer that question *functionally*, to answer it from a third person perspective. We can say that having sonar would give us a certain set of abilities that having sight does not give us. And we are confident that psychologists could create a myriad of clever experiments designed to tap into how bats process information with sonar, including details about the nature of the representations that sonar gives rise to and the processes that operate on those representations.

But although those would all be good questions to ask, our intrepid cognitive batologist would not be answering the question Nagel originally posed. For Nagel asked not how it is that bats work, or what makes bats tick. Nagel asked, "What is it like to be a bat?" What would it be like *experientially*? Nagel argued that there is no way for us to conceptualize the answer to that question. There is no way for us to understand, from the first person perspective, what it would be like to be a bat. We can no more understand the *experience* of sonar than a congenitally blind person can understand the experience of redness (Jackson, 1986).

Our emphasis on the self as a unique phenomenological perspective is not meant to discount the importance of narrative structure in understanding the nature of the self. Nor do we mean to set up a straw man by implying that others in this volume believe that phenomenology is irrelevant. Rather we hope to set up a point of emphasis. Narrative is important in establishing the continuity of the self. But it is not uniquely important. Rather, we believe that both narrative structure and subjective experience play a role in allowing us to develop a sense of self that exists continuously across time. Our experiences are our experiences because they all come to us with a unique phenomenological perspective, the perspective of being seen through our eyes and heard through our ears. And no matter how much we change over time, our experiences all have that unique phenomenological perspective that nobody else's experiences have for us. They happened to us, and we know they happened to us, because when things happen to other people we see them from a different vantage point, from a different perspective. When things happen to other people we feel the emotions, the pains and pleasures, the excitement and fear, only vicariously. We can only imagine what the experience looked like through their eyes, we can never fully experience it ourselves. It is, of course, this idea that underlies the source monitoring perspective developed by Marcia Johnson and her colleagues (Johnson, Hashtroudi, & Lindsay, 1993; Johnson & Raye, 1981). We believe this perspective is also central to our sense of personal identity.

DIACHRONIC DISUNITY

Thus far we have been considering the problem of personal identity by assuming that the self shows continuity across time and by trying to provide explanations for that sense of continuity. Indeed, in many ways the prevailing wisdom in cognitive and social psychology appears to be that personal identity is a function of autobiographical memory, that memory is the glue that binds the self together across time (Neimeyer & Rareshide, 1991; Riutort, Cuervo, Danion, Peretti, & Salame, 2003; Ross & Wilson, 2003). We believe that there is a good deal of truth in the prevailing wisdom. We believe that the majority of people, the majority of the time, experience the self as being unified across time and that for many people memory is an important component of self-definition (see for instance Hyman & Faries, 1992). However, we also believe that the prevailing wisdom is open to challenge, that some people, at least some of the time, describe discontinuities in their senses of self. We call this sense of discontinuity of the self across time diachronic disunity.

It is not difficult to find examples of people describing their selves as being discontinuous across time. In fact, such descriptions are commonplace. Conduct an exact phrase search for, "I'm not the same person," on your favorite Internet search engine and it will return thousands of web pages written by people who describe their experience in this manner. People tend to use phrases like this to describe profound personal changes. What do people mean when they say such things? Are they merely being metaphorical? Our own view is that people are indeed being metaphorical, but not *merely* so. We believe, as Lakoff and Johnson (1980, 1999) have argued so persuasively, that the conceptual metaphors people use when they construe reality are powerful. They shape cognition and in particular the metaphors people use to describe the self have profound implications for how they think about and remember the past.

So what do people mean exactly when they say things like, "I'm not the same person anymore"? They seem to mean something like when they look back on their lives in retrospect, the person they were back then just doesn't *feel* like them anymore. They feel like they don't even recognize who that person was. They can't imagine doing the things that person did or feeling the things that person felt. Now, of course it's the case that even people who feel this way about their lives recognize that they are *in some sense* the same person they were in the past. Nobody is arguing with that. Physically they are the same person. A picture of them from five years ago is still a picture of *them*. There is a causal connection between the things that happened to them in the past and their current self, even if they can't fully articulate those connections. Of course, all of those things are true. But in another important sense they feel as if they are not the same person anymore because when they look back on that old self, it doesn't *feel* like them. That is what we mean by the diachronic disunity experience. There is a *subjective* loss of diachronic unity.

Galen Strawson (1999; in press) provides a provocative discussion of the experience of disunity across time. Strawson was primarily interested in what it means to have a sense of self, and he argued that to answer this question one needed to understand what the minimal conditions are for a being to have a sense of self. If we were to attribute a self to any creature — to a bird or a bat or an orangutan — what would that creature minimally need to possess? Strawson considered a number of candidate possibilities. He pointed out that the self is often conceived of as a *mental thing* that is a subject of *experience* and *action*, that has a certain *character* or *personality* and that is unified both at the present time (*synchronically*) and across time (*diachronically*). Strawson asked, which of these conditions are really necessary for the self to be a coherent concept?

Many would argue that diachronic unity is a core feature of what we mean by saying that a being has a self. Consider what John Locke wrote in *An Essay Concerning Human Understanding*:

> This being premised, to find wherein personal identity exists, we must consider what "person" stands for; which, I think, is a thinking intelligent being that has reason and reflection and can consider itself as itself, the same thinking thing, in different times and places; which it does only by that consciousness which is inseparable from thinking, and it seems to me essential to it . . . and as far as this consciousness can be extended backwards to any past action or thought, so far reaches the identity of that person; it is the same self now it was then. . . . (Locke 1690/1994, pp. 246–247)

Strawson, however, argued that diachronic unity is not a necessary condition for having a self. In fact, he argued that a lack of diachronic unity is not merely a metaphysical possibility, but a perfectly common and healthy human experience.[2]

> One can be fully aware of that fact that one has long-term continuity as *a living human being* without *ipso facto* having any significant sense of the *mental self* or *subject of experience* as something that has long term continuity. (Strawson, 1999, p. 14, emphasis in the original)

Strawson (in press) has recently characterized diachronic unity in a manner akin to what psychologists would call an individual difference variable. Some people experience the self diachronically, some people don't. Moreover, for Strawson the distinction is not all or none. Individuals may experience some aspects of their lives diachronically and may fail to experience diachronic unity for other aspects of their lives. In the present chapter we too treat diachronic unity and disunity as a graded, rather than all or none, construct. However, it is not yet clear to us whether this perspective represents a transient or enduring disposition.

If some people do indeed experience diachronic disunity, an important question to ask is why this occurs. In the present work we propose the diachronic disunity occurs when people adopt a *discontinuity metaphor* of the self. The *discontinuity metaphor* of the self involves conceptualizing large-scale changes in terms of two separate persons acting at two separate times. As we will discuss in more detail in our concluding comments, we also believe that diachronic unity involves one of a number of metaphors (e.g., change = growth), and we refer to these as *continuity metaphors*. On our account, the particular metaphor adopted will be a function of how well the metaphor coheres with one's motives, experiences, and beliefs. In the next section we consider four variables that may influence the adoption of the continuity versus discontinuity metaphors.

VARIABLES THAT MAY INFLUENCE THE USE OF THE DISCONTINUITY METAPHOR

First, it seems possible that some people may adopt the discontinuity metaphor as a coping mechanism. The past is not always something that is pleasant to face. And for some people it is less pleasant than others. People hurt us sometimes, and it is not fun to acknowledge that. Sometimes we do things that we're not especially proud of. We may experience failures of significant dimensions. The past may be too painful, or embarrassing, or inconsistent with one's current view of the self to accept. People may sometimes deal with these inconsistencies and painful memories by making them somebody else's problem, even if that somebody else is merely a past version of themselves. It is important to note that in saying this we are not claiming that there is anything inherently pathological about diachronic disunity. But to take some liberties with Joyce (1934), for some people, *personal* history may be a nightmare from which they are trying to escape.

Second, people may adopt a discontinuity metaphor when they cannot create a narrative in which their past and present selves cohere. Establishing a coherent life story appears to minimally require developing a representation of the past self, a representation of the present self, and establishing causal connectivity between those representations (Habermas & Bluck, 2000). Some people may simply not be interested in drawing those connections. Others may desire to draw connections between their present and past, but be unable to do so. We may not always know why we did certain things in the past. Our own past motivations and beliefs may be difficult for us to reconstruct years or even decades later. The trajectory our lives take may not always be transparent, even to ourselves. Whatever the reason, a lack of causal connectivity between life events may leave one feeling disconnected with the past.

Third, the discontinuity metaphor may be inconsistent with the essentialist beliefs many hold about the self. Considerable evidence suggests that people are essentialists with regard to their understanding of many concepts (Medin & Ortony, 1989). That is, despite the theoretical arguments and empirical evidence that concepts rarely have defining features (Smith & Medin, 1981; Wittgenstein, 1963), many people persist in believing that concepts have some core or essence that defines them. Most people are probably essentialists with regard to their understanding of the self. Essentialist beliefs about the self would allow individuals to ignore discrepancies with their past self by appealing to some ineffable core that constitutes the *real* self. Moreover, the very concept of an *unalterable* core appears inconsistent with the discontinuity metaphor of self. People who report diachronic disunity may believe that essences are rubbish, or alternatively, may believe that certain transformational experiences may result in radical changes in those core essences.

Fourth, it is possible that the discontinuity metaphor is adopted when people's memories are qualitatively impoverished. Tulving (2002) has recently written that "mental time travel requires a mental time traveler." To the extent that one can mentally relive a past event in exquisite detail it may be difficult to disregard the strong inference that it must have been the same protagonist then as now. Marcia Johnson's (Johnson et al., 1993) source-monitoring perspective suggests that we identify memories as having been experienced by us, by making inferences based partly on the qualitative experience of those memories. To the extent that memories are experienced in a qualitatively impoverished form, it may seem to us as if the memories are not really ours. We believe that all of these factors play a role in the adopting of the discontinuity metaphor and in the development of diachronic disunity. Indeed, it seems likely to us that not everyone experiences diachronic disunity in the same way or for the same reasons.

In the section that follows we describe our initial work investigating diachronic disunity. The work is in its early stages and considerable work still needs to be done in terms of measurement, theory, and empirical findings. Indeed, much of this chapter is purposefully speculative in nature. We are far from having all the answers. However, as an initial pass we begin by examining how commonly people claim to experience diachronic disunity, and some of the factors that appear to be related to diachronic disunity. We then conclude by discussing empirical evidence we've collected on naive theories of the persistence conditions for the self.

EMPIRICAL STUDIES OF DIACHRONIC UNITY AND DISUNITY

Because our goal was to empirically investigate how people describe their continuity across time, we first needed to develop a measurement instrument. On the scale we ended up developing we asked people if they felt as though they were the same person today that they were at some point in the past. Because we did not want them to interpret that question as merely being a surrogate for the question, "Have you changed?" we also asked them how much they believed they have changed since that point in time. In particular, we emphasized that these were not the same question, that one person might feel like they have changed a great deal but are still basically the same person, whereas another person might feel like they have changed a great deal and are no longer the same person.

Figure 11.1 shows the scale that we developed. Participants were asked to think back to some point in the past and compare that person to the person they were today. For example, in most of our research people were asked to compare who they were that day to who they were 5 years ago. To ascertain the extent to which people felt they had changed over the past 5 years, they provided ratings on an 8-point Likert-type scale. On this scale, "haven't changed at all" was represented as −4 and "have changed a great deal" was represented as +4. To provide a measure of the continuity of the self over the past five years, the extent to which a person was or was not the same person was measured on the Y-axis. On this scale, −4 represented "I'm not the same person" and +4 represented "I'm the same person." Participants completed the form by placing a single mark on the graph (see Figure 11.1) to represent their responses to both questions. Participants found this scale simple and intuitive to use.

Directions: Some people have the sense that they have changed a lot over the last 5 years and other people feel that they have not changed much at all. That dimension, have you changed or haven't you changed is represented on the horizontal axis below.

Some people think of themselves as being a different person than they were 5 years ago. That dimension do you think of yourself as the same person you were 5 years ago, is represented on the vertical axis below.

Keep in mind that these are slightly different questions. For instance, you can believe you have changed a lot but still see yourself as basically the same person. Or you could think of yourself as actually being a different person than you were 5 years ago.

Below is a graph showing those two dimensions. Place an X in the location on the graph that best indicates both how much you believe you have changed in the past 5 years and the extent to which you see yourself as the same or a different person than you were 5 years ago.

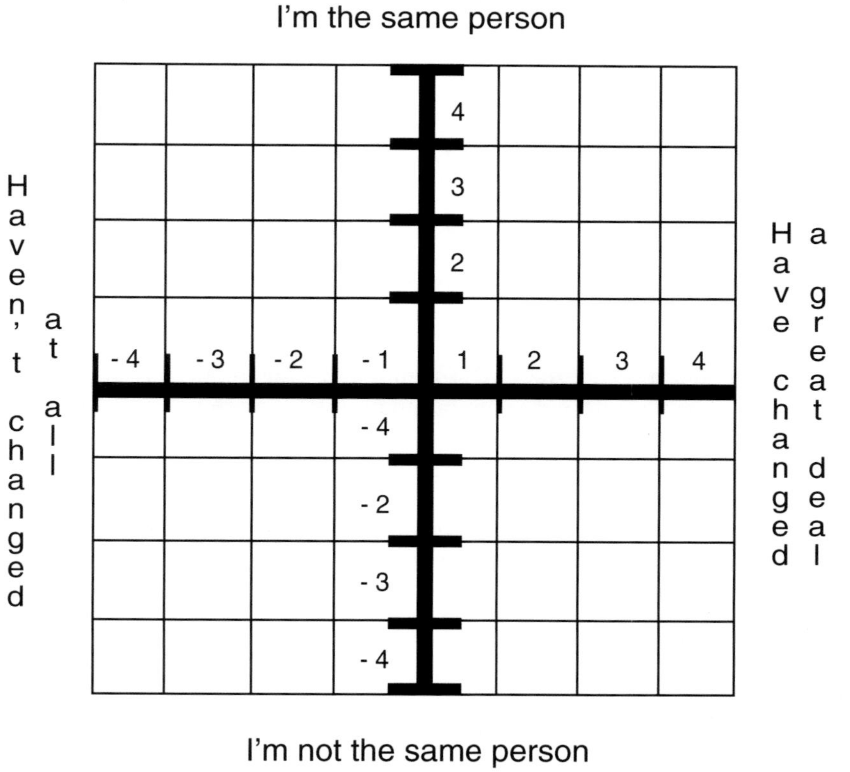

FIGURE 11.1. Diachronicity scale measuring degree of change and degree to which participant is the same person they were N years ago.

We use the term *diachronicity* to refer to the extent to which participants indicate that they are they same person now that they were in the past. For instance, a participant who indicates that they absolutely are the same person would be said to score high on diachronicity. A participant who said that they absolutely were not the same person would be said to score low on diachronicity. Note that consistent with the view that diachronic unity is not an all or none phenomenon, participants in our studies responded in a graded manner, indicating the degree to which they believed they were still the same person.

The Role of Temporal Distance

One straightforward prediction concerning diachronic disunity is that it should be more common the further back in time one goes. If I think back on the person I was 10 years ago I'm likely to feel less connected with that past self than if I think back on the person I was 1 year ago. As a general rule there should be a negative correlation between diachronicity and the temporal distance between the current self and the past self.

To address this issue we examined the relationship between participants' responses on our scale when they were cued to think back varying numbers of years into the past. The data we report here are based on responses of 224 participants who participated in one of three different studies (the details of two of those studies are reported later in the chapter). All participants came from a single participant pool and were tested in the same semester and in the same manner. In one study, participants were cued to think back 2, 4, 6, or 8 years into the past. In a second study participants were cued to think back 4 years into the past. And in the third study participants were cued to think back 5 years into the past.

In the analysis we treated diachronicity as the dependent variable and treated self-reported change, the number of years subjects were cued with, and gender as predictor variables. Table 11.1 shows the results of the regression. No significant effects of gender were observed. The Y-intercept of the regression was significantly above zero indicating that diachronic unity was more common than diachronic disunity. There was also a significant negative relationship between self-reported change and self-reported diachronicity. Participants who reported a great deal of change were more likely to say that they were not the same person any more. Consistent with our predictions, there was also a significant negative relationship between feelings of diachronicity and the number of years participants were cued to think back. The further back in time participants were asked to think about, the less likely they were to report a diachronically unified sense of self. These findings provide us with some initial evidence that diachronic disunity is a coherent construct. Responses on the diachronicity scale were predicted by temporal closeness, as they reasonably should be. Moreover, diachronicity does not seem to be merely equivalent to degree of change, as the cuing effect was statistically reliable even with self-reported degree of change regressed out.

To further understand the nature of diachronic unity and disunity, we conducted a small pilot study in which additional participants completed our measure.

TABLE 11.1. Results of Regression Analysis
from Temporal Cuing Experiment

Predictor variable	B	F	p
Intercept	3.47	30.56	<0.001
Temporal cue	–0.310	6.73	<0.01
Change score	–0.218	5.15	<0.05
Gender	0.11	0.26	n.s.

Note: Overall model significant at $F(3, 221) = 4.74$, $p < 0.01$.

All participants were primed to think back 5 years when rating how much they had changed and the extent to which they were the same or a different person. After completing the questionnaire, they provided explanations for their responses. Below are two examples of people who reported changing a great deal but who stressed that they still felt as though they were fundamentally the same person.

Diachronic Unity Example 1: I believe that I am the same person but have changed a great deal. I have had so many new experiences which have changed me, such as boyfriends and high school. However, I am still the same person. I still have the same religious beliefs. My experiences changed me, but I am still virtually the same on the inside.

Diachronic Unity Example 2: In the past five years I have done a lot of growing up while my life has changed in some drastic ways. My family moved to another town where my mom took on a new business. She put all of her time and money into it and my brothers and I were kind of on our own. This experience has taught me a lot and definitely changed me, but the core person is still the same. Also, I have changed naturally with age.

Both of these individuals highlighted changes that had occurred in their lives, but both still felt that they were the same person. Notice that in both examples, the individuals listed aspects of their lives that had changed, while at the same time they identified aspects of their lives that had remained the same. The first respondent says that she is the "same on the inside" and the second alludes to a "core" that remains constant. Although speculative, these descriptions are consistent with the notion that the two participants may be essentialists with regard to the self.

As expected, people who reported feelings of disunity on our measure provided rich explanations for why it was that they felt like they had become a different person.

Diachronic Disunity Example 1: I feel that I am not the same person I was five years ago, because I have changed spiritually. I am now a Christian, and I look at life completely differently from the way I did five years ago before I was saved. Because of my faith in Christ I no longer worry like I used to. I do not get stressed out as much.I do not get offended like I used to either.

> *Diachronic Disunity Example 2:* I am totally not the same person. Five years ago I was in the closet and very conservative. I was very unhappy and was in and out of hospitals for depression and suicide. Now that I have come out and told people I was gay, I am very happy. I do not worry about what people think about me anymore. I even have a boyfriend!

Both of these examples stress that some fundamental aspect of these individuals' senses of self had changed, and as a result they no longer felt as though they were the same person on that day that they were 5 years earlier. The two individuals who reported diachronic disunity report starkly different experiences of the self than the two individuals who reported diachronic unity. Indeed, all four individuals reported having changed a great deal, but the diachronically unified individuals emphatically stated that they were the same person.

Diachronicity and Individual Difference Measures

Given these initial results, we felt it important to provide a profile of what differences might exist between those individuals who report a diachronically unified sense of self and those who describe a diachronically disunified sense of self.

Diachronicity and Dissociation

In the present section we report research examining the relationship between diachronicity and dissociation, need for cognitive closure, and need for cognition. One obvious variable that might be related to diachronic disunity is dissociation. Dissociation by definition involves a split in the person that can impact self, memory, and identity (Halligan, Tanja, Clark, & Ehlers, 2003; Steinberg, 1995). It seems reasonable then that diachronic disunity and dissociation may be related.

To examine this possibility, 80 participants completed the Dissociative Experience Scale (DES; Carlson & Putnam, 1993) as well as our scale. We then performed a regression analysis in which we used standardized diachronicity scores, standardized change scores, and the interaction term as predictors of DES scores. Table 11.2 provides the results of this analysis. As we predicted, participants who reported experiencing diachronic disunity had significantly higher scores on the DES, indicating that diachronic disunity may be related to the person's overall tendency to dissociate. However, there was also a significant interaction, indicating that the effect was reduced in individuals who reported changing a great deal.

Recently Waller and colleagues (Waller, Putnam & Carlson, 1996; Waller & Ross, 1997) have argued that one can distinguish between pathological and nonpathological forms of dissociation using the DES. On Waller's account, the difference between the pathological and nonpathological variants of dissociation are taxonomic rather than merely quantitative. He and his colleagues have developed statistical techniques that involve using responses to particular DES questions in order to provide an estimate of the Bayesian probability that the test taker falls into the pathological group. Using their methods we derived the probability that each of our participants was pathologically dissociative. As can be seen in Figure 11.2, the

TABLE 11.2. Results of Regression Analyses of Relationship between Diachronicity and Individual Difference Variables

Predictor variable	B	F	p value
DES			
Intercept	16.43	190.94	< 0.001
Diachronicity	−4.12	11.99	< 0.001
Change	−1.56	1.80	n.s.
Diachronicity X Change	2.41	5.38	< 0.05
Decisiveness subscale (NFC)			
Intercept	24.77	1208.61	< 0.001
Diachronicity	1.62	5.09	< 0.05
Change	0.35	0.24	n.s.
Diachronicity X Change	−1.68	7.07	< 0.01
Discomfort with Ambiguity subscale (NFC)			
Intercept	37.65	3116.32	< 0.001
Diachronicity	−1.56	5.28	< 0.05
Change	−1.08	2.49	n.s.
Diachronicity X Change	1.07	3.21	< 0.08

Note: For DES overall model significant at $F(3,77) = 6.01$, $p < 0.01$; for Decisiveness overall model significant at $F(3,78) = 4.12$, $p < 0.01$; for Discomfort with Ambiguity overall model significant at $F(3,78) = 3.26$, $p < 0.05$. n.s. = not significant.

vast majority of participants in both groups appeared to be nonpathological (i.e. there is a low probability that they fall into the pathological taxon). It appears however, that the percentage of diachronically disunified individuals in the tail of the distribution is somewhat greater than the percentage of diachronically unified individuals. Although we would need a larger sample to say this definitively, it may be that few diachronically disunified individuals are pathologically dissociative (i.e. P(Pathological Dissociation|DD) is low), but that most pathologically dissociative individuals are diachronically disunified (i.e. P(DD|Pathological Dissociation) is high).

Need for Cognition and Need for Closure

Earlier we discussed the possibility that diachronic disunity may be a function of lack of causal connectivity between the current self and the past self. We speculated that this lack of connectivity could occur for two reasons. First, it seems possible that some people are simply uninterested in why events in their past happened to them and so simply lack the motivation needed to establish causal connectivity between temporally disparate events in their lives. The Need for Cognition Scale (Cacioppo & Petty, 1982) measures the degree to which people like engaging in cognitive effort and as such might provide an indication of whether this hypothesis is correct.

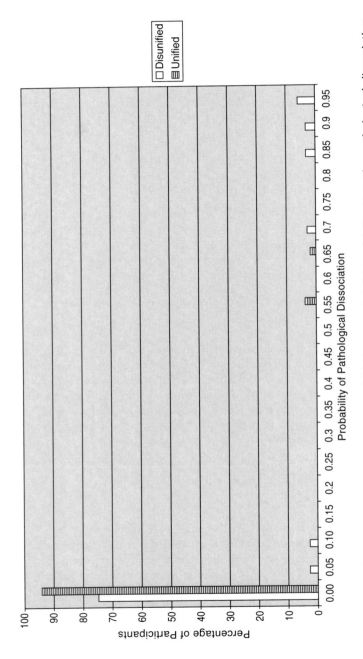

FIGURE 11.2. Percentage of participants with different probabilities of falling into the pathological dissociation taxon.

The second possibility we discussed in the introduction is that diachronic disunity may come about from a failure to achieve causal connectivity in one's life story, despite one's best efforts. Causal connectivity may be especially difficult for people to develop if they are bothered by the minor inconsistencies that exist in all people's lives. Imagine a person who is an honest, upright pillar of the community but as a teenager engaged in petty larceny with some frequency. This inconsistency between the current self and the past self may nag at someone who hasn't learned to reconcile the inherent contradictions that occur in a person's life. To examine this possibility participants were given the Need for Closure Scale (Webster & Kruglanski, 1994). Need for Closure refers to the degree to which people "seize and freeze" when making attributions (Kruglanski & Webster, 1996). The seizing component of need for closure refers to a desire to make attributions quickly, rather than remaining open minded. The freezing component of need for closure refers to a tendency to stick with an attribution once it is made rather than revisiting it (even in the face of disconfirming evidence). Significantly, people high in need for closure also show considerable discomfort with ambiguity. A person who is uncomfortable with ambiguity may be particularly ill at ease with aspects of their past self that are inconsistent with their current self and may respond to that discomfort by disowning their previous self.

To examine all of these issues, 81 participants completed the Need for Cognition scale and the Need for Closure Scale. The participants for this study were the same subjects we described above who had completed the DES and all of the scales were completed as part of a single session. We performed a series of regression analyses in which we used standardized diachronicity scores, standardized change scores, and the interaction term as predictors. The results of these analyses are shown in Table 11.2. Need for Cognition was not significantly related to diachronicity. This finding is inconsistent with the hypothesis that diachronically disunified individuals dislike cognitive effort. In Strawson's (in press) recent writings he makes a strong argument that people who experience diachronic disunity (he would call such people "episodics") have a full, rich mental life. The findings from the Need for Cognition scale seem consistent with that claim.

Overall results from the Need for Closure scale also failed to predict diachronic disunity. Inspection of the subscales suggested that this lack of an overall effect occurred because one subscale was associated with diachronic unity and another subscale was associated with diachronic disunity. On the one hand, participants who were high in diachronicity tended to score high on the decisiveness subscale. On the other hand, participants who reported experiencing diachronic disunity tended to have higher scores on the discomfort with ambiguity subscale. In both cases there were interactions between diachronicity and change, although this interaction was not statistically reliable for the discomfort with ambiguity analysis. The Need for Closure scale also has three additional subscales (i.e., closed-mindedness, preference for order, preference for predictability). None of these other subscales was significantly related to diachronicity.

Collectively these results highlight that the feeling of being a different self is more than simply feeling as though one has changed a considerable amount.

TABLE 11.3. Significant Correlations between MCQ Items and Diachronicity Scale

Positive memories from 6 years ago	Negative memories from 6 years ago
Participant/observer in event (r = 0.337, p = 0.022)	Participant/observer in event (r = 0.303, p = 0.041)
Trust accuracy of memory (r = 0.300, p = 0.043)	Trust accuracy of memory (r = 0.478, p = 0.001)
Verbal rehearsal (r = 0.362, p = 0.013)	Verbal rehearsal (r = 0.321, p =.029)
Mental rehearsal (r = 0.346, p = 0.018)	Amount of visual detail in memory (r = 0.336, p = 0.023)
Self-defining (r = 0.452, p = 0.002)	Presence of color in memory (r = 0.331, p = 0.025)
Positive affect (r = 0.478, p = 0.001)	Memory for event order (r = 0.302, p = 0.042)
	Implications at the time (r = 0.329 p = 0.041)

Note: There were no significant correlations between MCQ items and the diachronicity scale for participants' recent memories.

People who feel as though they are different selves tend to dislike ambiguity, are less decisive, and more prone to dissociation. These effects occur even with self-reported change scores statistically controlled for.

Memory Quality and the Past Self

As we argued above, one way diachronically unified and disunified individuals might differ is in terms of the qualities of their memories. To examine this possibility, we collected event memories from a group of 46 individuals who had previously been asked how much they changed in the past 4 years and whether they were the same person they were 4 years ago. Each participant provided four memories in a counterbalanced order. Two of the memories were from 6 years ago and two memories were from 1 year ago. In each case one of the memories was a positive memory and the other was a negative memory. Each memory was then rated using the Memory Characteristics Questionnaire (MCQ; Johnson, Foley, Suengas, & Raye, 1988). The version of the MCQ we used contained 38 questions concerning the vividness of the memory, its sensory qualities, the perspective from which it was originally experienced, how often one has spoken about this memory with others, as well as other aspects of the memory.

In Table 11.3 we report all of the significant correlations between diachronicity and the MCQ items. For the recent memories there were no significant correlations. Thus, it is not the case that people who experience diachronic disunity have globally impoverished memories. Instead our predictions were that diachronically disunified individuals would experience selective impairments to those portions of their past that had splintered off from their present sense of self. First consider the positive memories from 6 years ago. Participants who reported that they were the same person they were 4 years ago tended to report memories that were happier than those who claimed that they were a different person than they were 4 years ago. Unified individuals reported being active participants more than disunified individuals in the positive memories they chose to report. Diachronically unified individuals were more likely to see their memories as being self-defining. They were also more likely to report that they trusted the accuracy of their memories. And finally, unified individuals reported more rehearsal of these memories than disunified individuals. Next consider the negative memories from 6 years ago. Diachronically unified individuals reported memories that were more likely to include color and other visual details. They were more likely to report memories where the order of events was coherent. They were more likely to report memories in which they were participants. Diachronically unified individuals were more likely to report memories that at the time seemed to have serious implications. And as with their positive memories they were more likely to trust the accuracy of their memories and to have rehearsed them often.

These findings suggest that people who experience the self as being diachronically unified remember their past differently than those who experience the self in a disunified manner. There are two possible interpretations of these findings. First, it is possible that people infer the extent to which their past self is related to their current self by examining the qualities of their memories. Alternatively it is possible that the experience of diachronic disunity may result in impoverished memories. We take up these issues further in our concluding comments.

FOLK PSYCHOLOGICAL THEORIES OF PERSISTENCE

In this section we do not discuss research on diachronic disunity per se, but rather on participants' naive views of what conditions are relevant to the persistence of the self across time. In this experiment 177 participants were presented with scenarios in which they were asked to imagine certain transformations (e.g., imagine you woke and found you were the opposite gender) and were asked to indicate on a 6-point scale whether they would still be the same person if it happened to them. Low numbers on the scale indicated that the subject was absolutely certain that they would no longer be the same person and high numbers on the scale indicated that they were absolutely certain that they would be the same person.

The questionnaire we developed contained a total of 50 items. Our main interest in the present experiment was to test the claim that autobiographical memories play an important role as persistence conditions in people's naive theories of persistence. We examined that question in two ways. First, we developed four pairs of items in which the scenarios making up each pair were identical except for whether or not the person in the scenario retained their autobiographical memories. These item pairs are presented at the top of Table 11.4. In addition to these questions, we also included a single additional question to determine whether our participants believed that autobiographical memories are the sine qua non of personal identity, or whether they believed that other psychological processes are as important or more important in establishing personal continuity across time. This scenario can be seen in the bottom right corner of Table 11.4. In addition to the nine unique scenarios shown in Table 11.4, we also created an

TABLE 11.4. Persistence Condition Questions Relating to Memory Processes

Memory Present	Memory Absent
Is Memory a Persistence Condition?	
Imagine you entered a machine that caused the physical processes of your body to run in reverse such that when you left the machine you were only 3 years old. Despite being 3 years old, the person leaving the machine still retains all of your adult memories. Would the person leaving the machine be you? ($M = 4.33$, $s = 1.58$)	Imagine you entered a machine that caused the physical processes of your body to run in reverse such that when you left the machine you were only 3 years old. The person leaving the machine no longer retains any of your adult memories. Would the person leaving the machine be you? ($M = 3.16$, $s = 1.67$)
Imagine your soul were placed into the body of another person. Assume also that the person retains all of your memories. Would that person be you? ($M = 3.68$, $s = 1.53$)	Imagine your soul were placed into the body of another person. Assume that you have lost all your memories. Would that person be you? ($M = 2.23$, $s = 1.27$)
Imagine your soul were placed into the body of a horse. Assume also that the horse retains all of your memories. Would the horse be you? ($M = 2.95$, $s = 1.59$)	Imagine your soul were placed into the body of a horse. Assume that you have lost all your memories. Would the horse be you? ($M = 1.91$, $s = 1.22$)
Imagine you woke up tomorrow and your personality was the opposite of what it is now. You still have all your memories but your likes and dislikes have changed drastically including hating all the people you used to like and liking all the people you used to hate. Would you still be you? ($M = 2.66$, $s = 1.40$)	Imagine you woke up tomorrow and your personality was the opposite of what it is now. You have no memory at all for your previous life and your likes and dislikes have changed drastically including hating all the people you used to like and liking all the people you used to hate. Would you still be you? ($M = 1.80$, $s = 1.21$)
Is Memory or Personality More Important?	
Imagine you woke up tomorrow and your personality was the opposite of what it is now. You still have all your memories but your likes and dislikes have changed drastically including hating all the people you used to like and liking all the people you used to hate. Would you still be you? ($M = 2.66$, $s = 1.40$)	Imagine you woke up tomorrow and couldn't remember any specific events from your life, but you still had the same personality, you still had the same likes and dislikes, and still felt the same feelings for people close to you. Would you still be you? ($M = 4.21$, $s = 1.42$)

Note: Subjects responded on a 6-point scale where 6 indicated absolutely certain yes and 1 indicated absolutely certain no.

additional 41 scenarios that included various kinds of transformations. These included financial gains and losses, personal tragedies, religious conversions, changes in physical appearance, mad scientists putting brains into vats, cutting off and reattaching limbs, and so on. These questions were included to disguise the purpose of the experiment (although the responses to many of these scenarios were interesting in their own right). All 50 items were presented to participants in a random order.

Our analyses of this data set revealed three interesting results. First, our participants indicated that they believed some of the pairs of scenarios represented more significant challenges to the persistence of their physical identity than others, $F(3, 528) = 82.02$, $MSE = 1.98$. From top to bottom, the possible changes to the physical body presented in Table 11.2 are rank ordered from the least to the most threatening to the persistence of the self. Consistent with somaticist theories of persistence, bodily continuity seems quite important to our participants.

The second major finding in these results was that participants treated retention of autobiographical memories as a persistence condition. When people were asked to imagine losing their memories in addition to the above changes, they were even more likely to deny that they would be the same person, $F(1, 176) = 212.433$, $MSE = 2.12$. However memory was not a uniquely important factor. When we directly compared changes in personality with loss of memory (see bottom of Table 11.4), changes in personality appeared to produce a considerably stronger effect, $t(176) = 12.10$.

These results present important food for thought for us as psychologists. A good deal of theoretical work in psychology has suggested that autobiographical memory is central to self-definition. But when asked about their naive theories of persistence, our participants did not report this. Consider the scenario in which participants were asked to imagine losing all of their autobiographical memories, but retaining their personalities. The average rating provided in response to that scenario was 4.21, two tenths of a scale point above "Somewhat certain I would be the same person." On average, then, people believed that if they lost their memories but retained their personality, they would still be the same person. Of course, lay conceptions of the world and scientific accounts of the world do not always coalesce. However it is interesting to note that our participants see the self as being multifaceted, dependent upon both their physical continuity, and the continuity of a variety of psychological variables.

CONCLUDING COMMENTS

Identity is an odd word for identity. After all, it does not consist in our being *identical* from one period of time to another. Rather it involves a sense of continuity, a sense that despite change, the self persists. It is a sense that the person now is *numerically identical* with the person in the past (i.e., one person at two times), despite being *qualitatively* different from that person (Olson, 2002). Identity is an attitude taken toward a constant state of flux. But it is not the only attitude people take. Some people report feeling as if they are not the same person now that they were in the past. They report feeling disconnected from who they used to be. Are they mistaken when they report this feeling? Is it *really* the case, no matter what people think or say, that their self persists over time? The answer to this question turns on the metaphysical conclusions one draws about the nature of the self. What sort of a thing is a self anyway? Is it a physical thing localized in the brain somewhere (John, 2002; Llinas & Pare, 1991)? Is it a protagonist in a story we create to explain our lives (McAdams, 1993; this volume)? Is it, as Dennett (1992) has suggested, an "abstractum" that we create? These are questions for the philosophers to settle, not for us.

Our data suggest that the majority of people, the majority of time, report experiencing the self diachronically. When they describe how they have changed over time they say things like, "I have grown" or "I have evolved" or "I have changed but there is a core self that remains the same." These are not literal statements. They are metaphors of continuity. Other people describe their past by claiming a more radical break. They indicate on our questionnaires that they do not consider themselves to be the same person they used to be. Moreover, it is a simple matter to find examples where people spontaneously describe the self in this manner: "I'm not the same person anymore" or "It's like I'm a new man" or "I have been reborn." These too are metaphors, metaphors of discontinuity. The question for us is not so much whether the self *really* persists (we think it does) but whether the conceptual metaphors people use to describe the self have force. We believe that they do.[3]

Possible Causes of Diachronic Disunity

If people do differ in the conceptual metaphors they use to describe the self, what factors underlie the metaphor that is chosen? We have considered four possibilities. It is possible that people may sometimes feel motivated to push their pasts away in an attempt to forget about things that have happened to them, and by doing this they can become a 'new' person with a 'new' beginning. Although we do not currently have any direct evidence of a relationship between psychological trauma and diachronic disunity, it is worth noting that diachronic disunity and dissociation appear to be related and it has been argued that dissociation and trauma are related (e.g., Halligan et al., 2003; Steinberg, 1995). This, of course, does not demonstrate a relationship between low diachronicity and trauma, but it suggests a reasonable topic for investigation.

We also speculated that diachronic disunity might reflect the absence of narrative reconstruction. Narrative's primary role appears to be in providing meaningful interpretations of life events and in establishing causal connectivity between disconnected episodes (Basting, 2003; Brown, 2001; Shenk, Boyd, Peacock, & Moore, 2002). We argued that a lack of causal connectivity would be especially troubling for individuals who are bothered by ambiguity. Such individuals might feel troubled by inconsistencies in their lives. Absent a narrative that explains these inconsistencies, they may resolve the ambiguity by adopting a discontinuity metaphor to describe their experiences. Consistent with this interpretation, we found that diachronic disunity was more common among participants scoring high on the discomfort with ambiguity subscale of the NFC.

A third cause of diachronic disunity could be differences in people's naive theories of the self. Evidence suggests that many people are essentialists (Medin & Ortony, 1989). Applied to the self, this means believing that there is some unalterable core that defines us, regardless of the changes we go through. It could be that diachronically disunified individuals are not as likely to be essentialists and therefore do not believe that there is a central aspect to their being that maintains their identity. Without the belief in this core, these individuals may be more likely to feel that they have become an entirely different person as they have matured and changed throughout life. Although merely anecdotal, the two examples of diachronically unified individuals we presented earlier seemed to reflect essentialist thinking. If the essentialist account were correct it would suggest that diachronically unified individuals' sense of personal continuity should be robust across a greater range of possible transformations. We are examining this possibility in current research.

It is also possible that individuals experience diachronic disunity when their distant memories are chronically impoverished. In light of Johnson's source monitoring perspective (Johnson et al., 1993), we argued that individuals with diachronic disunity might have qualitatively different memories for events from the time period that they were split off from. The results of our experiment indicated the distant memories of diachronically disunified individuals differed along a number of dimensions from those of diachronically unified individuals. Those differences did not occur for more recent memories. Because this work was correlational in nature, it is unclear whether the feeling of disunity is caused by or causes impoverished memories of distant events. And we ourselves are torn between the two interpretations. On the one hand, if impoverished memory played a causal role in establishing diachronic disunity, it would provide an explanation of the phenomenon in terms of basic cognitive mechanisms. However, if diachronic disunity results in impoverished memories it would be consistent with a kind of memory reconstruction that is dependent on self-concept. Both accounts are appealing and we, as of yet, have no way of distinguishing between them.

Is Diachronic Disunity Pathological?

In this section we say a few words about whether diachronic disunity represents a pathological perspective on the past, or whether it is merely a different perspective on the past. It is important to note, first of all, that we do not yet have the final answer to that question. We have not, for instance, systematically looked for the prevalence of psychopathology among individuals who vary in their diachronicity. The measures we have looked at have been theoretically driven, but have not been numerous. Our own educated guess is that diachronic disunity may be a perfectly healthy response for some people under some circumstances and may be dysfunctional for other people under other circumstances.

These conclusions grow primarily out of the relationship we observed between diachronic disunity and dissociation. Our results showed that diachronically disunified individuals are more prone to dissociation, on average. Moreover, approximately 15% of the participants who described themselves as diachronically disunified had at least a 70% chance of falling into the pathologically dissociative taxon. None of the participants who described themselves as being diachronically unifed had that high of a probability. It is important to note, however, that the vast majority of people in both groups (diachronically unified and disunified) appeared to be clearly nonpathological with regard to dissociation (i.e., the individuals each had less than a 5% chance of falling into the pathological taxon).

Strawson has argued that diachronic disunity can, in some ways, be perfectly healthy. "If you had a girlfriend pinched off [at] you in the past, you might feel that that is something that still directly relates to you now, that you are still smarting from it. That's if you're diachronic. But if you are episodic, you just don't have that strong feeling. . . . I find I can't really do resentment. I just sort of forget about it. If I see the person again, I will feel not well-disposed toward them, but I feel relatively free of resentment" (quoted in Barss, 2001, p. A15). Consistent with this view, Beike, Kleinknecht, and Wirth-Beaumont (this volume) discuss the psychological benefits of obtaining closure on events and the psychological costs of keeping events open. For people who have gone through dramatic life changes, diachronic disunity may provide one avenue for achieving event closure.

Following McAdams (this volume; McAdams & Bowman, 2001; McAdams, Reynolds, Lewis, Patten, & Bowman, 2001) we speculate that diachronic disunity may occur in both redemptive and nonredemptive forms. Redemptive disunity can be seen in people who have had transformational experiences in which they change for the better and as a consequence no longer feel like they are the same person anymore. Consider, for instance, a drug addict who kicks their addiction and turns their life around. Years later they may feel that the drug addict they were has very little to do with who they are in the here and now. Or consider a person who has undergone a transformational religious experience. Their very conception of the nature of the universe is changed dramatically in a very short period of time. Think about a person struggling under the weight of clinical depression who has that burden lifted by psychotherapy and antidepressant medications. Are they not in some sense a new and different person afterwards? In *Listening to Prozac*, Kramer (1993) reports a patient who had been off Prozac for 8 months calling and complaining "I am not myself" (p. 18). The self from her depressed period was returning, and she perhaps wanted a dose of diachronic disunity.

The Centrality of Autobiographical Memory

Research on the topic of autobiographical memory has contributed a great deal to both cognitive and social psychology (Reese, 2002; Singer & Bluck, 2001; Thompson, 1998). But perhaps more important than any other contribution has been the realization that memory is not just for memorizing. Rather memory plays a number of other central and important roles in our lives (Baddeley, 1988; Hyman & Faries, 1992; Neisser, 1978; Pillemer, 1992; Robinson & Swanson, 1990). Research in the area of case-based reasoning has demonstrated the important role of autobiographical memory in problem solving (Schank, 1990). If my car breaks down, I am likely to think of other experiences I have had with broken cars and how I solved those problems. Autobiographical memory is used in regulating our moods (Pillemer, 1992). We can entertain ourselves by thinking of better times and better days (Josephson, Singer, & Salovey, 1996). We can also cause ourselves untold misery by dwelling on unpleasant events (Beike et al., this volume). Autobiographical memories can serve social bonding functions (Hyman & Faries, 1992; Pillemer, 1992). When getting together with friends it is amazing how often the same old stories are told, stories with no informational content, given that everybody knows them already. What function could these stories possibly serve but to strengthen the bonds of friendship? And for many people, autobiographical memories serve to help shape our conceptions of who we are (Blagov & Singer, 2004; Neisser, 1978; Singer & Blagov, this volume).

So what can diachronic disunity tell us about the relationship between self and memory? It seems clear to us that for most people memory plays a crucial role in their self-definition (Hyman & Faries, 1992; Neisser, 1978). Indeed, our data show that the majority of people experience the self in a diachronically unified fashion. As we stated in this chapter's opening remarks, we believe that the sense of personal continuity that most people appear to achieve, the continuity metaphor that they adopt, is a function of both memory quality and narrative reconstruction. Qualitatively compelling memories for past events gives the individual the subjective sense of the self being back in time experiencing the event anew. Narrative reconstruction provides causal connectivity between life episodes.

The research presented in this chapter also suggests that some people report experiencing diachronic disunity. People who experience diachronic disunity remember past events but they appear to do so in a qualitatively different manner. Their pasts are not as significant to them as are the pasts of diachronically unified individuals, or at least, they are not significant to them in the same way. They do not describe the past as being part of who they are in the here and now. We believe this occurs because, for a variety of reasons, they adopt a discontinuity metaphor to describe profound changes that they go through. An implication of this is that memory's role in self-definition, although important for many, may not be obligatory for all. Indeed, although responses to our persistence condition items suggested that many participants believed that loss of their autobiographical memories would impair their personal continuity, many others did not. In fact, our participants indicated that persistence of their personalities would likely play a larger role than the persistence of their memories in maintaining their sense of identity. Of course people's naive theories of self are not incorrigible. However taken together with our other findings, the results suggest that there may be avenues of research concerning the relationship between self-definition and the past that are yet to be fully explored. It is our hope that the research we report in this chapter, although speculative and in its early stages, may make some small contribution to that exploration.

ENDNOTES

1. A variety of sources (e.g., Earp, 2002) credit Ralph Waldo Emerson with writing, "To laugh often and much, to win the respect of intelligent people and the affection of children, to earn the appreciation of honest critics and endure the betrayal of false friends, to appreciate beauty, to find the best in others, to leave the world a bit better, whether by a healthy child, a garden patch, or a redeemed social condition; to know even one life has breathed easier because you have lived. This is to have succeeded!" However, whether this poem was actually written by Emerson is controversial among scholars (Myerson, 2000).

2. Strawson uses slightly different terminology than we adopt here, referring to those who experience the self as discontinuous across time as "episodics" and those who experience the self as unified across time as "diachronics." Because *episodic* has a particular meaning within psychology, especially memory psychology, we've adopted the terms diachronic disunity and diachronic unity.

3. The conceptual metaphor interpretation that we offer also suggests the possibility of cuing people to adopt different metaphors. This is a possibility that we are currently exploring.

REFERENCES

Baddeley, A. (1988). But what the hell is it for? In M. M. Gruneberg, P. E. Morris, & R. N. Sykes (Eds.), *Practical aspects of memory: Current research and issues* (pp. 3–8). Chichester, England: John Wiley & Sons.

Barclay, R. C., & DeCooke, P. A. (1988). Ordinary everyday memories: Some of the things of which selves are made. In U. Neisser & E. Winograd (Eds.), *Remembering reconsidered* (pp. 91–125). New York: Cambridge University Press.

Barss, P. (2001, January 24). Not feeling quite one self? *National Post*, A15.

Basting, A. D. (2003). Looking back from loss: Views of the self in Alzheimer's disease. *Journal of Aging Studies, 17*, 87–99.

Beike, D. R., Kleinknecht, E. E., & Wirth-Beaumont, E. T. (2004). Open versus closed event memory. In D. R. Beike, J. M. Lampinen, & D. A. Behrend (Eds.), *The self and memory*. New York: Psychology Press.

Blagov, P., & Singer, J. A. (2004). Four dimensions of self-defining memories (content, structure, meaning, and affect) and their relationship to socioemotional maturity, distress and repressive defensiveness. *Journal of Personality, 72*, 481–510.

Brewer, W. F. (1986). What is autobiographical memory? In D. C. Rubin (Ed.), *Autobiographical Memory* (pp. 25–49). Cambridge, England: Cambridge University Press.

Brown, M. T. (2001). Multiple personality and personal identity. *Philosophical Psychology, 14*, 435–447.

Burke, M. (1994). Preserving the principle of one object to a place: A novel account of the relations among objects, sorts, sortals, and persistence conditions. *Philosophy and Phenomenological Research, 54*, 591–624.

Cacioppo, J. T., & Petty, R. E. (1982). The need for cognition. *Journal of Personality and Social Psychology, 42*, 116–131.

Carlson, E. B., & Putnam, F. W. (1993). An update on the dissociative experiences scale. *Dissociation, 6*, 16–27.

Dennett, D. C. (1992). The self as a center of narrative gravity. In F. Kessel, P. Cole, & D. Johnson (Eds.), *Self and consciousness: Multiple perspectives* (pp. 103–115). Hillsdale, NJ: Erlbaum.

Earp, S. (2002, December 19). Abrams still challenging himself. *Jacksonville News.* URL: http://www.jaxnews.com/news/2002/jn-localnews-1219-searp-2l19l4134.htm.

Farley, C. J. (2001, September 17). Legend of Dylan. *Time 158*(11), 92.

Fivush, R. (1991). The social construction of personal narratives. *Merrill-Palmer Quarterly, 37,* 59–82.

Fivush, R. (1994). Constructing narrative, emotion, and self in parent-child conversations about the past. In U. Neisser & R. Fivush (Eds.), *The remembering self: Construction and accuracy in the self-narrative* (pp. 136–157). New York: Cambridge University Press.

Garrett, B. J. (1985). Noonan, Best Candidate Theories, and the Ship of Theseus. *Analysis, 45,* 212–215.

Habermas, T., & Bluck, S. (2000). Getting a life: The emergence of the life story in adolescence. *Psychological Bulletin, 126,* 748–769.

Halligan, S. L., Tanja, M., Clark, D. M., & Ehlers, A. (2003). Posttraumatic stress disorder following assault: The role of cognitive processing, trauma memory, and appraisals. *Journal of Consulting and Clinical Psychology, 71,* 419–431.

Haslanger, S. (1989). Persistence, change, and explanation. *Philosophical Studies, 56,* 1–28.

Heraclitus (2001). *Fragments: The collected wisdom of Heraclitus.* Translated by B. Haxton. New York: Penguin.

Hyman, I. E., Jr., & Faries, J. M. (1992). The functions of autobiographical memories. In M. A. Conway, D. C. Rubin, H. Spinnler, & W. A. Wagenaar (Eds.), *Theoretical perspectives on autobiographical memory* (pp. 207–221). Dordrecht, the Netherlands: Kluwer Academic Publishers.

Jackson, F. (1986). What Mary didn't know. *Journal of Philosophy, 85,* 291–295.

John, E. R. (2002). The neurophysics of consciousness. *Brain Research Reviews, 39,* 1–28.

Johnson, M. K., Foley, M. A., Suengas, A. G., & Raye, C. L. (1988). Phenomenal characteristics of memories for perceived and imagined autobiographical events. *Journal of Experimental Psychology: General, 117,* 371–376.

Johnson, M. K., Hashtroudi, S., & Lindsay, D. S. (1993). Source monitoring. *Psychological Bulletin, 114,* 3–28.

Johnson, M. K., & Raye, C. L. (1981). Reality monitoring. *Psychological Review, 88,* 67–83.

Josephson, B., Singer, J. A., & Salovey, P. (1996). Mood regulation and memory: Repairing sad moods with happy memories. *Cognition and Emotion, 10,* 437–444.

Joyce, J. (1934). *Ulysses.* New York: Random House.

Kramer, P. D. (1993). *Listening to Prozac.* New York: Viking.

Kruglanski, A. W., & Webster, D. M. (1996). Motivated closing of the mind: "Seizing" and "freezing." *Psychological Review, 103,* 263–283.

Lakoff, G., & Johnson, M. (1980). *Metaphors we live by.* Chicago: University of Chicago Press.

Lakoff, G., & Johnson, M. (1999). *Philosophy in the flesh: The embodied mind and its challenge to Western thought.* New York: Basic Books.

Llinas, R. R., & Pare, D. (1991). Of dreaming and wakefulness. *Neuroscience, 44,* 521–535.

Locke, J. (1690/1994). *An essay concerning human understanding.* Amherst, NY: Prometheus Books.

McAdams, D. P. (1993). *The stories we live by: Personal myths and the making of the self.* New York: William Morrow and Company.

McAdams, D. P. (2004). The redemptive self: Narrative identity in America today. In D. R. Beike, J. M. Lampinen, & D. A. Behrend (Eds.), *The self and memory.* New York: Psychology Press.

McAdams, D. P. & Bowman, P. J. (2001). Narrating life's turning points: Redemption and contamination. In D. P. McAdams, R. Josselson, & A. Lieblich (Eds.), *Turns in the road: Narrative studies of lives in transition* (pp. 3–34). Washington, D.C.: American Psychological Association.

McAdams, D. P., Reynolds, J., Lewis, M., Patten, A. H., & Bowman, P. J. (2001). When bad things turn good and good things turn bad: Sequences of redemption and contamination in life narrative and their relation to psychosocial adaptation in midlife adults and in students. *Personality and Social Psychology Bulletin, 27,* 474–485.

Medin, D. L., & Ortony, A. (1989). Psychological essentialism. In S. Vosniadou & A. Ortony (Eds.), *Similarity and analogical reasoning* (pp. 179–195). Cambridge, England: Cambridge University Press.

Merricks, T. (1999). Persistence, parts and presentism. *Noûs, 33,* 421–438.

Myerson, J. (2000). Emerson's "success" — Actually, it is not. *Emerson Society Papers, 11,* 1, 8.

Nagel, T. (1974). What is it like to be a bat? *Philosophical Review, 83,* 435–450.

Neimeyer, G. J., & Rareshide, M. B. (1991). Personal memories and personal identity: The impact of ego identity development on autobiographical memory recall. *Journal of Personality & Social Psychology, 60,* 562–569.

Neisser, U. (1978). Memory: What are the important questions? In M. M. Gruneberg, P. E. Morris, & R. N. Sykes (Eds.), *Practical aspects of memory* (pp. 3–24). San Diego CA: Academic Press.

Neisser, U. (1988). Five kinds of self-knowledge. *Philosophical Psychology, 1,* 35–59.

Neisser, U. (1994). Self-narratives: True and false. In U. Neisser & R. Fivush (Eds.), *The remembering self: Construction and accuracy in the self-narrative* (pp. 1–18). New York: Cambridge University Press.

Olson, E. T. (2002). Personal identity. In E. N. Zalta (Ed.), *The Stanford encyclopedia of philosophy.* URL: http://plato.stanford.edu/archives/fall2002/entries/identity-personal/.

Pillemer, D. B. (1992). Remembering personal circumstances: A functional analysis. In E. Winograd & U. Neisser (Eds.), *Affect and accuracy in recall: Studies of "flashbulb" memories* (pp. 236–264). New York: Cambridge University Press.

Plutarch (1992). *Lives of noble Grecians and Romans.* Translated by J. Dryden. New York: Modern Library.

Rea, M. (1995). The problem of material constitution. *The Philosophical Review, 104,* 525–552.

Reese, E. (2002). Social factors in the development of autobiographical memory: The state of the art. *Social Development, 11,* 124–142.

Riutort, M., Cuervo, C., Danion, J. M., Peretti, C. S., & Salame, P. (2003). Reduced levels of specific autobiographical memories in schizophrenia. *Psychiatry Research, 117,* 35–45.

Robinson, J. A., & Swanson, K. L. (1990). Autobiographical memory: The next phase. *Applied Cognitive Psychology, 4,* 321–335.

Ross, M., & Wilson, A. E. (2003). Autobiographical memory and conceptions of self: Getting better all the time. *Current Directions in Psychological Science, 12,* 66–69.

Scaltsas, T. (1980). The ship of Theseus. *Analysis, 40,* 152–157.

Schank, R. C. (1990). *Tell me a story: A new look at real and artificial memory.* New York: Charles Scribner & Sons.

Shenk, D., Boyd, D., Peacock, J. R., & Moore, L. (2002). Narrative and self-identity in later life: Two rural American older women. *Journal of Aging Studies, 16,* 401–413.

Singer, J. A., & Bluck, S. (2001). New perspectives on autobiographical memory: The integration of narrative processing and autobiographical reasoning. *Review of General Psychology, 5,* 91–99.

Smith, E. E., & Medin, D. L. (1981). *Categories and concepts.* Cambridge, MA: Harvard University Press.

Steinberg, M. (1995). *Handbook for the assessment of dissociation: A clinical guide.* Washington, D.C.: American Psychiatric Press.

Strawson, G. (1999). The self. In S. Gallagher & J. Shear (Eds.), *Models of the self* (pp. 1–24). Exeter, England: Imprint Academic.

Strawson, G. (in press). Against narrative. In G. Strawson (Ed.), *The self.* Oxford: Blackwell.

Thompson, C. P. (1998). The bounty of everyday memory. In C. P. Thompson, D. J. Herrmann, D. Bruce, J. D. Read, D. G. Payne, & M. P. Toglia (Eds.), *Autobiographical memory: Theoretical and applied perspectives* (pp. 29–43). Mahwah, NJ: Erlbaum.

Tulving, E. (2002). Episodic memory: From mind to brain. *Annual Review of Psychology, 53,* 1–25.

Waller, N., Putnam, F. W., & Carlson, E. B. (1996). Types of dissociation and dissociative types: A taxometric analysis of dissociative experiences. *Psychological Methods, 1,* 300–321.

Waller, N. G., & Ross, C. A. (1997). The prevalence and biometric structure of pathological dissociation in the general population: Taxometric and behavior genetic findings, *Journal of Abnormal Psychology, 106,* 499–510.

Webster, D. M., & Kruglanski, A. W. (1994). Individual differences in need for closure. *Journal of Personality and Social Psychology, 67,* 1049–1062.

Wiggins, D. (1967). *Identity and spatio-temporal continuity.* Oxford, England: Blackwell.

Wittgenstein, L. (1963). *Philosophical investigations.* New York: Macmillan.

Zimmerman, D. W. (1996). Persistence and presentism. *Philosophical Papers, 25,* 115–126.

12

The Self and Memory: It's about Time

JAMES M. LAMPINEN
DENISE R. BEIKE
DOUGLAS A. BEHREND
University of Arkansas

W ho we conceive ourselves to be depends crucially on how we remember our lives. How we remember our lives depends crucially on how we mentally represent who we are. And our mental (and perhaps physical) well-being depends crucially on both memory and self concept. These claims summarize a large body of research and theorizing in the area of autobiographical memory over the past quarter century. The authors represented in the present volume are some of the most important contributors to that body of knowledge.

THE SCIENCE OF HUMAN MEMORY: A LIFE STORY

Most of us who spend at least part of our professional lives trying to understand human memory were initially brought up on a very different tradition than that described above of what memory research was all about. We were brought up on a tradition of nonsense syllables, and word lists, and if we were good an occasional bedtime story. Indeed, one of us (JML) still spends most of his time with such materials and enjoys doing so (it beats working).

We were all brought up learning about Ebbinghaus (1885/1913) and his forgetting curve. Ebbinghaus's influence is still felt to this day, including in the study of autobiographical memory. He was, as all students of memory know, a careful experimentalist and true innovator. He single-handedly created the science of memory, at a time when many of his contemporaries believed that higher level cognition could not be scientifically studied at all. How's *that* for a line on your vita?

Those of us who study memory for a living were also brought up on the revolutionary work of Sir Fredric Bartlett (1932). Memory for Bartlett was not a mechanical process, but a meaning-making system. He argued that the main problem with Ebbinghaus and his followers was that they were making faulty assumptions about their subject matter. Ebbinghaus, with all the care and thoughtfulness of his work, seemed to believe that one could methodically tease apart the process of interpretation from the process of remembering. Bartlett believed that this was completely wrongheaded. Meaning and interpretation, in Bartlett's view, are obligatory parts of the process of remembering. It simply isn't possible to exaggerate the influence Bartlett has had on modern theorizing about memory.

We were also all raised on the computational metaphor underlying the cognitive revolution. Work on memory in the 1960s and 1970s focused on how people learn lists of words and other simple materials. This work continues to this day and provides an incredibly rich repository of knowledge about the basic principles by which memory operates. Each of these approaches, Ebbinghaus, Bartlett, and the information-processing revolution, provide important chapters in the life story of the science of human memory.

In the late 1970s another chapter was added to the life story of our field. The setting for this new chapter was a conference called the Practical Aspects of Memory conference. At this conference Neisser (1978) evaluated traditional memory research and found it lacking. In fact, he seemed to find it almost entirely without merit (a view with which we disagree). Neisser opened the conference with a talk entitled "Memory: What Are the Important Questions?" In that talk he famously remarked, "If X is an interesting or socially significant aspect of memory, then psychologists have hardly ever studied X."

Needless to say this talk sparked a great range of debate within the memory community, most notably inspiring a spirited reply from Banaji and Crowder (1989) about a decade later. It's worthwhile, however, to take some time and look more closely at Neisser's argument and the influence that it had. Neisser seemed to be making three basic arguments in his influential paper. He argued that many of the issues addressed in traditional memory research were trivial issues. He argued that human memory was deeply contextually bound, such that investigating memory outside of its naturally occurring context was unlikely to be especially illuminating. Neisser argued, "I think that 'memory' in general does not exist either. It is a concept left over from a medieval psychology that partitioned the mind into independent faculties. . . . Let's give it up and begin to ask our questions different ways." Lastly, and most interestingly, he argued that exclusive reliance on laboratory research led us to ask a very narrow range of questions. We become, in Neisser's words, like the "legendary drunk who kept looking for his money under the streetlamp although he had dropped it ten yards away in the dark. As he correctly pointed out, the light was better where he was looking."

Neisser wanted memory psychologists to study the "important questions." He argued that once one decides to move out of the laboratory and examine memory in more naturalistic settings, questions arise that might never have arisen otherwise.

Some of the questions Neisser felt were being neglected included: How does one remember the source of information? How long do students remember information from their classes? What are the functions that memory is used for? How is memory used in self-definition? And a host of other questions as well. These questions are the type of question that naturally arise in the naturalistic study of memory, but are less likely to arise in a laboratory setting.

It's unclear to us whether Neisser inspired what followed, or whether he was merely representing an emerging zeitgeist, but in the 1980s and 1990s scores of psychologists jumped into the fray. Psychologists began to develop theories of the organizational principles under which autobiographical memory operates (Barsalou, 1988; Conway, 1992; Conway & Bekerian, 1987; Reiser, Black, & Abelson, 1985). They began to examine flashbulb memories and the relationship between affect and accuracy more generally (Brown & Kulik, 1977; McCloskey, Wible, & Cohen, 1988; Neisser & Harsch, 1992; Pillemer, 1984; Wright & Gaskell, 1995). They began to systematically examine the functions served by autobiographical memories (Baddeley, 1988; Hyman & Faries, 1992; Pillemer, 1992). Scientists began to explore the relationship between narrative ability and autobiographical memory (Fivush, 1991; McAdams, 1997; Nelson, 1993; Pillemer, 1998). And with the advent of the recovered memory controversy scores of research scientists explored false memories, and memory for traumatic events (e.g., Hyman & Kleinknecht, 1999).

The 1990s were a time of continued growth in addressing these important questions, but also a time of continued diversification. Indeed, as we were putting together the conference on which this volume is based, we hoped to capture the diversity of approaches that are inherent in the study of autobiographical memory. But we were also concerned: What if we ended up with something rather like a bad blind date, where we have absolutely nothing to say to each other?

Gladly that is not how things turned out. Indeed, the conference and the work included in the present volume illustrate quite clearly how the research of cognitive, social, developmental, personality, and clinical psychologists could be mutually informative. Speakers from very different perspectives each spoke of common themes. Indeed, the themes mentioned in the introductory chapter, issues related to emotional well-being, narrative coherence, conceptions of time, and emergence of self, themselves emerged naturally during the course of the presentations. The coherence was clear to everyone, and planned by absolutely no one (so of course, we intend to take credit for it!). This sense of coherence was undoubtedly aided by the recent publication of the *Psychological Review* article by Conway and Pleydell-Pearce (2000).

We now have four strands of memory research to teach our students about. The groundbreaking work of Ebbinghaus demonstrated convincingly that memory was a tractable topic for scientific inquiry. The revolutionary work of Bartlett demonstrated that memory and interpretation could not always be so easily separated. The information-processing perspective generated important understanding of the basic cognitive principles through which memory operates. Added to those perspectives were the perspectives gained by the rich and growing literature on the topic of self-relevant memories. We find each of these traditions interesting and important, and borrow heavily from each in our own work.

MEMORY AND THE SELF: "WHAT ARE THE IMPORTANT QUESTIONS?"

Life stories, as Dan McAdams (this volume) teaches us, are not just about the past but they are also about the anticipated future. Where does the life story of our discipline go from here? Or in Neisser's apt phrase, "What are the important questions?" If you were to ask every participant at the Self and Memory conference, you would probably get a somewhat different answer from each as to what the unanswered questions are. In this section we outline three questions that we believe deserve attention in the coming years.

What Is a Self?

Everybody seems to agree that people have things called selves. And most people agree that memory and the self are in some sense related. But what exactly is a self anyway? As we pointed out in the introductory chapter, the term itself seems to be polysemous. Selves can be thought of in terms of actors, moral agents, subjects of experience, representations of traits, synchronically unified entities, diachronically unified entities, I's and me's (goo goo ga joob). Is the self a physical thing? Is it a mental thing? Is it an illusion as Hume (1739/1979) seemed to think it was? Is it a social construct? Is it an evolutionary adaptation? Or is it something more abstract? Is it all of these things, or none of these things? Are these things the same thing or different things? To what extent is the *self* a coherent unified construct?

Consider the way the words *I*, *me*, and *self* are used in ordinary language. People say things like "I am not myself today." What on earth could that possibly mean if the self is a unified construct? Or people say, "I'm not the same person I was back then." A very peculiar expression. How can we make sense of it? One possibility is to assume that the words themselves have multiple senses.

Several years ago the philosophy department at our university hosted a debate between David Chalmers and Daniel Dennett. The two debated about their differing views concerning the nature of consciousness. Chalmers (1995) is famous, among other things, for arguing that consciousness is vexingly ineffable. Dennett (1991) is famous, among other things, for writing a book claiming to "explain" consciousness. Needless to say, they didn't quite see eye to eye. Dennett told the story of a great magician who challenged other magicians to figure out how he did a particular trick. The magicians watched as he did the trick, first looking to see if he might be using a trapped door. No such luck. They watched again, this time seeing if it was done with mirrors. They were wrong again. They watched again, seeing if there were any wires being used. Nope. Eventually after striking out again and again, the magicians gave up. When asked how he did it, the brilliant magician replied, "Simple, it wasn't one trick, it was a bunch of different tricks."

Dennett wondered if consciousness was a lot like that. Not one big complicated trick, but a bunch of different relatively simple tricks evolved to solve different problems. We wonder if the self may be a bunch of different loosely connected tricks as well. Is the sense of self that is involved in autobiographical memory related to the sense of self involved in navigation and planning? Does self-esteem relate to the ability to find surreptitiously applied rouge on your face when looking in the mirror? One could easily come up with arguments for how the components are related, and equally plausible arguments for how they might be dissociable. These are interesting questions, questions on which some headway has been made, but where even more progress could be made. New information emerging from brain imaging studies may be a particularly apt source of information in this regard (see, e.g., Craik, Moroz, Moscovitch, Stuss, Winocur, Tulving, et al., 1999).

SELF, MEMORY, AND LANGUAGE

Research on autobiographical memory necessarily involves asking people to describe relatively complex structured events. It is important to ask whether the structure and content of the memory reports reflect how memory is organized or how verbal reports are produced. As Lampinen, Neuschatz, and Payne (1998) argued with regard to memory phenomenology, self-reports of experience necessarily involve memory mechanisms, language abilities, and pragmatic social constraints on reporting. A full understanding of the relationship between self and memory will require developing better ways of deconfounding memory, language, and pragmatic constraints.

Obviously this is easier said than done, and we have no easy answers in this regard. Consider, for instance, research showing that depression is associated with autobiographical memory reports that are overgeneral (Watkins & Teasdale, 2001). What are we to make of these findings? Do depressed individuals report more general memories because they encode fewer events or encode them more sparsely? Do depressed individuals report more general memories because of impoverished retrieval? Is it possible that depressed individuals just don't care for talking? or feel like no one would be interested in their memories? From our reading of the literature it appears that the answers to these questions have not been fully worked out. Research in the area of autobiographical memory is replete with these sorts of interpretative difficulties, and an important area for future research is to try to devise ways of deconfounding these variables.

MEMORY AND MORALITY?

Autobiographical memory has been studied in terms of its cognitive, social, and clinical implications, but an area that is relatively untouched involves the moral implications of remembering and forgetting. Yet upon reflection it is quite clear that people often view memory as having a moral component. We remember things that are significant to us, but do we not also mark things as significant by remembering them? Do people see themselves as having a moral duty to remember some events? Do people believe it is sometimes wrong to forget?

When we tell a lover "I will always remember this moment" we are not making a statement about forgetting curves, cue dependent retrieval, or savings in relearning. We are saying we value them, and the time we shared together. When someone we love passes away, or when a significant loss occurs in our community or nation, we hold memorials. We do so not to provide another rehearsal opportunity, but rather, through the act of remembering, to say that this was important, and not only was this important, it continues to be important still. To remember is to validate; to forget is not merely a mechanical act, but an implicit assessment: "This doesn't matter to me anymore."

The act of saying that something is of significance by remembering it, or saying that something is insignificant by forgetting it, is not a value-free action. Nothing cuts quite as deeply as a friend forgetting a shared event that was significant to us. And when we ourselves forget such an event, guilt is not an unusual response. It may be that this moral component of remembering underlies why people cling to their memories at times. When one puts something behind them, it's as if they are saying, "That didn't matter." And saying "It didn't matter" is a moral/ethical decision.

CONCLUDING REMARKS

These are but a few of the important questions we think face the field of self and memory in the future. Many questions remain open and yet we have come a long way toward answering other vital questions about the self and memory. For example, consider Baddeley's (1988) question about memory in general: "But what the hell is it for?" What is personal memory for? As the contributors to this volume make clear, a well-tuned personal memory system serves a number of (probably related) functions: it provides the building blocks of identity, it informs the sense of time passage, it allows smooth social functioning, it contributes to intelligent decision making, it facilitates emotion regulation. But perhaps most importantly, personal memory is the currency of everyday thought and interaction. Conversational English is replete with personal memories. After all, the word most frequently used in spoken English is "I," often a signal that a personal memory is about to be shared. From our earliest conversations with caregivers to the mainly introspective life review process in old age, personal memories are the coin of the realm.

A quarter of a century and the dawn of a new millenium have passed since Neisser initially challenged professional memory scientists to examine memory in more naturalistic settings. His challenge has been well met by all of the contributors to this volume. As we look toward future challenges, this is an exciting time to be a researcher exploring memory and the self.

REFERENCES

Baddeley, A. (1988). But what the hell is it for? In M. M. Gruneberg & R. N. Sykes (Eds.), *Practical aspects of memory* (Vol. 1, pp. 3–18). New York: Wiley.

Banaji, M. R., & Crowder, R. G. (1989). The bankruptcy of everyday memory. *American Psychologist, 44,* 1185–1193.

Barsalou, L. W. (1988). The content and organization of autobiographical memories. In U. Neisser & E. Winograd (Eds.), *Remembering reconsidered: Ecological and traditional approaches to the study of memory* (pp. 193–243). Cambridge, England: Cambridge University Press.

Bartlett, F. C. (1932). *Remembering: An experimental and social study.* Cambridge, England: Cambridge University Press.

Brown, R., & Kulik, J. (1977). Flashbulb memories. *Cognition, 5,* 73–99.

Chalmers, D. J. (1995). The puzzle of conscious experience. *Scientific American, 237(6),* 62–68.

Conway, M. A., & Bekerian, D. A. (1987). Organization in autobiographical memory. *Memory and Cognition, 15,* 119–132.

Conway, M. A. (1992). A structural model of autobiographical memory. In M. A. Conway, D. C. Rubin, H. Spinler, & W. Wagenaar (Eds.), *Theoretical perspectives on autobiographical memory* (pp. 167–193). Amsterdam: Kluwer Academic Publishers.

Conway, M. A., & Pleydell-Pearce, C. W. (2000). The construction of autobiographical memories in the self memory system. *Psychological Review, 107,* 261–288.

Craik, F. I. M., Moroz, T. M., Moscovitch, M., Stuss, D. T., Winocur, G., Tulving, E., et al. (1999). In search of the self: A positron emission tomography study. *Psychological Science, 10,* 26–34.

Dennett, D. C. (1991). *Consciousness explained.* Boston: Little Brown.

Ebbinghaus, H. (1885/1913). *Memory. A contribution to experimental psychology.* New York: Teachers College, Columbia University.

Fivush, R. (1991). The social construction of personal narratives. *Merrill-Palmer Quarterly, 37,* 59–82.

Hume, D. (1739/1979). *A treatise of human nature.* In R. I. Watson (Ed.), *Basic writings in the history of psychology* (pp. 51–62). New York: Oxford University Press.

Hyman, I. E., Jr., & Faries, J. M. (1992). The functions of autobiographical memories. In M. A. Conway, D. C. Rubin, H. Spinnler, & W. A. Wagenaar (Eds.), *Theoretical perspectives on autobiographical memory* (pp. 207–221). Dordrecht, the Netherlands: Kluwer Academic Publishers.

Hyman, I. E., Jr., & Kleinknecht, E. E. (1999). False childhood memories: Research, theory, and application. In L. M. Williams & V. L. Banyard (Eds.), *Trauma and memory* (pp. 175–188). Thousand Oaks, CA: Sage.

Lampinen, J. M., Neuschatz, J. S., & Payne, D. G. (1998). Memory illusions and consciousness: Examining the phenomenology of true and false memories. *Current Psychology, 16,* 181–223.

McAdams, D. (1997). *The stories we live by: Personal myths and the making of the self.* New York: Guilford Press.

McCloskey, M., Wible, C. G., & Cohen, N. J. (1988). Is there a special flashbulb-memory mechanism? *Journal of Experimental Psychology: General, 117,* 171–181.

Neisser, U. (1978). Memory: What are the important questions? In M. M. Gruneberg, P. E. Morris, & R. N. Sykes (Eds.), *Practical aspects of memory* (pp. 3–24). San Diego, CA: Academic Press.

Neisser, U., & Harsch, N. (1992). Phantom flashbulbs: False recollections of hearing the news about Challenger. In E. Winograd & U. Neisser (Eds.), *Affect and accuracy in recall: Studies of "flashbulb" memories* (pp. 9–31). New York: Cambridge University Press.

Nelson, K. (1993). The psychological and social origins of autobiographical memory. *Psychological Science 4*, 7–14.

Pillemer, D. B. (1984). Flashbulb memories of the assassination attempt on President Reagan. *Cognition, 16*, 63–80.

Pillemer, D. B. (1992). Remembering personal circumstances: A functional analysis. In E. Winograd & U. Neisser (Eds.), *Affect and accuracy in recall: Studies of "flashbulb" memories* (pp. 236–264). New York: Cambridge University Press.

Pillemer, D. B. (1998). *Momentous events, vivid memories.* Cambridge, MA: Harvard University Press.

Reiser, B. J., Black, J. B., & Abelson, R. P. (1985). Knowledge structures in the organization and retrieval of autobiographical memories. *Cognitive Psychology, 17*, 89–137.

Watkins, E., & Teasdale, J. D. (2001). Rumination and overgeneral memory in depression: effects of self-focus and analytic thinking. *Journal of Abnormal Psychology, 110*, 333–357.

Wright, D. B., & Gaskell, G. D. (1995). Flashbulb memories: Conceptual and methodological issues. *Memory, 3*, 67–80.

Index